Ceph Cookbook

Second Edition

Practical recipes to design, implement, operate, and manage
Ceph storage systems

Vikhyat Umrao
Michael Hackett
Karan Singh

BIRMINGHAM - MUMBAI

Ceph Cookbook

Second Edition

First published: February 2016

Second edition: November 2017

Production reference: 1221117

Published by Packt Publishing Ltd.
Livery Place
35 Livery Street
Birmingham
B3 2PB, UK.

ISBN 978-1-78839-106-1

www.packtpub.com

Credits

Authors
Vikhyat Umrao
Michael Hackett
Karan Singh

Copy Editors
Safis Editing
Juliana Nair

Reviewer
Álvaro Soto

Project Coordinator
Judie Jose

Commissioning Editor
Gebin George

Proofreader
Safis Editing

Acquisition Editor
Shrilekha Inani

Indexer
Pratik Shirodkar

Content Development Editor
Nikita Pawar

Graphics
Tania Dutta

Technical Editor
Mohd Riyan Khan

Production Coordinator
Deepika Naik

Disclaimer

The views expressed in this book are those of the authors and not of Red Hat.

Foreword

Since Ceph's inception and posting to GitHub in 2008, Sage Weil's creation has grown from an individual idea to a successful open source project with over 87,000 commits from almost 900 different contributors from dozens of companies. Originally incubated as a skunkworks project inside DreamHost, an earlier Sage startup focused on web hosting. In 2012, it was spun off into a new company, Inktank, dedicated to focusing exclusively on the development and support of Ceph. Inktank's reputation was built upon the stellar customer support its employees provided, from on-site installation and configuration, to highly complex bug troubleshooting, through patch development, and ultimate problem resolution. The DNA of the company was a dedication to customer success, even when it required a senior developer to join a customer support teleconference at short notice, or even Sage himself to remotely log in to a server and assist in diagnosing the root cause of an issue.

This focus on the customer was elevated even further after Inktank's acquisition by Red Hat in 2014. If Red Hat is known for anything, it's for making CIOs comfortable with open source software. Members of Red Hat's customer experience and engagement team are some of the most talented individuals I've had the pleasure to work with. They possess the unique ability to blend the technical troubleshooting skills necessary to support a complex distributed storage system with the soft relational skills required to be on the front lines engaging with a customer, who in many cases is in an extremely stressful situation where production clusters are out of operation.

The authors of this book are two of the finest exemplars of this unique crossing of streams. Inside this work, Vikhyat and Michael share some of their hard-earned best practices in successfully installing, configuring, and supporting a Ceph cluster. Vikhyat has 9 years of experience providing sustaining engineering support for distributed storage products with a focus on Ceph for over 3 years. Michael has been working in the storage industry for over 12 years and has been focused on Ceph for close to 3 years. They both have the uncommon ability to calmly work through complex customer escalations, providing a first class experience with Ceph under even the most stressful of situations. Between the two of them, you're in good hands—the ones that have seen some of the hairiest, most difficult-to-diagnose problems and have come out the other side to share their hard-earned wisdom with you.

If there's been one frequent critique of Ceph over the years, it's been that it's too complex for a typical administrator to work with. Our hope is that the ones who might be intimidated by the thought of setting up their first Ceph cluster will find comfort and gain confidence from reading this book. After all, there's no time like the present to start playing with The Future of Storage™. :-)

Ian R. Colle

Global Director of Software Engineering, Red Hat Ceph Storage

About the Authors

Vikhyat Umrao has 9 years of experience with distributed storage products as a sustenance engineer and in the last couple of years, he has been working on software-defined storage technology, with specific expertise in Ceph Unified Storage. He has been working on Ceph for over 3 years now and in his current position at Red Hat, he focuses on the support and development of Ceph to solve Red Hat Ceph storage customer issues and upstream reported issues.

He is based in the Greater Boston area, where he is a principal software maintenance engineer for Red Hat Ceph Storage. Vikhyat lives with his wife, Pratima, and he likes to explore new places.

I'd like to thank my wife, Pratima, for keeping me motivated so that I could write this book and give time I could have spent with her to this book. I would also like to thank my family (mom and dad) and both my sisters (Khyati and Pragati) for their love, support, and belief in me that I would do better in my life.

I would also like to thank Red Hat for giving me an opportunity to work on such a wonderful storage product, and my colleagues who make a great team. I would like to thank the Ceph community and developers for constantly developing, improving, and supporting Ceph.

I would like to thank Michael—my friend, colleague, and co-author of this book—for making a great team for this book as we make a great team at Red Hat. I would also like to thank Karan, who wrote the first version of this book, for giving us the base for version two.

Finally, I would like to thank the entire team at Packt and a team of technical reviewers for giving us this opportunity, and the hard work they put in beside us while we wrote this book.

Michael Hackett is a storage and SAN expert in customer support. He has been working on Ceph and storage-related products for over 12 years. Apart from this, he holds several storage and SAN-based certifications, and prides himself on his ability to troubleshoot and adapt to new complex issues.

Michael is currently working at Red Hat, based in Massachusetts, where he is a principal software maintenance engineer for Red Hat Ceph and the technical product lead for the global Ceph team.

Michael lives in Massachusetts with his wife, Nicole, his two sons, and their dog. He is an avid sports fan and enjoys time with his family.

I'd like to thank my wife, Nicole, for putting up with some long nights while I was working on this book and understanding the hard work and dedication—a role in the software industry requires. I would also like to thank my two young sons for teaching me more about patience and myself than I ever thought was possible (love you more than you will ever know L and C). Also thank you to my family (mom and dad) and in-laws (Gary and Debbie) for the constant and continued support in everything I do. I would also like to thank Red Hat and my colleagues who truly make each day of work a pleasure. Working at Red Hat is a passion and the drive to make software better is within every Red Hatter. I would like to thank the Ceph community and the developers for constantly developing, improving, and supporting Ceph. Finally, I would like to thank the entire team at Packt and the team of technical reviewers for giving us this opportunity, and the hard work they put in beside us, while we wrote this book.

Karan Singh devotes a part of his time in learning emerging technologies and enjoys the challenges that come with it. He loves tech writing and is an avid blogger. He also authored the first edition of *Learning Ceph* and *Ceph Cookbook*, Packt Publishing. You can reach him on Twitter at `@karansingh010`.

I'd like to thank my wife, Monika, for giving me wings to fly.

I'd also like to thank my employer, Red Hat, for giving me an opportunity to work on cutting-edge technologies and to be a part of the world class team I work with.
Finally, special thanks to Vikhyat and Michael for putting great effort into the continued success of Ceph Cookbook.

About the Reviewer

Álvaro Soto is a cloud and open source enthusiast. He was born in Chile, but he has been living in Mexico for more than 10 years now. He is an active member of OpenStack and Ceph communities in Mexico. He holds an engineering degree in computer science from Instituto Politécnico Nacional (IPN México) and he is on his way to getting a master's degree in computer science at Instituto Tecnológico Autónomo de México (ITAM).

Álvaro currently works as a Ceph consultant at Sentinel.la doing architecting, implementing, and performance tuning on Ceph clusters, data migration, and new ways to adopt Ceph solutions.

He enjoys his time reading about distributing systems, automation, Linux, security-related papers and books.
You can always contact him by email `alsotoes@gmail.com`, on IRC using the nickname `khyr0n`, or on Twitter `@alsotoes`.

> *I would like to thank Haidee, my partner in life, and Nico for his affect and pleasant company while reviewing this book.*
>
> *To the guys at Sentinel.la, their advices and work for OpenStack and Ceph communities.*

www.PacktPub.com

For support files and downloads related to your book, please visit www.PacktPub.com.

Did you know that Packt offers eBook versions of every book published, with PDF and ePub files available? You can upgrade to the eBook version at www.PacktPub.com and as a print book customer, you are entitled to a discount on the eBook copy. Get in touch with us at service@packtpub.com for more details.

At www.PacktPub.com, you can also read a collection of free technical articles, sign up for a range of free newsletters and receive exclusive discounts and offers on Packt books and eBooks.

https://www.packtpub.com/mapt

Get the most in-demand software skills with Mapt. Mapt gives you full access to all Packt books and video courses, as well as industry-leading tools to help you plan your personal development and advance your career.

Why subscribe?

- Fully searchable across every book published by Packt
- Copy and paste, print, and bookmark content
- On demand and accessible via a web browser

Customer Feedback

Thanks for purchasing this Packt book. At Packt, quality is at the heart of our editorial process. To help us improve, please leave us an honest review on this book's Amazon page at `https://www.amazon.com/dp/1788391063`.

If you'd like to join our team of regular reviewers, you can email us at `customerreviews@packtpub.com`. We award our regular reviewers with free eBooks and videos in exchange for their valuable feedback. Help us be relentless in improving our products!

Table of Contents

Preface

So long are the days past of massively expensive black boxes and their large data center footprints. The current data-driven world we live in demands the ability to handle large-scale data growth at a more economical cost. Day-by-day data continues to grow exponentially and the need to store this data increases. This is where software-defined storage enters the picture.

The idea behind a software-defined storage solution is to utilize the intelligence of software combined with the use of commodity hardware to solve our future computing problems, including where to store all this data the human race is compiling, from music to insurance documents. The software-defined approach should be the answer to the future's computing problems and Ceph is the future of storage.

Ceph is a true open source, software-defined storage solution, purposely built to handle unprecedented data growth with linear performance improvement. It provides a unified storage experience for file, object, and block storage interfaces from the same system. The beauty of Ceph is its distributed, scalable nature and performance; reliability and robustness come along with these attributes. And furthermore it is pocket-friendly, that is, economical, providing you greater value for each dollar you spent.

Ceph is capable of providing block, object, and file access from a single storage solution, and its enterprise-class features such as scalability, reliability, erasure coding, and cache tiering have led organizations such as CERN, Yahoo!, and DreamHost to deploy and run Ceph highly successfully, for years. It is also currently being deployed in all flash storage scenarios, where low latency / high performance workloads, database workloads, storage for containers, and Hyper Converge Infrastructure as well. With Ceph BlueStore on the very near horizon, the best is truly yet to come for Ceph.

In this book, we will take a deep dive to understand Ceph—covering components and architecture, including its working. The Ceph Cookbook focuses on hands-on knowledge by providing you with step-by-step guidance with the help of recipes. Right from the first chapter, you will gain practical experience of Ceph by following the recipes. With each chapter, you will learn and play around with interesting concepts in Ceph. By the end of this book, you will feel competent regarding Ceph, both conceptually as well as practically, and you will be able to operate your Ceph storage infrastructure with confidence and success.

Best of luck in your future endeavors with Ceph!

What this book covers

Chapter 1, *Ceph - Introduction and Beyond*, covers an introduction to Ceph, gradually moving toward RAID and its challenges, and a Ceph architectural overview. Finally, we will go through Ceph installation and configuration.

Chapter 2, *Working with Ceph Block Device*, covers an introduction to the Ceph Block Device and provisioning of the Ceph block device. We will also go through RBD snapshots and clones, as well as implementing a disaster-recovery solution with RBD mirroring.

Chapter 3, *Working with Ceph and Openstack,* covers configuring Openstack clients for use with Ceph, as well as storage options for OpenStack using cinder, glance, and nova.

Chapter 4, *Working with Ceph Object Storage*, covers a deep dive into Ceph object storage, including RGW setup and configuration, S3, and OpenStack Swift access. Finally, we will set up RGW with the Hadoop S3A plugin.

Chapter 5, *Working with Ceph Object Storage Multi-Site V2*, helps you to deep dive into the new Multi-site V2, while configuring two Ceph clusters to mirror objects between them in an object disaster recovery solution.

Chapter 6, *Working with the Ceph Filesystem*, covers an introduction to CephFS, deploying and accessing MDS and CephFS via kerenel, FUSE, and NFS-Ganesha.

Chapter 7, *Monitoring Ceph Clusters*, covers classic ways of monitoring Ceph via the Ceph command-line tools. You will also be introduced to Ceph Metrics and Grafana, and learn how to configure Ceph Metrics to monitor a Ceph cluster.

Chapter 8, *Operating and Managing a Ceph Cluster*, covers Ceph service management with systemd, and scaling up and scaling down a Ceph cluster. This chapter also includes failed disk replacement and upgrading Ceph infrastructures.

Chapter 9, *Ceph under the Hood*, explores the Ceph CRUSH map, understanding the internals of the CRUSH map and CRUSH tunables, followed by Ceph authentication and authorization. This chapter also covers dynamic cluster management and understanding Ceph PG. Finally, we create the specifics required for specific hardware.

Chapter 10, *Production Planning and Performance Tuning for Ceph*, covers the planning of cluster production deployment and HW and SW planning for Ceph. This chapter also includes Ceph recommendation and performance tuning. Finally, this chapter covers erasure coding and cache tuning.

Chapter 11, *The Virtual Storage Manager for Ceph*, speaks about Virtual Storage Manager (VSM), covering it's introduction and architecture. We will also go through the deployment of VSM and then the creation of a Ceph cluster, using VSM to manage it.

Chapter 12, *More on Ceph*, covers Ceph benchmarking, Ceph troubleshooting using admin socket, API, and the ceph-objectstore tool. This chapter also covers the deployment of Ceph using Ansible and Ceph memory profiling. Furthermore, it covers health checking your Ceph cluster using Ceph Medic and the new experimental backend Ceph BlueStore.

Chapter 13, *An Introduction to Troubleshooting Ceph*, covers troubleshooting common issues seen in Ceph clusters detailing methods to troubleshoot each component. This chapter also covers what to look for to determine where an issue is in the cluster and what the possible cause could be.

Chapter 14, *Upgrading Your Ceph Cluster from Hammer to Jewel*, covers upgrading the core components in your Ceph cluster from the Hammer release to the Jewel release.

What you need for this book

The various software components required to follow the instructions in the chapters are as follows:

- VirtualBox 4.0 or higher (https://www.virtualbox.org/wiki/Downloads)

- GIT (http://www.git-scm.com/downloads)

- Vagrant 1.5.0 or higher (https://www.vagrantup.com/downloads.html)

- CentOS operating system 7.0 or higher (http://wiki.centos.org/Download)

- Ceph software Jewel packages Version 10.2.0 or higher (http://ceph.com/resources/downloads/)

- S3 Client, typically S3cmd (http://s3tools.org/download)

- Python-swift client

- NFS Ganesha

- Ceph Fuse

- CephMetrics (https://github.com/ceph/cephmetrics)

- Ceph-Medic (`https://github.com/ceph/ceph-medic`)

- Virtual Storage Manager 2.0 or higher (`https://github.com/01org/virtual-storagemanager/releases/tag/v2.1.0`)

- Ceph-Ansible (`https://github.com/ceph/ceph-ansible`)

- OpenStack RDO (`http://rdo.fedorapeople.org/rdo-release.rpm`)

Who this book is for

This book is aimed at storage and cloud system engineers, system administrators, and technical architects and consultants who are interested in building software-defined storage solutions around Ceph to power their cloud and virtual infrastructure. If you have a basic knowledge of GNU/Linux and storage systems, with no experience of software-defined storage solutions and Ceph, but are eager to learn, this book is for you.

Sections

In this book, you will find several headings that appear frequently (Getting ready, How to do it…, How it works…, There's more…, and See also). To give clear instructions on how to complete a recipe, we use these sections as follows:

Getting ready

This section tells you what to expect in the recipe, and describes how to set up any software or any preliminary settings required for the recipe.

How to do it...

This section contains the steps required to follow the recipe.

How it works...

This section usually consists of a detailed explanation of what happened in the previous section.

There's more…

This section consists of additional information about the recipe in order to make the reader more knowledgeable about the recipe.

See also

This section provides helpful links to other useful information for the recipe.

Conventions

In this book, you will find a number of text styles that distinguish between different kinds of information. Here are some examples of these styles and an explanation of their meaning. Code words in text, database table names, folder names, filenames, file extensions, pathnames, dummy URLs, user input, and Twitter handles are shown as follows: "Verify the `installrc` file" A block of code is set as follows:

```
AGENT_ADDRESS_LIST="192.168.123.101 192.168.123.102 192.168.123.103"
        CONTROLLER_ADDRESS="192.168.123.100"
```

Any command-line input or output is written as follows:

```
# VBoxManage --version
```

New terms and **important words** are shown in bold. Words that you see on the screen, for example, in menus or dialog boxes, appear in the text like this: "Select **System info** from the **Administration** panel."

Warnings or important notes appear like this.

Tips and tricks appear like this.

Reader feedback

Feedback from our readers is always welcome. Let us know what you think about this book-what you liked or disliked. Reader feedback is important for us as it helps us develop titles that you will really get the most out of. To send us general feedback, simply e-mail feedback@packtpub.com, and mention the book's title in the subject of your message. If there is a topic that you have expertise in and you are interested in either writing or contributing to a book, see our author guide at www.packtpub.com/authors .

Customer support

Now that you are the proud owner of a Packt book, we have a number of things to help you to get the most from your purchase.

Downloading the example code

You can download the example code files for this book from your account at http://www.packtpub.com. If you purchased this book elsewhere, you can visit http://www.packtpub.com/support and register to have the files e-mailed directly to you. You can download the code files by following these steps:

1. Log in or register to our website using your e-mail address and password.
2. Hover the mouse pointer on the **SUPPORT** tab at the top.
3. Click on **Code Downloads & Errata**.
4. Enter the name of the book in the **Search** box.
5. Select the book for which you're looking to download the code files.
6. Choose from the drop-down menu where you purchased this book from.
7. Click on **Code Download**.

You can also download the code files by clicking on the **Code Files** button on the book's webpage at the Packt Publishing website. This page can be accessed by entering the book's name in the **Search** box. Please note that you need to be logged in to your Packt account. Once the file is downloaded, please make sure that you unzip or extract the folder using the latest version of:

- WinRAR / 7-Zip for Windows
- Zipeg / iZip / UnRarX for Mac
- 7-Zip / PeaZip for Linux

The code bundle for the book is also hosted on GitHub at `https://github.com/PacktPublishing/Ceph-Cookbook-Second-Edition`. We also have other code bundles from our rich catalog of books and videos available at `https://github.com/PacktPublishing/`. Check them out!

Downloading the color images of this book

We also provide you with a PDF file that has color images of the screenshots/diagrams used in this book. The color images will help you better understand the changes in the output. You can download this file from `https://www.packtpub.com/sites/default/files/downloads/CephCookbookSecondEdition_ColorImages.pdf`.

Errata

Although we have taken every care to ensure the accuracy of our content, mistakes do happen. If you find a mistake in one of our books-maybe a mistake in the text or the code-we would be grateful if you could report this to us. By doing so, you can save other readers from frustration and help us improve subsequent versions of this book. If you find any errata, please report them by visiting `http://www.packtpub.com/submit-errata`, selecting your book, clicking on the **Errata Submission Form** link, and entering the details of your errata. Once your errata are verified, your submission will be accepted and the errata will be uploaded to our website or added to any list of existing errata under the **Errata** section of that title. To view the previously submitted errata, go to `https://www.packtpub.com/books/content/support` and enter the name of the book in the search field. The required information will appear under the **Errata** section.

Piracy

Piracy of copyrighted material on the Internet is an ongoing problem across all media. At Packt, we take the protection of our copyright and licenses very seriously. If you come across any illegal copies of our works in any form on the Internet, please provide us with the location address or website name immediately so that we can pursue a remedy. Please contact us at `copyright@packtpub.com` with a link to the suspected pirated material. We appreciate your help in protecting our authors and our ability to bring you valuable content.

Questions

If you have a problem with any aspect of this book, you can contact us at `questions@packtpub.com`, and we will do our best to address the problem.

1
Ceph – Introduction and Beyond

In this chapter, we will cover the following recipes:

- Ceph – the beginning of a new era
- RAID – the end of an era
- Ceph – the architectural overview
- Planning a Ceph deployment
- Setting up a virtual infrastructure
- Installing and configuring Ceph
- Scaling up your Ceph cluster
- Using Ceph clusters with a hands-on approach

Introduction

Ceph is currently the hottest **software-defined storage** (**SDS**) technology and is shaking up the entire storage industry. It is an open source project that provides unified software-defined solutions for *block*, *file*, and *object* storage. The core idea of Ceph is to provide a distributed storage system that is massively scalable and high performing with no single point of failure. From the roots, it has been designed to be highly scalable (up to the *exabyte* level and beyond) while running on general-purpose commodity hardware.

Ceph is acquiring most of the traction in the storage industry due to its open, scalable, and reliable nature. This is the era of cloud computing and software-defined infrastructure, where we need a storage backend that is purely software-defined and, more importantly, cloud-ready. Ceph fits in here very well, regardless of whether you are running a public, private, or hybrid cloud.

Today's software systems are very smart and make the best use of commodity hardware to run gigantic-scale infrastructures. Ceph is one of them; it intelligently uses commodity hardware to provide enterprise-grade robust and highly reliable storage systems.

Ceph has been raised and nourished with the help of the Ceph upstream community with an architectural philosophy that includes the following:

- Every component must scale linearly
- There should not be any single point of failure
- The solution must be software-based, open source, and adaptable
- The Ceph software should run on readily available commodity hardware
- Every component must be self-managing and self-healing wherever possible

The foundation of Ceph lies in objects, which are its building blocks. Object storage such as Ceph is the perfect provision for current and future needs for unstructured data storage. Object storage has its advantages over traditional storage solutions; we can achieve platform and hardware independence using object storage. Ceph plays meticulously with objects and replicates them across the cluster to avail reliability; in Ceph, objects are not tied to a physical path, making object location independent. This flexibility enables Ceph to scale linearly from the petabyte to the *exabyte* level.

Ceph provides great performance, enormous scalability, power, and flexibility to organizations. It helps them get rid of expensive proprietary storage silos. Ceph is indeed an enterprise-class storage solution that runs on commodity hardware; it is a low-cost yet feature-rich storage system. Ceph's universal storage system provides block, file, and object storage under one hood, enabling customers to use storage as they want.

In the following section we will learn about Ceph releases.

Ceph is being developed and improved at a rapid pace. On July 3, 2012, Sage announced the first LTS release of Ceph with the code name Argonaut. Since then, we have seen 12 new releases come up. Ceph releases are categorized as **Long Term Support (LTS)**, and stable releases and every alternate Ceph release are LTS releases. For more information, visit `https://Ceph.com/category/releases/`.

Ceph release name	Ceph release version	Released On
Argonaut	V0.48 (LTS)	July 3, 2012
Bobtail	V0.56 (LTS)	January 1, 2013
Cuttlefish	V0.61	May 7, 2013
Dumpling	V0.67 (LTS)	August 14, 2013
Emperor	V0.72	November 9, 2013
Firefly	V0.80 (LTS)	May 7, 2014
Giant	V0.87.1	Feb 26, 2015
Hammer	V0.94 (LTS)	April 7, 2015
Infernalis	V9.0.0	May 5, 2015
Jewel	V10.0.0 (LTS)	Nov, 2015
Kraken	V11.0.0	June 2016
Luminous	V12.0.0 (LTS)	Feb 2017

Here is a fact: Ceph release names follow an alphabetic order; the next one will be an *M* release. The term *Ceph* is a common nickname given to pet octopuses and is considered a short form of *Cephalopod*, which is a class of marine animals that belong to the mollusk phylum. Ceph has octopuses as its mascot, which represents Ceph's highly parallel behavior, similar to octopuses.

Ceph – the beginning of a new era

Data storage requirements have grown explosively over the last few years. Research shows that data in large organizations is growing at a rate of 40 to 60 percent annually, and many companies are doubling their data footprint each year. IDC analysts have estimated that worldwide, there were 54.4 exabytes of total digital data in the year 2000. By 2007, this reached 295 exabytes, and by 2020, it's expected to reach 44 zettabytes worldwide. Such data growth cannot be managed by traditional storage systems; we need a system such as Ceph, which is distributed, scalable and most importantly, economically viable. Ceph has been especially designed to handle today's as well as the future's data storage needs.

Software-defined storage – SDS

SDS is what is needed to reduce TCO for your storage infrastructure. In addition to reduced storage cost, SDS can offer flexibility, scalability, and reliability. Ceph is a true SDS solution; it runs on commodity hardware with no vendor lock-in and provides low cost per GB. Unlike traditional storage systems, where hardware gets married to software, in SDS, you are free to choose commodity hardware from any manufacturer and are free to design a heterogeneous hardware solution for your own needs. Ceph's software-defined storage on top of this hardware provides all the intelligence you need and will take care of everything, providing all the enterprise storage features right from the software layer.

Cloud storage

One of the drawbacks of a cloud infrastructure is the storage. Every cloud infrastructure needs a storage system that is reliable, low-cost, and scalable with a tighter integration than its other cloud components. There are many traditional storage solutions out there in the market that claim to be cloud-ready, but today, we not only need cloud readiness, but also a lot more beyond that. We need a storage system that should be fully integrated with cloud systems and can provide lower TCO without any compromise to reliability and scalability. Cloud systems are software-defined and are built on top of commodity hardware; similarly, it needs a storage system that follows the same methodology, that is, being software-defined on top of commodity hardware, and Ceph is the best choice available for cloud use cases.

Ceph has been rapidly evolving and bridging the gap of a true cloud storage backend. It is grabbing the center stage with every major open source cloud platform, namely OpenStack, CloudStack, and OpenNebula. Moreover, Ceph has succeeded in building up beneficial partnerships with cloud vendors such as Red Hat, Canonical, Mirantis, SUSE, and many more. These companies are favoring Ceph big time and including it as an official storage backend for their cloud OpenStack distributions, thus making Ceph a red-hot technology in cloud storage space.

The OpenStack project is one of the finest examples of open source software powering public and private clouds. It has proven itself as an end-to-end open source cloud solution. OpenStack is a collection of programs, such as Cinder, Glance, and Swift, which provide storage capabilities to OpenStack. These OpenStack components require a reliable, scalable, and all in one storage backend such as Ceph. For this reason, OpenStack and Ceph communities have been working together for many years to develop a fully compatible Ceph storage backend for the OpenStack.

Cloud infrastructure based on Ceph provides much-needed flexibility to service providers to build *Storage-as-a-Service* and *Infrastructure-as-a-Service* solutions, which they cannot achieve from other traditional enterprise storage solutions as they are not designed to fulfill cloud needs. Using Ceph, service providers can offer low-cost, reliable cloud storage to their customers.

Unified next-generation storage architecture

The definition of unified storage has changed lately. A few years ago, the term *unified storage* referred to providing file and block storage from a single system. Now because of recent technological advancements, such as *cloud computing*, *big data*, and *internet of Things*, a new kind of storage has been evolving, that is, object storage. Thus, all storage systems that do not support object storage are not really unified storage solutions. A true unified storage is like Ceph; it supports blocks, files, and object storage from a single system.

In Ceph, the term *unified storage* is more meaningful than what existing storage vendors claim to provide. It has been designed from the ground up to be future-ready, and it's constructed such that it can handle enormous amounts of data. When we call Ceph *future ready*, we mean to focus on its object storage capabilities, which is a better fit for today's mix of unstructured data rather than blocks or files. Everything in Ceph relies on intelligent objects, whether it's block storage or file storage. Rather than managing blocks and files underneath, Ceph manages objects and supports block-and-file-based storage on top of it. Objects provide enormous scaling with increased performance by eliminating metadata operations. Ceph uses an algorithm to dynamically compute where the object should be stored and retrieved from.

The traditional storage architecture of SAN and NAS systems is very limited. Basically, they follow the tradition of controller high availability; that is, if one storage controller fails, it serves data from the second controller. But, what if the second controller fails at the same time, or even worse, if the entire disk shelf fails? In most cases, you will end up losing your data. This kind of storage architecture, which cannot sustain multiple failures, is definitely what we do not want today. Another drawback of traditional storage systems is their data storage and access mechanism. They maintain a central lookup table to keep track of metadata, which means that every time a client sends a request for a read or write operation, the storage system first performs a lookup in the huge metadata table, and after receiving the real data location, it performs the client operation. For a smaller storage system, you might not notice performance hits, but think of a large storage cluster—you would definitely be bound by performance limits with this approach. This would even restrict your scalability.

Ceph does not follow this traditional storage architecture; in fact, the architecture has been completely reinvented. Rather than storing and manipulating metadata, Ceph introduces a newer way: the CRUSH algorithm. CRUSH stands for **Controlled Replication Under Scalable Hashing**. Instead of performing a lookup in the metadata table for every client request, the CRUSH algorithm computes on demand where the data should be written to or read from. By computing metadata, the need to manage a centralized table for metadata is no longer there. Modern computers are amazingly fast and can perform a CRUSH lookup very quickly; moreover, this computing load, which is generally not too much, can be distributed across cluster nodes, leveraging the power of distributed storage. In addition to this, CRUSH has a unique property, which is infrastructure awareness. It understands the relationship between various components of your infrastructure and stores your data in a unique failure zone, such as a disk, node, rack, row, and data center room, among others. CRUSH stores all the copies of your data such that it is available even if a few components fail in a failure zone. It is due to CRUSH that Ceph can handle multiple component failures and provide reliability and durability.

The CRUSH algorithm makes Ceph self-managing and self-healing. In the event of component failure in a failure zone, CRUSH senses which component has failed and determines the effect on the cluster. Without any administrative intervention, CRUSH self-manages and self-heals by performing a recovering operation for the data lost due to failure. CRUSH regenerates the data from the replica copies that the cluster maintains. If you have configured the Ceph CRUSH map in the correct order, it makes sure that at least one copy of your data is always accessible. Using CRUSH, we can design a highly reliable storage infrastructure with no single point of failure. This makes Ceph a highly scalable and reliable storage system that is future-ready. CRUSH is covered more in detail in Chapter 9, *Ceph Under the Hood*.

RAID – the end of an era

The RAID technology has been the fundamental building block for storage systems for years. It has proven successful for almost every kind of data that has been generated in the last 3 decades. But all eras must come to an end, and this time, it's RAID's turn. These systems have started showing limitations and are incapable of delivering to future storage needs. In the course of the last few years, cloud infrastructures have gained a strong momentum and are imposing new requirements on storage and challenging traditional RAID systems. In this section, we will uncover the limitations imposed by RAID systems.

RAID rebuilds are painful

The most painful thing in a RAID technology is its super-lengthy rebuild process. Disk manufacturers are packing lots of storage capacity per disk. They are now producing an extra-large capacity of disk drives at a fraction of the price. We no longer talk about 450 GB, 600 GB, or even 1 TB disks, as there is a larger capacity of disks available today. The newer enterprise disk specification offers disks up to 4 TB, 6 TB, and even 10 TB disk drives, and the capacities keep increasing year by year.

Think of an enterprise RAID-based storage system that is made up of numerous 4 TB or 6 TB disk drives. Unfortunately, when such a disk drive fails, RAID will take several hours and even up to days to repair a single failed disk. Meanwhile, if another drive fails from the same RAID group, then it would become a chaotic situation. Repairing multiple large disk drives using RAID is a cumbersome process.

RAID spare disks increases TCO

The RAID system requires a few disks as hot spare disks. These are just free disks that will be used only when a disk fails; else, they will not be used for data storage. This adds extra cost to the system and increases TCO. Moreover, if you're running short of spare disks and immediately a disk fails in the RAID group, then you will face a severe problem.

RAID can be expensive and hardware dependent

RAID requires a set of identical disk drivers in a single RAID group; you would face penalties if you change the disk size, rpm, or disk type. Doing so would adversely affect the capacity and performance of your storage system. This makes RAID highly choosy about the hardware.

Also, enterprise RAID-based systems often require expensive hardware components, such as RAID controllers, which significantly increases the system cost. These RAID controllers will become single points of failure if you do not have many of them.

The growing RAID group is a challenge

RAID can hit a dead end when it's not possible to grow the RAID group size, which means that there is no scale-out support. After a point, you cannot grow your RAID-based system, even though you have money. Some systems allow the addition of disk shelves but up to a very limited capacity; however, these new disk shelves put a load on the existing storage controller. So, you can gain some capacity but with a performance trade-off.

The RAID reliability model is no longer promising

RAID can be configured with a variety of different types; the most common types are RAID5 and RAID6, which can survive the failure of one and two disks, respectively. RAID cannot ensure data reliability after a two-disk failure. This is one of the biggest drawbacks of RAID systems.

Moreover, at the time of a RAID rebuild operation, client requests are most likely to starve for I/O until the rebuild completes. Another limiting factor with RAID is that it only protects against disk failure; it cannot protect against a failure of the network, server hardware, OS, power, or other data center disasters.

After discussing RAID's drawbacks, we can come to the conclusion that we now need a system that can overcome all these drawbacks in a performance and cost-effective way. The Ceph storage system is one of the best solutions available today to address these problems. Let's see how.

For reliability, Ceph makes use of the data replication method, which means it does not use RAID, thus overcoming all the problems that can be found in a RAID-based enterprise system. Ceph is a software-defined storage, so we do not require any specialized hardware for data replication; moreover, the replication level is highly customized by means of commands, which means that the Ceph storage administrator can manage the replication factor of a minimum of one and a maximum of a higher number, totally depending on the underlying infrastructure.

In an event of one or more disk failures, Ceph's replication is a better process than RAID. When a disk drive fails, all the data that was residing on that disk at that point of time starts recovering from its peer disks. Since Ceph is a distributed system, all the data copies are scattered on the entire cluster of disks in the form of objects, such that no two object's copies should reside on the same disk and must reside in a different failure zone defined by the CRUSH map. The good part is that all the cluster disks participate in data recovery. This makes the recovery operation amazingly fast with the least performance problems. Furthermore, the recovery operation does not require any spare disks; the data is simply replicated to other Ceph disks in the cluster. Ceph uses a weighting mechanism for its disks, so different disk sizes is not a problem.

In addition to the replication method, Ceph also supports another advanced way of data reliability: using the erasure-coding technique. Erasure-coded pools require less storage space compared to replicated pools. In erasure-coding, data is recovered or regenerated algorithmically by erasure code calculation. You can use both the techniques of data availability, that is, replication as well as erasure-coding, in the same Ceph cluster but over different storage pools. We will learn more about the erasure-coding technique in the upcoming chapters.

Ceph – the architectural overview

The Ceph internal architecture is pretty straightforward, and we will learn about it with the help of the following diagram:

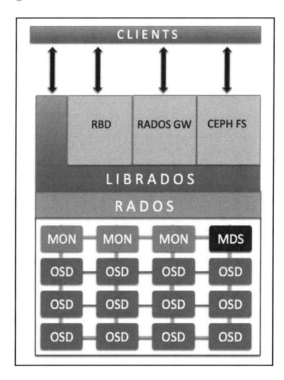

- **Ceph monitors (MON)**: Ceph monitors track the health of the entire cluster by keeping a map of the cluster state. They maintain a separate map of information for each component, which includes an OSD map, MON map, PG map (discussed in later chapters), and CRUSH map. All the cluster nodes report to monitor nodes and share information about every change in their state. The monitor does not store actual data; this is the job of the OSD.
- **Ceph object storage device (OSD)**: As soon as your application issues a write operation to the Ceph cluster, data gets stored in the OSD in the form of objects.

This is the only component of the Ceph cluster where actual user data is stored, and the same data is retrieved when the client issues a read operation. Usually, one OSD daemon is tied to one physical disk in your cluster. So in general, the total number of physical disks in your Ceph cluster is the same as the number of OSD daemons working underneath to store user data on each physical disk.

- **Ceph metadata server (MDS)**: The MDS keeps track of file hierarchy and stores metadata only for the CephFS filesystem. The Ceph block device and RADOS gateway do not require metadata; hence, they do not need the Ceph MDS daemon. The MDS does not serve data directly to clients, thus removing the single point of failure from the system.

- **RADOS**: The **Reliable Autonomic Distributed Object Store (RADOS)** is the foundation of the Ceph storage cluster. Everything in Ceph is stored in the form of objects, and the RADOS object store is responsible for storing these objects irrespective of their data types. The RADOS layer makes sure that data always remains consistent. To do this, it performs data replication, failure detection, and recovery, as well as data migration and rebalancing across cluster nodes.

- **librados**: The librados library is a convenient way to gain access to RADOS with support to the PHP, Ruby, Java, Python, C, and C++ programming languages. It provides a native interface for the Ceph storage cluster (RADOS) as well as a base for other services, such as RBD, RGW, and CephFS, which are built on top of librados. librados also supports direct access to RADOS from applications with no HTTP overhead.

- **RADOS block devices (RBDs)**: RBDs, which are now known as the Ceph block device, provide persistent block storage, which is thin-provisioned, resizable, and stores data striped over multiple OSDs. The RBD service has been built as a native interface on top of librados.

- **RADOS gateway interface (RGW)**: RGW provides object storage service. It uses librgw (the Rados Gateway Library) and librados, allowing applications to establish connections with the Ceph object storage. The RGW provides RESTful APIs with interfaces that are compatible with Amazon S3 and OpenStack Swift.

- **CephFS**: The Ceph filesystem provides a POSIX-compliant filesystem that uses the Ceph storage cluster to store user data on a filesystem. Like RBD and RGW, the CephFS service is also implemented as a native interface to librados.

- **Ceph manager**: The *Ceph manager* daemon (ceph-mgr) was introduced in the Kraken release, and it runs alongside monitor daemons to provide additional monitoring and interfaces to external monitoring and management systems.

Planning a Ceph deployment

A Ceph storage cluster is created on top of the commodity hardware. This commodity hardware includes industry-standard servers loaded with physical disk drives that provide storage capacity and some standard networking infrastructure. These servers run standard Linux distributions and Ceph software on top of them. The following diagram helps you understand the basic view of a Ceph cluster:

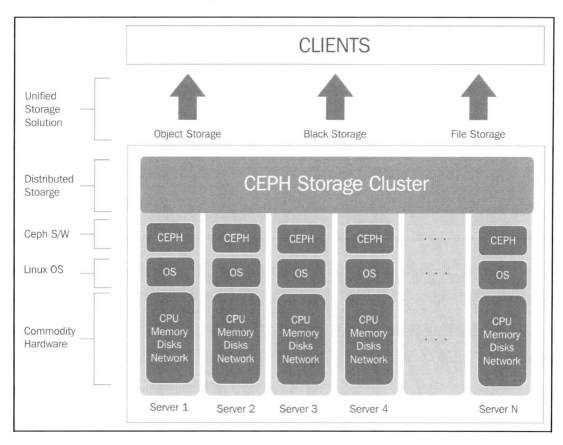

As explained earlier, Ceph does not have a very specific hardware requirement. For the purpose of testing and learning, we can deploy a Ceph cluster on top of virtual machines. In this section and in the later chapters of this book, we will be working on a Ceph cluster that is built on top of virtual machines. It's very convenient to use a virtual environment to test Ceph, as it's fairly easy to set up and can be destroyed and recreated anytime. It's good to know that a virtual infrastructure for the Ceph cluster should not be used for a production environment, and you might face serious problems with this.

Setting up a virtual infrastructure

To set up a virtual infrastructure, you will require open source software, such as Oracle VirtualBox and Vagrant, to automate virtual machine creation for you. Make sure you have the software installed and working correctly on your host machine. The installation processes of the software are beyond the scope of this book; you can follow their respective documentation in order to get them installed and working correctly.

Getting ready

You will need the following software to get started:

- **Oracle VirtualBox**: This is an open source virtualization software package for host machines based on x86 and AMD64/Intel64. It supports Microsoft Windows, Linux, and Apple macOS X host operating systems. Make sure it's installed and working correctly. More information can be found at https://www.virtualbox.org.

  Once you have installed VirtualBox, run the following command to ensure the installation was successful:

  ```
  # VBoxManage --version
  ```

  ```
  [vumrao@ceph-jewel ~]$
  [vumrao@ceph-jewel ~]$ VBoxManage --version
  5.1.26r117224
  [vumrao@ceph-jewel ~]$
  ```

- **Vagrant**: This is software meant for creating virtual development environments. It works as a wrapper around virtualization software, such as VirtualBox, VMware, KVM, and so on. It supports the Microsoft Windows, Linux, and Apple macOS X host operating systems. Make sure it's installed and working correctly. More information can be found at `https://www.vagrantup.com/`. Once you have installed Vagrant, run the following command to ensure the installation was successful:

```
# vagrant --version
```

```
[vumrao@ceph-jewel ~]$
[vumrao@ceph-jewel ~]$ vagrant --version
Vagrant 1.9.1
[vumrao@ceph-jewel ~]$
```

- **Git**: This is a distributed revision control system and the most popular and widely adopted version control system for software development. It supports Microsoft Windows, Linux, and Apple macOS X operating systems. Make sure it's installed and working correctly. More information can be found at `http://git-scm.com/`.

Once you have installed Git, run the following command to ensure the installation was successful:

```
# git --version
```

```
[vumrao@ceph-jewel ~]$
[vumrao@ceph-jewel ~]$ git --version
git version 2.13.3
[vumrao@ceph-jewel ~]$
```

How to do it...

Once you have installed the mentioned software, we will proceed with virtual machine creation:

1. `git clone` ceph-cookbook repositories to your VirtualBox host machine:

   $ git clone
   https://github.com/PacktPublishing/Ceph-Cookbook-Second-Edition

```
[vumrao@ceph-jewel Projects]$
[vumrao@ceph-jewel Projects]$ git clone https://github.com/PacktPublishing/Ceph-Cookbook-Second-Edition
Cloning into 'Ceph-Cookbook-Second-Edition'...
remote: Counting objects: 33, done.
remote: Compressing objects: 100% (29/29), done.
remote: Total 33 (delta 8), reused 26 (delta 3), pack-reused 0
Unpacking objects: 100% (33/33), done.
[vumrao@ceph-jewel Projects]$
```

2. Under the cloned directory, you will find `vagrantfile`, which is our Vagrant configuration file that basically instructs VirtualBox to launch the VMs that we require at different stages of this book. Vagrant will automate the VM's creation, installation, and configuration for you; it makes the initial environment easy to set up:

   $ cd Ceph-Cookbook-Second-Edition ; ls -l

```
[vumrao@ceph-jewel Projects]$
[vumrao@ceph-jewel Projects]$ cd Ceph-Cookbook-Second-Edition/
[vumrao@ceph-jewel Ceph-Cookbook-Second-Edition]$ ls -l
total 56
-rw-rw-r--. 1 vumrao vumrao   215 Sep 15 13:51 keystonerc_admin
-rw-rw-r--. 1 vumrao vumrao   180 Sep 15 13:51 keystonerc_demo
-rw-rw-r--. 1 vumrao vumrao  1062 Sep 15 13:51 LICENSE
-rw-rw-r--. 1 vumrao vumrao   972 Sep 15 13:51 post-deploy.sh
-rw-rw-r--. 1 vumrao vumrao   646 Sep 15 13:51 rbdmap
-rw-rw-r--. 1 vumrao vumrao   327 Sep 15 13:51 rbd-mount.service
-rw-rw-r--. 1 vumrao vumrao 24657 Sep 15 13:51 Vagrantfile
drwxrwxr-x. 2 vumrao vumrao  4096 Sep 15 13:51 vsm
[vumrao@ceph-jewel Ceph-Cookbook-Second-Edition]$
```

3. Next, we will launch three VMs using Vagrant; they are required throughout this chapter:

   $ vagrant up ceph-node1 ceph-node2 ceph-node3

If the default Vagrant provider is not set to VirtualBox, set it to VirtualBox. To make it permanent, it can be added to user `.bashrc` file:

```
# export VAGRANT_DEFAULT_PROVIDER=virtualbox
# echo $VAGRANT_DEFAULT_PROVIDER
```

```
[vumrao@ceph-jewel Ceph-Cookbook-Second-Edition]$
[vumrao@ceph-jewel Ceph-Cookbook-Second-Edition]$ export VAGRANT_DEFAULT_PROVIDER=virtualbox
[vumrao@ceph-jewel Ceph-Cookbook-Second-Edition]$ echo $VAGRANT_DEFAULT_PROVIDER
virtualbox
[vumrao@ceph-jewel Ceph-Cookbook-Second-Edition]$
```

4. Run `vagrant up ceph-node1 ceph-node2 ceph-node3`:

```
[vumrao@ceph-jewel Ceph-Cookbook-Second-Edition]$
[vumrao@ceph-jewel Ceph-Cookbook-Second-Edition]$ vagrant up ceph-node1 ceph-node2 ceph-node3
Bringing machine 'ceph-node1' up with 'virtualbox' provider...
Bringing machine 'ceph-node2' up with 'virtualbox' provider...
Bringing machine 'ceph-node3' up with 'virtualbox' provider...
==> ceph-node1: Importing base box 'centos7-standard'...
==> ceph-node1: Matching MAC address for NAT networking...
==> ceph-node1: Setting the name of the VM: ceph-node1
==> ceph-node1: Clearing any previously set network interfaces...
==> ceph-node1: Preparing network interfaces based on configuration...
    ceph-node1: Adapter 1: nat
    ceph-node1: Adapter 2: hostonly
==> ceph-node1: Forwarding ports...
    ceph-node1: 22 (guest) => 2222 (host) (adapter 1)
==> ceph-node1: Running 'pre-boot' VM customizations...
==> ceph-node1: Booting VM...
==> ceph-node1: Waiting for machine to boot. This may take a few minutes...
    ceph-node1: SSH address: 127.0.0.1:2222
    ceph-node1: SSH username: vagrant
    ceph-node1: SSH auth method: private key
    ceph-node1:
    ceph-node1: Vagrant insecure key detected. Vagrant will automatically replace
    ceph-node1: this with a newly generated keypair for better security.
    ceph-node1:
    ceph-node1: Inserting generated public key within guest...
    ceph-node1: Removing insecure key from the guest if it's present...
    ceph-node1: Key inserted! Disconnecting and reconnecting using new SSH key...
==> ceph-node1: Machine booted and ready!
==> ceph-node1: Checking for guest additions in VM...
    ceph-node1: The guest additions on this VM do not match the installed version of
    ceph-node1: VirtualBox! In most cases this is fine, but in rare cases it can
    ceph-node1: prevent things such as shared folders from working properly. If you see
    ceph-node1: shared folder errors, please make sure the guest additions within the
    ceph-node1: virtual machine match the version of VirtualBox you have installed on
    ceph-node1: your host and reload your VM.
    ceph-node1:
    ceph-node1: Guest Additions Version: 4.3.22
    ceph-node1: VirtualBox Version: 5.1
==> ceph-node1: Setting hostname...
==> ceph-node1: Configuring and enabling network interfaces...
==> ceph-node1: Running provisioner: shell...
    ceph-node1: Running: /tmp/vagrant-shell20170915-15795-iyuutx.sh
==> ceph-node2: Importing base box 'centos7-standard'...
```

5. Check the status of your virtual machines:

```
$ vagrant status ceph-node1 ceph-node2 ceph-node3
```

```
[vumrao@ceph-jewel Ceph-Cookbook-Second-Edition]$
[vumrao@ceph-jewel Ceph-Cookbook-Second-Edition]$ vagrant status ceph-node1 ceph-node2 ceph-node3
Current machine states:

ceph-node1                running (virtualbox)
ceph-node2                running (virtualbox)
ceph-node3                running (virtualbox)

This environment represents multiple VMs. The VMs are all listed
above with their current state. For more information about a specific
VM, run `vagrant status NAME`.
[vumrao@ceph-jewel Ceph-Cookbook-Second-Edition]$
```

 The username and password that Vagrant uses to configure virtual machine is `vagrant`, and Vagrant has `sudo` rights. The default password for the root user is `vagrant`.

6. Vagrant will, by default, set up hostnames as `ceph-node<node_number>` and IP address subnet as `192.168.1.X` and will create three additional disks that will be used as OSDs by the Ceph cluster. Log in to each of these machines one by one and check whether the hostname, networking, and additional disks have been set up correctly by Vagrant:

```
$ vagrant ssh ceph-node1
$ ip addr show
$ sudo fdisk -l
$ exit
```

7. Vagrant is configured to update `hosts` file on the VMs. For convenience, update the `/etc/hosts` file on your host machine with the following content:

```
192.168.1.101 ceph-node1
192.168.1.102 ceph-node2
192.168.1.103 ceph-node3
```

```
[vumrao@ceph-jewel Ceph-Cookbook-Second-Edition]$
[vumrao@ceph-jewel Ceph-Cookbook-Second-Edition]$ sudo vim /etc/hosts
[vumrao@ceph-jewel Ceph-Cookbook-Second-Edition]$ cat /etc/hosts | grep -i ceph-node
192.168.1.101 ceph-node1
192.168.1.102 ceph-node2
192.168.1.103 ceph-node3
[vumrao@ceph-jewel Ceph-Cookbook-Second-Edition]$
```

8. Update all the three VM's to the latest CentOS release and reboot to the latest kernel:

```
[vumrao@ceph-jewel Ceph-Cookbook-Second-Edition]$
[vumrao@ceph-jewel Ceph-Cookbook-Second-Edition]$ vagrant ssh ceph-node1
Last login: Fri Sep 15 21:24:41 2017 from 10.0.2.2
[vagrant@ceph-node1 ~]$ sudo yum update -y
```

9. Generate root SSH keys for `ceph-node1` and copy the keys to `ceph-node2` and `ceph-node3`. The password for the root user on these VMs is `vagrant`. Enter the root user password when asked by the `ssh-copy-id` command and proceed with the default settings:

```
$ vagrant ssh ceph-node1
$ sudo su -
# ssh-keygen
# ssh-copy-id root@ceph-node1
# ssh-copy-id root@ceph-node2
# ssh-copy-id root@ceph-node3
```

```
[root@ceph-node1 ~]#
[root@ceph-node1 ~]# ssh-copy-id root@ceph-node2
The authenticity of host 'ceph-node2 (192.168.1.102)' can't be established.
ECDSA key fingerprint is af:2a:a5:74:a7:0b:f5:5b:ef:c5:4b:2a:fe:1d:30:8e.
Are you sure you want to continue connecting (yes/no)? yes
/bin/ssh-copy-id: INFO: attempting to log in with the new key(s), to filter out any that are already installed
/bin/ssh-copy-id: INFO: 1 key(s) remain to be installed -- if you are prompted now it is to install the new keys
root@ceph-node2's password:

Number of key(s) added: 1

Now try logging into the machine, with:   "ssh 'root@ceph-node2'"
and check to make sure that only the key(s) you wanted were added.

[root@ceph-node1 ~]#
```

10. Once the SSH keys are copied to `ceph-node2` and `ceph-node3`, the root user from `ceph-node1` can do an `ssh` login to VMs without entering the password:

```
# ssh ceph-node2 hostname
# ssh ceph-node3 hostname
```

```
[root@ceph-node1 ~]#
[root@ceph-node1 ~]# ssh ceph-node2 hostname
ceph-node2
[root@ceph-node1 ~]# ssh ceph-node3 hostname
ceph-node3
[root@ceph-node1 ~]#
```

11. Enable ports that are required by the Ceph MON, OSD, and MDS on the operating system's firewall. Execute the following commands on all VMs:

```
# firewall-cmd --zone=public --add-port=6789/tcp --permanent
# firewall-cmd --zone=public --add-port=6800-7100/tcp --permanent
# firewall-cmd --reload
# firewall-cmd --zone=public --list-all
```

```
[root@ceph-node1 ~]#
[root@ceph-node1 ~]# firewall-cmd --zone=public --add-port=6789/tcp --permanent
success
[root@ceph-node1 ~]# firewall-cmd --zone=public --add-port=6800-7100/tcp --permanent
success
[root@ceph-node1 ~]# firewall-cmd --reload
success
[root@ceph-node1 ~]# firewall-cmd --zone=public --list-all
public (active)
  target: default
  icmp-block-inversion: no
  interfaces: enp0s3 enp0s8
  sources:
  services: dhcpv6-client ssh
  ports: 6789/tcp 6800-7100/tcp
  protocols:
  masquerade: no
  forward-ports:
  sourceports:
  icmp-blocks:
  rich rules:

[root@ceph-node1 ~]#
```

12. Install and configure NTP on all VMs:

```
# yum install ntp ntpdate -y
# ntpdate pool.ntp.org
# systemctl restart ntpdate.service
# systemctl restart ntpd.service
# systemctl enable ntpd.service
# systemctl enable ntpdate.service
```

Installing and configuring Ceph

To deploy our first Ceph cluster, we will use the `ceph-ansible` tool to install and configure Ceph on all three virtual machines. The `ceph-ansible` tool is a part of the Ceph project, which is used for easy deployment and management of your Ceph storage cluster. In the previous section, we created three virtual machines with CentOS 7, which have connectivity with the internet over NAT, as well as private host-only networks.

We will configure these machines as Ceph storage clusters, as mentioned in the following diagram:

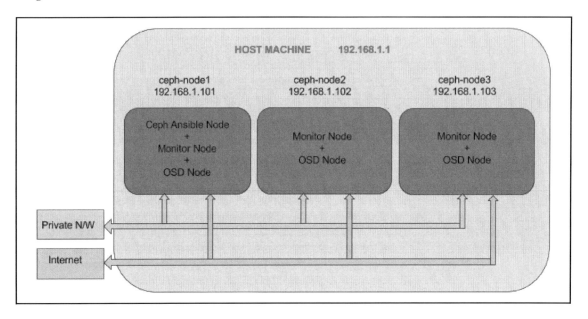

Creating the Ceph cluster on ceph-node1

We will first install Ceph and configure `ceph-node1` as the Ceph monitor and the Ceph OSD node. Later recipes in this chapter will introduce `ceph-node2` and `ceph-node3`.

How to do it...

Copy `ceph-ansible` package on `ceph-node1` from the `Ceph-Cookbook-Second-Edition` directory.

1. Use `vagrant` as the password for the root user:

   ```
   # cd Ceph-Cookbook-Second-Edition
   # scp ceph-ansible-2.2.10-38.g7ef908a.el7.noarch.rpm root@ceph-node1:/root
   ```

   ```
   [vumrao:~]$ cd /home/vumrao/Projects/Ceph-Cookbook-Second-Edition
   [vumrao:...eph-Cookbook-Second-Edition]$ pwd
   /home/vumrao/Projects/Ceph-Cookbook-Second-Edition
   [vumrao:...eph-Cookbook-Second-Edition]$
   [vumrao:...eph-Cookbook-Second-Edition]$ scp ceph-ansible-2.2.10-38.g7ef908a.el7.noarch.rpm root@ceph-node1:/root
   root@ceph-node1's password:
   ceph-ansible-2.2.10-38.g7ef908a.el7.noarch.rpm
   [vumrao:...eph-Cookbook-Second-Edition]$
   [vumrao:...eph-Cookbook-Second-Edition]$
   ```

2. Log in to `ceph-node1` and install `ceph-ansible` on `ceph-node1`:

   ```
   [root@ceph-node1 ~]#
   yum install ceph-ansible-2.2.10-38.g7ef908a.el7.noarch.rpm -y
   ```

   ```
   Running transaction
     Installing : python-passlib-1.6.5-2.el7.noarch
     Installing : ansible-2.3.2.0-2.el7.noarch
     Installing : ceph-ansible-2.2.10-38.g7ef908a.el7.noarch
     Verifying  : ansible-2.3.2.0-2.el7.noarch
     Verifying  : ceph-ansible-2.2.10-38.g7ef908a.el7.noarch
     Verifying  : python-passlib-1.6.5-2.el7.noarch

   Installed:
     ceph-ansible.noarch 0:2.2.10-38.g7ef908a.el7

   Dependency Installed:
     ansible.noarch 0:2.3.2.0-2.el7                          python-passlib.noarch 0:1.6.5-2.el7
   ```

3. Update the Ceph hosts to `/etc/ansible/hosts`:

   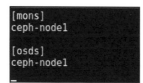

   ```
   [mons]
   ceph-node1

   [osds]
   ceph-node1
   ```

4. Verify that Ansible can reach the Ceph hosts mentioned in
   `/etc/ansible/hosts`:

```
[root@ceph-node1 ~]#
[root@ceph-node1 ~]# ansible all -m ping
ceph-node1 | SUCCESS => {
    "changed": false,
    "ping": "pong"
}
[root@ceph-node1 ~]#
```

5. Create a directory under the root home directory so Ceph Ansible can use it for
   storing the keys:

```
[root@ceph-node1 ~]#
[root@ceph-node1 ~]# mkdir ceph-ansible-keys
[root@ceph-node1 ~]#
```

6. Create a symbolic link to the Ansible `group_vars` directory in the
   `/etc/ansible/` directory:

```
[root@ceph-node1 ~]#
[root@ceph-node1 ~]# ln -s /usr/share/ceph-ansible/group_vars /etc/ansible/group_vars
[root@ceph-node1 ~]#
```

7. Go to `/etc/ansible/group_vars` and copy an `all.yml` file from the
   `all.yml.sample` file and open it to define configuration options' values:

```
[root@ceph-node1 ~]#
[root@ceph-node1 ~]# cd /etc/ansible/group_vars
[root@ceph-node1 group_vars]# cp all.yml.sample all.yml
[root@ceph-node1 group_vars]# vim all.yml
[root@ceph-node1 group_vars]#
```

8. Define the following configuration options in `all.yml` for the latest jewel version
   on CentOS 7:

```
fetch_directory: ~/ceph-ansible-keys
centos_package_dependencies:
  - python-pycurl
  - hdparm
  - epel-release
  - python-setuptools
  - libselinux-python
ceph_origin: 'upstream' # or 'distro' or 'local'
ceph_stable: true # use ceph stable branch
ceph_stable_release: jewel # ceph stable release
ceph_stable_redhat_distro: el7
cephx: true
monitor_interface: enp0s8
journal_size: 2048 # OSD journal size in MB
public_network: 192.168.1.0/24
cluster_network: 192.168.1.0/24
osd_mkfs_type: xfs
osd_mkfs_options_xfs: -f -i size=2048
osd_mount_options_xfs: noatime,largeio,inode64,swalloc
```

9. Go to `/etc/ansible/group_vars` and copy an `osds.yml` file from the `osds.yml.sample` file and open it to define configuration options' values:

```
[root@ceph-node1 group_vars]#
[root@ceph-node1 group_vars]# cp osds.yml.sample osds.yml
[root@ceph-node1 group_vars]# vim osds.yml
[root@ceph-node1 group_vars]# _
```

10. Define the following configuration options in `osds.yml` for OSD disks; we are co-locating an OSD journal in the OSD data disk:

```
devices:
  - /dev/sdb
  - /dev/sdc
  - /dev/sdd
journal_collocation: true
```

11. Go to `/usr/share/ceph-ansible` and add `retry_files_save_path` option in `ansible.cfg` in the `[defaults]` tag:

```
[root@ceph-node1 ~]#
[root@ceph-node1 ~]# cd /usr/share/ceph-ansible
[root@ceph-node1 ceph-ansible]# vim ansible.cfg
[root@ceph-node1 ceph-ansible]# cat ansible.cfg | grep retry_files_save
retry_files_save_path = ~/
[root@ceph-node1 ceph-ansible]#
```

12. Run Ansible playbook in order to deploy the Ceph cluster on `ceph-node1`:

To run the playbook, you need `site.yml`, which is present in the same path: `/usr/share/ceph-ansible/`. You should be in the `/usr/share/ceph-ansible/` path and should run following commands:

```
# cp site.yml.sample site.yml
# ansible-playbook site.yml
```

```
[root@ceph-node1 ceph-ansible]#
[root@ceph-node1 ceph-ansible]# cp site.yml.sample site.yml
[root@ceph-node1 ceph-ansible]# ansible-playbook site.yml
[DEPRECATION WARNING]: docker is kept for backwards compatibility but usage is discouraged. The module documentation details page may explain more about this rationale.
This feature will be removed in a future
release. Deprecation warnings can be disabled by setting deprecation_warnings=False in ansible.cfg.

PLAY [mons,agents,osds,mdss,rgws,nfss,restapis,rbdmirrors,clients,mgrs] ********************************************************
```

Once playbook completes the Ceph cluster installation job and plays the recap with `failed=0`, it means `ceph-ansible` has deployed the Ceph cluster, as shown in the following screenshot:

```
PLAY RECAP *********************************************************************************************
ceph-node1                     : ok=126   changed=24   unreachable=0   failed=0

[root@ceph-node1 ceph-ansible]#
[root@ceph-node1 ceph-ansible]# ceph -s
    cluster 8e396f0b-81ba-4a79-8bf2-7d29be9de05b
     health HEALTH_WARN
            64 pgs degraded
            64 pgs undersized
            too few PGs per OSD (21 < min 30)
     monmap e1: 1 mons at {ceph-node1=192.168.1.101:6789/0}
            election epoch 3, quorum 0 ceph-node1
     osdmap e13: 3 osds: 3 up, 3 in
            flags sortbitwise,require_jewel_osds
      pgmap v24: 64 pgs, 1 pools, 0 bytes data, 0 objects
            101816 kB used, 55163 MB / 55262 MB avail
                  64 undersized+degraded+peered
[root@ceph-node1 ceph-ansible]# ceph osd tree
ID WEIGHT  TYPE NAME          UP/DOWN REWEIGHT PRIMARY-AFFINITY
-1 0.05278 root default
-2 0.05278     host ceph-node1
 0 0.01759         osd.0           up  1.00000          1.00000
 1 0.01759         osd.1           up  1.00000          1.00000
 2 0.01759         osd.2           up  1.00000          1.00000
[root@ceph-node1 ceph-ansible]#
```

You have all three OSD daemons and one monitor daemon up and running in `ceph-node1`.

Here's how you can check the Ceph jewel release installed version. You can run the `ceph -v` command to check the installed ceph version:

```
[root@ceph-node1 ceph-ansible]#
[root@ceph-node1 ceph-ansible]# ceph -v
ceph version 10.2.9 (2ee413f77150c0f375ff6f10edd6c8f9c7d060d0)
[root@ceph-node1 ceph-ansible]#
```

Scaling up your Ceph cluster

At this point, we have a running Ceph cluster with one MON and three OSDs configured on `ceph-node1`. Now we will scale up the cluster by adding `ceph-node2` and `ceph-node3` as MON and OSD nodes.

How to do it...

A Ceph storage cluster requires at least one monitor to run. For high availability, a Ceph storage cluster relies on an odd number of monitors and more than one, for example, 3 or 5, to form a quorum. It uses the Paxos algorithm to maintain quorum majority. You will notice that your Ceph cluster is currently showing `HEALTH_WARN`; this is because we have not configured any OSDs other than `ceph-node1`. By default, the data in a Ceph cluster is replicated three times, that too on three different OSDs hosted on three different nodes.

Since we already have one monitor running on `ceph-node1`, let's create two more monitors for our Ceph cluster and configure OSDs on `ceph-node2` and `ceph-node3`:

1. Update the Ceph hosts `ceph-node2` and `ceph-node3` to `/etc/ansible/hosts`:

```
[mons]
ceph-node1
ceph-node2
ceph-node3

[osds]
ceph-node1
ceph-node2
ceph-node3
```

2. Verify that Ansible can reach the Ceph hosts mentioned in
   `/etc/ansible/hosts`:

```
[root@ceph-node1 ceph-ansible]#
[root@ceph-node1 ceph-ansible]# ansible all -m ping
ceph-node3 | SUCCESS => {
    "changed": false,
    "ping": "pong"
}
ceph-node2 | SUCCESS => {
    "changed": false,
    "ping": "pong"
}
ceph-node1 | SUCCESS => {
    "changed": false,
    "ping": "pong"
}
[root@ceph-node1 ceph-ansible]#
```

3. Run Ansible playbook in order to scale up the Ceph cluster on `ceph-node2` and
   `ceph-node3`:

```
[root@ceph-node1 ceph-ansible]#
[root@ceph-node1 ceph-ansible]# ansible-playbook site.yml
[DEPRECATION WARNING]: docker is kept for backwards compatibility but usage is discouraged. The module documentation details page may explain more about this rationale..
This feature will be removed in a future
release. Deprecation warnings can be disabled by setting deprecation_warnings=False in ansible.cfg.

PLAY [mons,agents,osds,mdss,rgws,nfss,restapis,rbdmirrors,clients,mgrs] *********************************************

TASK [check for python2] *******************************************************
ok: [ceph-node3]
ok: [ceph-node2]
ok: [ceph-node1]
```

Once playbook completes the ceph cluster scaleout job and plays the recap with `failed=0`, it means that the Ceph ansible has deployed more Ceph daemons in the cluster, as shown in the following screenshot.

You have three more OSD daemons and one more monitor daemon running in `ceph-node2` and three more OSD daemons and one more monitor daemon running in `ceph-node3`. Now you have total nine OSD daemons and three monitor daemons running on three nodes:

```
PLAY RECAP **********************************************************************************************************
ceph-node1                 : ok=123   changed=2    unreachable=0    failed=0
ceph-node2                 : ok=119   changed=4    unreachable=0    failed=0
ceph-node3                 : ok=120   changed=4    unreachable=0    failed=0

[root@ceph-node1 ceph-ansible]# ceph -s
    cluster 8e396f0b-81ba-4a79-8bf2-7d29be9de05b
     health HEALTH_WARN
            too few PGs per OSD (21 < min 30)
     monmap e3: 3 mons at {ceph-node1=192.168.1.101:6789/0,ceph-node2=192.168.1.102:6789/0,ceph-node3=192.168.1.103:6789/0}
            election epoch 10, quorum 0,1,2 ceph-node1,ceph-node2,ceph-node3
     osdmap e34: 9 osds: 9 up, 9 in
            flags sortbitwise,require_jewel_osds
      pgmap v64: 64 pgs, 1 pools, 0 bytes data, 0 objects
            302 MB used, 161 GB / 161 GB avail
                  64 active+clean
[root@ceph-node1 ceph-ansible]# ceph osd tree
ID WEIGHT  TYPE NAME            UP/DOWN REWEIGHT PRIMARY-AFFINITY
-1 0.15834 root default
-2 0.05278     host ceph-node1
 0 0.01759         osd.0            up  1.00000          1.00000
 1 0.01759         osd.1            up  1.00000          1.00000
 2 0.01759         osd.2            up  1.00000          1.00000
-3 0.05278     host ceph-node3
 3 0.01759         osd.3            up  1.00000          1.00000
 5 0.01759         osd.5            up  1.00000          1.00000
 7 0.01759         osd.7            up  1.00000          1.00000
-4 0.05278     host ceph-node2
 4 0.01759         osd.4            up  1.00000          1.00000
 6 0.01759         osd.6            up  1.00000          1.00000
 8 0.01759         osd.8            up  1.00000          1.00000
[root@ceph-node1 ceph-ansible]# ceph osd pool set rbd pg_num 128
set pool 0 pg_num to 128
[root@ceph-node1 ceph-ansible]# ceph osd pool set rbd pgp_num 128
set pool 0 pgp_num to 128
[root@ceph-node1 ceph-ansible]# ceph -s
    cluster 8e396f0b-81ba-4a79-8bf2-7d29be9de05b
     health HEALTH_OK
     monmap e3: 3 mons at {ceph-node1=192.168.1.101:6789/0,ceph-node2=192.168.1.102:6789/0,ceph-node3=192.168.1.103:6789/0}
            election epoch 10, quorum 0,1,2 ceph-node1,ceph-node2,ceph-node3
     osdmap e38: 9 osds: 9 up, 9 in
            flags sortbitwise,require_jewel_osds
      pgmap v77: 128 pgs, 1 pools, 0 bytes data, 0 objects
            306 MB used, 161 GB / 161 GB avail
                 128 active+clean
[root@ceph-node1 ceph-ansible]#
```

4. We were getting a `too few PGs per OSD` warning and because of that, we increased the default RBD pool PGs from 64 to 128. Check the status of your Ceph cluster; at this stage, your cluster is healthy. PGs - placement groups are covered in detail in `Chapter 9`, *Ceph Under the Hood*.

Using the Ceph cluster with a hands-on approach

Now that we have a running Ceph cluster, we will perform some hands-on practice to gain experience with Ceph using some basic commands.

How to do it...

Below are some of the common commands used by Ceph admins:

1. Check the status of your Ceph installation:

   `# ceph -s or # ceph status`

2. Check Ceph's health detail:

   `# ceph health detail`

3. Watch the cluster health:

   `# ceph -w`

4. Check Ceph's monitor quorum status:

   `# ceph quorum_status --format json-pretty`

5. Dump Ceph's monitor information:

   `# ceph mon dump`

6. Check the cluster usage status:

   `# ceph df`

7. Check the Ceph monitor, OSD, pool, and placement group stats:

   ```
   # ceph mon stat
   # ceph osd stat
   # ceph osd pool stats
   # ceph pg stat
   ```

8. List the placement group:

   ```
   # ceph pg dump
   ```

9. List the Ceph pools in detail:

   ```
   # ceph osd pool ls detail
   ```

10. Check the CRUSH map view of OSDs:

    ```
    # ceph osd tree
    ```

11. Check Ceph's OSD usage:

    ```
    # ceph osd df
    ```

12. List the cluster authentication keys:

    ```
    # ceph auth list
    ```

These were some basic commands that you learned in this section. In the upcoming chapters, you will learn advanced commands for Ceph cluster management.

2
Working with Ceph Block Device

In this chapter, we will cover the following recipes:

- Configuring Ceph client
- Creating Ceph Block Device
- Mapping Ceph Block Device
- Resizing Ceph RBD
- Working with RBD snapshots
- Working with RBD clones
- Disaster recovery replication using RBD mirroring
- Configuring pools for RBD mirroring with one way replication
- Configuring image mirroring
- Configuring two-way mirroring
- Recovering from a disaster!

Introduction

Once you have installed and configured your Ceph storage cluster, the next task is performing storage provisioning. Storage provisioning is the process of assigning storage space or capacity to physical or virtual servers, either in the form of block, file, or object storage. A typical computer system or server comes with a limited local storage capacity that might not be enough for your data storage needs.

Storage solutions such as Ceph provide virtually unlimited storage capacity to these servers, making them capable of storing all your data and making sure that you do not run out of space. Using a dedicated storage system instead of local storage gives you the much-needed flexibility in terms of scalability, reliability, and performance.

Ceph can provision storage capacity in a unified way, which includes block, filesystem, and object storage. The following diagram shows storage formats supported by Ceph, and depending on your use case, you can select one or more storage options:

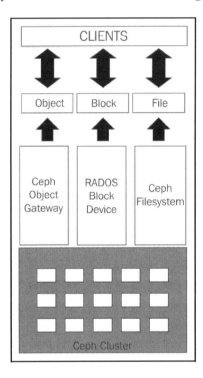

We will discuss each of these options in detail in this book, but in this chapter, we will focus on Ceph block storage.

The **Ceph Block Device**, formerly known as **RADOS Block Device**, provides reliable, distributed, and high-performance block storage disks to clients. A RADOS Block Device makes use of the `librbd` library and stores a block of data in sequential form striped over multiple OSDs in a Ceph cluster. RBD is backed by the RADOS layer of Ceph, thus every block device is spread over multiple Ceph nodes, delivering high performance and excellent reliability. RBD has native support for Linux kernel, which means that RBD drivers are well integrated with the Linux kernel since the past few years. In addition to reliability and performance, RBD also provides enterprise features such as full and incremental snapshots, thin provisioning, Copy-On-Write cloning, dynamic resizing, and so on. RBD also supports in-memory caching, which drastically improves its performance:

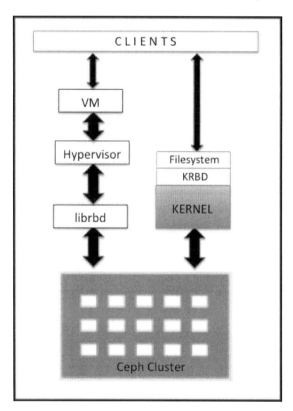

Industry-leading open source hypervisors, such as KVM and Xen, provide full support to RBD and leverage its features on their guest virtual machines. Other proprietary hypervisors, such as VMware and Microsoft Hyper-V will be supported very soon. There has been a lot of work going on in the community to support these hypervisors. The Ceph Block Device provides full support to cloud platforms such as OpenStack, CloudStack, as well as others. It has been proven successful and feature-rich for these cloud platforms. In OpenStack, you can use the Ceph Block Device with Cinder (block) and Glance (imaging) components. Doing so, you can spin thousands of **virtual machines** (**VMs**) in very little time, taking advantage of the Copy-On-Write feature of the Ceph Block Storage.

All these features make RBD an ideal candidate for cloud platforms such as OpenStack and CloudStack. We will now learn how to create a Ceph Block Device and make use of it.

Configuring Ceph client

Any regular Linux host (RHEL or Debian-based) can act as a Ceph client. The client interacts with the Ceph storage cluster over the network to store or retrieve user data. Ceph RBD support has been added to the Linux mainline kernel, starting with 2.6.34 and later versions.

How to do it...

As we did earlier, we will set up a Ceph client machine using Vagrant and VirtualBox. We will use the same `Vagrantfile` that we cloned in the last chapter. Vagrant will then launch a CentOS 7.3 virtual machine that we will configure as a Ceph client:

1. From the directory where we cloned the `Ceph-Cookbook-Second-Edition` GitHub repository, launch the client virtual machine using Vagrant:

```
$ vagrant status client-node1
$ vagrant up client-node1
```

```
[mhackett@localhost ceph-cookbook]$ vagrant up --provider=virtualbox client-node1
Bringing machine 'client-node1' up with 'virtualbox' provider...
==> client-node1: Importing base box 'centos7-standard'...
==> client-node1: Matching MAC address for NAT networking...
==> client-node1: Setting the name of the VM: client-node1
==> client-node1: Fixed port collision for 22 => 2222. Now on port 2202.
==> client-node1: Clearing any previously set network interfaces...
==> client-node1: Preparing network interfaces based on configuration...
```

2. Log in to `client-node1` and update the node:

```
$ vagrant ssh client-node1
$ sudo yum update -y
```

 The username and password that Vagrant uses to configure virtual machines is `vagrant`, and Vagrant has `sudo` rights. The default password for the root user is `vagrant`.

3. Check OS and kernel release (this is optional):

```
# cat /etc/centos-release
# uname -r
```

4. Check for RBD support in the kernel:

```
# sudo modprobe rbd
```

```
[root@client-node1 ~]# cat /etc/centos-release
CentOS Linux release 7.3.1611 (Core)
[root@client-node1 ~]# uname -r
3.10.0-514.26.2.el7.x86_64
[root@client-node1 ~]# modprobe rbd
[root@client-node1 ~]# echo $?
0
[root@client-node1 ~]# 
```

5. Allow `ceph-node1` monitor machine to access `client-node1` over SSH. To do this, copy root SSH keys from `ceph-node1` to `client-node1` Vagrant user. Execute the following commands from `ceph-node1` machine until otherwise specified:

```
## Log in to the ceph-node1 machine
$ vagrant ssh ceph-node1
$ sudo su -
# ssh-copy-id vagrant@client-node1
```

Provide a one-time Vagrant user password, that is, vagrant, for client-node1. Once the SSH keys are copied from ceph-node1 to client-node1, you should able to log in to client-node1 without a password.

6. Using Ansible, we will create the ceph-client role which will copy the Ceph configuration file and administration keyring to the client node. On our Ansible administration node, ceph-node1, add a new section [clients] to the /etc/ansible/hosts file:

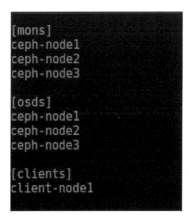

7. Go to the /etc/ansible/group_vars directory on ceph-node1 and create a copy of clients.yml from the clients.yml.sample:

```
# cp clients.yml.sample clients.yml
```

You can instruct the ceph-client to create pools and clients by updating the clients.yml file. By uncommenting the user_config and setting to true you have the ability to define customer pools and client names altogether with Cephx capabilities.

Chapter 2

8. Run the Ansible playbook from `ceph-node1`:

```
root@ceph-node1 ceph-ansible # ansible-playbook site.yml
```

```
PLAY RECAP *******************************************************************
*****
ceph-node1                     : ok=124   changed=2    unreachable=0    failed=0

ceph-node2                     : ok=118   changed=2    unreachable=0    failed=0

ceph-node3                     : ok=119   changed=2    unreachable=0    failed=0

client-node1                   : ok=40    changed=13   unreachable=0    failed=0


[root@ceph-node1 ceph-ansible]#
```

9. On `client-node1` check and validate that the `keyring` and `ceph.conf` file were populated into the `/etc/ceph` directory by Ansible:

```
[root@client-node1 ~]# cd /etc/ceph
[root@client-node1 ceph]# ls
ceph.client.admin.keyring  ceph.conf  ceph.d  rbdmap
[root@client-node1 ceph]#
```

10. On `client-node1` you can validate that the Ceph client packages were installed by Ansible:

```
[root@client-node1 ceph]# rpm -qa |grep ceph
ceph-fuse-10.2.9-0.el7.x86_64
python-cephfs-10.2.9-0.el7.x86_64
ceph-selinux-10.2.9-0.el7.x86_64
ceph-base-10.2.9-0.el7.x86_64
libcephfs1-10.2.9-0.el7.x86_64
ceph-common-10.2.9-0.el7.x86_64
[root@client-node1 ceph]#
```

11. The client machine will require Ceph keys to access the Ceph cluster. Ceph creates a default user, `client.admin`, which has full access to the Ceph cluster and Ansible copies the `client.admin` key to client nodes. It's not recommended to share `client.admin` keys with client nodes. A better approach is to create a new Ceph user with separate keys and allow access to specific Ceph pools. In our case, we will create a Ceph user, `client.rbd`, with access to the RBD `pool`. By default, Ceph Block Devices are created on the RBD `pool`:

```
[root@ceph-node1 ~]# ceph auth get-or-create client.rbd mon 'allow r' osd
'allow class-read object_prefix rbd_children, allow rwx pool=rbd'
[client.rbd]
        key = AQC7fbBZb9p/MxAAJiWeI+3RrokobUgTy7wNIQ==
[root@ceph-node1 ~]#
```

12. Add the key to `client-node1` machine for `client.rbd` user:

```
[root@ceph-node1 ~]# ceph auth get-or-create client.rbd | ssh vagrant@clie
nt-node1 sudo tee /etc/ceph/ceph.client.rbd.keyring
vagrant@client-node1's password:
[client.rbd]
        key = AQC7fbBZb9p/MxAAJiWeI+3RrokobUgTy7wNIQ==
[root@ceph-node1 ~]#
```

13. By this step, `client-node1` should be ready to act as a Ceph client. Check the cluster status from the `client-node1` machine by providing the username and secret key:

```
# cat /etc/ceph/ceph.client.rbd.keyring >> /etc/ceph/keyring
### Since we are not using the default user client.admin we
need to supply username that will connect to the Ceph cluster
# ceph -s --name client.rbd
```

```
[root@client-node1 ~]# cat /etc/ceph/ceph.client.rbd.keyring >> /etc/ceph/
keyring
[root@client-node1 ~]# ceph -s --name client.rbd
    cluster f90d2a73-29b1-4c81-b598-cd3a74541833
    health HEALTH_OK
    monmap e1: 3 mons at {ceph-node1=10.19.1.101:6789/0,ceph-node2=10.19.
1.102:6789/0,ceph-node3=10.19.1.103:6789/0}
            election epoch 6, quorum 0,1,2 ceph-node1,ceph-node2,ceph-node
3
    osdmap e30: 9 osds: 9 up, 9 in
            flags sortbitwise,require_jewel_osds
      pgmap v59: 128 pgs, 1 pools, 690 bytes data, 4 objects
            307 MB used, 161 GB / 161 GB avail
                  128 active+clean
[root@client-node1 ~]# █
```

Creating Ceph Block Device

Up to now, we have configured Ceph client, and now we will demonstrate creating a Ceph Block Device from the client-node1 machine.

How to do it...

1. Create a RADOS Block Device named rbd1 of size 10240 MB:

   ```
   # rbd create rbd1 --size 10240 --name client.rbd
   ```

2. There are multiple options that you can use to list RBD images:

   ```
   ## The default pool to store block device images is "rbd",
      you can also specify the pool name with the rbd
      command using -p option:
   # rbd ls --name client.rbd
   # rbd ls -p rbd --name client.rbd
   # rbd list --name client.rbd
   ```

3. Check the details of the RBD image:

```
# rbd --image rbd1 info --name client.rbd
```

```
[root@client-node1 ~]# rbd create rbd1 --size 10240 --name client.rbd
[root@client-node1 ~]# rbd ls --name client.rbd
rbd1
[root@client-node1 ~]# rbd --image rbd1 info --name client.rbd
rbd image 'rbd1':
        size 10240 MB in 2560 objects
        order 22 (4096 kB objects)
        block_name_prefix: rbd_data.110e238e1f29
        format: 2
        features: layering, exclusive-lock, object-map, fast-diff, deep-fl
atten
        flags:
[root@client-node1 ~]#
```

Mapping Ceph Block Device

Now that we have created a block device on a Ceph cluster, in order to use this block device, we need to map it to the client machine. To do this, execute the following commands from the client-node1 machine.

How to do it...

1. Map the block device to the client-node1:

```
# rbd map --image rbd1 --name client.rbd
```

```
[root@client-node1 ~]# rbd map --image rbd1 --name client.rbd
rbd: sysfs write failed
RBD image feature set mismatch. You can disable features unsupported by th
e kernel with "rbd feature disable".
In some cases useful info is found in syslog - try "dmesg | tail" or so.
rbd: map failed: (6) No such device or address
```

 Notice the mapping of the images has failed due to a feature set mismatch!

2. With Ceph Jewel the new default format for RBD images is 2 and Ceph Jewel default configuration includes the following default Ceph Block Device features:

- `layering`: layering support
- `exclusive-lock`: exclusive locking support
- `object-map`: object map support (requires `exclusive-lock`)
- `deep-flatten`: snapshot flatten support
- `fast-diff`: fast diff calculations (requires `object-map`)

Using the **krbd (kernel rbd)** client on `client-node1` we will be unable to map the block device image on CentOS kernel 3.10 as this kernel does not support `object-map`, `deep-flatten` and `fast-diff` (support was introduced in kernel 4.9). In order to work around this we will disable the unsupported features, there are several options to do this:

- Disable the unsupported features dynamically (this is the option we will be using):

```
# rbd feature disable rbd1
    exclusive-lock object-map
    deep-flatten fast-diff
```

- When creating the RBD image initially utilize the `--image-feature layering` option with the `rbd create` command which will only enable the layering feature:

```
# rbd create rbd1 --size 10240
    --image-feature layering
    --name client.rbd
```

- Disable the feature in the Ceph configuration file:

```
rbd_default_features = 1
```

All these features work for the user-space RBD client librbd.

```
[root@client-node1 ~]# rbd feature disable rbd1 exclusive-lock object-
map deep-flatten fast-diff
[root@client-node1 ~]# rbd --image rbd1 info --name client.rbd
rbd image 'rbd1':
        size 10240 MB in 2560 objects
        order 22 (4096 kB objects)
        block_name_prefix: rbd_data.1128238e1f29
        format: 2
        features: layering
        flags:
[root@client-node1 ~]#
```

3. Retry mapping the block device with the unsupported features now disabled:

    ```
    # rbd map --image rbd1 --name client.rbd
    ```

4. Check the mapped block device:

    ```
    rbd showmapped --name client.rbd
    ```

    ```
    [root@client-node1 ~]# rbd map --image rbd1 --name client.rbd
    /dev/rbd0
    [root@client-node1 ~]# rbd showmapped --name client.rbd
    id pool image snap device
    0  rbd  rbd1   -    /dev/rbd0
    [root@client-node1 ~]#
    ```

5. To make use of this block device, we should create a filesystem on this and mount it:

    ```
    # fdisk -l /dev/rbd0
    # mkfs.xfs /dev/rbd0
    # mkdir /mnt/ceph-disk1
    # mount /dev/rbd0 /mnt/ceph-disk1
    # df -h /mnt/ceph-disk1
    ```

```
[root@client-node1 ~]# fdisk -l /dev/rbd0

Disk /dev/rbd0: 10.7 GB, 10737418240 bytes, 20971520 sectors
Units = sectors of 1 * 512 = 512 bytes
Sector size (logical/physical): 512 bytes / 512 bytes
I/O size (minimum/optimal): 4194304 bytes / 4194304 bytes

[root@client-node1 ~]# mkfs.xfs /dev/rbd0
meta-data=/dev/rbd0               isize=512    agcount=17, agsize=162816 bl
ks
         =                        sectsz=512   attr=2, projid32bit=1
         =                        crc=1        finobt=0, sparse=0
data     =                        bsize=4096   blocks=2621440, imaxpct=25
         =                        sunit=1024   swidth=1024 blks
naming   =version 2               bsize=4096   ascii-ci=0 ftype=1
log      =internal log            bsize=4096   blocks=2560, version=2
         =                        sectsz=512   sunit=8 blks, lazy-count=1
realtime =none                    extsz=4096   blocks=0, rtextents=0
[root@client-node1 ~]# mkdir /mnt/ceph-disk1
[root@client-node1 ~]# mount /dev/rbd0 /mnt/ceph-disk1
[root@client-node1 ~]# df -h /mnt/ceph-disk1
Filesystem     Size  Used Avail Use% Mounted on
/dev/rbd0       10G   33M   10G   1% /mnt/ceph-disk1
[root@client-node1 ~]#
```

6. Test the block device by writing data to it:

```
dd if=/dev/zero of=/mnt/ceph-disk1/file1 count=100 bs=1M
```

```
[root@client-node1 ~]# dd if=/dev/zero of=/mnt/ceph-disk1/file1 count=100
bs=1M
100+0 records in
100+0 records out
104857600 bytes (105 MB) copied, 1.18044 s, 88.8 MB/s
[root@client-node1 ~]# df -h /mnt/ceph-disk1
Filesystem     Size  Used Avail Use% Mounted on
/dev/rbd0       10G  133M  9.9G   2% /mnt/ceph-disk1
[root@client-node1 ~]#
```

7. To map the block device across reboots, we will need to create and configure a services file:

    1. Create a new file in the `/usr/local/bin` directory for mounting and unmounting and include the following:

```
# cd /usr/local/bin
# vim rbd-mount
```

```
#!/bin/bash

# Pool name where block device image is stored
export poolname=rbd

# Disk image name
export rbdimage=rbd1

# Mounted directory
export mountpoint=/mnt/ceph-disk1

# Image mount/unmount and pool are passed from the systemd service as
arguments
# Are we are mounting or unmounting
if [ "$1" == "m" ]; then
    modprobe rbd
    rbd feature disable $rbdimage exclusive-lock object-map fast-diff d
eep-flatten
    rbd map $rbdimage --id rbd --keyring /etc/ceph/ceph.client.rbd.keyr
ing
    mkdir -p $mountpoint
    mount /dev/rbd/$poolname/$rbdimage $mountpoint
fi
if [ "$1" == "u" ]; then
    umount $mountpoint
    rbd unmap /dev/rbd/$poolname/$rbdimage
fi
~
```

    2. Save the file and make it executable:

```
# sudo chmod +x rbd-mount
```

This can be done automatically by grabbing the `rbd-mount` script from the `Ceph-Cookbook-Second-Edition` repository and making it executable:

```
# wget https://raw.githubusercontent.com/PacktPublishing/
  Ceph-Cookbook-Second-Edition/master/
  rbdmap -O /usr/local/bin/rbd-mount
# chmod +x /usr/local/bin/rbd-mount
```

3. Go to the `systemd` directory and create the service file, include the following in the file `rbd-mount.service`:

```
# cd /etc/systemd/system/
# vim rbd-mount.service
```

```
[Unit]
Description=RADOS block device mapping for $rbdimage in pool $poolname"
Conflicts=shutdown.target
Wants=network-online.target
After=NetworkManager-wait-online.service
[Service]
Type=oneshot
RemainAfterExit=yes
ExecStart=/usr/local/bin/rbd-mount m
ExecStop=/usr/local/bin/rbd-mount u
[Install]
WantedBy=multi-user.target
~
~
~
```

This can be done automatically by grabbing the service file from the `Ceph-Cookbook-Second-Edition` repository:

```
# wget https://raw.githubusercontent.com/PacktPublishing/
  Ceph-Cookbook-Second-Edition/master/rbd-mount.service
```

4. After saving the file and exiting Vim, reload the `systemd` files and enable the `rbd-mount.service` to start at boot time:

```
# systemctl daemon-reload
# systemctl enable rbd-mount.service
```

8. Reboot `client-node1` and verify that block device `rbd0` is mounted to `/mnt/ceph-disk1` after the reboot:

```
root@client-node1 # reboot -f
# df -h
```

```
[root@client-node1 system]# df -h
Filesystem                Size  Used Avail Use% Mounted on
/dev/mapper/centos-root   6.7G  1.7G  5.1G  25% /
devtmpfs                  234M     0  234M   0% /dev
tmpfs                     245M     0  245M   0% /dev/shm
tmpfs                     245M  4.3M  241M   2% /run
tmpfs                     245M     0  245M   0% /sys/fs/cgroup
/dev/sda1                 497M  193M  305M  39% /boot
/dev/rbd0                  10G  133M  9.9G   2% /mnt/ceph-disk1
tmpfs                      49M     0   49M   0% /run/user/0
[root@client-node1 system]#
```

Resizing Ceph RBD

Ceph supports thin provisioned block devices, which means that the physical storage space will not get occupied until you begin storing data on the block device. The Ceph Block Device is very flexible; you can increase or decrease the size of an RBD on the fly from the Ceph storage end. However, the underlying filesystem should support resizing. Advance filesystems such as XFS, Btrfs, EXT, ZFS, and others support filesystem resizing to a certain extent. Please follow filesystem specific documentation to know more about resizing.

XFS does not currently support shrinking, Btrfs, and ext4 do support shrinking but should be done with caution!

How to do it...

To increase or decrease the Ceph RBD image size, use the `--size <New_Size_in_MB>` option with the `rbd resize` command, this will set the new size for the RBD image:

1. The original size of the RBD image that we created earlier was 10 GB. We will now increase its size to 20 GB:

   ```
   # rbd resize --image rbd1 --size 20480 --name client.rbd
   # rbd info --image rbd1 --name client.rbd
   ```

   ```
   [root@client-node1 system]# rbd resize --image rbd1 --size 20480 --name cl
   ient.rbd
   Resizing image: 100% complete...done.
   [root@client-node1 system]# rbd info --image rbd1 --name client.rbd
   rbd image 'rbd1':
           size 20480 MB in 5120 objects
           order 22 (4096 kB objects)
           block_name_prefix: rbd_data.110e238e1f29
           format: 2
           features: layering, exclusive-lock
           flags:
   [root@client-node1 system]# 
   ```

2. Grow the filesystem so that we can make use of increased storage space. It's worth knowing that the filesystem resize is a feature of the OS as well as the device filesystem. You should read filesystem documentation before resizing any partition. The XFS filesystem supports online resizing. Check system messages to know the filesystem size change (you will notice df -h shows the original 10G size even though we resized, as the filesystem still see's the original size):

```
# df -h
# lsblk
# dmesg | grep -i capacity
# xfs_growfs -d /mnt/ceph-disk1
```

```
[root@client-node1 system]# df -h
Filesystem                Size  Used Avail Use% Mounted on
/dev/mapper/centos-root   6.7G  1.7G  5.1G  25% /
devtmpfs                  234M     0  234M   0% /dev
tmpfs                     245M     0  245M   0% /dev/shm
tmpfs                     245M  4.3M  241M   2% /run
tmpfs                     245M     0  245M   0% /sys/fs/cgroup
/dev/sda1                 497M  193M  305M  39% /boot
/dev/rbd0                  10G  133M  9.9G   2% /mnt/ceph-disk1
tmpfs                      49M     0   49M   0% /run/user/0
[root@client-node1 system]# lsblk
NAME             MAJ:MIN RM  SIZE RO TYPE MOUNTPOINT
sda                8:0    0    8G  0 disk
├─sda1             8:1    0  500M  0 part /boot
└─sda2             8:2    0  7.5G  0 part
  ├─centos-swap  253:0    0  820M  0 lvm  [SWAP]
  └─centos-root  253:1    0  6.7G  0 lvm  /
sr0               11:0    1 1024M  0 rom
rbd0             252:0    0   20G  0 disk /mnt/ceph-disk1
[root@client-node1 system]# dmesg |grep -i capacity
[    9.783649] rbd: rbd0: capacity 10737418240 features 0x5
[ 1882.993946] rbd0: detected capacity change from 10737418240 to 214748364
80
[root@client-node1 system]# xfs_growfs -d /mnt/ceph-disk1
meta-data=/dev/rbd0              isize=512    agcount=17, agsize=162816 blk
s
         =                       sectsz=512   attr=2, projid32bit=1
         =                       crc=1        finobt=0 spinodes=0
data     =                       bsize=4096   blocks=2621440, imaxpct=25
         =                       sunit=1024   swidth=1024 blks
naming   =version 2             bsize=4096   ascii-ci=0 ftype=1
log      =internal              bsize=4096   blocks=2560, version=2
         =                       sectsz=512   sunit=8 blks, lazy-count=1
realtime =none                   extsz=4096   blocks=0, rtextents=0
data blocks changed from 2621440 to 5242880
[root@client-node1 system]# df -h
Filesystem                Size  Used Avail Use% Mounted on
/dev/mapper/centos-root   6.7G  1.7G  5.1G  25% /
devtmpfs                  234M     0  234M   0% /dev
tmpfs                     245M     0  245M   0% /dev/shm
tmpfs                     245M  4.3M  241M   2% /run
tmpfs                     245M     0  245M   0% /sys/fs/cgroup
/dev/sda1                 497M  193M  305M  39% /boot
/dev/rbd0                  20G  134M   20G   1% /mnt/ceph-disk1
tmpfs                      49M     0   49M   0% /run/user/0
[root@client-node1 system]#
```

Working with RBD snapshots

Ceph extends full support to snapshots, which are point-in-time, read-only copies of an RBD image. You can preserve the state of a Ceph RBD image by creating snapshots and restoring the snapshot to get the original data.

If you take a snapshot of an RBD image while I/O is in progress to the image the snapshot may be inconsistent. If this occurs you will be required to clone the snapshot to a new image for it to be mountable. When taking snapshots it is recommended to cease I/O from the application to the image before taking the snapshot. This can be done by customizing the application to issue a freeze before a snapshot or can manually be done using the `fsfreeze` command (man page for `fsfreeze` details this command further).

How to do it...

Let's see how a snapshot works with Ceph:

1. To test the snapshot functionality of Ceph, let's create a file on the block device that we created earlier:

   ```
   # echo "Hello Ceph This is snapshot test"
     > /mnt/ceph-disk1/snapshot_test_file
   ```

   ```
   [root@client-node1 system]# echo "Hello Ceph This is snapshot test" > /mnt
   /ceph-disk1/snapshot_test_file
   [root@client-node1 system]# ls -l /mnt/ceph-disk1
   total 102404
   -rw-r--r-- 1 root root 104857600 Sep  7 03:50 file1
   -rw-r--r-- 1 root root        33 Sep  7 05:10 snapshot_test_file
   [root@client-node1 system]# cat /mnt/ceph-disk1/snapshot_test_file
   Hello Ceph This is snapshot test
   [root@client-node1 system]# 
   ```

2. Create a snapshot for the Ceph Block Device. Syntax for the same is as follows:

   ```
   # rbd snap create <pool name>/<image name>@<snap name>
   # rbd snap create rbd/rbd1@snapshot1
   ```

3. To list the snapshots of an image, use the following syntax:

   ```
   # rbd snap ls <pool name>/<image name>
   # rbd snap ls rbd/rbd1
   ```

```
[root@client-node1 system]# rbd snap create rbd/rbd1@snapshot1 --name clie
nt.rbd
[root@client-node1 system]# rbd snap ls rbd/rbd1 --name client.rbd
SNAPID NAME       SIZE
     4 snapshot1 20480 MB
[root@client-node1 system]#
```

4. To test the snapshot restore functionality of Ceph RBD, let's delete files from the filesystem:

   ```
   # rm -f /mnt/ceph-disk1/*
   ```

5. We will now restore the Ceph RBD snapshot to get back the files that we deleted in the last step. Please note that a rollback operation will overwrite the current version of the RBD image and its data with the snapshot version. You should perform this operation carefully. The syntax is as follows:

   ```
   # rbd snap rollback <pool-name>/<image-name>@<snap-name>
   # umount /mnt/ceph-disk1
   # rbd snap rollback rbd/rbd1@snapshot1 --name client.rbd
   ```

Prior to the rollback operation the filesystem was unmounted to validate a refreshed filesystem state after the rollback.

6. Once the snapshot rollback operation is completed, remount the Ceph RBD filesystem to refresh the filesystem state. You should be able to get your deleted files back:

   ```
   # mount /dev/rbd0 /mnt/ceph-disk1
   # ls -l /mnt/ceph-disk1
   ```

```
[root@client-node1 ~]# ls -l /mnt/ceph-disk1
total 102400
-rw-r--r-- 1 root root 104857600 Sep  7 05:50 file1
-rw-r--r-- 1 root root         0 Sep  7 05:52 snapshot_test_file
[root@client-node1 ~]# rm -f /mnt/ceph-disk1/*
[root@client-node1 ~]# ls -l /mnt/ceph-disk1
total 0
[root@client-node1 ~]# umount /mnt/ceph-disk1
[root@client-node1 ~]# rbd snap rollback rbd/rbd1@snapshot1 --name client.rbd
Rolling back to snapshot: 100% complete...done.
[root@client-node1 ~]# mount /dev/rbd0 /mnt/ceph-disk1
[root@client-node1 ~]# ls -l /mnt/ceph-disk1
total 102400
-rw-r--r-- 1 root root 104857600 Sep  7 05:50 file1
-rw-r--r-- 1 root root         0 Sep  7 05:52 snapshot_test_file
[root@client-node1 ~]#
```

7. You are also able to rename snapshots if you so choose. The syntax is as follows:

```
#rbd snap rename <pool-name>/<image-name>@<original-snapshot-
  name> <pool-name>/<image-name>@<new-snapshot-name>
# rbd snap rename rbd/rbd1@snapshot1 rbd/rbd1@snapshot1_new
```

8. When you no longer need snapshots, you can remove a specific snapshot using the following syntax. Deleting the snapshot will not delete your current data on the Ceph RBD image:

```
# rbd snap rm <pool-name>/<image-name>@<snap-name>
# rbd snap rm rbd/rbd1@snapshot1 --name client.rbd
```

9. If you have multiple snapshots of an RBD image and you wish to delete all the snapshots with a single command, then use the `purge` subcommand. The syntax is as follows:

```
# rbd snap purge <pool-name>/<image-name>
# rbd snap purge rbd/rbd1 --name client.rbd
```

Working with RBD clones

Ceph supports a very nice feature for creating **Copy-On-Write** (**COW**) clones from RBD snapshots. This is also known as *snapshot layering* in Ceph. Layering allows clients to create multiple instant clones of Ceph RBD. This feature is extremely useful for cloud and virtualization platforms such as OpenStack, CloudStack, Qemu/KVM, and so on. These platforms usually protect Ceph RBD images containing an OS/VM image in the form of a snapshot. Later, this snapshot is cloned multiple times to spawn new virtual machines / instances. Snapshots are read-only, but COW clones are fully writable; this feature of Ceph provides a greater level of flexibility and is extremely useful in cloud platforms. In the later chapters, we will discover more on COW clones for spawning OpenStack instances:

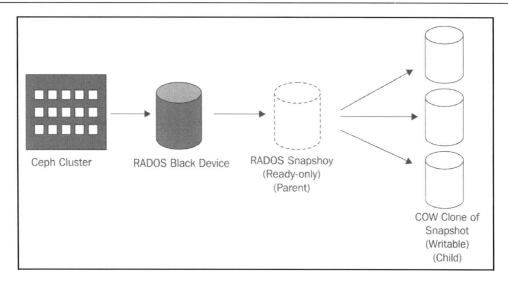

Ceph Cluster   RADOS Black Device   RADOS Snapshoy
(Ready-only)
(Parent)

COW Clone of
Snapshot
(Writable)
(Child)

Every cloned image (child image) stores references of its parent snapshot to read image data. Hence, the parent snapshot should be protected before it can be used for cloning. At the time of data writing on the COW cloned image, it stores new data references to itself. COW cloned images are as good as RBD. They are quite flexible like RBD, which means that they are writable, resizable, and support snapshots and further cloning.

In Ceph RBD, images are of two types: format-1 and format-2. The RBD snapshot feature is available on both types, that is, in format-1 as well as in format-2 RBD images. However, the layering feature (the COW cloning feature) is available only for the RBD image with format-2. The default RBD image format in Jewel is format-2.

How to do it...

To demonstrate RBD cloning, we will intentionally create an RBD image (specifying the layering feature) then create and protect its snapshot, and finally, create COW clones out of it:

1. Create an RBD image with `layering` feature specified and check it's details:

   ```
   # rbd create rbd2 --size 10240
     --image-feature layering --name client.rbd
   # rbd info --image rbd2 --name client.rbd
   ```

   ```
   [root@client-node1 ~]# rbd create rbd2 --size 10240 --image-feature layering --na
   me client.rbd
   [root@client-node1 ~]# rbd info --image rbd2 --name client.rbd
   rbd image 'rbd2':
           size 10240 MB in 2560 objects
           order 22 (4096 kB objects)
           block_name_prefix: rbd_data.373e2ae8944a
           format: 2
           features: layering
           flags:
   [root@client-node1 ~]#
   ```

2. Create a snapshot of this RBD image:

   ```
   # rbd snap create rbd/rbd2@snapshot_for_cloning
     --name client.rbd
   ```

3. To create a COW clone, protect the snapshot. This is an important step, we should protect the snapshot because if the snapshot gets deleted, all the attached COW clones will be destroyed:

   ```
   # rbd snap protect rbd/rbd2@snapshot_for_cloning
     --name client.rbd
   ```

4. Next, we will create a cloned RBD image, specifying the `layering` feature, using this snapshot. The syntax is as follows:

   ```
   # rbd clone <pool-name>/<parent-image-name>@<snap-name>
     <pool-name>/<child_image-name>
     --image-feature <feature-name>
   # rbd clone rbd/rbd2@snapshot_for_cloning rbd/clone_rbd2
     --image-feature layering --name client.rbd
   ```

5. Creating a clone is a quick process. Once it's completed, check the new image information. You will notice that its parent pool, image, and snapshot information will be displayed:

```
# rbd info rbd/clone_rbd2 --name client.rbd
```

The clients do not always provide equivalent functionality, for example the fuse client supports `client-enforced` quotas while the kernel client does not:

```
[root@client-node1 ~]# rbd snap create rbd/rbd2@snapshot_for_cloning --name clien
t.rbd
[root@client-node1 ~]# rbd snap protect rbd/rbd2@snapshot_for_cloning --name clie
nt.rbd
[root@client-node1 ~]# rbd clone rbd/rbd2@snapshot_for_cloning rbd/clone_rbd2 --i
mage-feature layering --name client.rbd
[root@client-node1 ~]# rbd info rbd/clone_rbd2 --name client.rbd
rbd image 'clone_rbd2':
        size 10240 MB in 2560 objects
        order 22 (4096 kB objects)
        block_name_prefix: rbd_data.37483d1b58ba
        format: 2
        features: layering
        flags:
        parent: rbd/rbd2@snapshot_for_cloning
        overlap: 10240 MB
[root@client-node1 ~]#
```

6. You also have the ability to list children of a snapshot. To list the children of a snapshot execute the following:

```
# rbd children rbd/rbd2@snapshot_for_cloning
```

We now have a cloned RBD image that is dependent on it's parent image. To split this cloned image from it's parent snapshot we will need to flatten the image which would require copying all the data from the parent snapshot image to the clone. Flattening may take awhile to complete and depends on the size of the parent snapshot image. One the cloned image is flattened there is no longer a relationship between the parent snapshot and the RBD clone. Please note that a flattened image will contain all information from the snapshot and will use more space than a clone.

7. To initiate the flattening process, use the following:

```
# rbd flatten rbd/clone_rbd2 --name client.rbd
# rbd info --image clone_rbd2 --name client.rbd
```

After the completion of the flattening process, if you check image information, you will notice that the parent image/snapshot name is not present and the clone is independent:

```
[root@client-node1 ~]# rbd flatten rbd/clone_rbd2 --name client.rbd
Image flatten: 100% complete...done.
[root@client-node1 ~]# rbd info --image clone_rbd2 --name client.rbd
rbd image 'clone_rbd2':
        size 10240 MB in 2560 objects
        order 22 (4096 kB objects)
        block_name_prefix: rbd_data.37483d1b58ba
        format: 2
        features: layering
        flags:
[root@client-node1 ~]#
```

If the `deep-flatten` feature is enabled on an image the image clone is dissociated from it's parent by default.

8. You can also remove the parent image snapshot if you no longer require it. Before removing the snapshot, you first have to unprotect it:

    ```
    # rbd snap unprotect rbd/rbd2@snapshot_for_cloning
      --name client.rbd
    ```

9. Once the snapshot is unprotected, you can remove it:

    ```
    # rbd snap rm rbd/rbd2@snapshot_for_cloning --name client.rbd
    ```

Disaster recovery replication using RBD mirroring

RBD mirroring is an asynchronous replication of RBD images between multiple Ceph clusters. RBD mirroring validates a point-in-time consistent replica of any change to an RBD image, including snapshots, clones, read and write IOPS and block device resizing. RBD mirroring can run in an active+active setup or an active+passive setup. RBD mirroring utilizes the RBD journaling and exclusive lock features which enables the RBD image to record all changes to the image in order of which they occur. These features validate that a crash-consistent copy of the remote image is available locally. Before mirroring can be enabled on a Ceph cluster the journaling feature must be enabled on the RBD image.

The daemon responsible for ensuring point-in-time consistency from one Ceph cluster to the other is the `rbd-mirror` daemon. Depending on your chosen type of replication the rbd-mirror daemon runs on either a single cluster or an each participating in the mirroring:

- **One way replication**: Data is mirrored from primary site to secondary site. RBD mirror runs only on secondary site.
- **Two-way replication**: Active-Active configuration. Data is mirrored from primary site to secondary site and mirrored back from a primary site to secondary site. RBD mirror runs on both primary and secondary sites.

Since we store the RBD images on both local and remote pools it is best practices to ensure the CRUSH hierarchy backing the mirrored pool is the same speed, size and type media. Also, proper bandwidth should be allocated between sites to handle the mirroring traffic.

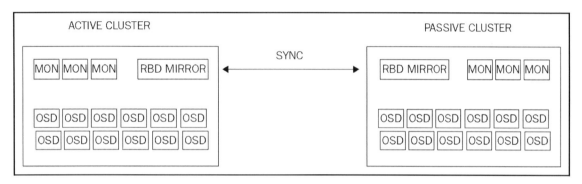

How to do it...

For this recipe, we will be configuring a second Ceph cluster with Ceph nodes `ceph-node5`, `ceph-node6`, and `ceph-node7`. The previous `Chapter 1`, *Ceph – Introduction and Beyond*, can be referenced for setting up your second Ceph cluster using Ansible with nodes 5, 6, and 7 taking the place of 1, 2, and 3 in the recipes, some highlights and changes that must be made before running the playbook on the secondary cluster are below:

1. Your `/etc/ansible/hosts` file from each of your Ansible configuration nodes (`ceph-node1` and `ceph-node5`) should look as follows:

```
#Primary site (ceph-node1):
 [mons]
 ceph-node1
 ceph-node2
```

```
ceph-node3
[osds]
ceph-node1
ceph-node2
ceph-node3
#Secondary site (ceph-node5):
[mons]
 ceph-node5
 ceph-node6
 ceph-node7
 [osds]
 ceph-node5
 ceph-node6
 ceph-node7
```

2. Your cluster will require a distinct name, the default cluster naming is `ceph`. Since our primary cluster is named `ceph` our secondary cluster must be named something different. For this recipe, we will name the secondary cluster as `backup`. We will need to edit the `all.yml` file on `ceph-node5` to reflect this change prior to deploying by commenting out cluster and renaming backup:

   root@ceph-node5 group_vars # vim all.yml

```
###########
# GENERAL #
###########

fetch_directory: ~/ceph-ansible-keys

# The 'cluster' variable determines the name of the cluster.
# Changing the default value to something else means that you will
# need to change all the command line calls as well, for example if
# your cluster name is 'foo':
# "ceph health" will become "ceph --cluster foo health"
#
# An easier way to handle this is to use the environment variable CEPH_ARGS
# So run: "export CEPH_ARGS="--cluster foo"
# With that you will be able to run "ceph health" normally
cluster: backup
```

It is possible to mirror RBD images between two clusters of the same name this requires changing the name of one of the clusters in the `/etc/sysconfig/ceph` file to a name other then Ceph and then creating a symlink to the `ceph.conf` file.

3. Run Ansible to install the second Ceph cluster with the distinct name of backup:

```
root@ceph-node5 ceph-ansible # ansible-playbook site.yml
```

4. When the playbook competes set the Ceph environment variable to use cluster name of `backup`:

```
# export CEPH_ARGS="--cluster backup"
```

5. In each of the clusters create a pool called data, this pool will be mirrored between the sites:

```
root@ceph-node1 # ceph osd pool create data 64
root@ceph-node5 # ceph osd pool create data 64
```

6. Create the user `client.local` on the `ceph` Ceph cluster and give it a `rwx` access to data pool:

```
root@ceph-node1 # ceph auth get-or-create client.local
mon 'allow r' osd 'allow class-read object_prefix rbd_children,
allow rwx pool=data' -o /etc/ceph/ceph.client.local.keyring
--cluster ceph
```

7. Create the user `client.remote` on the `backup` cluster and give it a `rwx` access to data pool:

```
root@ceph-node5 # ceph auth get-or-create client.remote
mon 'allow r' osd 'allow class-read object_prefix rbd_children,
allow rwx pool=data' -o /etc/ceph/backup.client.remote.keyring
--cluster backup
```

8. Copy the Ceph configuration file from each of the clusters into the `/etc/ceph` directory of the corresponding peer cluster:

```
root@ceph-node1 # scp /etc/ceph/ceph.conf
root@ceph-node5:/etc/ceph/ceph.conf
root@ceph-node5 # scp /etc/ceph/backup.conf
root@ceph.node1:/etc/ceph/backup.conf
```

9. Copy the keyrings for the user `client.local` and `client.remote` from each of the clusters into the `/etc/ceph` directory of the corresponding peer cluster:

```
root@ceph-node1 # scp /etc/ceph/ceph.client.local.keyring
root@ceph-node5:/etc/ceph/ceph.client.local.keyring
root@ceph-node5 # scp /etc/ceph/backup.client.remote.keyring
root@ceph-node1:/etc/ceph/backup.client.remote.keyring
```

We now have two Ceph clusters, with a `client.local` and a `client.remote` user, copies of their peer `ceph.conf` file in the `etc/ceph` directory and keyrings for the corresponding users on each peer cluster. In the next recipe we will configure mirroring on the data pool.

Configuring pools for RBD mirroring with one way replication

RBD mirroring is configured by enabling it on a pool basis in a primary and secondary Ceph cluster. There are two modes that can be configured with RBD mirroring depending on what level of data you choose to mirror. Note that the enabled RBD mirroring configuration must be the same per pool on primary and secondary clusters.

- **Pool mode**: Any image in a pool with journaling enabled is mirrored to the secondary cluster.
- **Image mode**: Only specifically chosen images with mirroring enabled will be mirrored to the secondary cluster. This requires the image to have mirroring enabled for it.

How to do it...

Before any data can be mirrored from the Ceph cluster to the `backup` cluster we first need install the `rbd-mirror` daemon on the `backup` cluster, enable mirroring on the data pool and then add a peer cluster to the pool:

1. On `ceph-node5` in the `backup` cluster install and configure the `rbd-mirror`. The client ID of remote (our user) is what the `rbd-mirror` daemon will use:

```
root@ceph-node5 # yum install -y rbd mirror
                # systemctl enable ceph-rbd-mirror.target
                # systemctl enable ceph-rbd-mirror@remote
                # systemctl start ceph-rbd-mirror@remote
```

2. Enable mirroring of the whole pool named data in cluster `ceph`. The syntax is as follows:

```
                # rbd mirror pool enable <pool> <mode>
root@ceph-node1 # rbd mirror pool enable data pool
```

3. Enable mirroring of the whole pool named `rbd` in the cluster `backup`:

```
root@ceph-node5 # rbd mirror pool enable data pool
```

4. For the `rbd-mirror` daemon to discover it's peer cluster, we now must register the peer to the pool. We will need to add the `ceph` cluster as a peer to the `backup` cluster. The syntax is as follows:

```
                # rbd mirror pool peer add <pool>
                  <client-name@cluster-name>
root@ceph-node5 # rbd mirror pool peer add
                  data client.local@ceph
```

5. Next, we will validate the peer relationship between the pools and the cluster. The syntax is as follows:

```
                # rbd mirror pool info <pool>
root@ceph-node5 # rbd mirror pool info rbd
```

```
[root@ceph-node5 ceph-ansible]# rbd mirror pool info data
Mode: pool
Peers:
  UUID                                     NAME CLIENT
  a786a03b-f91a-46e3-a053-93c1f5adc324 ceph client.local
[root@ceph-node5 ceph-ansible]#
```

Mirroring is now enabled at the pool level for pool data in the `ceph` and `backup` clusters and a pool peer is configured for the data pool in the cluster `backup`.

6. Review the data pool in each cluster and see there are currently no RBD images in either site. Once verified we will create three new RBD images in the data pool with `exclusive-lock` and journaling enabled and watch them sync to the secondary `backup` cluster:

```
# rbd ls data
# rbd create image-1 --size 1024 --pool data
  --image-feature exclusive-lock,journaling
```

1. Pool mirrors can be polled for a status of the images as they sync to the `backup` cluster:

```
# rbd mirror pool status data
```

```
[root@ceph-node1 ceph]# rbd -p data ls
[root@ceph-node1 ceph]# rbd create image-1 --size 1024 --pool data --image-feature exclusive-lock,journ
aling
[root@ceph-node1 ceph]# rbd create image-2 --size 1024 --pool data --image-feature exclusive-lock,journ
aling
[root@ceph-node1 ceph]# rbd create image-3 --size 1024 --pool data --image-feature exclusive-lock,journ
aling
[root@ceph-node1 ceph]# rbd -p data ls
image-1
image-2
image-3
```

2. Viewing the remote site for before and after on the `data` pool:

```
[root@ceph-node5 ceph-ansible]# rbd -p data ls
[root@ceph-node5 ceph-ansible]# rbd -p data ls
image-1
image-2
image-3
```

3. Viewing the image sync status on the remote site:

```
[root@ceph-node5 ceph-ansible]# rbd mirror pool status data
health: WARNING
images: 3 total
    3 syncing
```

4. Viewing the healthy state of the journal replaying the image on the remote site:

```
[root@ceph-node5 ceph-ansible]# rbd mirror pool status data
health: OK
images: 3 total
    3 replaying
```

Replaying is the image state we want to see as this means the `rbd-mirror` daemon sees the images in sync and is replaying the journals for any changes to the images that need to be sync.

7. We will now delete the three images from the `ceph` cluster and watch as they are removed from the `backup` cluster:

```
# rbd rm -p data image-<num>
```

```
[root@ceph-node1 ceph]# rbd rm -p data image-1
Removing image: 100% complete...done.
[root@ceph-node1 ceph]# rbd rm -p data image-2
Removing image: 100% complete...done.
[root@ceph-node1 ceph]# rbd rm -p data image-3
Removing image: 100% complete...done.
[root@ceph-node1 ceph]# rbd ls -p data
[root@ceph-node1 ceph]# 
```

8. Viewing the `pool` status to validate the images are removed from the remote site:

```
# rbd mirror pool status data
```

```
[root@ceph-node5 ceph-ansible]# rbd mirror pool status data
health: OK
images: 0 total
```

If at any point and time you choose to disable mirroring on a pool this can be done via the `rbd mirror peer remove` and `rbd mirror pool disable` commands for the chosen pool. Please note when mirroring is disabled for a pool you also disable mirroring on any images residing in the pool.

Following is the syntax for removing mirroring:

1. To remove peer:

```
# rbd mirror peer remove <pool-name> <peer-uuid>
```

2. To remove mirroring on pool:

```
# rbd mirror pool disable <pool>
```

Configuring image mirroring

Image mirroring can be used when you choose to only want to mirror a specific subset of images and not an entire pool. The next recipe we will enable mirroring on a single image in the data pool and not mirror the other two images in the pool. This recipe requires you to have completed step 1 - step 9 in *Disaster recovery replication using RBD mirroring* recipe and have `rbd-mirror` running on backup site:

How to do it...

1. Create three images in the `ceph` cluster as we did in the previous recipe:

```
# rbd create image-1 --size 1024 --pool data
  --image-feature exclusive-lock,journaling
```

2. Enable image mirroring on the data pool on the `ceph` and `backup` clusters:

```
# rbd mirror pool enable data image
```

3. Add `ceph` cluster as a peer to `backup` cluster:

```
root@ceph-node5 # rbd mirror pool peer add
                  data client.local@ceph
```

4. Validate that peer is successfully added:

```
# rbd mirror pool info
```

```
[root@ceph-node5 ceph-ansible]# rbd mirror pool enable data image
[root@ceph-node5 ceph-ansible]# rbd mirror pool peer add data client.local
@ceph
7a5c3404-02bf-4b94-8944-f0b733d47473
[root@ceph-node5 ceph-ansible]# rbd mirror pool info
Mode: pool
Peers:
  UUID                                  NAME CLIENT
  4204c228-643f-4e3d-a206-0e07aff355ea ceph client.rbd
```

5. In the `ceph` cluster, enable image mirroring on `image-1`, `image-2` and `image-3` will not be mirrored:

    root@ceph-node1 # rbd mirror image enable data/image-1

```
[root@ceph-node1 ceph]# rbd mirror pool enable data image
[root@ceph-node1 ceph]# rbd mirror image enable data/image-1
Mirroring enabled
[root@ceph-node1 ceph]# rbd ls -p data
image-1
image-2
image-3
[root@ceph-node1 ceph]# 
```

6. Check mirror status in `backup` cluster to verify single image being mirrored:

    # rbd mirror pool status

7. Check the image status in the `backup` cluster to validate the statue of this image and that image being mirrored is `image-1`:

    # rbd mirror image status data/image-1

```
[root@ceph-node5 ceph-ansible]# rbd mirror pool status data
health: OK
images: 1 total
    1 replaying
[root@ceph-node5 ceph-ansible]# rbd mirror image status data/image-1
image-1:
  global_id:   712afcbe-4514-4a6c-89ef-0eef74766f66
  state:       up+replaying
  description: replaying, master_position=[object_number=3, tag_tid=2, ent
ry_tid=3], mirror_position=[object_number=3, tag_tid=2, entry_tid=3], entr
ies_behind_master=0
  last_update: 2017-09-10 06:10:55
[root@ceph-node5 ceph-ansible]# 
```

Configuring two-way mirroring

Two-way mirroring requires a `rbd-mirror` daemon running on both clusters, the primary and the secondary. With two way mirroring it is possible to mirror data or images from the primary site to a secondary site, and the secondary site can mirror data or images back to the primary site.

We will not be demoing this configuration in this book at it is very similar to one-way configuration, but we will highlight the changes needed for two way replication at the pool level, these steps are covered in the one-way replication recipe.

How to do it...

1. Both clients must have the `rbd-mirror` installed and running:

```
# yum install rbd-mirror
# systemctl enable ceph-rbd-mirror.target
# systemctl enable ceph-rbd-mirror@<client-id>
# systemctl start ceph-rbd-mirror@<client-id>
```

2. As with one way mirroring, both clients must have copies of the respective cluster configuration files and keyrings for client users for the mirrored pools.

3. The pools to be replicated must have mirroring enabled at the pool or image level in *both* clusters:

```
# rbd mirror pool enable <pool> <replication type>
# rbd mirror pool enable <pool> <replication type>
```

4. Validate that mirroring has been successfully enabled:

```
# rbd mirror pool status data
```

5. The pools to be replicated must have a peer registered for mirroring in *both* clusters:

```
# rbd mirror pool peer add <pool>
  client.<user>@<primary cluster name>
# rbd mirror pool peer add <pool>
  client.<user>@<secondary cluster name>
```

See also

For more information, please refer to: `http://docs.ceph.com/docs/master/rbd/rbd-mirroring/`.

Recovering from a disaster!

The following recipes will show how to fail over to the mirrored data on the `backup` cluster after the primary cluster `ceph` has encountered a disaster and how to failback once the `ceph` cluster has recovered. There are two methods for failover when dealing with a disaster:

- **Orderly**: Failover after an orderly shutdown. This would be a proper shutdown of the cluster and demotion and promotion of the image.
- **Non-orderly**: Failover after a non-orderly shutdown. This would be a complete loss of the primary cluster. In this case, the failback would require a resynchronizing of the image.

How to do it...

1. How to properly failover after an orderly shutdown:
   - Stop all client's that are writing to the primary image
   - Demote the primary image located on the `ceph` cluster:

     ```
     # rbd mirror image demote data/image-1
     ```

   - Promote the non-primary image located on the `backup` cluster:

     ```
     # rbd-mirror image promote data/image-1
     ```

   - Validate image has become primary on the `backup` cluster:

     ```
     # rbd mirror image status data/image-1
     ```

- Resume client access to the image:

```
[root@ceph-node1 ceph]# rbd mirror image demote data/image-1
Image demoted to non-primary
[root@ceph-node1 ceph]#
```

```
[root@ceph-node5 ceph-ansible]# rbd mirror image promote data/image-1
Image promoted to primary
[root@ceph-node5 ceph-ansible]# rbd mirror image status data/image-1
image-1:
  global_id:   712afcbe-4514-4a6c-89ef-0eef74766f66
  state:       up+stopped
  description: remote image is non-primary or local image is primary
  last_update: 2017-09-10 06:35:25
[root@ceph-node5 ceph-ansible]#
```

2. How to properly failover after a non-orderly shutdown:
    - Validate that the primary cluster is in a down state
    - Stop all client access to the ceph cluster that accesses the primary image
    - Promote the non-primary image using the FORCE option on the backup cluster, as the demotion cannot be propagated to the down ceph cluster:

    ```
    # rbd-mirror image promote data/image-1
    ```

    - Resume client access to the peer image
3. How to failback from a disaster:
    - If there was a non-orderly shutdown on the ceph cluster then demote the old primary image on the ceph cluster once it returns:

    ```
    # rbd mirror image demote data/image-1
    ```

    - Resynchronize the image *only* if there was a non-orderly shutdown:

    ```
    # rbd mirror image resync data/image-1
    ```

- Validate that the re-synchronization has completed and image is in up+replaying state:

```
# rbd mirror image status data/image-1
```

- Demote the secondary image on the `backup` cluster:

```
# rbd mirror image demote data/image-1
```

- Promote the formerly primary image on `ceph` cluster:

```
# rbd mirror image promotion data/image-1
```

3
Working with Ceph and OpenStack

In this chapter we will cover the following recipes:

- Ceph – the best match for OpenStack
- Setting up OpenStack
- Configuring OpenStack as Ceph clients
- Configuring Glance for Ceph backend
- Configuring Cinder for Ceph backend
- Configuring Nova to boot instances from Ceph RBD
- Configuring Nova to attach Ceph RBD

Introduction

OpenStack is an open source software platform for building and managing public and private cloud infrastructure. It is being governed by an independent, non-profit foundation known as *The OpenStack Foundation*. It has the largest and the most active community, which is backed by technology giants such as HP, Red Hat, Dell-EMC, Cisco, IBM, Rackspace, and many more.

OpenStack's idea for a cloud is that it should be simple to implement and massively scalable.

OpenStack is considered as the cloud operating system where users are allowed to instantly deploy hundreds of virtual machines in an automated way. It also provides an efficient way of hassle-free management of these machines. OpenStack is known for its dynamic scale up, scale out, and distributed architecture capabilities, making your cloud environment robust and future-ready. OpenStack provides an enterprise-class **Infrastructure-as-a-Service** (**IaaS**) platform for all your cloud needs. As shown in the following high-level diagram, OpenStack is made up of several different software components that work together to provide cloud services:

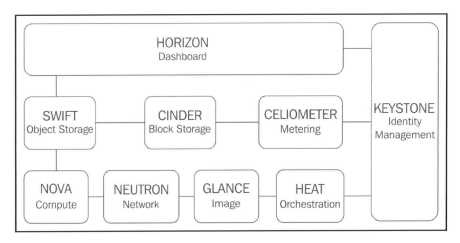

Out of all these components, in this chapter, we will focus on Cinder and Glance, which provide block storage and image services respectively. For more information on OpenStack components, please visit `http://www.openstack.org/`.

Ceph – the best match for OpenStack

OpenStack adoption continues to rise at an incredible rate, and it is incredibly popular as it's based on software-defined on a wide range, whether it's computing, networking, or even storage. And when you talk about storage for OpenStack, Ceph will get all the attention. An OpenStack user survey, conducted in April 2017, showed Ceph dominating the block storage driver market with a whopping 65% usage, 41% higher (Source - `https://www.openstack.org/assets/survey/April2017SurveyReport.pdf`) than the next storage driver.

Ceph provides the robust, reliable storage backend that OpenStack was looking for. Its seamless integration with OpenStack components such as Cinder, Glance, Nova, and Keystone provides an all-in-one cloud storage backend for OpenStack. Here are some key benefits that make Ceph the best match for OpenStack:

- Ceph provides an enterprise-grade, feature-rich storage backend at a very low cost per gigabyte, which helps to keep the OpenStack cloud deployment price down

- Ceph is a unified storage solution for block, file, or object storage for OpenStack, allowing applications to use storage as they need

- Ceph provides advance block storage capabilities for OpenStack clouds, which includes the easy and quick spawning of instances, as well as the backup and cloning of VMs

- It provides default persistent volumes for OpenStack instances that can work like traditional servers, where data will not flush on rebooting the VMs

- Ceph supports OpenStack in being host-independent by supporting VM migrations, scaling up storage components without affecting VMs

- It provides the snapshot feature to OpenStack volumes, which can also be used as a means of backup

- Ceph's *copy-on-write* cloning feature provides OpenStack to spin up several instances at once, which helps the provisioning mechanism function faster

- Ceph supports rich APIs for both Swift and S3 object storage interfaces

The Ceph and OpenStack communities continue to work to make the integration more seamless and to make use of new features as they emerge.

OpenStack is a modular system that has a unique component for a specific set of tasks. There are several components that require a reliable storage backend, such as Ceph and extend full integration to it, as shown in the following diagram:

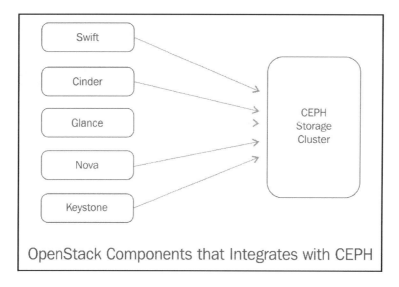

Each of these components uses Ceph in their own way to store block devices and objects. The majority of cloud deployment based on OpenStack and Ceph use the Cinder, Glance, and the Swift integrations with Ceph. Keystone integration is used when you need an S3-compatible object storage on the Ceph backend. Nova integration allows boot from Ceph volume capabilities for your OpenStack instances.

Setting up OpenStack

OpenStack setup and configuration is beyond the scope of this book, however, for ease of demonstration, we will use a virtual machine that is preinstalled with the OpenStack RDO Juno release. If you like, you can also use your own OpenStack environment and can perform Ceph integration.

How to do it...

In this recipe, we will demonstrate setting up a preconfigured OpenStack environment using Vagrant and accessing it via CLI and GUI:

1. Launch `openstack-node1` using `vagrantfile` as we did for Ceph nodes in the last chapter. Make sure that you are on the host machine and are under the `Ceph-Cookbook-Second-Edition` repository before bringing up `openstack-node1` using Vagrant:

   ```
   # cd Ceph-Cookbook-Second-Edition
   # vagrant up openstack-node1
   ```

```
[vumrao@ceph-jewel Ceph-Cookbook-Second-Edition]$ vagrant up openstack-node1
Bringing machine 'openstack-node1' up with 'virtualbox' provider...
==> openstack-node1: Box 'openstack' could not be found. Attempting to find and install...
    openstack-node1: Box Provider: virtualbox
    openstack-node1: Box Version: >= 0
==> openstack-node1: Box file was not detected as metadata. Adding it directly...
==> openstack-node1: Adding box 'openstack' (v0) for provider: virtualbox
    openstack-node1: Downloading: https://www.dropbox.com/s/azww4ud3ti910os/openstack.box?dl=1
==> openstack-node1: Successfully added box 'openstack' (v0) for 'virtualbox'!
==> openstack-node1: Importing base box 'openstack'...
Progress: 40%
```

2. Log in to the OpenStack node with the following `vagrant` command:

   ```
   # vagrant status openstack-node1
   $ vagrant ssh openstack-node1
   ```

```
[vumrao@ceph-jewel Ceph-Cookbook-Second-Edition]$
[vumrao@ceph-jewel Ceph-Cookbook-Second-Edition]$ vagrant status openstack-node1
Current machine states:

openstack-node1           running (virtualbox)

The VM is running. To stop this VM, you can run `vagrant halt` to
shut it down forcefully, or you can run `vagrant suspend` to simply
suspend the virtual machine. In either case, to restart it again,
simply run `vagrant up`.
[vumrao@ceph-jewel Ceph-Cookbook-Second-Edition]$
```

3. We assume that you have some knowledge of OpenStack and are aware of its operations. We will source the `keystone_admin` file, which has been placed under `/root`, and to do this, we need to switch to root:

```
$ sudo su -
$ source keystonerc_admin
```

We will now run some native OpenStack commands to make sure that OpenStack is set up correctly. Please note that some of these commands do not show any information since this is a fresh OpenStack environment and does not have instances or volumes created:

```
# nova list
# cinder list
# glance image-list
```

```
[root@os-node1 ~]# source keystonerc_admin
[root@os-node1 ~(keystone_admin)]# nova list
+----+------+--------+------------+-------------+----------+
| ID | Name | Status | Task State | Power State | Networks |
+----+------+--------+------------+-------------+----------+
+----+------+--------+------------+-------------+----------+
[root@os-node1 ~(keystone_admin)]# cinder list
+----+--------+--------------+------+-------------+----------+-------------+
| ID | Status | Display Name | Size | Volume Type | Bootable | Attached to |
+----+--------+--------------+------+-------------+----------+-------------+
+----+--------+--------------+------+-------------+----------+-------------+
[root@os-node1 ~(keystone_admin)]# glance image-list
+--------------------------------------+--------+-------------+------------------+----------+--------+
| ID                                   | Name   | Disk Format | Container Format | Size     | Status |
+--------------------------------------+--------+-------------+------------------+----------+--------+
| 5c261af7-9388-44ad-a8ce-f9ebdad2e5cb | cirros | qcow2       | bare             | 13200896 | active |
+--------------------------------------+--------+-------------+------------------+----------+--------+
[root@os-node1 ~(keystone_admin)]#
```

4. You can also log into the OpenStack horizon web interface
   (`https://192.168.1.111/dashboard`) using the username `admin` and the
   password `vagrant`:

5. After logging in, the **Overview** page opens:

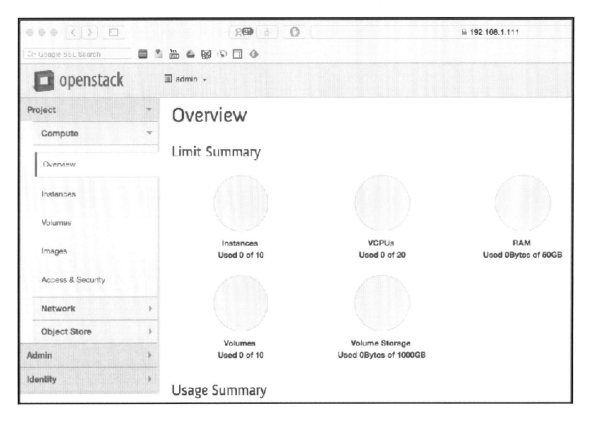

OpenStack Dashboard Overview

Configuring OpenStack as Ceph clients

OpenStack nodes should be configured as Ceph clients in order to access the Ceph cluster. To do this, install Ceph packages on OpenStack nodes and make sure it can access the Ceph cluster.

How to do it...

In this recipe, we are going to configure OpenStack as a Ceph client, which will be later used to configure Cinder, Glance, and Nova:

1. Install `ceph-common` the Ceph client-side package in OpenStack node and then copy `ceph.conf` from `ceph-node1` to the OpenStack node – `os-nod1`.

2. Create an SSH tunnel between the monitor node `ceph-node1` and OpenStack `os-node1`:

```
[root@ceph-node1 group_vars]#
[root@ceph-node1 group_vars]# ssh-copy-id root@os-node1
/usr/bin/ssh-copy-id: INFO: Source of key(s) to be installed: "/root/.ssh/id_rsa.pub"
The authenticity of host 'os-node1 (192.168.1.111)' can't be established.
ECDSA key fingerprint is SHA256:LKEJvMiROJpoHqwTWm1X8kuT9Mg1jkfXE6WjQ4MrogU.
ECDSA key fingerprint is MD5:af:2a:a5:74:a7:0b:f5:5b:ef:c5:4b:2a:fe:1d:30:8e.
Are you sure you want to continue connecting (yes/no)? yes
/usr/bin/ssh-copy-id: INFO: attempting to log in with the new key(s), to filter out any that are already installed
/usr/bin/ssh-copy-id: INFO: 1 key(s) remain to be installed -- if you are prompted now it is to install the new key
root@os-node1's password:

Number of key(s) added: 1

Now try logging into the machine, with:   "ssh 'root@os-node1'"
and check to make sure that only the key(s) you wanted were added.

[root@ceph-node1 group_vars]#
```

3. Copy the Ceph repository file from `ceph-node1` to `os-node1`:

```
[root@ceph-node1 group_vars]#
[root@ceph-node1 group_vars]# scp /etc/yum.repos.d/ceph_stable.repo os-node1:/etc/yum.repos.d/.
ceph_stable.repo
[root@ceph-node1 group_vars]#
```

4. Install `ceph-common` package in `os-node1`:

```
[root@os-node1 ~(keystone_admin)]#
[root@os-node1 ~(keystone_admin)]# yum install ceph-common -y
Loaded plugins: fastestmirror, priorities
base
ceph_stable
```

5. Once it completes, you will have the following message:

6. Copy `ceph.conf` from `ceph-node1` to `os-node1`:

```
[root@ceph-node1 group_vars]#
[root@ceph-node1 group_vars]# scp /etc/ceph/ceph.conf os-node1:/etc/ceph/
ceph.conf
[root@ceph-node1 group_vars]#
```

7. Create Ceph pools for Cinder, Glance, and Nova from monitor node `ceph-node1`. You may use any available pool, but it's recommended that you create separate pools for OpenStack components:

```
# ceph osd pool create images 128
# ceph osd pool create volumes 128
# ceph osd pool create vms 128
```

```
[root@ceph-node1 ceph]# ceph osd pool create images 128
pool 'images' created
[root@ceph-node1 ceph]# ceph osd pool create volumes 128
pool 'volumes' created
[root@ceph-node1 ceph]# ceph osd pool create vms 128
pool 'vms' created
[root@ceph-node1 ceph]# ceph osd lspools
0 rbd,1 images,2 volumes,3 vms,
[root@ceph-node1 ceph]#
```

 We have used 128 as PG number for these three pools. For the PG calculation, for your pools, you can use Ceph PGcalc tool `http://ceph.com/pgcalc/`.

8. Set up client authentication by creating a new user for Cinder and Glance:

```
# ceph auth get-or-create client.cinder mon 'allow r' osd
    'allow class-read object_prefix rbd_children, allow rwx
pool=volumes,
        allow rwx pool=vms, allow rx pool=images'

# ceph auth get-or-create client.glance mon 'allow r' osd
    'allow class-read object_prefix rbd_children, allow rwx
pool=images'
```

```
[root@ceph-node1 ~]#
[root@ceph-node1 ~]# ceph auth get-or-create client.cinder mon 'allow r' osd 'allow class-read object_prefix rbd_children, allow rwx pool=volumes, allow rwx pool=vms, allow rx pool=images'
[client.cinder]
        key = AQAjOclZx/d5IxAAAD07JU1PaQXfrqin6fPPnQ==
[root@ceph-node1 ~]# ceph auth get-or-create client.glance mon 'allow r' osd 'allow class-read object_prefix rbd_children, allow rwx pool=images'
[client.glance]
        key = AQAwOclZwet1MRAAi5ER7wKOeWj7YmMqK8zC1w==
[root@ceph-node1 ~]#
```

9. Add the keyrings to `os-node1` and change their ownership:

```
# ceph auth get-or-create client.glance |
    ssh os-node1 sudo tee /etc/ceph/ceph.client.glance.keyring
# ssh os-node1 sudo chown glance:glance
    /etc/ceph/ceph.client.glance.keyring
# ceph auth get-or-create client.cinder |
    ssh os-node1 sudo tee /etc/ceph/ceph.client.cinder.keyring
# ssh os-node1 sudo chown cinder:cinder
    /etc/ceph/ceph.client.cinder.keyring
```

```
[root@ceph-node1 ~]#
[root@ceph-node1 ~]# ceph auth get-or-create client.glance | ssh os-node1 sudo tee /etc/ceph/ceph.client.glance.keyring
[client.glance]
        key = AQAwOclZwet1MRAAi5ER7wKOeWj7YmMqK8zC1w==
[root@ceph-node1 ~]# ssh os-node1 sudo chown glance:glance /etc/ceph/ceph.client.glance.keyring
[root@ceph-node1 ~]# ceph auth get-or-create client.cinder | ssh os-node1 sudo tee /etc/ceph/ceph.client.cinder.keyring
[client.cinder]
        key = AQAjOclZx/d5IxAAAD07JU1PaQXfrqin6fPPnQ==
[root@ceph-node1 ~]# ssh os-node1 sudo chown cinder:cinder /etc/ceph/ceph.client.cinder.keyring
```

10. The `libvirt` process requires accessing the Ceph cluster while attaching or detaching a block device from Cinder. We should create a temporary copy of the `client.cinder` key that will be needed for the Cinder and Nova configuration later in this chapter:

```
# ceph auth get-key client.cinder |
    ssh os-node1 tee /etc/ceph/temp.client.cinder.key
```

11. At this point, you can test the previous configuration by accessing the Ceph cluster from `os-node1` using the `client.glance` and `client.cinder` Ceph users.

    Log in to `os-node1` and run the following commands:

    ```
    $ vagrant ssh openstack-node1
    $ sudo su -
    # ceph -s --id glance
    # ceph -s --id cinder
    ```

```
[root@os-node1 ~]# ceph -s --id glance
    cluster 585ce77b-476c-4f52-b147-93fe9424eb2a
     health HEALTH_OK
     monmap e1: 3 mons at {ceph-node1=192.168.1.101:6789/0,ceph-node2=192.168.1.102:6789/0,ceph-node3=192.168.1.103:6789/0}
            election epoch 6, quorum 0,1,2 ceph-node1,ceph-node2,ceph-node3
     osdmap e90: 9 osds: 9 up, 9 in
            flags sortbitwise,require_jewel_osds
      pgmap v2566: 600 pgs, 15 pools, 4161 bytes data, 183 objects
            352 MB used, 161 GB / 161 GB avail
                 600 active+clean
[root@os-node1 ~]#
[root@os-node1 ~]#
[root@os-node1 ~]# ceph -s --id cinder
    cluster 585ce77b-476c-4f52-b147-93fe9424eb2a
     health HEALTH_OK
     monmap e1: 3 mons at {ceph-node1=192.168.1.101:6789/0,ceph-node2=192.168.1.102:6789/0,ceph-node3=192.168.1.103:6789/0}
            election epoch 6, quorum 0,1,2 ceph-node1,ceph-node2,ceph-node3
     osdmap e90: 9 osds: 9 up, 9 in
            flags sortbitwise,require_jewel_osds
      pgmap v2566: 600 pgs, 15 pools, 4161 bytes data, 183 objects
            352 MB used, 161 GB / 161 GB avail
                 600 active+clean
[root@os-node1 ~]# _
```

12. Finally, generate UUID, then create, define, and set the secret key to `libvirt` and remove temporary keys:

    1. Generate a UUID by using the following command:

       ```
       # cd /etc/ceph
       # uuidgen
       ```

    2. Create a `secret` file and set this UUID number to it:

       ```
       cat > secret.xml <<EOF
       <secret ephemeral='no' private='no'>
       <uuid>e279566e-bc97-46d0-bd90-68080a2a0ad8</uuid>
       <usage type='ceph'>
       <name>client.cinder secret</name>
       </usage>
       </secret>
       EOF
       ```

Make sure that you use your own UUID generated for your environment.

```
[root@os-node1 ceph]#
[root@os-node1 ceph]# cd /etc/ceph/
[root@os-node1 ceph]# uuidgen
e279566e-bc97-46d0-bd90-68080a2a0ad8
[root@os-node1 ceph]# cat > secret.xml << EOF
> <secret ephemeral='no' private='no'>
>   <uuid>e279566e-bc97-46d0-bd90-68080a2a0ad8</uuid>
>   <usage type='ceph'>
>     <name>client.cinder secret</name>
>   </usage>
> </secret>
> EOF
[root@os-node1 ceph]#
```

3. Define the secret and keep the generated secret value safe. We will require this secret value in the next steps:

```
# virsh secret-define --file secret.xml
```

```
[root@os-node1 ceph]#
[root@os-node1 ceph]# virsh secret-define --file secret.xml
Secret e279566e-bc97-46d0-bd90-68080a2a0ad8 created

[root@os-node1 ceph]# _
```

4. Set the secret value that was generated in the last step to `virsh` and delete temporary files. Deleting the temporary files is optional; it's done just to keep the system clean:

```
# virsh secret-set-value
--secret e279566e-bc97-46d0-bd90-68080a2a0ad8
--base64 $(cat temp.client.cinder.key) &&
rm temp.client.cinder.key secret.xml
# virsh secret-list
```

```
[root@os-node1 ceph]#
[root@os-node1 ceph]# virsh secret-define --file secret.xml
Secret e279566e-bc97-46d0-bd90-68080a2a0ad0 created

[root@os-node1 ceph]#
[root@os-node1 ceph]# virsh secret-set-value --secret e279566e-bc97-46d0-bd90-68080a2a0ad8 --base64 $(cat temp.client.cinder.key) && rm temp.client.cinder.key secret.xml
Secret value set

rm: remove regular file 'temp.client.cinder.key'? y
rm: remove regular file 'secret.xml'? y
[root@os-node1 ceph]#
[root@os-node1 ceph]# virsh secret-list
 UUID                                  Usage
--------------------------------------------------------------------------------
 e279566e-bc97-46d0-bd90-68080a2a0ad8 ceph client.cinder secret

[root@os-node1 ceph]# _
```

Configuring Glance for Ceph backend

We have completed the configuration required from the Ceph side. In this recipe, we will configure the OpenStack Glance to use Ceph as a storage backend.

How to do it...

This recipe talks about configuring the Glance component of OpenStack to store virtual machine images on Ceph RBD:

1. Log in to `os-node1`, which is our Glance node, and edit `/etc/glance/glance-api.conf` for the following changes:
    1. Under the `[DEFAULT]` section, make sure that the following lines are present:

    ```
    default_store=rbd
    show_image_direct_url=True
    ```

2. Execute the following command to verify entries:

```
# cat /etc/glance/glance-api.conf |
egrep -i "default_store|image_direct"
```

```
[root@os-node1 ceph]# cat /etc/glance/glance-api.conf | egrep -i "default_store|image_direct"
default_store=rbd
show_image_direct_url=True
[root@os-node1 ceph]#
```

3. Under the [glance_store] section, make sure that the following lines are present under RBD store options:

```
stores = rbd
rbd_store_ceph_conf=/etc/ceph/ceph.conf
rbd_store_user=glance
rbd_store_pool=images
rbd_store_chunk_size=8
```

4. Execute the following command to verify the previous entries:

```
# cat /etc/glance/glance-api.conf |
  egrep -v "#|default" | grep -i rbd
```

```
[root@os-node1 ceph]# cat /etc/glance/glance-api.conf | egrep -v "#|default" | grep -i rbd
stores = rbd
rbd_store_ceph_conf=/etc/ceph/ceph.conf
rbd_store_user=glance
rbd_store_pool=images
rbd_store_chunk_size=8
[root@os-node1 ceph]#
```

2. Restart the OpenStack Glance services:

```
# service openstack-glance-api restart
```

3. Source the `keystone_admin` file for OpenStack and list the Glance images:

```
# source /root/keystonerc_admin
# glance image-list
```

```
[root@os-node1 ~]# source /root/keystonerc_admin
[root@os-node1 ~(keystone_admin)]# glance image-list
+--------------------------------------+--------+-------------+------------------+----------+--------+
| ID                                   | Name   | Disk Format | Container Format | Size     | Status |
+--------------------------------------+--------+-------------+------------------+----------+--------+
| 5c261af7-9388-44ad-a8ce-f9ebdad2e5cb | cirros | qcow2       | bare             | 13200896 | active |
+--------------------------------------+--------+-------------+------------------+----------+--------+
[root@os-node1 ~(keystone_admin)]#
```

4. Download the cirros image from the internet, which will later be stored in Ceph:

```
# wget http://download.cirros-cloud.net/0.3.1/cirros-0.3.1-
x86_64-disk.img
```

5. Add a new Glance image using the following command:

```
# glance image-create --name cirros_image --is-public=true
  --disk-format=qcow2 --container-format=bare
   < cirros-0.3.1-x86_64-disk.img
```

```
[root@os-node1 ~(keystone_admin)]#
[root@os-node1 ~(keystone_admin)]# glance image-create --name cirros_image --is-public=true --disk-format=qcow2 --container-format=bare < cirros-0.3.1-x86_64-disk.img
+------------------+--------------------------------------+
| Property         | Value                                |
+------------------+--------------------------------------+
| checksum         | d972013792949d0d3ba628fbe8685bce     |
| container_format | bare                                 |
| created_at       | 2017-09-25T18:00:49                  |
| deleted          | False                                |
| deleted_at       | None                                 |
| disk_format      | qcow2                                |
| id               | b1c39f06-5330-4b04-ae0f-0b1d5e901e5b |
| is_public        | True                                 |
| min_disk         | 0                                    |
| min_ram          | 0                                    |
| name             | cirros_image                         |
| owner            | c9f87abe43ea49239313565ca74ebaa0     |
| protected        | False                                |
| size             | 13147648                             |
| status           | active                               |
| updated_at       | 2017-09-25T18:00:50                  |
| virtual_size     | None                                 |
+------------------+--------------------------------------+
[root@os-node1 ~(keystone_admin)]#
```

6. List the Glance images using the following command; you will notice there are now two Glance images:

```
# glance image-list
```

```
[root@os-node1 ~(keystone_admin)]#
[root@os-node1 ~(keystone_admin)]# glance image-list
+--------------------------------------+-------------+-------------+------------------+----------+--------+
| ID                                   | Name        | Disk Format | Container Format | Size     | Status |
+--------------------------------------+-------------+-------------+------------------+----------+--------+
| 5c261af7-9388-44ad-a8ce-f9ebdad2e5cb | cirros      | qcow2       | bare             | 13200896 | active |
| b1c39f06-5330-4b04-ae0f-0b1d5e901e5b | cirros_image | qcow2      | bare             | 13147648 | active |
+--------------------------------------+-------------+-------------+------------------+----------+--------+
[root@os-node1 ~(keystone_admin)]#
```

7. You can verify that the new image is stored in Ceph by querying the image ID in the Ceph images pool:

```
# rbd -p images ls --id glance
# rbd info images/<image name> --id glance
```

```
[root@os-node1 ~(keystone_admin)]#
[root@os-node1 ~(keystone_admin)]# rbd -p images ls --id glance
b1c39f06-5330-4b04-ae0f-0b1d5e901e5b
[root@os-node1 ~(keystone_admin)]# rbd info images/b1c39f06-5330-4b04-ae0f-0b1d5e901e5b --id glance
rbd image 'b1c39f06-5330-4b04-ae0f-0b1d5e901e5b':
        size 12839 kB in 2 objects
        order 23 (8192 kB objects)
        block_name_prefix: rbd_data.278a23b69012
        format: 2
        features: layering
        flags:
[root@os-node1 ~(keystone_admin)]#
```

8. Since we have configured Glance to use Ceph for its default storage, all the Glance images will now be stored in Ceph. You can also try creating images from the OpenStack horizon dashboard:

9. Finally, we will try to launch an instance using the image that we have created earlier:

```
# nova boot --flavor 1 --image b1c39f06-5330-4b04-ae0f-0b1d5e901e5b vm1
```

```
[root@os-node1 ~(keystone_admin)]#
[root@os-node1 ~(keystone_admin)]# nova boot --flavor 1 --image b1c39f06-5330-4b04-ae0f-0b1d5e901e5b vm1
+--------------------------------------+------------------------------------------------------+
| Property                             | Value                                                |
+--------------------------------------+------------------------------------------------------+
| OS-DCF:diskConfig                    | MANUAL                                               |
| OS-EXT-AZ:availability_zone          | nova                                                 |
| OS-EXT-SRV-ATTR:host                 | -                                                    |
| OS-EXT-SRV-ATTR:hypervisor_hostname  | -                                                    |
| OS-EXT-SRV-ATTR:instance_name        | instance-00000001                                    |
| OS-EXT-STS:power_state               | 0                                                    |
| OS-EXT-STS:task_state                | scheduling                                           |
| OS-EXT-STS:vm_state                  | building                                             |
| OS-SRV-USG:launched_at               | -                                                    |
| OS-SRV-USG:terminated_at             | -                                                    |
| accessIPv4                           |                                                      |
| accessIPv6                           |                                                      |
| adminPass                            | 265PXYcotdev                                         |
| config_drive                         |                                                      |
| created                              | 2017-09-25T18:53:05Z                                 |
| flavor                               | m1.tiny (1)                                          |
| hostId                               |                                                      |
| id                                   | cee98754-de7b-440d-b20c-10e2620e8217                 |
| image                                | cirros_image (b1c39f06-5330-4b04-ae0f-0b1d5e901e5b)  |
| key_name                             | -                                                    |
| metadata                             | {}                                                   |
| name                                 | vm1                                                  |
| os-extended-volumes:volumes_attached | []                                                   |
| progress                             | 0                                                    |
| security_groups                      | default                                              |
| status                               | BUILD                                                |
| tenant_id                            | c9f87abe43ea49239313565ca74ebaa0                     |
| updated                              | 2017-09-25T18:53:05Z                                 |
| user_id                              | 58e7a4c12d4f44ed865b2bf8ddf2f8f4                     |
+--------------------------------------+------------------------------------------------------+
```

10. You can check with the Nova list command:

```
[root@os-node1 ~(keystone_admin)]#
[root@os-node1 ~(keystone_admin)]# nova list
+--------------------------------------+------+--------+------------+-------------+---------------------+
| ID                                   | Name | Status | Task State | Power State | Networks            |
+--------------------------------------+------+--------+------------+-------------+---------------------+
| cee98754-de7b-440d-b20c-10e2620e8217 | vm1  | ACTIVE | -          | Running     | public=172.24.4.227 |
+--------------------------------------+------+--------+------------+-------------+---------------------+
[root@os-node1 ~(keystone_admin)]#
```

While you are adding new Glance images or creating an instance from the Glance image stored on Ceph, you can check the IO on the Ceph cluster by monitoring it and using the # `watch ceph -s` command.

Configuring Cinder for Ceph backend

The Cinder program of OpenStack provides block storage to virtual machines. In this recipe, we will configure OpenStack Cinder to use Ceph as a storage backend. OpenStack Cinder requires a driver to interact with the Ceph Block Device. On the OpenStack node, edit the `/etc/cinder/cinder.conf` configuration file by adding the code snippet given in the following section.

How to do it...

In the last recipe, we learned to configure Glance to use Ceph. In this recipe, we will learn to use the Ceph RBD with the Cinder service of OpenStack:

1. Since in this demonstration we are not using multiple backend cinder configurations, comment the `enabled_backends` option from the `/etc/cinder/cinder.conf` file:

2. Navigate to the options defined in `cinder.volume.drivers.rbd` section of the `/etc/cinder/cinder.conf` file and add the following (replace the secret UUID with your environments value):

```
volume_driver = cinder.volume.drivers.rbd.RBDDriver
rbd_pool = volumes
rbd_user = cinder
rbd_secret_uuid = e279566e-bc97-46d0-bd90-68080a2a0ad8
rbd_ceph_conf = /etc/ceph/ceph.conf
rbd_flatten_volume_from_snapshot = false
rbd_max_clone_depth = 5
rbd_store_chunk_size = 4
rados_connect_timeout = -1
glance_api_version = 2
```

3. Execute the following command to verify the previous entries:

   ```
   # cat /etc/cinder/cinder.conf | egrep "rbd|rados|version" |
     grep -v "#"
   ```

```
[root@os-node1 ~(keystone_admin)]#
[root@os-node1 ~(keystone_admin)]# cat /etc/cinder/cinder.conf | egrep "rbd|rados|version" | grep -v "#"
volume_driver = cinder.volume.drivers.rbd.RBDDriver
rbd_pool = volumes
rbd_user = cinder
rbd_secret_uuid = e279566e-bc97-46d0-bd90-68080a2a0ad8
rbd_ceph_conf = /etc/ceph/ceph.conf
rbd_flatten_volume_from_snapshot = false
rbd_max_clone_depth = 5
rbd_store_chunk_size = 4
rados_connect_timeout = -1
glance_api_version = 2
[root@os-node1 ~(keystone_admin)]#
```

4. Comment enabled_backend=lvm option in /etc/cinder/cinder.conf:

```
[root@os-node1 ~(keystone_admin)]#
[root@os-node1 ~(keystone_admin)]# cat /etc/cinder/cinder.conf | grep enabled_backend
#enabled_backends=<None>
#enabled_backends=lvm
[root@os-node1 ~(keystone_admin)]#
```

5. Restart the OpenStack Cinder services:

   ```
   # service openstack-cinder-volume restart
   ```

6. Source the keystone_admin files for OpenStack:

   ```
   # source /root/keystonerc_admin
   # cinder list
   ```

7. To test this configuration, create your first Cinder volume of 2 GB, which should now be created on your Ceph cluster:

   ```
   # cinder create --display-name ceph-volume01
     --display-description "Cinder volume on CEPH storage" 2
   ```

```
[root@os-node1 ~]# source /root/keystonerc_admin
[root@os-node1 ~(keystone_admin)]# cinder list
+----+--------+--------------+------+-------------+----------+-------------+
| ID | Status | Display Name | Size | Volume Type | Bootable | Attached to |
+----+--------+--------------+------+-------------+----------+-------------+
+----+--------+--------------+------+-------------+----------+-------------+
[root@os-node1 ~(keystone_admin)]# cinder create --display-name ceph-volume01 --display-description "Cinder volume on CEPH storage" 2
+---------------------+--------------------------------------+
|       Property      |                Value                 |
+---------------------+--------------------------------------+
|     attachments     |                  []                  |
|  availability_zone  |                 nova                 |
|       bootable      |                false                 |
|      created_at     |      2017-09-25T19:47:42.488505      |
| display_description |    Cinder volume on CEPH storage     |
|     display_name    |            ceph-volume01             |
|      encrypted      |                False                 |
|          id         | 7443e2b6-0674-4950-9371-49094a1702a7 |
|       metadata      |                  {}                  |
|         size        |                  2                   |
|     snapshot_id     |                 None                 |
|     source_volid    |                 None                 |
|        status       |               creating               |
|     volume_type     |                 None                 |
+---------------------+--------------------------------------+
[root@os-node1 ~(keystone_admin)]#
```

8. Check the volume by listing the Cinder and Ceph volumes pool:

   # cinder list

```
[root@os-node1 ~(keystone_admin)]#
[root@os-node1 ~(keystone_admin)]# cinder list
+--------------------------------------+-----------+--------------+------+-------------+----------+-------------+
|                  ID                  |  Status   | Display Name | Size | Volume Type | Bootable | Attached to |
+--------------------------------------+-----------+--------------+------+-------------+----------+-------------+
| 7443e2b6-0674-4950-9371-49094a1702a7 | available | ceph-volume01|  2   |    None     |  false   |             |
+--------------------------------------+-----------+--------------+------+-------------+----------+-------------+
[root@os-node1 ~(keystone_admin)]#
```

   # rbd -p volumes ls --id cinder

   # rbd info volumes/volume-7443e2b6-0674-4950-9371-49094a1702a7
     --id cinder

```
[root@os-node1 ~(keystone_admin)]#
[root@os-node1 ~(keystone_admin)]# rbd -p volumes ls --id cinder
volume-7443e2b6-0674-4950-9371-49094a1702a7
[root@os-node1 ~(keystone_admin)]# rbd info volumes/volume-7443e2b6-0674-4950-9371-49094a1702a7 --id cinder
rbd image 'volume-7443e2b6-0674-4950-9371-49094a1702a7':
        size 2048 MB in 512 objects
        order 22 (4096 kB objects)
        block_name_prefix: rbd_data.2ad7f3d9bcfab
        format: 2
        features: layering
        flags:
[root@os-node1 ~(keystone_admin)]#
```

9. Similarly, try creating another volume using the OpenStack horizon dashboard.

Configuring Nova to boot instances from Ceph RBD

In order to boot all OpenStack instances into Ceph, that is, for the *boot-from-volume* feature, we should configure an ephemeral backend for Nova. To do this, edit `/etc/nova/nova.conf` on the OpenStack node and perform the following changes.

How to do it...

This recipe deals with configuring Nova to store the entire virtual machines on the Ceph RBD:

1. Navigate to the `[libvirt]` section and add the following:

   ```
   inject_partition=-2
   images_type=rbd
   images_rbd_pool=vms
   images_rbd_ceph_conf=/etc/ceph/ceph.conf
   rbd_user=cinder
   rbd_secret_uuid= e279566e-bc97-46d0-bd90-68080a2a0ad8
   ```

2. Verify your changes:

   ```
   # cat /etc/nova/nova.conf|egrep "rbd|partition" | grep -v "#"
   ```

   ```
   [root@os-node1 ~(keystone_admin)]#
   [root@os-node1 ~(keystone_admin)]# cat /etc/nova/nova.conf|egrep "rbd|partition" | grep -v "#"
   inject_partition=-2
   images_type=rbd
   images_rbd_pool=vms
   images_rbd_ceph_conf=/etc/ceph/ceph.conf
   rbd_user=cinder
   rbd_secret_uuid=e279566e-bc97-46d0-bd90-68080a2a0ad8
   [root@os-node1 ~(keystone_admin)]#
   ```

3. Restart the OpenStack Nova services:

```
# service openstack-nova-compute restart
```

4. To boot a virtual machine in Ceph, the Glance image format must be RAW. We will use the same cirros image that we downloaded earlier in this chapter and convert this image from the QCOW to the RAW format (this is important). You can also use any other image, as long as it's in the RAW format:

```
# qemu-img convert -f qcow2 -O raw cirros-0.3.1-x86_64-disk.img
cirros-0.3.1-x86_64-disk.raw
```

5. Create a Glance image using a RAW image:

```
# glance image-create --name cirros_raw_image
  --is-public=true --disk-format=raw
  --container-format=bare < cirros-0.3.1-x86_64-disk.raw
```

6. To test the boot from the Ceph volume feature, create a bootable volume:

```
# nova image-list
# cinder create --image-id 78e1fd35-aa65-447b-954e-1b072e9a17ec
              --display-name cirros-ceph-boot-volume 1
```

```
[root@os-node1 ~(keystone_admin)]# cinder create --image-id 78e1fd35-aa65-447b-954e-1b072e9a17ec --display-name cirros-ceph-boot-volume 1
+---------------------+--------------------------------------+
|       Property      |                Value                 |
+---------------------+--------------------------------------+
|     attachments     |                  []                  |
|  availability_zone  |                 nova                 |
|       bootable      |                false                 |
|      created_at     |      2017-09-26T01:29:20.869107      |
| display_description |                 None                 |
|     display_name    |        cirros-ceph-boot-volume       |
|      encrypted      |                False                 |
|          id         | d3a3eb50-6b3a-4a93-b90c-b17d01e10b64 |
|       image_id      | 78e1fd35-aa65-447b-954e-1b072e9a17ec |
|       metadata      |                  {}                  |
|         size        |                  1                   |
|     snapshot_id     |                 None                 |
|     source_volid    |                 None                 |
|        status       |               creating               |
|     volume_type     |                 None                 |
+---------------------+--------------------------------------+
[root@os-node1 ~(keystone_admin)]#
```

7. List Cinder volumes to check if the bootable field is `true`:

```
# cinder list
```

```
[root@os-node1 ~(keystone_admin)]# cinder list
+--------------------------------------+-----------+-------------------------+------+-------------+----------+-------------+
|                  ID                  |   Status  |       Display Name      | Size | Volume Type | Bootable | Attached to |
+--------------------------------------+-----------+-------------------------+------+-------------+----------+-------------+
| 21bb3f31-6f9e-4d26-9afd-5eec3f450034 | available |      ceph-volume01      |  2   |     None    |   false  |             |
| d3a3eb50-6b3a-4a93-b90c-b17d01e10b64 | available | cirros-ceph-boot-volume |  1   |     None    |   true   |             |
+--------------------------------------+-----------+-------------------------+------+-------------+----------+-------------+
[root@os-node1 ~(keystone_admin)]#
[root@os-node1 ~(keystone_admin)]# rbd info volumes/volume-d3a3eb50-6b3a-4a93-b90c-b17d01e10b64 --id cinder
rbd image 'volume-d3a3eb50-6b3a-4a93-b90c-b17d01e10b64':
        size 1024 MB in 256 objects
        order 22 (4096 kB objects)
        block_name_prefix: rbd_data.35a5f72c334e2
        format: 2
        features: layering
        flags:
        parent: images/78e1fd35-aa65-447b-954e-1b072e9a17ec@snap
        overlap: 40162 kB
[root@os-node1 ~(keystone_admin)]#
```

8. Now, we have a bootable volume, which is stored on Ceph, so let's launch an instance with this volume:

   1. We have a known issue with `qemu-kvm` package which is causing nova boot to fail:

      ```
      Log - "libvirtError: internal error: process exited
      while connecting to monitor: ... Unknown protocol"
      ```

2. We have the following packages installed in the `os-node1` VM which have this issue:

```
qemu-kvm-1.5.3-60.el7_0.11.x86_64
qemu-kvm-common-1.5.3-60.el7_0.11.x86_64
qemu-img-1.5.3-60.el7_0.11.x86_64
```

3. Please upgrade the `qemu-kvm`, `qemu-kvm-common` and `qemu-img` packages:

$ yum update qemu-kvm qemu-img -y

4. It will install the following packages:

```
qemu-kvm-common-1.5.3-141.el7_4.2.x86_64
qemu-kvm-1.5.3-141.el7_4.2.x86_64
qemu-img-1.5.3-141.el7_4.2.x86_64
```

```
Updated:
  qemu-img.x86_64 10:1.5.3-141.el7_4.2                                qemu-kvm.x86_64 10:1.5.3-141.el7_4.2
```

```
# nova boot --flavor 1 --block_device_mapping
 vda=d3a3eb50-6b3a-4a93-b90c-b17d01e10b64::0
--image 78e1fd35-aa65-447b-954e-1b072e9a17ec
  vm2_on_ceph
--block_device_mapping vda = <cinder bootable
volume id >
--image = <Glance image associated with the bootable
 volume>
```

```
[root@os-node1 ~(keystone_admin)]#
[root@os-node1 ~(keystone_admin)]# nova boot --flavor 1 --block_device_mapping vda=d3a3eb50-6b3a-4a93-b90c-b17d01e10b64 --image 78e1fd35-aa65-447b-954e-1b072e9a17ec vm2_on_ceph
+-------------------------------------+----------------------------------------------------+
| Property                            | Value                                              |
+-------------------------------------+----------------------------------------------------+
| OS-DCF:diskConfig                   | MANUAL                                             |
| OS-EXT-AZ:availability_zone         | nova                                              |
| OS-EXT-SRV-ATTR:host                | -                                                 |
| OS-EXT-SRV-ATTR:hypervisor_hostname | -                                                 |
| OS-EXT-SRV-ATTR:instance_name       | instance-00000033                                 |
| OS-EXT-STS:power_state              | 0                                                 |
| OS-EXT-STS:task_state               | scheduling                                        |
| OS-EXT-STS:vm_state                 | building                                          |
| OS-SRV-USG:launched_at              | -                                                 |
| OS-SRV-USG:terminated_at            | -                                                 |
| accessIPv4                          |                                                   |
| accessIPv6                          |                                                   |
| adminPass                           | gAtgzhu2or9T                                      |
| config_drive                        |                                                   |
| created                             | 2017-09-26T03:32:57Z                              |
| flavor                              | m1.tiny (1)                                        |
| hostId                              |                                                   |
| id                                  | 45c2f1a6-80ce-4ff4-8adf-237de30ca332              |
| image                               | cirros_raw_image (78e1fd35-aa65-447b-954e-1b072e9a17ec) |
| key_name                            | -                                                 |
| metadata                            | {}                                                |
| name                                | vm2_on_ceph                                        |
| os-extended-volumes:volumes_attached | [{"id": "d3a3eb50-6b3a-4a93-b90c-b17d01e10b64"}]  |
| progress                            | 0                                                 |
| security_groups                     | default                                           |
| status                              | BUILD                                             |
| tenant_id                           | c9f87abe43ea49239313565ca74ebaa0                  |
| updated                             | 2017-09-26T03:32:57Z                              |
| user_id                             | 58e7a4c12d4f44ed865b2bf8ddf2f8f4                  |
+-------------------------------------+----------------------------------------------------+
```

9. Finally, check the instance status:

```
# nova list
```

```
[root@os-node1 ~(keystone_admin)]#
[root@os-node1 ~(keystone_admin)]# nova list
+--------------------------------------+------------+--------+------------+-------------+---------------------+
| ID                                   | Name       | Status | Task State | Power State | Networks            |
+--------------------------------------+------------+--------+------------+-------------+---------------------+
| 45c2f1a6-80ce-4ff4-8adf-237de30ca332 | vm2_on_ceph | ACTIVE | -          | Running     | public=172.24.4.231 |
+--------------------------------------+------------+--------+------------+-------------+---------------------+
[root@os-node1 ~(keystone_admin)]#
```

10. At this point, we have an instance running from a Ceph volume. Let's do a boot from image:

```
# nova boot --flavor 1
          --image 78e1fd35-aa65-447b-954e-1b072e9a17ec
          vm1_on_ceph
```

```
[root@os-node1 ~(keystone_admin)]# nova boot --flavor 1 --image 78e1fd35-aa65-447b-954e-1b072e9a17ec vm1_on_ceph
+--------------------------------------+----------------------------------------------------------+
| Property                             | Value                                                    |
+--------------------------------------+----------------------------------------------------------+
| OS-DCF:diskConfig                    | MANUAL                                                   |
| OS-EXT-AZ:availability_zone          | nova                                                     |
| OS-EXT-SRV-ATTR:host                 | -                                                        |
| OS-EXT-SRV-ATTR:hypervisor_hostname  | -                                                        |
| OS-EXT-SRV-ATTR:instance_name        | instance-00000034                                        |
| OS-EXT-STS:power_state               | 0                                                        |
| OS-EXT-STS:task_state                | scheduling                                               |
| OS-EXT-STS:vm_state                  | building                                                 |
| OS-SRV-USG:launched_at               | -                                                        |
| OS-SRV-USG:terminated_at             | -                                                        |
| accessIPv4                           |                                                          |
| accessIPv6                           |                                                          |
| adminPass                            | e2onrYJVs6Yh                                             |
| config_drive                         |                                                          |
| created                              | 2017-09-26T03:50:54Z                                     |
| flavor                               | m1.tiny (1)                                              |
| hostId                               |                                                          |
| id                                   | 31000c20-5847-48eb-b2e3-6b681f5df46c                     |
| image                                | cirros_raw_image (78e1fd35-aa65-447b-954e-1b072e9a17ec)  |
| key_name                             | -                                                        |
| metadata                             | {}                                                       |
| name                                 | vm1_on_ceph                                              |
| os-extended-volumes:volumes_attached | []                                                       |
| progress                             | 0                                                        |
| security_groups                      | default                                                  |
| status                               | BUILD                                                    |
| tenant_id                            | c9f87abe43ea49239313565ca74ebaa0                         |
| updated                              | 2017-09-26T03:50:55Z                                     |
| user_id                              | 58e7a4c12d4f44ed865b2bf8ddf2f8f4                         |
+--------------------------------------+----------------------------------------------------------+
[root@os-node1 ~(keystone_admin)]#
```

11. Finally, check the instance status:

```
# nova list
```

```
[root@os-node1 ~(keystone_admin)]#
[root@os-node1 ~(keystone_admin)]# nova list
+--------------------------------------+-------------+--------+------------+-------------+----------------------+
| ID                                   | Name        | Status | Task State | Power State | Networks             |
+--------------------------------------+-------------+--------+------------+-------------+----------------------+
| 31000c20-5847-48eb-b2e3-6b681f5df46c | vm1_on_ceph | ACTIVE | -          | Running     | public=172.24.4.232  |
| 45c2f1a6-80ce-4ff4-8adf-237de30ca332 | vm2_on_ceph | ACTIVE | -          | Running     | public=172.24.4.231  |
+--------------------------------------+-------------+--------+------------+-------------+----------------------+
[root@os-node1 ~(keystone_admin)]# _
```

12. Check if the instance is stored in Ceph:

```
[root@os-node1 ~(keystone_admin)]#
[root@os-node1 ~(keystone_admin)]# nova list
+--------------------------------------+-------------+--------+------------+-------------+----------------------+
| ID                                   | Name        | Status | Task State | Power State | Networks             |
+--------------------------------------+-------------+--------+------------+-------------+----------------------+
| 31000c20-5847-48eb-b2e3-6b681f5df46c | vm1_on_ceph | ACTIVE | -          | Running     | public=172.24.4.232  |
| 45c2f1a6-80ce-4ff4-8adf-237de30ca332 | vm2_on_ceph | ACTIVE | -          | Running     | public=172.24.4.231  |
+--------------------------------------+-------------+--------+------------+-------------+----------------------+
[root@os-node1 ~(keystone_admin)]#
[root@os-node1 ~(keystone_admin)]# rbd -p vms ls --id cinder
31000c20-5847-48eb-b2e3-6b681f5df46c_disk
[root@os-node1 ~(keystone_admin)]# rbd info vms/31000c20-5847-48eb-b2e3-6b681f5df46c_disk --id cinder
rbd image '31000c20-5847-48eb-b2e3-6b681f5df46c_disk':
        size 1024 MB in 256 objects
        order 22 (4096 kB objects)
        block_name_prefix: rbd_data.3a1e1238e1f29
        format: 2
        features: layering, exclusive-lock, object-map, fast-diff, deep-flatten
        flags:
[root@os-node1 ~(keystone_admin)]#
```

Configuring Nova to attach Ceph RBD

In order to attach the Ceph RBD to OpenStack instances, we should configure the Nova component of OpenStack by adding the RBD user and UUID information that it needs to connect to the Ceph cluster. To do this, we need to edit /etc/nova/nova.conf on the OpenStack node and perform the steps that are given in the following section.

How to do it...

The Cinder service that we configured in the last recipe creates volumes on Ceph, however, to attach these volumes to OpenStack instances, we need to configure Nova:

1. We have already configured the following options to enable volume attachment:

   ```
   rbd_user=cinder
   rbd_secret_uuid= e279566e-bc97-46d0-bd90-68080a2a0ad8
   ```

2. To test this configuration, we will attach the Cinder volume to an OpenStack instance. List the instance and volumes to get the ID:

   ```
   # nova list
   # cinder list
   ```

3. Attach the volume to the instance:

   ```
   # nova volume-attach 31000c20-5847-48eb-b2e3-6b681f5df46c
   21bb3f31-6f9e-4d26-9afd-5eec3f450034
   # cinder list
   ```

4
Working with Ceph Object Storage

In this chapter, we will cover the following recipes:

- Understanding Ceph object storage
- RADOS Gateway standard setup, installation, and configuration
- Creating the radosgw user
- Accessing the Ceph object storage using the S3 API
- Accessing the Ceph object storage using the Swift API
- Integrating RADOS Gateway with OpenStack Keystone
- Integrating RADOS Gateway with Hadoop S3A plugin

Introduction

Object-based storage has been getting a lot of industry attention as organizations are looking for flexibility for their enormous data. Object storage is an approach to store data in the form of objects rather than traditional files and blocks, and each object stores data, metadata, and a unique identifier. In this chapter, we will understand the object storage part of Ceph and gain practical knowledge by configuring the Ceph RADOS Gateway.

Understanding Ceph object storage

Object storage cannot be directly accessed by an operating system as a disk of a filesystem. Rather, it can only be accessed via API at the application level. Ceph is a distributed object storage system that provides an object storage interface via the Ceph object gateway, also known as the **RADOS Gateway** (**RGW**) interface, which has been built on top of the Ceph RADOS layer. The RGW uses librgw (RADOS Gateway Library) and librados, allowing applications to establish a connection with the Ceph object storage. The RGW provides applications with a RESTful S3 / Swift-compatible API interface to store data in the form of objects in the Ceph cluster. Ceph also supports multitenant object storage, accessible via RESTful API. In addition to this, the RGW also supports Ceph Admin APIs that can be used to manage the Ceph storage cluster using native API calls.

The librados software libraries are very flexible and can allow user applications to directly access the Ceph storage cluster via C, C++, Java, Python, and PHP bindings. Ceph object storage also has multisite capabilities, that is, it provides solutions for disaster recovery.

The following image represents a Ceph object storage:

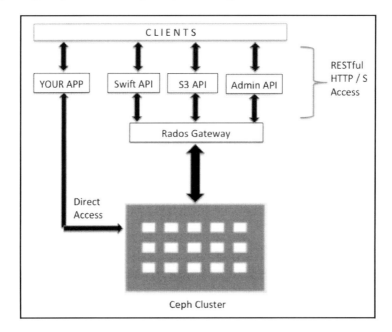

RADOS Gateway standard setup, installation, and configuration

For a production environment, it's recommended that you configure the RGW on a physical, dedicated machine. However, if your object storage workload is not too much, you can consider using any of the monitor machines as an RGW node. The RGW is a separate service that externally connects to a Ceph cluster and provides object storage access to its clients. In a production environment, it's recommended that you run more than one instance of the RGW, masked by a **Load Balancer**, as shown in the following diagram:

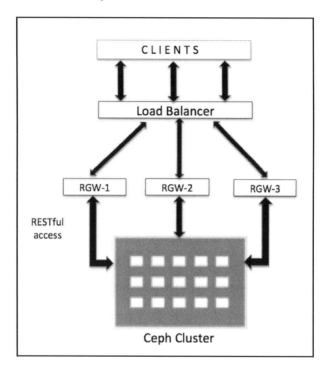

Starting with the Firefly release of Ceph, a new RGW frontend had been introduced: Civetweb, which is a lightweight standalone web server. Civetweb has been embedded directly into the `ceph-radosgw` service, making the Ceph object storage service deployment quicker and easier.

In the following recipes, we will demonstrate the RGW configuration using Civetweb on a virtual machine that will interact with the same Ceph cluster that we have created in Chapter 1, *Ceph – Introduction and Beyond*.

Setting up the RADOS Gateway node

To run the Ceph object storage service, we should have a running Ceph cluster and the RGW node should have access to the Ceph network.

Like you should have it as you created in Chapter 1, *Ceph – Introduction and Beyond* with following Ceph status:

```
[root@ceph-node2 ~]#
[root@ceph-node2 ~]# ceph -s
    cluster 585ce77b-476c-4f52-b147-93fe9424eb2a
     health HEALTH_OK
     monmap e1: 3 mons at {ceph-node1=192.168.1.101:6789/0,ceph-node2=192.168.1.102:6789/0,ceph-node3=192.168.1.103:6789/0}
            election epoch 4, quorum 0,1,2 ceph-node1,ceph-node2,ceph-node3
     osdmap e36: 9 osds: 9 up, 9 in
            flags sortbitwise,require_jewel_osds
      pgmap v80: 128 pgs, 1 pools, 0 bytes data, 0 objects
            307 MB used, 161 GB / 161 GB avail
                 128 active+clean
[root@ceph-node2 ~]#
```

How to do it...

As demonstrated in the earlier chapters, we will boot up a virtual machine using Vagrant and configure that as our RGW node:

1. Launch rgw-node1 using vagrantfile, as we have done for Ceph nodes in Chapter 1, *Ceph – Introduction and Beyond*. Make sure you are on the host machine and under the Ceph-Cookbook-Second-Edition repository before bringing up rgw-node1 using Vagrant:

    ```
    # cd Ceph-Cookbook-Second-Edition
    # vagrant up rgw-node1
    ```

2. Once `rgw-node1` is up, check the Vagrant status, and log into the node:

```
$ vagrant status rgw-node1
```

```
[vumrao@ceph-jewel Ceph-Cookbook-Second-Edition]$
[vumrao@ceph-jewel Ceph-Cookbook-Second-Edition]$ vagrant status rgw-node1
Current machine states:

rgw-node1                 running (virtualbox)

The VM is running. To stop this VM, you can run `vagrant halt` to
shut it down forcefully, or you can run `vagrant suspend` to simply
suspend the virtual machine. In either case, to restart it again,
simply run `vagrant up`.
[vumrao@ceph-jewel Ceph-Cookbook-Second-Edition]$
```

```
$ vagrant ssh rgw-node1
```

3. Upgrade to the latest CentOS 7.4, you can use the following command:

```
$ sudo yum update -y
```

4. Check if `rgw-node1` can reach the Ceph cluster nodes:

```
# ping ceph-node1 -c 3
# ping ceph-node2 -c 3
# ping ceph-node3 -c 3
```

5. Verify the localhost file entries, hostname, and FQDN for `rgw-node1`:

```
# cat /etc/hosts | grep -i rgw
# hostname
# hostname -f
```

```
[vagrant@rgw-node1 ~]$
[vagrant@rgw-node1 ~]$ cat /etc/hosts | grep -i rgw
127.0.0.1        rgw-node1.cephcookbook.com        rgw-node1
192.168.1.106 rgw-node1.cephcookbook.com rgw-node1
[vagrant@rgw-node1 ~]$ hostname
rgw-node1.cephcookbook.com
[vagrant@rgw-node1 ~]$ hostname -f
rgw-node1.cephcookbook.com
[vagrant@rgw-node1 ~]$
```

Installing and configuring the RADOS Gateway

The previous recipe was about setting up a virtual machine for RGW. In this recipe, we will learn to set up the `ceph-radosgw` service on this node.

How to do it...

1. To install and configure the Ceph RGW, we will use the `ceph-ansbile` from `ceph-node1`, which is our `ceph-ansible` and one of the monitor node. Log in to the `ceph-node1` and perform the following commands:
   1. Make sure that the `ceph-node1` can reach the `rgw-node1` over the network by using the following command:

      ```
      # ping rgw-node1 -c 1
      ```

   2. Allow `ceph-node1` a password-less SSH login to `rgw-node1` and test the connection.

 The root password for `rgw-node1` is the same as earlier, that is, `vagrant`.
```
# ssh-copy-id rgw-node1
# ssh rgw-node1 hostname
```

2. Add `rgw-node1` to the `ceph-ansible` hosts file and test the Ansible `ping` command:

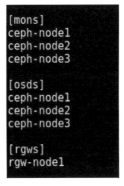

```
[mons]
ceph-node1
ceph-node2
ceph-node3

[osds]
ceph-node1
ceph-node2
ceph-node3

[rgws]
rgw-node1
```

```
# ansible all -m ping
```

```
[root@ceph-node1 ~]#
[root@ceph-node1 ~]# ansible all -m ping
ceph-node1 | SUCCESS => {
    "changed": false,
    "ping": "pong"
}
ceph-node3 | SUCCESS => {
    "changed": false,
    "ping": "pong"
}
rgw-node1 | SUCCESS => {
    "changed": false,
    "ping": "pong"
}
ceph-node2 | SUCCESS => {
    "changed": false,
    "ping": "pong"
}
[root@ceph-node1 ~]#
```

3. Update `all.yml` file to install and configure the Ceph RGW in the VM `rgw-node1`:

```
[root@ceph-node1 ceph-ansible]# cd /usr/share/
                                 ceph-ansible/group_vars/
[root@ceph-node1 group_vars]# vim all.yml
```

4. Enable the `radosgw_civetweb_port` and `radosgw_civetweb_bind_ip` option. In this book, `rgw-node1` has IP `192.168.1.106` and we are using port `8080`:

```
[root@ceph-node1 group_vars]#
[root@ceph-node1 group_vars]# cat all.yml | egrep 'radosgw_civetweb_port|radosgw_civetweb_bind_ip'
radosgw_civetweb_port: 8080
radosgw_civetweb_bind_ip: 192.168.1.106 # when using ipv6 enclose with brackets: "[{{ ansible_default_ipv6.address }}]"
#radosgw_civetweb_options: "port={{ radosgw_civetweb_bind_ip }}:{{ radosgw_civetweb_port }} num_threads={{ radosgw_civetweb_num_threads }}"
[root@ceph-node1 group_vars]#
```

5. Change the directory back to `/usr/share/ceph-ansible` and then run the playbook, it will install and configure the RGW in `rgw-node1`:

```
$ cd ..
$ ansible-playbook site.yml
```

```
[root@ceph-node1 group_vars]# cd ..
[root@ceph-node1 ceph-ansible]# ansible-playbook site.yml
[DEPRECATION WARNING]: docker is kept for backwards compatibility but usage is discouraged.
This feature will be removed in a future
 release. Deprecation warnings can be disabled by setting deprecation_warnings=False in ansi

PLAY [mons,agents,osds,mdss,rgws,nfss,restapis,rbdmirrors,clients,mgrs] ********************

TASK [check for python2] ******************************************************************
ok: [ceph-node3]
ok: [rgw-node1]
ok: [ceph-node2]
ok: [ceph-node1]
```

6. Once `ceph-ansible` finishes the installation and configuration, you will have the following recap output:

```
PLAY RECAP ********************************************************************************
ceph-node1                 : ok=127   changed=6    unreachable=0    failed=0
ceph-node2                 : ok=121   changed=6    unreachable=0    failed=0
ceph-node3                 : ok=122   changed=6    unreachable=0    failed=0
rgw-node1                  : ok=46    changed=14   unreachable=0    failed=0

[root@ceph-node1 ceph-ansible]#
```

7. Once it completes, you will have the `radosgw` daemon running in `rgw-node1`:

```
[root@rgw-node1 ~]#
[root@rgw-node1 ~]# ps -ef | grep rados
ceph      3558    1  0 22:27 ?        00:00:00 /usr/bin/radosgw -f --cluster ceph --name client.rgw.rgw-node1 --setuser ceph --setgroup ceph
root      3771 1149  0 22:31 pts/0    00:00:00 grep --color=auto rados
[root@rgw-node1 ~]#
```

8. And you will notice in the following screenshot that we now have more pools which got created for RGW:

```
[root@ceph-node2 ~]# ceph -s
    cluster 585ce77b-476c-4f52-b147-93fe9424eb2a
     health HEALTH_OK
     monmap e1: 3 mons at {ceph-node1=192.168.1.101:6789/0,ceph-node2=192.168.1.102:6789/0,ceph-node3=192.168.1.103:6789/0}
            election epoch 6, quorum 0,1,2 ceph-node1,ceph-node2,ceph-node3
     osdmap e74: 9 osds: 9 up, 9 in
            flags sortbitwise,require_jewel_osds
      pgmap v205: 176 pgs, 7 pools, 1588 bytes data, 171 objects
            317 MB used, 161 GB / 161 GB avail
                 176 active+clean
[root@ceph-node2 ~]# ceph osd pool ls
rbd
.rgw.root
default.rgw.control
default.rgw.data.root
default.rgw.gc
default.rgw.log
default.rgw.users.uid
```

9. The Civetweb web server that is embedded into the `radosgw` daemon should now be running on the specified port, `8080`:

```
[root@rgw-node1 ~]#
[root@rgw-node1 ~]# netstat -tnlp | grep radosgw
tcp        0      0 192.168.1.106:8080      0.0.0.0:*               LISTEN      3558/radosgw
[root@rgw-node1 ~]#
```

10. You will have the following entries related to this RGW in `rgw-node1` VM `/etc/ceph/ceph.conf`:

```
[client.rgw.rgw-node1]
host = rgw-node1
keyring = /var/lib/ceph/radosgw/ceph-rgw.rgw-node1/keyring
rgw socket path = /tmp/radosgw-rgw-node1.sock
log file = /var/log/ceph/ceph-rgw-rgw-node1.log
rgw data = /var/lib/ceph/radosgw/ceph-rgw.rgw-node1
rgw frontends = civetweb port=192.168.1.106:8080 num_threads=100
rgw resolve cname = False
```

Creating the radosgw user

To use the Ceph object storage, we should create an initial Ceph object gateway user for the S3 interface and then create a subuser for the Swift interface.

How to do it...

Following steps will help you to create `radosgw` user:

1. Make sure that the `rgw-node1` is able to access the Ceph cluster:

   ```
   # ceph -s -k /var/lib/ceph/radosgw/ceph-rgw.rgw-node1/keyring
     --name client.rgw.rgw-node1
   ```

2. Create a RADOS Gateway user for the S3 access:

   ```
   # radosgw-admin user create --uid=pratima
     --display-name="Pratima Umrao"
     --email=pratima@cephcookbook.com
     -k /var/lib/ceph/radosgw/ceph-rgw.rgw-node1/keyring
     --name client.rgw.rgw-node1
   ```

```json
{
    "user_id": "pratima",
    "display_name": "Pratima Umrao",
    "email": "pratima@cephcookbook.com",
    "suspended": 0,
    "max_buckets": 1000,
    "auid": 0,
    "subusers": [],
    "keys": [
        {
            "user": "pratima",
            "access_key": "7L0HXU1F6DK9RTB8HK8M",
            "secret_key": "kNcVjuMUWxnNv3enKDCHGAkZu5oeYqKKbjiUKfSI"
        }
    ],
    "swift_keys": [],
    "caps": [],
    "op_mask": "read, write, delete",
    "default_placement": "",
    "placement_tags": [],
    "bucket_quota": {
        "enabled": false,
        "max_size_kb": -1,
        "max_objects": -1
    },
    "user_quota": {
        "enabled": false,
        "max_size_kb": -1,
        "max_objects": -1
    },
    "temp_url_keys": []
}
```

3. The values keys (`access_key`) and the keys (`secret_key`) would be required later in this chapter for access validation.

4. To use Ceph object storage with the Swift API, we need to create a Swift subuser on the Ceph RGW:

```
# radosgw-admin subuser create --uid=pratima
  --subuser=pratima:swift --access=full
  -k /var/lib/ceph/radosgw/ceph-rgw.rgw-node1/keyring
  --name client.rgw.rgw-node1
```

```
{
    "user_id": "pratima",
    "display_name": "Pratima Umrao",
    "email": "pratima@cephcookbook.com",
    "suspended": 0,
    "max_buckets": 1000,
    "auid": 0,
    "subusers": [
        {
            "id": "pratima:swift",
            "permissions": "full-control"
        }
    ],
    "keys": [
        {
            "user": "pratima",
            "access_key": "7L0HXU1F6DK9RTB8HK8M",
            "secret_key": "kNcVjuMUWxnNv3enKDCHGAkZu5oeYqKKbjiUKfSI"
        }
    ],
    "swift_keys": [
        {
            "user": "pratima:swift",
            "secret_key": "whUTYlKFeKvKO59O6wFOANoyoH37SUJEjBD9cQmH"
        }
    ],
    "caps": [],
    "op_mask": "read, write, delete",
    "default_placement": "",
    "placement_tags": [],
    "bucket_quota": {
        "enabled": false,
        "max_size_kb": -1,
        "max_objects": -1
    },
    "user_quota": {
        "enabled": false,
        "max_size_kb": -1,
        "max_objects": -1
    },
    "temp_url_keys": []
}
```

See also...

The *Accessing the Ceph object storage using the Swift API* recipe.

Accessing the Ceph object storage using S3 API

Amazon Web Services offer **Simple Storage Service** (**S3**) that provides storage through web interfaces such as REST. Ceph extends its compatibility with S3 through the RESTful API. S3 client applications can access Ceph object storage based on access and secret keys.

S3 also requires a DNS server in place as it uses the virtual host bucket naming convention, that is, `<object_name>`.`<RGW_Fqdn>`. For example, if you have a bucket named `jupiter`, then it would be accessible over HTTP via the URL, `http://jupiter.rgw-node1.cephcookbook.com`.

How to do it...

Perform the following steps to configure DNS on the `rgw-node1` node. If you have an existing DNS server, you can skip the DNS configuration and use your DNS server.

Configuring DNS

1. Install bind packages on the `ceph-rgw` node:

   ```
   # yum install bind* -y
   ```

2. Edit `/etc/named.conf` and add information for IP addresses, IP range, and zone, which are mentioned as follows. You can match the changes from the author's version of the `named.conf` file provided with this book:

   ```
   listen-on port 53 { 127.0.0.1;192.168.1.106; };
   ### Add DNS IP ###
   allow-query { localhost;192.168.1.0/24; };
   ### Add IP Range ###
   ```

```
options {
        listen-on port 53 { 127.0.0.1;192.168.1.106; };  ### Add DNS IP ###
        listen-on-v6 port 53 { ::1; };
        directory       "/var/named";
        dump-file       "/var/named/data/cache_dump.db";
        statistics-file "/var/named/data/named_stats.txt";
        memstatistics-file "/var/named/data/named_mem_stats.txt";
        allow-query     { localhost;192.168.1.0/24; };     ### Add IP Range ###
```

```
### Add new zone for the domain cephcookbook.com before EOF ###
zone "cephcookbook.com" IN {
type master;
file "db.cephcookbook.com";
allow-update { none; };
};
```

```
### Add new zone for domain cephcookbook.com before EOF   ###
zone "cephcookbook.com" IN {
type master;
file "db.cephcookbook.com";
allow-update { none; };
};
include "/etc/named.rfc1912.zones";
include "/etc/named.root.key";
```

3. Create the zone file /var/named/db.cephcookbook.com, with the following content:

```
@ 86400 IN SOA cephcookbook.com. root.cephcookbook.com. (
20091028 ; serial yyyy-mm-dd
10800 ; refresh every 15 min
3600 ; retry every hour
3600000 ; expire after 1 month +
86400 ); min ttl of 1 day
@ 86400 IN NS cephbookbook.com.
@ 86400 IN A 192.168.1.106
* 86400 IN CNAME @
```

```
[root@rgw-node1 named]#
[root@rgw-node1 named]# cat /var/named/db.cephcookbook.com
@ 86400 IN SOA cephcookbook.com. root.cephcookbook.com. (
20091028 ; serial yyyy-mm-dd
10800 ; refresh every 15 min
3600 ; retry every hour
3600000 ; expire after 1 month +
86400 ); min ttl of 1 day
@ 86400 IN NS cephbookbook.com.
@ 86400 IN A 192.168.1.106
* 86400 IN CNAME @
[root@rgw-node1 named]#
```

4. Edit `/etc/resolve.conf` and add the following content on top of the file:

```
search cephcookbook.com
nameserver 192.168.1.106
```

```
[root@rgw-node1 named]# cat /etc/resolv.conf
# Generated by NetworkManager
search cephcookbook.com
nameserver 192.168.1.106
search redhat.com cephcookbook.com
nameserver 10.0.2.3
[root@rgw-node1 named]#
```

5. Start the named service:

```
# systemctl start named.service
```

6. Test the DNS configuration files for any syntax errors:

```
# named-checkconf /etc/named.conf
# named-checkzone cephcookbook.com
                  /var/named/db.cephcookbook.com
```

```
[root@rgw-node1 named]#
[root@rgw-node1 named]# named-checkconf /etc/named.conf
[root@rgw-node1 named]# named-checkzone cephcookbook.com /var/named/db.cephcookbook.com
zone cephcookbook.com/IN: loaded serial 20091028
OK
[root@rgw-node1 named]#
```

7. Test the DNS server:

```
# dig rgw-node1.cephcookbook.com
# nslookup rgw-node1.cephcookbook.com
```

Configuring the s3cmd client

To access Ceph object storage via the S3 API, we should configure the client machine with s3cmd as well as the DNS client settings. Perform the following steps to configure the s3cmd client machine:

1. Bring up the `client-node1` virtual machine using Vagrant. This virtual machine will be used as a client machine for S3 object storage.

2. Go to the `Ceph-Cookbook-Second-Edition` repository directory and run the following command:

```
$ vagrant up client-node1
$ vagrant ssh client-node1
```

3. Upgrade the `client-node1` to the latest CentOS 7.4:

```
$ sudo yum update -y
$reboot
$ vagrant ssh client-node1
```

4. Install the `bind-utils` package:

```
# yum install bind-utils -y
```

5. On the `client-node1` machine, update `/etc/resolve.conf` with the DNS server entries on top of the file:

```
search cephcookbook.com
nameserver 192.168.1.106
```

6. Test the DNS settings on the `client-node1`:

```
# dig rgw-node1.cephcookbook.com
# nslookup rgw-node1.cephcookbook.com
```

7. `client-node1` should be able to resolve all the subdomains for `rgw-node1.cephcookbook.com`:

```
# ping mj.rgw-node1.cephcookbook.com -c 1
# ping anything.rgw-node1.cephcookbook.com -c 1
```

Configure the S3 client (s3cmd) on client-node1

Following commands are used for configuring s3cmd on the `client-node1`:

1. Install s3cmd using the following command:

```
# yum install s3cmd -y
```

2. Configure s3cmd by providing the access_key and secret_key of the user, pratima, which we created earlier in this chapter. Execute the following command and follow the prompts:

```
# s3cmd --configure
```

```
[root@client-node1 ~]#
[root@client-node1 ~]# s3cmd --configure

Enter new values or accept defaults in brackets with Enter.
Refer to user manual for detailed description of all options.

Access key and Secret key are your identifiers for Amazon S3. Leave them empty for using the env variables.
Access Key: 7L0HXU1F6DK9RTB8HK8M
Secret Key: kNcVjuMUWxnNv3enKDCHGAkZu5oeYqKKbjiUKfSI
Default Region [US]:

Encryption password is used to protect your files from reading
by unauthorized persons while in transfer to S3
Encryption password:
Path to GPG program [/bin/gpg]:

When using secure HTTPS protocol all communication with Amazon S3
servers is protected from 3rd party eavesdropping. This method is
slower than plain HTTP, and can only be proxied with Python 2.7 or newer
Use HTTPS protocol [Yes]: no

On some networks all internet access must go through a HTTP proxy.
Try setting it here if you can't connect to S3 directly
HTTP Proxy server name:

New settings:
  Access Key: 7L0HXU1F6DK9RTB8HK8M
  Secret Key: kNcVjuMUWxnNv3enKDCHGAkZu5oeYqKKbjiUKfSI
  Default Region: US
  Encryption password:
  Path to GPG program: /bin/gpg
  Use HTTPS protocol: False
  HTTP Proxy server name:
  HTTP Proxy server port: 0

Test access with supplied credentials? [Y/n] n

Save settings? [y/N] y
Configuration saved to '/root/.s3cfg'
[root@client-node1 ~]#
```

The s3cmd --configure command will create /root/.s3cfg.

3. Edit this file for the RGW host details. Modify `host_base` and `host_bucket`, as shown. Make sure these lines do not have trailing spaces at the end:

```
host_base = rgw-node1.cephcookbook.com:8080
host_bucket = %(bucket).rgw-node1.cephcookbook.com:8080
```

```
[root@client-node1 ~]#
[root@client-node1 ~]# cat .s3cfg | egrep "access_key|secret_key|host_base|host_bucket"
access_key = 7L0HXU1F6DK9RTB8HK8M
host_base = rgw-node1.cephcookbook.com:8080
host_bucket = %(bucket).rgw-node1.cephcookbook.com:8080
secret_key = kNcVjuMUWxnNv3enKDCHGAkZu5oeYqKKbjiUKfSI
[root@client-node1 ~]#
```

4. Finally, we will create buckets and put objects into them:

```
# s3cmd mb s3://first-bucket
# s3cmd ls
# s3cmd put /etc/hosts s3://first-bucket
# s3cmd ls s3://first-bucket
```

```
[root@client-node1 ~]#
[root@client-node1 ~]# s3cmd mb s3://first-bucket
Bucket 's3://first-bucket/' created
[root@client-node1 ~]# s3cmd ls
2017-09-24 22:53  s3://first-bucket
[root@client-node1 ~]#
[root@client-node1 ~]# s3cmd put /etc/hosts s3://first-bucket
upload: '/etc/hosts' -> 's3://first-bucket/hosts'  [1 of 1]
 789 of 789   100% in    1s    538.43 B/s  done
[root@client-node1 ~]#
[root@client-node1 ~]# s3cmd ls s3://first-bucket
2017-09-24 22:53       789    s3://first-bucket/hosts
[root@client-node1 ~]#
```

Accessing the Ceph object storage using the Swift API

Ceph supports RESTful API that is compatible with the basic data access model of the Swift API. In the last section, we covered accessing the Ceph cluster via the S3 API; in this section, we will learn to access it via the Swift API.

How to do it...

To use Ceph object storage with the Swift API, we need the Swift subuser and secret keys that we created earlier in this chapter. This user information will then be passed using the Swift CLI tool in order to access the Ceph object storage:

1. On the `client-node1`, a virtual machine installs the Python Swift client:

```
# easy_install pip
# pip install --upgrade setuptools
# pip install --upgrade python-swiftclient
```

2. Get the swift subuser and secret keys from the RGW node:

```
# radosgw-admin user info --uid pratima
-k /var/lib/ceph/radosgw/ceph-rgw.rgw-node1/keyring
--name client.rgw.rgw-node1
```

3. Access Ceph object storage by listing the default bucket:

```
# swift -A http://192.168.1.106:8080/auth/1.0
-U pratima:swift
-K whUTYlKFeKvKO59O6wFOANoyoH37SUJEjBD9cQmH list
```

4. Add a new bucket, `second-bucket`:

```
# swift -A http://192.168.1.106:8080/auth/1.0
-U pratima:swift
-K whUTYlKFeKvKO59O6wFOANoyoH37SUJEjBD9cQmH post second-bucket
```

5. List the buckets; it should show the new `second-bucket` as well:

```
# swift -A http://192.168.1.106:8080/auth/1.0
-U pratima:swift
-K whUTYlKFeKvKO59O6wFOANoyoH37SUJEjBD9cQmH list
```

```
[root@client-node1 ~]#
[root@client-node1 ~]# swift -A http://192.168.1.106:8080/auth/1.0 -U pratima:swift -K whUTYlKFeKvKO59O6wFOANoyoH37SUJEjBD9cQmH list
first-bucket
[root@client-node1 ~]# swift -A http://192.168.1.106:8080/auth/1.0 -U pratima:swift -K whUTYlKFeKvKO59O6wFOANoyoH37SUJEjBD9cQmH post second-bucket
[root@client-node1 ~]# swift -A http://192.168.1.106:8080/auth/1.0 -U pratima:swift -K whUTYlKFeKvKO59O6wFOANoyoH37SUJEjBD9cQmH list
first-bucket
second-bucket
[root@client-node1 ~]#
```

Integrating RADOS Gateway with OpenStack Keystone

Ceph can be integrated with the OpenStack identity management service, *Keystone*. With this integration, the Ceph RGW is configured to accept Keystone tokens for user authority. So, any user who is validated by Keystone will get rights to access the RGW.

How to do it...

Execute the following command on your `openstack-node1`, unless otherwise specified:

1. Configure OpenStack to point to the Ceph RGW by creating the service and its endpoints:

   ```
   # keystone service-create --name swift --type object-store
     --description "ceph object store"
   ```

   ```
   # keystone endpoint-create --service-id
   6614554878344bbeaa7fec0d5dccca7f --publicurl
   http://192.168.1.106:8080/swift/v1 --internalurl
   http://192.168.1.106:8080/swift/v1 --adminurl
   http://192.168.1.106:8080/swift/v1 --region RegionOne
   ```

2. Get the Keystone admin token, which will be used for the RGW configuration:

   ```
   # cat /etc/keystone/keystone.conf | grep -i admin_token
   ```

3. Create a directory for certificates:

   ```
   # mkdir -p /var/ceph/nss
   ```

4. Generate OpenSSL certificates:

   ```
   # openssl x509 -in /etc/keystone/ssl/certs/ca.pem
   -pubkey|certutil -d /var/ceph/nss -A -n ca -t "TCu,Cu,Tuw"
   # openssl x509 -in /etc/keystone/ssl/certs/signing_cert.pem
   -pubkey | certutil -A -d /var/ceph/nss -n signing_cert
   -t "P,P,P"
   ```

```
[root@os-node1 ~{keystone_admin}]# cat /etc/keystone/keystone.conf | grep -i admin_token
#admin_token=ADMIN
admin_token=f72adb0238d74bb885005744ce526148
[root@os-node1 ~{keystone_admin}]#
[root@os-node1 ~{keystone_admin}]# mkdir -p /var/ceph/nss
[root@os-node1 ~{keystone_admin}]# openssl x509 -in /etc/keystone/ssl/certs/ca.pem -pubkey|certutil -d /var/ceph/nss -A -n ca -t "TCu,Cu,Tuw"
Notice: Trust flag u is set automatically if the private key is present.
[root@os-node1 ~{keystone_admin}]#
[root@os-node1 ~{keystone_admin}]# openssl x509 -in /etc/keystone/ssl/certs/signing_cert.pem -pubkey | certutil -A -d /var/ceph/nss -n signing_cert -t "P,P,P"
[root@os-node1 ~{keystone_admin}]# ls -l /var/ceph/nss/
total 76
-rw------- 1 root root 65536 Sep 26 07:19 cert8.db
-rw------- 1 root root 16384 Sep 26 07:19 key3.db
-rw------- 1 root root 16384 Sep 26 07:19 secmod.db
[root@os-node1 ~{keystone_admin}]#
```

5. Create the /var/ceph/nss directory on rgw-node1:

   ```
   # mkdir -p /var/ceph/nss
   ```

6. From openstack-node1, copy OpenSSL certificates to rgw-node1. If you are logging in for the first time, you will get an SSH confirmation; type yes and then type the root password, which is vagrant for all the machines:

   ```
   # scp /var/ceph/nss/* rgw-node1:/var/ceph/nss
   ```

7. Update /etc/ceph/ceph.conf on rgw-node1 with the following entries under the [client.rgw.rgw-node1] section:

   ```
   rgw keystone url = http://192.168.1.111:5000
   rgw keystone admin token = f72adb0238d74bb885005744ce526148
   rgw keystone accepted roles = admin, Member, swiftoperator
   rgw keystone token cache size = 500
   rgw keystone revocation interval = 60
   rgw s3 auth use keystone = true
   nss db path = /var/ceph/nss
   ```

rgw keystone url must be the Keystone management URL that can be gotten from the # keystone endpoint-list command. rgw keystone admin token is the token value that we saved in *step 2* of this recipe.

8. Finally, restart the ceph-radosgw service:

```
# systemctl restart ceph-radosgw.target
```

9. Now, to test the Keystone and Ceph integration, switch back to openstack-node1 and run the basic Swift commands, and it should not ask for any user keys:

```
# export OS_STORAGE_URL=http://192.168.1.106:8080/swift/v1
# swift list
# swift post swift-test-bucket
# swift list
```

```
[root@os-node1 ~(keystone_admin)]#
[root@os-node1 ~(keystone_admin)]# export OS_STORAGE_URL=http://192.168.1.106:8080/swift/v1
[root@os-node1 ~(keystone_admin)]# swift list
[root@os-node1 ~(keystone_admin)]# swift post swift-test-bucket
[root@os-node1 ~(keystone_admin)]# swift list
swift-test-bucket
[root@os-node1 ~(keystone_admin)]# swift stat swift-test-bucket
                   Account: v1
                 Container: swift-test-bucket
                   Objects: 0
                     Bytes: 0
                  Read ACL:
                 Write ACL:
                   Sync To:
                  Sync Key:
             Accept-Ranges: bytes
           X-Storage-Policy: default-placement
X-Container-Bytes-Used-Actual: 0
               X-Timestamp: 1506400950.36066
                X-Trans-Id: tx00000000000000000000c-0059c9dabf-4405b-default
              Content-Type: text/plain; charset=utf-8
[root@os-node1 ~(keystone_admin)]#
```

10. Let us verify if the container swift-test-bucket got created in the RGW:

```
[root@rgw-node1 ~]#
[root@rgw-node1 ~]# radosgw-admin bucket list -k /var/lib/ceph/radosgw/ceph-rgw.rgw-node1/keyring --name client.rgw.rgw-node1
[
    "first-bucket",
    "swift-test-bucket",
    "second-bucket"
]
[root@rgw-node1 ~]#
```

Integrating RADOS Gateway with Hadoop S3A plugin

For data analytics applications that require **Hadoop Distributed File System** (**HDFS**) access, the Ceph object gateway can be accessed using the Apache S3A connector for Hadoop. The S3A connector is an open source tool that presents S3 compatible object storage as an HDFS file system with HDFS file system read and write semantics to the applications while data is stored in the Ceph object gateway.

Ceph object gateway Jewel version 10.2.9 is fully compatible with the S3A connector that ships with Hadoop 2.7.3.

How to do it...

You can use `client-node1` to configure Hadoop S3A client.

1. Install Java packages in the `client-node1`:

   ```
   # yum install java* -y
   ```

   ```
   Installed:
     java-1.6.0-openjdk.x86_64 1:1.6.0.41-1.13.13.1.el7_3
     java-1.6.0-openjdk-devel.x86_64 1:1.6.0.41-1.13.13.1.el7_3
     java-1.6.0-openjdk-src.x86_64 1:1.6.0.41-1.13.13.1.el7_3
     java-1.7.0-openjdk-accessibility.x86_64 1:1.7.0.151-2.6.11.1.el7_4
     java-1.7.0-openjdk-devel.x86_64 1:1.7.0.151-2.6.11.1.el7_4
     java-1.7.0-openjdk-javadoc.noarch 1:1.7.0.151-2.6.11.1.el7_4
     java-1.8.0-openjdk.x86_64 1:1.8.0.144-0.b01.el7_4
     java-1.8.0-openjdk-accessibility-debug.x86_64 1:1.8.0.144-0.b01.el7_4
     java-1.8.0-openjdk-demo.x86_64 1:1.8.0.144-0.b01.el7_4
     java-1.8.0-openjdk-devel.x86_64 1:1.8.0.144-0.b01.el7_4
     java-1.8.0-openjdk-headless.x86_64 1:1.8.0.144-0.b01.el7_4
     java-1.8.0-openjdk-javadoc.noarch 1:1.8.0.144-0.b01.el7_4
     java-1.8.0-openjdk-javadoc-zip.noarch 1:1.8.0.144-0.b01.el7_4
     java-1.8.0-openjdk-src.x86_64 1:1.8.0.144-0.b01.el7_4
     java-atk-wrapper.x86_64 0:0.30.4-5.el7
     java-dirq-javadoc.noarch 0:1.8-1.el7
     java-oauth-javadoc.noarch 0:20100601-13.el7
     java_cup-javadoc.noarch 1:0.11a-16.el7
     javacc.noarch 0:5.0-10.el7
     javacc-javadoc.noarch 0:5.0-10.el7
     javacc-maven-plugin.noarch 0:2.6-17.el7
     javamail.noarch 0:1.4.6-8.el7
     javapackages-tools.noarch 0:3.4.1-11.el7
     javaparser-javadoc.noarch 0:1.0.11-3.el7
     javassist-javadoc.noarch 0:3.16.1-10.el7
     javawriter.noarch 0:2.5.1-4.el7
   ```

2. Download the Hadoop `.tar` file from `https://archive.apache.org/dist/` `hadoop/core/hadoop-2.7.3/hadoop-2.7.3.tar.gz`:

```
[root@client-node1 ~]# wget https://archive.apache.org/dist/hadoop/core/hadoop-2.7.3/hadoop-2.7.3.tar.gz
--2017-09-27 05:25:52--  https://archive.apache.org/dist/hadoop/core/hadoop-2.7.3/hadoop-2.7.3.tar.gz
Resolving archive.apache.org (archive.apache.org)... 163.172.17.199
Connecting to archive.apache.org (archive.apache.org)|163.172.17.199|:443... connected.
HTTP request sent, awaiting response... 200 OK
Length: 214092195 (204M) [application/x-gzip]
Saving to: 'hadoop-2.7.3.tar.gz'

100%[===================================================================================================>]

2017-09-27 05:26:44 (4.03 MB/s) - 'hadoop-2.7.3.tar.gz' saved [214092195/214092195]

[root@client-node1 ~]#
```

 We have also uploaded the `hadoop-2.7.3.tar.gz` file in GitHub - `https://github.com/PacktPublishing/Ceph-Cookbook-Second-Edition/raw/master/hadoop-2.7.3.tar.gz` if it will be removed from `http://archive.apache.org/`.

3. Extract the Hadoop `.tar` file:

   ```
   # tar -xvf hadoop-2.7.3.tar.gz
   ```

   ```
   [root@client-node1 ~]#
   [root@client-node1 ~]# cd hadoop-2.7.3
   [root@client-node1 hadoop-2.7.3]# ll
   total 116
   drwxr-xr-x 2 root root  4096 Aug 18  2016 bin
   drwxr-xr-x 3 root root    19 Aug 18  2016 etc
   drwxr-xr-x 2 root root   101 Aug 18  2016 include
   drwxr-xr-x 3 root root    19 Aug 18  2016 lib
   drwxr-xr-x 2 root root  4096 Aug 18  2016 libexec
   -rw-r--r-- 1 root root 84854 Aug 18  2016 LICENSE.txt
   -rw-r--r-- 1 root root 14978 Aug 18  2016 NOTICE.txt
   -rw-r--r-- 1 root root  1366 Aug 18  2016 README.txt
   drwxr-xr-x 2 root root  4096 Aug 18  2016 sbin
   drwxr-xr-x 4 root root    29 Aug 18  2016 share
   [root@client-node1 hadoop-2.7.3]#
   ```

4. Add the following in the `.bashrc` file:

   ```
   export JAVA_HOME=/usr/lib/jvm/jre-1.8.0-openjdk
   export
   PATH=/usr/local/sbin:/usr/local/bin:/usr/sbin:/usr/bin:/root/
                                    bin:/root/hadoop-2.7.3/bin
   ```

```
[root@client-node1 ~]#
[root@client-node1 ~]# cat .bashrc | grep export
export JAVA_HOME=/usr/lib/jvm/jre-1.8.0-openjdk
export PATH=/usr/local/sbin:/usr/local/bin:/usr/sbin:/usr/bin:/root/bin:/root/hadoop-2.7.3/bin
[root@client-node1 ~]#
```

5. Update the `/root/hadoop-2.7.3/etc/hadoop/core-site.xml` file with the following details. Add the RGW node IP and Port and we have the RGW user `pratima` as the access key and secret key.

```xml
<!-- Put site-specific property overrides in this file. -->

<configuration>

<!-- RGW node IP and Port. -->

<property>
  <name>fs.s3a.endpoint</name>
  <value>192.168.1.106:8080</value>
</property>

<!-- RGW user pratima access key. -->

<property>
  <name>fs.s3a.access.key</name>
  <value>7L0HXU1F6DK9RTB8HK8M</value>
</property>

<!-- RGW user pratima secret key. -->

<property>
  <name>fs.s3a.secret.key</name>
  <value>kNcVjuMUWxnNv3enKDCHGAkZu5oeYqKKbjiUKfSI</value>
</property>

<property>
  <name>fs.s3a.buffer.dir</name>
  <value>${hadoop.tmp.dir}/s3a</value>
</property>

<property>
  <name>test.fs.s3a.encryption.enabled</name>
  <value>false</value>
</property>

<property>
  <name>fs.s3a.connection.ssl.enabled</name>
  <value>false</value>
</property>

<property>
  <name>fs.s3a.multipart.size</name>
  <value>104857600</value>
</property>

<!-- necessary for Hadoop to load our filesystem driver -->
<property>
  <name>fs.s3a.impl</name>
  <value>org.apache.hadoop.fs.s3a.S3AFileSystem</value>
</property>

</configuration>
```

6. You can now upload a file using the `hadoop distcp` command to your RGW
   `first-bucket`:

   ```
   # hadoop distcp /root/anaconda-ks.cfg s3a://first-bucket/
   ```

   You will have initial map logs in the command line:

```
[root@client-node1 ~]# hadoop distcp /root/anaconda-ks.cfg s3a://first-bucket/

17/09/27 05:41:45 INFO tools.DistCp: Input Options: DistCpOptions{atomicCommit=false, syncFolder=false, deleteMissing=false, ignoreFailures=false, m
'uniformsize', sourceFileListing=null, sourcePaths=[/root/anaconda-ks.cfg], targetPath=s3a://first-bucket/, targetPathExists=true, preserveRawXattrs
17/09/27 05:41:45 INFO Configuration.deprecation: session.id is deprecated. Instead, use dfs.metrics.session-id
17/09/27 05:41:45 INFO jvm.JvmMetrics: Initializing JVM Metrics with processName=JobTracker, sessionId=
17/09/27 05:41:51 INFO Configuration.deprecation: io.sort.mb is deprecated. Instead, use mapreduce.task.io.sort.mb
17/09/27 05:41:51 INFO Configuration.deprecation: io.sort.factor is deprecated. Instead, use mapreduce.task.io.sort.factor
17/09/27 05:41:51 INFO jvm.JvmMetrics: Cannot initialize JVM Metrics with processName=JobTracker, sessionId= - already initialized
17/09/27 05:41:51 INFO mapreduce.JobSubmitter: number of splits:1
17/09/27 05:41:51 INFO mapreduce.JobSubmitter: Submitting tokens for job: job_local967237231_0001
17/09/27 05:41:51 INFO mapreduce.Job: The url to track the job: http://localhost:8080/
17/09/27 05:41:51 INFO tools.DistCp: DistCp job-id: job_local967237231_0001
17/09/27 05:41:51 INFO mapreduce.Job: Running job: job_local967237231_0001
17/09/27 05:41:51 INFO mapred.LocalJobRunner: OutputCommitter set in config null
17/09/27 05:41:51 INFO output.FileOutputCommitter: File Output Committer Algorithm version is 1
17/09/27 05:41:51 INFO mapred.LocalJobRunner: OutputCommitter is org.apache.hadoop.tools.mapred.CopyCommitter
17/09/27 05:41:52 INFO mapred.LocalJobRunner: Waiting for map tasks
17/09/27 05:41:52 INFO mapred.LocalJobRunner: Starting task: attempt_local967237231_0001_m_000000_0
17/09/27 05:41:52 INFO output.FileOutputCommitter: File Output Committer Algorithm version is 1
17/09/27 05:41:52 INFO mapred.Task:  Using ResourceCalculatorProcessTree : [ ]
17/09/27 05:41:52 INFO mapred.MapTask: Processing split: file:/tmp/hadoop-root/mapred/staging/root1557284174/.staging/_distcp-1998956257/fileList.se
17/09/27 05:41:52 INFO output.FileOutputCommitter: File Output Committer Algorithm version is 1
17/09/27 05:41:52 INFO mapreduce.Job: Job job_local967237231_0001 running in uber mode : false
17/09/27 05:41:52 INFO mapreduce.Job:  map 0% reduce 0%
17/09/27 05:41:57 INFO mapred.CopyMapper: Copying file:/root/anaconda-ks.cfg to s3a://first-bucket/anaconda-ks.cfg
17/09/27 05:42:01 INFO mapred.LocalJobRunner: Copying file:/root/anaconda-ks.cfg to s3a://first-bucket/anaconda-ks.cfg > map
17/09/27 05:42:01 INFO mapreduce.Job:  map 100% reduce 0%
17/09/27 05:42:15 INFO mapred.RetriableFileCopyCommand: Creating temp file: s3a://first-bucket/.distcp.tmp.attempt_local967237231_0001_m_000000_0
17/09/27 05:42:19 INFO mapred.LocalJobRunner: 100.0% Copying file:/root/anaconda-ks.cfg to s3a://first-bucket/anaconda-ks.cfg [815.0B/815.0B] > map
17/09/27 05:42:22 INFO mapred.LocalJobRunner: 100.0% Copying file:/root/anaconda-ks.cfg to s3a://first-bucket/anaconda-ks.cfg [815.0B/815.0B] > map
17/09/27 05:43:09 INFO mapred.LocalJobRunner: 100.0% Copying file:/root/anaconda-ks.cfg to s3a://first-bucket/anaconda-ks.cfg [815.0B/815.0B] > map
```

Once it will finish the upload, you will have the following logs:

```
        File System Counters
                FILE: Number of bytes read=130262
                FILE: Number of bytes written=416919
                FILE: Number of read operations=0
                FILE: Number of large read operations=0
                FILE: Number of write operations=0
                S3A: Number of bytes read=0
                S3A: Number of bytes written=815
                S3A: Number of read operations=14
                S3A: Number of large read operations=0
                S3A: Number of write operations=3
        Map-Reduce Framework
                Map input records=1
                Map output records=0
                Input split bytes=157
                Spilled Records=0
                Failed Shuffles=0
                Merged Map outputs=0
                GC time elapsed (ms)=22
                Total committed heap usage (bytes)=16564224
        File Input Format Counters
                Bytes Read=235
        File Output Format Counters
                Bytes Written=8
        org.apache.hadoop.tools.mapred.CopyMapper$Counter
                BYTESCOPIED=815
                BYTESEXPECTED=815
                COPY=1
[root@client-node1 ~]#
```

7. Now you can verify if the `anaconda-ks.cfg` file got uploaded to the `first-bucket`:

```
[root@client-node1 ~]#
[root@client-node1 ~]# s3cmd ls
2017-09-24 22:53  s3://first-bucket
2017-09-25 02:50  s3://second-bucket
[root@client-node1 ~]# s3cmd ls s3://first-bucket
2017-09-27 02:42        815  s3://first-bucket/anaconda-ks.cfg
2017-09-24 22:53        789  s3://first-bucket/hosts
[root@client-node1 ~]#
```

5
Working with Ceph Object Storage Multi-Site v2

In this chapter, we will cover the following recipes:

- Functional changes from Hammer federated configuration
- RGW multi-site v2 requirement
- Installing the Ceph RGW multi-site v2 environment
- Configuring Ceph RGW multi-site v2
- Testing user, bucket, and object sync between master and secondary sites

Introduction

A single zone configuration typically consists of one zone group, containing one zone and one or more RGW instances, where you may load balance gateway client requests between instances. In a single zone configuration, typically, multiple gateway instances point to a single Ceph storage cluster. With the Jewel release, Ceph supports several multi-site configuration options for the Ceph Object Gateway:

- **Zone**: In a zone, one or more Ceph Object Gateways are logically grouped.
- **Zone group**: A zone group is a container of multiple zones. In a multi-site configuration there should be a master zone group. All the changes to configurations are handled by the master zone group.
- **Realm**: A realm can have multiple zone groups. It allows separation of the zone groups themselves between clusters. There can be multiple realms for having different configurations in the same cluster.

- **Period**: Every realm has a corresponding current period. Each period is a container of an epoch and an unique id. A period holds the current state of configuration of the zone groups and object storage strategies. Each period's commit operation, as well as any configuration change for a non-master zone, will increment the period's epoch.

Following is the diagrammatic representation of zone configuration:

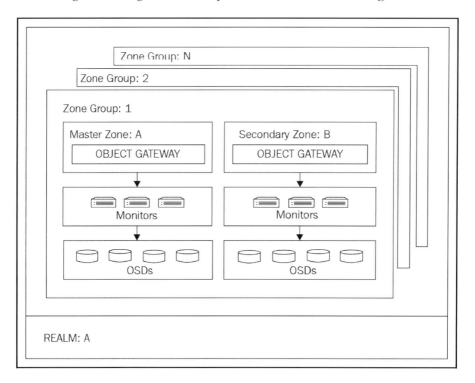

Functional changes from Hammer federated configuration

In Jewel, you can configure each Ceph Object Gateway to work in an active-active zone configuration, allowing for writes to non-master zones.

The multi-site configuration is stored within a container known as a realm. It stores zones, zone groups, and a time period with multiple epochs for tracking changes to the configuration. In Jewel, the `ceph-radosgw` daemons handle the synchronization by eliminating the need for a separate synchronization agent. Also, the new approach to synchronization allows the Ceph Object Gateway to operate with an active-active configuration instead of active-passive.

RGW multi-site v2 requirement

In this recipe, you need a minimum of two Ceph clusters and a minimum of two object gateways (one for each Ceph cluster). This is a minimum requirement for RGW multi-site.

This recipe assumes two Ceph object Gateway servers, named `us-east-1` and `us-west-1`, with two respective Ceph clusters.

In a multi-site configuration, a master zone group and a master zone are required. Additionally, each zone group requires a master zone. Zone groups may have one or more secondary, or non-master, zones.

In this recipe, the `us-east-1` host will serve as the master zone of the master zone group; the `us-west-1` host will serve as the secondary zone of the master zone group.

Installing the Ceph RGW multi-site v2 environment

You need to install two clusters, and on each cluster, you need to install a minimum of one RGW daemon for client I/O and for RGW replication.

How to do it...

In this recipe, we will use the `ceph-node1`, `ceph-node2`, and `ceph-node3` VMs for the first cluster, and in this cluster, we will use the `us-east-1` VM for the RGW node. In the second cluster, we will use the `ceph-node4`, `ceph-node5`, and `ceph-node5` VMs for cluster nodes and the `us-west-1` VM for the RGW node.

You should use Chapter 1, *Ceph – Introduction and Beyond,* for installing both clusters and Chapter 4, *Working with Ceph Object Storage,* for installing RGW nodes in both clusters:

1. Bring up all eight VMs with the help of the vagrant up command:

   ```
   $ vagrant up ceph-node1 ceph-node2 ceph-node3 ceph-node4 ceph-node5
     ceph-node6 us-east-1 us-west-1
   ```

   ```
   [vumrao@ceph-jewel Ceph-Cookbook-Second-Edition]$ vagrant up ceph-node1 ceph-node2 ceph-node3 ceph-node4 ceph-node5 ceph-node6 us-east-1 us-west-1
   Bringing machine 'ceph-node1' up with 'virtualbox' provider...
   Bringing machine 'ceph-node2' up with 'virtualbox' provider...
   Bringing machine 'ceph-node3' up with 'virtualbox' provider...
   Bringing machine 'ceph-node4' up with 'virtualbox' provider...
   Bringing machine 'ceph-node5' up with 'virtualbox' provider...
   Bringing machine 'ceph-node6' up with 'virtualbox' provider...
   Bringing machine 'us-east-1' up with 'virtualbox' provider...
   Bringing machine 'us-west-1' up with 'virtualbox' provider...
   ==> ceph-node1: Clearing any previously set forwarded ports...
   ==> ceph-node1: Clearing any previously set network interfaces...
   ==> ceph-node1: Preparing network interfaces based on configuration...
   ```

2. Once all VMs come up, log in and update to CentOS release 7.4 and then reboot to CentOS 7.4:

   ```
   # vagrant ssh <vm-name>
   #sudo su -
   # yum update -y
   # reboot
   ```

   You should configure firewall settings and NTP settings, as given in Chapter 1, *Ceph – Introduction and Beyond,* in all the nodes used in the multi-site configuration.

Create the primary cluster and primary RGW node us-east-1:

1. Install the ceph-ansible and ansible package, as given in Chapter 1, *Ceph – Introduction and Beyond,* and then update /etc/ansible/hosts for cluster 1 VMs:

```
[mons]
ceph-node1
ceph-node2
ceph-node3

[osds]
ceph-node1
ceph-node2
ceph-node3

[rgws]
us-east-1
```

2. You should copy the `ceph-node1` ssh key to all cluster 1 nodes, including RGW node `us-east-1`.

3. Update `all.yml` and `osds.yml` and other Ansible configuration files, as given in *Chapter 1*, *Ceph – Introduction and Beyond*. For the `us-east-1` RGW node, you should enable the following options in `all.yml`:

```
radosgw_civetweb_port: 8080
radosgw_civetweb_bind_ip: 192.168.1.107
```

4. After this configuration, you should run the `ansible-playbook` to install cluster 1 with the `us-east-1` RGW node:

   ansible-playbook site.yml

5. Once the `ansible-playbook` finishes installing the cluster, you will have the following cluster running; please notice the monitor names:

```
[root@ceph-node1 ~]#
[root@ceph-node1 ~]# ceph -s
    cluster 15e6d769-958f-412d-bd98-67a3852263cd
     health HEALTH_OK
     monmap e1: 3 mons at {ceph-node1=192.168.1.101:6789/0,ceph-node2=192.168.1.102:6789/0,ceph-node3=192.168.1.103:6789/0}
            election epoch 12, quorum 0,1,2 ceph-node1,ceph-node2,ceph-node3
     osdmap e42: 9 osds: 9 up, 9 in
            flags sortbitwise,require_jewel_osds
      pgmap v177: 112 pgs, 7 pools, 1588 bytes data, 171 objects
            313 MB used, 161 GB / 161 GB avail
                 112 active+clean
[root@ceph-node1 ~]#
```

Create the secondary cluster and primary RGW node `us-west-1`:

1. Install the `ceph-ansible` and `ansible` package, as given in Chapter 1, *Ceph – Introduction and Beyond*, and then update `/etc/ansible/hosts` for the cluster 2 VMs:

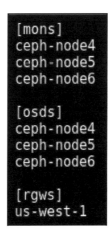

```
[mons]
ceph-node4
ceph-node5
ceph-node6

[osds]
ceph-node4
ceph-node5
ceph-node6

[rgws]
us-west-1
```

You should copy the `ceph-node4` ssh key to all cluster 2 nodes, including the RGW node `us-west-1`.

2. Update `all.yml` and `osds.yml` and other Ansible configuration files, as given in Chapter 1, *Ceph – Introduction and Beyond*. For the `us-west-1` RGW node, you should enable the following options in `all.yml`:

```
radosgw_civetweb_port: 8080
radosgw_civetweb_bind_ip: 192.168.1.108
```

3. After this configuration, you should run the `ansible-playbook` to install cluster 1 with the `us-west-1` RGW node:

    ansible-playbook site.yml

4. Once the ansible-playbook finishes installing the cluster, you will have the following cluster running; please notice the monitor names:

```
[root@ceph-node4 ~]#
[root@ceph-node4 ~]# ceph -s
    cluster 5234b0c8-d7a2-4ae1-b06d-14d3238e705f
     health HEALTH_OK
     monmap e1: 3 mons at {ceph-node4=192.168.1.104:6789/0,ceph-node5=192.168.1.115:6789/0,ceph-node6=192.168.1.116:6789/0}
            election epoch 8, quorum 0,1,2 ceph-node4,ceph-node5,ceph-node6
     osdmap e62: 9 osds: 9 up, 9 in
            flags sortbitwise,require_jewel_osds
      pgmap v160: 112 pgs, 7 pools, 1588 bytes data, 171 objects
            313 MB used, 161 GB / 161 GB avail
                 112 active+clean
[root@ceph-node4 ~]#
```

Configuring Ceph RGW multi-site v2

In the following sections, you will be configuring the master zone and secondary zone for RGW active-active multi-site; this means you can write data on both of the sites and it will be replicated to the other site cluster. Metadata operations like user creation should only be performed on the primary site.

How to do it...

We will use the following steps to configure the RGW multi-site v2 master zone and the secondary zone:

Configuring a master zone

All RADOS Gateways in a multi-site v2 configuration will get their configuration from a `radosgw` daemon on a node within the master zone group and master zone. To configure your RADOS Gateways in a multi-site v2 configuration, you need to choose a `radosgw` instance to configure the master zone group and master zone. You should be using the `us-east-1` RGW instance to configure your master zone:

1. Create an RGW keyring in the `/etc/ceph` path and check if you are able to access the cluster with user RGW Cephx:

   ```
   # cp /var/lib/ceph/radosgw/ceph-rgw.us-east-1/
     keyring /etc/ceph/ceph.client.rgw.us-east-1.keyring
   # cat /etc/ceph/ceph.client.rgw.us-east-1.keyring
   # ceph -s --id rgw.us-east-1
   ```

   ```
   [root@us-east-1 ~]#
   [root@us-east-1 ~]# cp /var/lib/ceph/radosgw/ceph-rgw.us-east-1/keyring /etc/ceph/ceph.client.rgw.us-east-1.keyring
   [root@us-east-1 ~]# cat /etc/ceph/ceph.client.rgw.us-east-1.keyring
   [client.rgw.us-east-1]
           key = AQBXLstZpee7KhAAYhfn2S59EY5FH+XP5G8Jpg==
   [root@us-east-1 ~]#
   [root@us-east-1 ~]#
   [root@us-east-1 ~]# ceph -s --id rgw.us-east-1
       cluster 15e6d769-958f-412d-bd98-67a3852263cd
        health HEALTH_OK
        monmap e1: 3 mons at {ceph-node1=192.168.1.101:6789/0,ceph-node2=192.168.1.102:6789/0,ceph-node3=192.168.1.103:6789/0}
               election epoch 16, quorum 0,1,2 ceph-node1,ceph-node2,ceph-node3
        osdmap e50: 9 osds: 9 up, 9 in
               flags sortbitwise,require_jewel_osds
         pgmap v1680: 112 pgs, 7 pools, 1588 bytes data, 171 objects
               346 MB used, 161 GB / 161 GB avail
                   112 active+clean
   [root@us-east-1 ~]#
   ```

   Now you should be able to use this RGW Cephx user to run `radosgw-admin` commands in cluster 1.

2. Create the RGW multi-site v2 realm. Run the following command in the `us-east-1` RGW node to create a realm:

   ```
   # radosgw-admin realm create --rgw-realm=cookbookv2
                                --default --id rgw.us-east-1
   ```

   ```
   [root@us-east-1 ~]#
   [root@us-east-1 ~]# radosgw-admin realm create --rgw-realm=cookbookv2 --default --id rgw.us-east-1
   2017-09-28 00:23:11.899968 7f9f6aa259c0  1 error read_lastest_epoch .rgw.root:periods.12f916f0-3ce8-4f6c-ad8c-e08a6e0cfad8.latest_epoch
   {
       "id": "9a66b241-eda4-4577-b5d5-aaf3d259168f",
       "name": "cookbookv2",
       "current_period": "12f916f0-3ce8-4f6c-ad8c-e08a6e0cfad8",
       "epoch": 1
   }

   [root@us-east-1 ~]#
   ```

You can ignore the error message given in the preceding screenshot; it will be fixed in the future release of Jewel. It is a known issue; it is not an error, but an information message declared as an error message. This will not cause any issues in configuring RGW multi-site v2.

3. Create a master zone group. An RGW realm must have at least one RGW zone group, which will serve as the master zone group for the realm.

   Run the following command in the `us-east-1` RGW node to create a master zone group:

   ```
   # radosgw-admin zonegroup create --rgw-zonegroup=us
     --endpoints=http://us-east-1.cephcookbook.com:8080
     --rgw-realm=cookbookv2 --master --default
     --id rgw.us-east-1
   ```

   ```
   {
       "id": "f5152481-422f-4ae5-a75d-7eaeae5c2b60",
       "name": "us",
       "api_name": "us",
       "is_master": "true",
       "endpoints": [
           "http:\/\/us-east-1.cephcookbook.com:8080"
       ],
       "hostnames": [],
       "hostnames_s3website": [],
       "master_zone": "",
       "zones": [],
       "placement_targets": [],
       "default_placement": "",
       "realm_id": "9a66b241-eda4-4577-b5d5-aaf3d259168f"
   }
   ```

4. Create a master zone. An RGW zone group must have at least one RGW zone. Run the following command in the `us-east-1` RGW node to create a master zone:

```
# radosgw-admin zone create --rgw-zonegroup=us
  --rgw-zone=us-east-1 --master --default
  --endpoints=http://us-east-1.cephcookbook.com:8080
  --id rgw.us-east-1
```

```
{
    "id": "286299f7-73eb-4da3-96ae-f0c6a0288d09",
    "name": "us-east-1",
    "domain_root": "us-east-1.rgw.data.root",
    "control_pool": "us-east-1.rgw.control",
    "gc_pool": "us-east-1.rgw.gc",
    "log_pool": "us-east-1.rgw.log",
    "intent_log_pool": "us-east-1.rgw.intent-log",
    "usage_log_pool": "us-east-1.rgw.usage",
    "user_keys_pool": "us-east-1.rgw.users.keys",
    "user_email_pool": "us-east-1.rgw.users.email",
    "user_swift_pool": "us-east-1.rgw.users.swift",
    "user_uid_pool": "us-east-1.rgw.users.uid",
    "system_key": {
        "access_key": "",
        "secret_key": ""
    },
    "placement_pools": [
        {
            "key": "default-placement",
            "val": {
                "index_pool": "us-east-1.rgw.buckets.index",
                "data_pool": "us-east-1.rgw.buckets.data",
                "data_extra_pool": "us-east-1.rgw.buckets.non-ec",
                "index_type": 0
            }
        }
    ],
    "metadata_heap": "",
    "realm_id": "9a66b241-eda4-4577-b5d5-aaf3d259168f"
}
```

5. Remove default zone group and zone information from cluster 1:

```
# radosgw-admin zonegroup remove --rgw-zonegroup=default
  --rgw-zone=default --id rgw.us-east-1
# radosgw-admin zone delete --rgw-zone=default
  --id rgw.us-east-1
# radosgw-admin zonegroup delete --rgw-zonegroup=default
  --id rgw.us-east-1
```

Finally, update the period with the new us zone group and `us-east-1` zone which will be used for multi-site v2:

```
# radosgw-admin period update --commit --id rgw.us-east-1
```

6. Remove the RGW default pools:

```
[root@us-east-1 ~]#
[root@us-east-1 ~]# rados lspools --id rgw.us-east-1
rbd
.rgw.root
default.rgw.control
default.rgw.data.root
default.rgw.gc
default.rgw.log
default.rgw.users.uid
[root@us-east-1 ~]#
```

```
# for i in `ceph osd pool ls --id rgw.us-east-1 |
  grep default.rgw`; do ceph osd pool delete $i $i
  --yes-i-really-really-mean-it --id rgw.us-east-1; done
```

```
[root@us-east-1 ~]#
[root@us-east-1 ~]# for i in `ceph osd pool ls --id rgw.us-east-1 | grep default.rgw`; do ceph osd pool delete $i $i --yes-i-really-really-mean-it --id rgw.us-east-1; done
pool 'default.rgw.control' removed
pool 'default.rgw.data.root' removed
pool 'default.rgw.gc' removed
pool 'default.rgw.log' removed
pool 'default.rgw.users.uid' removed
[root@us-east-1 ~]#
```

7. Create an RGW multi-site v2 system user. In the master zone, create a system user to establish authentication between multi-site `radosgw` daemons:

```
# radosgw-admin user create --uid="replication-user"
  --display-name="Multisite v2 replication user"
  --system --id rgw.us-east-1
```

```
{
    "user_id": "replication-user",
    "display_name": "Multisite v2 replication user",
    "email": "",
    "suspended": 0,
    "max_buckets": 1000,
    "auid": 0,
    "subusers": [],
    "keys": [
        {
            "user": "replication-user",
            "access_key": "ZYCDNTEASHKREV4X9BUJ",
            "secret_key": "4JbC4OC4vC6fy6EY6Pfp8rPZMrpDnYmETZxNyyu9"
        }
    ],
    "swift_keys": [],
    "caps": [],
    "op_mask": "read, write, delete",
    "system": "true",
    "default_placement": "",
    "placement_tags": [],
    "bucket_quota": {
        "enabled": false,
        "max_size_kb": -1,
        "max_objects": -1
    },
    "user_quota": {
        "enabled": false,
        "max_size_kb": -1,
        "max_objects": -1
    },
    "temp_url_keys": []
}
```

Make a note of the access key and secret key for the system user named `"replication-user"` because you need to use the same access key and secret key in the secondary zone.

8. Finally, update the period with this system user information:

```
# radosgw-admin zone modify --rgw-zone=us-east-1
--access-key=ZYCDNTEASHKREV4X9BUJ
--secret=4JbC4OC4vC6fy6EY6Pfp8rPZMrpDnYmETZxNyyu9
--id rgw.us-east-1
# radosgw-admin period update --commit --id rgw.us-east-1
```

9. You also need to update the [client.rgw.us-east-1] section of ceph.conf with the rgw_zone=us-east-1 option:

```
[client.rgw.us-east-1]
rgw_zone = us-east-1
host = us-east-1
keyring = /var/lib/ceph/radosgw/ceph-rgw.us-east-1/keyring
rgw socket path = /tmp/radosgw-us-east-1.sock
log file = /var/log/ceph/ceph-rgw-us-east-1.log
rgw data = /var/lib/ceph/radosgw/ceph-rgw.us-east-1
rgw frontends = civetweb port=192.168.1.107:8080 num_threads=100
rgw resolve cname = False
```

10. Restart the us-east-1 RGW daemon:

```
#   systemctl restart ceph-radosgw.target
```

Configuring a secondary zone

In RGW, multi-site zones replicate all data within a zone group to ensure that each zone has the same set data. In this section, you will be configuring the secondary zone. You should be using the us-west-1 RGW instance to configure your secondary zone:

1. Create an RGW keyring in the /etc/ceph path and check if you are able to access the cluster with user RGW Cephx:

```
# cp /var/lib/ceph/radosgw/ceph-rgw.us-west-1/
keyring /etc/ceph/ceph.client.rgw.us-west-1.keyring
# cat /etc/ceph/ceph.client.rgw.us-west-1.keyring
# ceph -s --id rgw.us-west-1
```

```
[root@us-west-1 ~]#
[root@us-west-1 ~]# cp /var/lib/ceph/radosgw/ceph-rgw.us-west-1/keyring /etc/ceph/ceph.client.rgw.us-west-1.keyring
[root@us-west-1 ~]#
[root@us-west-1 ~]# cat /etc/ceph/ceph.client.rgw.us-west-1.keyring
[client.rgw.us-west-1]
        key = AQCTNstZZAeuDBAA3Njk/HvQMsnhBlgOFwmgAQ==
[root@us-west-1 ~]#
[root@us-west-1 ~]# ceph -s --id rgw.us-west-1
    cluster 5234b0c8-d7a2-4ae1-b06d-14d3238e705f
     health HEALTH_OK
     monmap e1: 3 mons at {ceph-node4=192.168.1.104:6789/0,ceph-node5=192.168.1.115:6789/0,ceph-node6=192.168.1.116:6789/0}
            election epoch 16, quorum 0,1,2 ceph-node4,ceph-node5,ceph-node6
     osdmap e71: 9 osds: 9 up, 9 in
            flags sortbitwise,require_jewel_osds
      pgmap v1367: 112 pgs, 7 pools, 1588 bytes data, 171 objects
            344 MB used, 161 GB / 161 GB avail
                 112 active+clean
[root@us-west-1 ~]#
```

You should be running the following steps in the secondary site RGW node us-west-1:

2. First of all, you need to pull the RGW realm.

You need to use the RGW endpoint URL path and the access key and secret key of the master zone in the master zone group to pull the realm to the secondary zone RGW node:

```
# radosgw-admin realm pull
  --url=http://us-east-1.cephcookbook.com:8080
  --access-key=ZYCDNTEASHKREV4X9BUJ
  --secret=4JbC4OC4vC6fy6EY6Pfp8rPZMrpDnYmETZxNyyu9
  --id rgw.us-west-1
```

```
{
    "id": "9a66b241-eda4-4577-b5d5-aaf3d259168f",
    "name": "cookbookv2",
    "current_period": "e4844523-625e-4ce3-a0b9-c4e7635a8cf0",
    "epoch": 2
}
```

3. As this is the default realm for this RGW multi-site setup, you need to make it default:

```
# radosgw-admin realm default --rgw-realm=cookbookv2
                              --id rgw.us-west-1
```

4. You need to pull the period from the master site, because you need to get the latest version of the zone group and zone configurations for the realm:

```
# radosgw-admin period pull
  --url=http://us-east-1.cephcookbook.com:8080
  --access-key=ZYCDNTEASHKREV4X9BUJ
  --secret=4JbC4OC4vC6fy6EY6Pfp8rPZMrpDnYmETZxNyyu9
  --id rgw.us-west-1
```

5. Create a secondary zone. Your secondary zone RGW node is `us-west-1` and you need to run the following command in the secondary zone RGW node `us-west-1`:

```
# radosgw-admin zone create --rgw-zonegroup=us
  --rgw-zone=us-west-1 --access-key=ZYCDNTEASHKREV4X9BUJ
  --secret=4JbC4OC4vC6fy6EY6Pfp8rPZMrpDnYmETZxNyyu9
  --endpoints=http://us-west-1.cephcookbook.com:8080
  --id rgw.us-west-1
```

```
{
    "id": "66dbedf3-1068-43c9-bc63-e4daea1fab17",
    "name": "us-west-1",
    "domain_root": "us-west-1.rgw.data.root",
    "control_pool": "us-west-1.rgw.control",
    "gc_pool": "us-west-1.rgw.gc",
    "log_pool": "us-west-1.rgw.log",
    "intent_log_pool": "us-west-1.rgw.intent-log",
    "usage_log_pool": "us-west-1.rgw.usage",
    "user_keys_pool": "us-west-1.rgw.users.keys",
    "user_email_pool": "us-west-1.rgw.users.email",
    "user_swift_pool": "us-west-1.rgw.users.swift",
    "user_uid_pool": "us-west-1.rgw.users.uid",
    "system_key": {
        "access_key": "ZYCDNTEASHKREV4X9BUJ",
        "secret_key": "4JbC4OC4vC6fy6EY6Pfp8rPZMrpDnYmETZxNyyu9"
    },
    "placement_pools": [
        {
            "key": "default-placement",
            "val": {
                "index_pool": "us-west-1.rgw.buckets.index",
                "data_pool": "us-west-1.rgw.buckets.data",
                "data_extra_pool": "us-west-1.rgw.buckets.non-ec",
                "index_type": 0
            }
        }
    ],
    "metadata_heap": "",
    "realm_id": "9a66b241-eda4-4577-b5d5-aaf3d259168f"
}
```

6. Remove the default zone from the secondary site, as you are not using it:

```
# radosgw-admin zone delete --rgw-zone=default
                            --id rgw.us-west-1
```

7. Finally, update the period on the secondary site:

```
# radosgw-admin period update --commit
  --id rgw.us-west-1
```

8. Remove the RGW default pools:

```
# for i in `ceph osd pool ls --id rgw.us-west-1 |
  grep default.rgw`; do ceph osd pool delete $i $i
  --yes-i-really-really-mean-it --id rgw.us-west-1; done
```

```
[root@us-west-1 ~]# for i in `ceph osd pool ls --id rgw.us-west-1 | grep default.rgw`; do ceph osd pool delete $i $i --yes-i-really-really-mean-it --id rgw.us-west-1; done
pool 'default.rgw.control' removed
pool 'default.rgw.data.root' removed
pool 'default.rgw.gc' removed
pool 'default.rgw.log' removed
pool 'default.rgw.users.uid' removed
[root@us-west-1 ~]#
[root@us-west-1 ~]#
[root@us-west-1 ~]#
[root@us-west-1 ~]# rados lspools --id rgw.us-west-1
rbd
.rgw.root
us-west-1.rgw.control
us-west-1.rgw.data.root
us-west-1.rgw.gc
us-west-1.rgw.log
[root@us-west-1 ~]#
```

9. You also need to update the [client.rgw.us-west-1] section of ceph.conf with the rgw_zone=us-west-1 option:

```
[client.rgw.us-west-1]
rgw_zone = us-west-1
host = us-west-1
keyring = /var/lib/ceph/radosgw/ceph-rgw.us-west-1/keyring
rgw socket path = /tmp/radosgw-us-west-1.sock
log file = /var/log/ceph/ceph-rgw-us-west-1.log
rgw data = /var/lib/ceph/radosgw/ceph-rgw.us-west-1
rgw frontends = civetweb port=192.168.1.108:8080 num_threads=100
rgw resolve cname = False
```

10. Then, restart the us-west-1 RGW daemon:

```
#  systemctl restart ceph-radosgw.target
```

With this, you have both the master and secondary site up and running with active-active asynchronous replication, and now you can check the synchronization status on both of the sites.

Checking the synchronization status

The following commands will be used for checking the status between the master zone and the secondary zone:

1. Cluster 1 master zone `us-east-1` synchronization status:

   ```
   # radosgw-admin sync status --id rgw.us-east-1
   ```

   ```
            realm 9a66b241-eda4-4577-b5d5-aaf3d259168f (cookbookv2)
        zonegroup f5152481-422f-4ae5-a75d-7eaeae5c2b60 (us)
             zone 286299f7-73eb-4da3-96ae-f0c6a0288d09 (us-east-1)
     metadata sync no sync (zone is master)
         data sync source: 66dbedf3-1068-43c9-bc63-e4daea1fab17 (us-west-1)
                          syncing
                          full sync: 0/128 shards
                          incremental sync: 128/128 shards
                          data is caught up with source
   ```

2. Cluster 2 secondary zone `us-west-1` synchronization status:

   ```
   # radosgw-admin sync status --id rgw.us-west-1
   ```

```
     realm 9a66b241-eda4-4577-b5d5-aaf3d259168f (cookbookv2)
 zonegroup f5152481-422f-4ae5-a75d-7eaeae5c2b60 (us)
      zone 66dbedf3-1068-43c9-bc63-e4daea1fab17 (us-west-1)
metadata sync syncing
          full sync: 0/64 shards
          incremental sync: 64/64 shards
          metadata is caught up with master
  data sync source: 286299f7-73eb-4da3-96ae-f0c6a0288d09 (us-east-1)
              syncing
              full sync: 0/128 shards
              incremental sync: 128/128 shards
              data is caught up with source
```

Testing user, bucket, and object sync between master and secondary sites

By this time, you should have configured RGW multi-site V2. In this recipe, you will test user, bucket, and object synchronization between the master and secondary sites.

How to do it...

We will use the following commands for testing user, bucket, and object sync between the master and secondary zones:

1. Let's create an s3 user in the master site and check if it gets synced to the secondary site. You should run the following commands in the master site RGW node us-east-1:

    ```
    # radosgw-admin user create --uid=pratima
                                --display-name="Pratima Umrao"
                                --id rgw.us-east-1
    ```

```
{
    "user_id": "pratima",
    "display_name": "Pratima Umrao",
    "email": "",
    "suspended": 0,
    "max_buckets": 1000,
    "auid": 0,
    "subusers": [],
    "keys": [
        {
            "user": "pratima",
            "access_key": "AH6X7HQWBGT8TB8K1P62",
            "secret_key": "bL6TUS8wOmW1h4ViIMUmJz1JwYRXxaFaPcVTXt9k"
        }
    ],
    "swift_keys": [],
    "caps": [],
    "op_mask": "read, write, delete",
    "default_placement": "",
    "placement_tags": [],
    "bucket_quota": {
        "enabled": false,
        "max_size_kb": -1,
        "max_objects": -1
    },
    "user_quota": {
        "enabled": false,
        "max_size_kb": -1,
        "max_objects": -1
    },
    "temp_url_keys": []
}
```

2. Check the number of users in the master site:

```
# radosgw-admin metadata list user --id rgw.us-east-1
```

```
[
    "pratima",
    "replication-user"
]
```

3. Let's verify that the user "pratima" got synced to the secondary site. You should run the following commands in the secondary site RGW node us-west-1:

```
# radosgw-admin metadata list user --id rgw.us-west-1
```

```
[
    "pratima",
    "replication-user"
]
```

```
# radosgw-admin user info --uid=pratima --id rgw.us-west-1
```

```
{
    "user_id": "pratima",
    "display_name": "Pratima Umrao",
    "email": "",
    "suspended": 0,
    "max_buckets": 1000,
    "auid": 0,
    "subusers": [],
    "keys": [
        {
            "user": "pratima",
            "access_key": "AH6X7HQWBGT8TB8K1P62",
            "secret_key": "bL6TUS8wOmW1h4ViIMUmJz1JwYRXxaFaPcVTXt9k"
        }
    ],
    "swift_keys": [],
    "caps": [],
    "op_mask": "read, write, delete",
    "default_placement": "",
    "placement_tags": [],
    "bucket_quota": {
        "enabled": false,
        "max_size_kb": -1,
        "max_objects": -1
    },
    "user_quota": {
        "enabled": false,
        "max_size_kb": -1,
        "max_objects": -1
    },
    "temp_url_keys": []
}
[root@us-west-1 ~]# _
```

We will use the s3cmd application in both sites to create the buckets and upload the objects to these buckets and see if the buckets and objects are getting synced on both the sites.

4. Install and configure s3cmd at the master site us-east-1 node:

```
[root@us-east-1 ~]#
[root@us-east-1 ~]# yum install s3cmd -y
Loaded plugins: fastestmirror
base
ceph_stable
epel/x86_64/metalink
extras
updates
Loading mirror speeds from cached hostfile
 * base: mirrors.rit.edu
 * epel: mirror.math.princeton.edu
 * extras: mirror.cogentco.com
 * updates: mirrors.cmich.edu
Resolving Dependencies
--> Running transaction check
---> Package s3cmd.noarch 0:1.6.1-1.el7 will be installed
--> Processing Dependency: python-magic for package: s3cmd-1.6.1-1.el7.noarch
--> Processing Dependency: python-dateutil for package: s3cmd-1.6.1-1.el7.noarc
--> Running transaction check
---> Package python-dateutil.noarch 0:1.5-7.el7 will be installed
---> Package python-magic.noarch 0:5.11-33.el7 will be installed
--> Finished Dependency Resolution

Dependencies Resolved

================================================================================
 Package                                              Arch
================================================================================
Installing:
 s3cmd                                                noarch
```

5. Configure s3cmd at the master site in the us-east-1 RGW node:

```
[root@us-east-1 ~]# s3cmd --configure

Enter new values or accept defaults in brackets with Enter.
Refer to user manual for detailed description of all options.

Access key and Secret key are your identifiers for Amazon S3. Leave them empty for using the env variables.
Access Key: AH6X7HQWBGT8TB8K1P62
Secret Key: bL6TUS8wOmW1h4ViIMUmJz1JwYRXxaFaPcVTXt9k
Default Region [US]:

Encryption password is used to protect your files from reading
by unauthorized persons while in transfer to S3
Encryption password:
Path to GPG program [/bin/gpg]:

When using secure HTTPS protocol all communication with Amazon S3
servers is protected from 3rd party eavesdropping. This method is
slower than plain HTTP, and can only be proxied with Python 2.7 or newer
Use HTTPS protocol [Yes]: No

On some networks all internet access must go through a HTTP proxy.
Try setting it here if you can't connect to S3 directly
HTTP Proxy server name:

New settings:
  Access Key: AH6X7HQWBGT8TB8K1P62
  Secret Key: bL6TUS8wOmW1h4ViIMUmJz1JwYRXxaFaPcVTXt9k
  Default Region: US
  Encryption password:
  Path to GPG program: /bin/gpg
  Use HTTPS protocol: False
  HTTP Proxy server name:
  HTTP Proxy server port: 0

Test access with supplied credentials? [Y/n] n

Save settings? [y/N] y
Configuration saved to '/root/.s3cfg'
[root@us-east-1 ~]# _
```

6. Update .s3cfg file options host_base and host_bucket with the master site
   RGW node hostname us-east-1.cephcookbook.com:

```
[root@us-east-1 ~]#
[root@us-east-1 ~]# cat .s3cfg | egrep "host_base|host_bucket"
host_base = us-east-1.cephcookbook.com:8080
host_bucket = %(bucket).us-east-1.cephcookbook.com:8080
[root@us-east-1 ~]#
```

7. Install and configure s3cmd at the secondary site `us-west-1` node:

```
[root@us-west-1 ~]#
[root@us-west-1 ~]# yum install s3cmd -y
Loaded plugins: fastestmirror
base
ceph_stable
epel/x86_64/metalink
epel
extras
updates
(1/8): base/7/x86_64/group_gz
(2/8): ceph_stable/x86_64/primary_db
(3/8): base/7/x86_64/primary_db
(4/8): epel/x86_64/updateinfo
(5/8): epel/x86_64/group_gz
(6/8): extras/7/x86_64/primary_db
(7/8): epel/x86_64/primary_db
(8/8): updates/7/x86_64/primary_db
Determining fastest mirrors
 * base: mirror.linux.duke.edu
 * epel: fedora-epel.mirrors.tds.net
 * extras: mirror.vtti.vt.edu
 * updates: centos.localmsp.org
Resolving Dependencies
--> Running transaction check
---> Package s3cmd.noarch 0:1.6.1-1.el7 will be installed
--> Processing Dependency: python-magic for package: s3cmd-1.6.1-1.el7.noarch
--> Processing Dependency: python-dateutil for package: s3cmd-1.6.1-1.el7.noarch
--> Running transaction check
---> Package python-dateutil.noarch 0:1.5-7.el7 will be installed
---> Package python-magic.noarch 0:5.11-33.el7 will be installed
--> Finished Dependency Resolution

Dependencies Resolved

================================================================================
 Package                                              Arch
================================================================================
Installing:
 s3cmd                                                noarch
```

8. Configure s3cmd at the secondary site in the `us-west-1` RGW node:

```
[root@us-west-1 ~]#
[root@us-west-1 ~]# s3cmd --configure

Enter new values or accept defaults in brackets with Enter.
Refer to user manual for detailed description of all options.

Access key and Secret key are your identifiers for Amazon S3. Leave them empty for using the env variables.
Access Key: AH6X7HQWBGT8TB8K1P62
Secret Key: bL6TUS8wOmW1h4ViIMUmJz1JwYRXxaFaPcVTXt9k
Default Region [US]:

Encryption password is used to protect your files from reading
by unauthorized persons while in transfer to S3
Encryption password:
Path to GPG program [/bin/gpg]:

When using secure HTTPS protocol all communication with Amazon S3
servers is protected from 3rd party eavesdropping. This method is
slower than plain HTTP, and can only be proxied with Python 2.7 or newer
Use HTTPS protocol [Yes]: no

On some networks all internet access must go through a HTTP proxy.
Try setting it here if you can't connect to S3 directly
HTTP Proxy server name:

New settings:
  Access Key: AH6X7HQWBGT8TB8K1P62
  Secret Key: bL6TUS8wOmW1h4ViIMUmJz1JwYRXxaFaPcVTXt9k
  Default Region: US
  Encryption password:
  Path to GPG program: /bin/gpg
  Use HTTPS protocol: False
  HTTP Proxy server name:
  HTTP Proxy server port: 0

Test access with supplied credentials? [Y/n] n

Save settings? [y/N] y
Configuration saved to '/root/.s3cfg'
[root@us-west-1 ~]#
```

9. Update `.s3cfg` file options `host_base` and `host_bucket` with the master site RGW node hostname `us-west-1`.

```
[root@us-west-1 ~]#
[root@us-west-1 ~]# cat .s3cfg | egrep "host_base|host_bucket"
host_base = us-west-1.cephcookbook.com:8080
host_bucket = %(bucket).us-west-1.cephcookbook.com:8080
[root@us-west-1 ~]#
```

10. Create the `test-bucket-master` and `upload: '/etc/hosts'` object in the bucket `test-bucket-master`:

```
[root@us-east-1 ~]# s3cmd mb s3://test-bucket-master
Bucket 's3://test-bucket-master/' created

[root@us-east-1 ~]# s3cmd ls
2017-09-28 03:45   s3://test-bucket-master

[root@us-east-1 ~]# radosgw-admin bucket list --id rgw.us-east-1
[
    "test-bucket-master"
]

[root@us-east-1 ~]# s3cmd put /etc/hosts s3://test-bucket-master
upload: '/etc/hosts' -> 's3://test-bucket-master/hosts'  [1 of 1]
 800 of 800   100% in    1s    560.59 B/s   done

[root@us-east-1 ~]# s3cmd ls s3://test-bucket-master
2017-09-28 03:46       800   s3://test-bucket-master/hosts
[root@us-east-1 ~]#
```

11. You can now check in the secondary site that the bucket and objects are synced:

```
[root@us-west-1 ~]#
[root@us-west-1 ~]# radosgw-admin bucket list --id rgw.us-west-1
[
    "test-bucket-master"
]
[root@us-west-1 ~]# s3cmd ls
2017-09-28 03:45   s3://test-bucket-master

[root@us-west-1 ~]# s3cmd ls s3://test-bucket-master
2017-09-28 03:46       800   s3://test-bucket-master/hosts
[root@us-west-1 ~]#
```

12. Now you can do the opposite to check the active-active replication; for this you need to create the `test-bucket-secondary` and `upload: '/root/anaconda-ks.cfg'` objects in the bucket `test-bucket-secondary` at the secondary RGW node `us-west-1`:

```
[root@us-west-1 ~]#
[root@us-west-1 ~]# s3cmd mb s3://test-bucket-secondary
Bucket 's3://test-bucket-secondary/' created

[root@us-west-1 ~]# s3cmd ls
2017-09-28 03:45  s3://test-bucket-master
2017-09-28 03:56  s3://test-bucket-secondary

[root@us-west-1 ~]# s3cmd put /root/anaconda-ks.cfg s3://test-bucket-secondary
upload: '/root/anaconda-ks.cfg' -> 's3://test-bucket-secondary/anaconda-ks.cfg'  [1 of 1]
 815 of 815   100% in    0s    59.05 kB/s  done

[root@us-west-1 ~]# s3cmd ls s3://test-bucket-secondary
2017-09-28 03:56        815   s3://test-bucket-secondary/anaconda-ks.cfg
[root@us-west-1 ~]#
```

13. You can now check in the master site that the bucket test-bucket-secondary and anaconda-ks.cfg objects are synced:

```
[root@us-east-1 ~]# radosgw-admin bucket list --id rgw.us-east-1
[
    "test-bucket-master",
    "test-bucket-secondary"
]
[root@us-east-1 ~]#

[root@us-east-1 ~]# s3cmd ls
2017-09-28 03:45  s3://test-bucket-master
2017-09-28 03:56  s3://test-bucket-secondary

[root@us-east-1 ~]# s3cmd ls s3://test-bucket-secondary
2017-09-28 03:56        815   s3://test-bucket-secondary/anaconda-ks.cfg
[root@us-east-1 ~]#
```

You can see that the bucket test-bucket-secondary and anaconda-ks.cfg objects are synced to the master site us-east-1. This is the behavior of active-active replication.

6
Working with the Ceph Filesystem

In this chapter, we will cover the following recipes:

- Understanding the Ceph Filesystem and MDS
- Deploying Ceph MDS
- Accessing Ceph FS through kernel driver
- Accessing Ceph FS through FUSE client
- Exporting the Ceph Filesystem as NFS
- Ceph FS – a drop-in replacement for HDFS

Introduction

The Ceph Filesystem, also known as Ceph FS, is a POSIX-compliant filesystem that uses the Ceph storage cluster to store user data. Ceph FS supports the native Linux kernel driver, which makes Ceph FS highly adaptive across any flavor of the Linux OS. In this chapter, we will cover the Ceph Filesystem in detail, including its deployment, understanding the kernel driver and FUSE.

Understanding the Ceph Filesystem and MDS

The Ceph Filesystem offers the POSIX-compliant distributed filesystem of any size that uses Ceph RADOS to store its data. To implement the Ceph Filesystem, you need a running Ceph storage cluster and at least one Ceph **Metadata Server** (**MDS**) to manage its metadata and keep it separated from data, which helps in reducing complexity and improves reliability. The following diagram depicts the architectural view of Ceph FS and its interfaces:

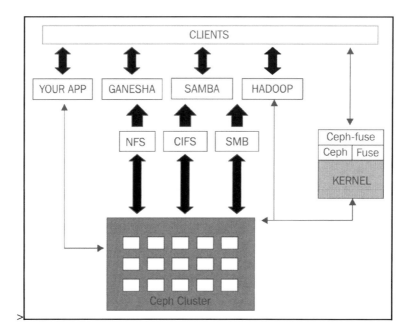

The `libcephfs` libraries play an important role in supporting its multiple client implementations. It has the native Linux kernel driver support, and thus clients can use native filesystem mounting, for example, using the mount command. It has tight integration with SAMBA and support for CIFS and SMB. Ceph FS extends its support to **Filesystem in USErspace** (**FUSE**) using `cephfuse` modules. It also allows direct application interaction with the RADOS cluster using the `libcephfs` libraries. Ceph FS is gaining popularity as a replacement for Hadoop HDFS. Previous versions of HDFS only supported the single name node, which impacts its scalability and creates a single point of failure; however, this has been changed in the current versions of HDFS. Unlike HDFS, Ceph FS can be implemented over multiple MDS in an active-active state, thus making it highly scalable, high performing, and with no single point of failure.

Ceph MDS is required only for the Ceph FS; other storage methods' block and object-based storage does not require MDS services. Ceph MDS operates as a daemon, which allows the client to mount a POSIX filesystem of any size. MDS does not serve any data directly to the client; data serving is done only by the OSD. MDS provides a shared coherent filesystem with a smart caching layer, hence drastically reducing reads and writes. It extends its benefits towards dynamic subtree partitioning and a single MDS for a piece of metadata. It is dynamic in nature; daemons can join and leave, and the takeover to failed nodes is quick.

MDS does not store local data, which is quite useful in some scenarios. If an MDS daemon dies, we can start it up again on any system that has cluster access. The Metadata Server's daemons are configured as active or passive. The primary MDS node becomes active and the rest will go into *standby*. In the event of primary MDS failure, the second node takes charge and is promoted to active. For even faster recovery, you can specify that a standby node should follow one of your active nodes, which will keep the same data in memory to pre-populate the cache.

Jewel (v10.2.0) is the first Ceph release to include stable Ceph FS code and fsck/repair tools, although multiple active MDS is running safely, and snapshots are still experimental. Ceph FS development continues to go at a very fast pace, and we can expect it to be fully production-ready in the Luminous release. For your non-critical workloads, you can consider using Ceph FS with single MDS and no snapshots.

In the coming sections, we will cover recipes for configuring both kernel and FUSE clients. Which client you choose to use is based on your use case. But the FUSE client is the easiest way to get up-to-date code, while the kernel client will often give better performance. Also, the clients do not always provide equivalent functionality; for example, the FUSE client supports client-enforced quotas while the kernel client does not.

Deploying Ceph MDS

To configure the Metadata Server for the Ceph Filesystem, you should have a running Ceph cluster. In the earlier chapters, we learned to deploy the Ceph storage cluster using Ansible; we will use the same cluster and Ansible for the MDS deployment.

How to do it...

Deploying an MDS server through `ceph-ansible` is quite easy, let's review the steps on how this is done:

1. Using Ansible from `ceph-node1`, we will deploy and configure MDS on `ceph-node2`. On our Ansible configuration node `ceph-node1`, add a new section `[mdss]` to the `/etc/ansible/hosts` file:

2. Navigate to the Ansible configuration directory on `ceph-node1`, `/usr/share/ceph-ansible`:

   ```
   root@ceph-node1 # cd /usr/share/ceph-ansible
   ```

3. Run the Ansible playbook to deploy the MDS on `ceph-node2`:

   ```
   # ansible-playbook site.yml
   ```

4. Once the playbook completes successfully, you can validate that the MDS is `up` and `active`, that we have created two pools, `cephfs_data` and `cephfs_metadata`, and that the Ceph Filesystem was created successfully:

```
# ceph mds stat
# ceph osd pool ls
# ceph fs ls
```

```
[root@ceph-node1 ceph]# ceph mds stat
e5: 1/1/1 up {0=ceph-node2=up:active}
[root@ceph-node1 ceph]# ceph osd pool ls
rbd
cephfs_data
cephfs_metadata
[root@ceph-node1 ceph]# ceph fs ls
name: cephfs, metadata pool: cephfs_metadata, data pools: [cephfs_data ]
[root@ceph-node1 ceph]#
```

5. It's recommended that you don't share `client.admin` user `keyring` with Ceph clients, so we will create a user `client.cephfs` on the Ceph cluster and will allow this user access to the Ceph FS pools, then we will transfer the `keyring` we created to `client-node1`:

```
root@ceph-node1 # ceph auth get-or-create client.cephfs
                    mon 'allow r'
mds 'allow r, allow rw path=/' osd 'allow rw pool=cephfs_data'
-o ceph.client.cephfs.keyring
```

```
[root@ceph-node1 ceph]# ceph auth get-or-create client.cephfs mon 'allow r' mds 'allow r, allow rw path=/' osd 'allow rw
pool=cephfs_data' -o ceph.client.cephfs.keyring
[root@ceph-node1 ceph]#
```

```
root@client-node1 # scp root@ceph-node1:/etc/ceph/
ceph.client.cephfs.keyring /etc/ceph/ceph.client.cephfs.keyring
root@client-node1 cat /etc/ceph/client.cephfs.keyring
```

```
[root@client-node1 ceph]# scp root@ceph-node1:/etc/ceph/ceph.client.cephfs.keyring /etc/
ceph/ceph.client.cephfs.keyring
root@ceph-node1's password:
ceph.client.cephfs.keyring                           100%   64     0.1KB/s   00:00
[root@client-node1 ceph]# cat /etc/ceph/ceph.client.cephfs.keyring
[client.cephfs]
    key = AQAimbFZAFAVOBAAsKsSAO9rtD9+dVWoj0CDDA==
[root@client-node1 ceph]#
```

Accessing Ceph FS through kernel driver

Native support for Ceph has been added in the Linux kernel 2.6.34 and the later versions. In this recipe, we will demonstrate how to access Ceph FS through the Linux kernel driver on `client-node1`.

How to do it...

In order for our client to have access to Ceph FS, we need to configure the client for accessing the cluster and mounting Ceph FS. Let's review how this is done:

1. Check your client's Linux kernel version:

   root@client-node1 # uname -r

2. Create a mount point directory in which you want to mount the filesystem:

   # mkdir /mnt/cephfs

3. Get the keys for the `client.cephfs` user, which we created in the last section. Execute the following command from the Ceph monitor node to get the user keys:

   # ceph auth get-key client.cephfs

4. Mount Ceph FS using the native Linux mount call with the following syntax:

   Syntax: # mount -t ceph <monitor _IP:Monitor_port>:/ <mount_point_name> -o name=admin,secret=<admin_user_key>

   # mount -t ceph ceph-node1:6789:/ /mnt/cephfs
   -o name=cephfs,secret=AQAimbFZAFAVOBAAsksSA09rtD9+dVWoj0CDDA==

```
[root@client-node1 ceph]# uname -r
3.10.0-514.26.2.el7.x86_64
[root@client-node1 ceph]# mkdir /mnt/cephfs
[root@client-node1 ceph]# ceph auth get-key client.cephfs
AQAimbFZAFAVOBAAsKsSA09rtD9+dVWoj0CDDA==[root@client-node1 ceph]#
[root@client-node1 ceph]# mount -t ceph ceph-node1:6789:/ /mnt/cephfs -o name=cephfs,sec
ret=AQAimbFZAFAVOBAAsKsSA09rtD9+dVWoj0CDDA==
[root@client-node1 ceph]# df -h /mnt/cephfs
Filesystem          Size  Used Avail Use% Mounted on
10.19.1.101:6789:/  162G  1.1G  161G   1% /mnt/cephfs
[root@client-node1 ceph]#
```

5. To mount Ceph FS more securely and avoid the admin key being visible in the command history, store the admin `keyring` as plain text in a separate file and use this file as a mount option for `secretkey`:

```
# echo AQAimbFZAFAVOBAAsksSA09rtD9+dVWoj0CDDA==
  > /etc/ceph/cephfskey
# mount -t ceph ceph-node1:6789:/ /mnt/cephfs
-o name=cephfs,secretfile=/etc/ceph/cephfskey
```

6. To allow the Ceph FS mount during the OS startup, add the following lines in the `/etc/fstab` file on `client-node1`:

Syntax: `<Mon_ipaddress>:<Monitor_port>:/ <mount_point>`
`<filesystem_name>`
`[name=username,secret=secretkey|secretfile=/<path/to/secretfile`
`],[{mount.options}]`

```
# echo "ceph-node1:6789:/ /mnt/cephfs ceph
  name=cephfs,secretfile=/etc/ceph/
       cephfskey,_netdev,noatime 0 0" >>
  /etc/fstab
```

Use the `_netdev` option to ensure that the filesystem is mounted after the networking subsystem to prevent networking issues.

7. `umount` and `mount` the Ceph FS again to validate clean mount:

```
# umount /mnt/cephfs
# mount /mnt/cephfs
```

```
[root@client-node1 ceph]# echo "ceph-node1:6789:/ /mnt/cephfs ceph name=cephfs,secretfil
e=/etc/ceph/cephfskey,_netdev,noatime 0 0" >> /etc/fstab
[root@client-node1 ceph]# cat /etc/fstab |grep -i cephfs
ceph-node1:6789:/ /mnt/cephfs ceph name=cephfs,secretfile=/etc/ceph/cephfskey,_netdev,no
atime 0 0
[root@client-node1 ceph]# umount /mnt/cephfs
[root@client-node1 ceph]# mount /mnt/cephfs
[root@client-node1 ceph]# df -h /mnt/cephfs
Filesystem          Size  Used Avail Use% Mounted on
10.19.1.101:6789:/  162G  1.1G  161G   1% /mnt/cephfs
[root@client-node1 ceph]#
```

8. Perform some I/O on the Ceph Filesystem and then umount it:

```
# dd if=/dev/zero of=/mnt/cephfs/file1 bs=1M count=1024
# umount /mnt/cephfs
```

```
[root@client-node1 ceph]# dd if=/dev/zero of=/mnt/cephfs/file1 bs=1M count=1024
1024+0 records in
1024+0 records out
1073741824 bytes (1.1 GB) copied, 14.8411 s, 72.3 MB/s
[root@client-node1 ceph]# ls -l /mnt/cephfs/file1
-rw-r--r-- 1 root root 1073741824 Sep  7 22:58 /mnt/cephfs/file1
[root@client-node1 ceph]# umount /mnt/cephfs
[root@client-node1 ceph]#
```

Accessing Ceph FS through FUSE client

The Ceph Filesystem is natively supported by the LINUX kernel; however, if your host is running on a lower kernel version or if you have any application dependency, you can always use the FUSE client for Ceph to mount Ceph FS.

How to do it...

Let's review how to configure FUSE client for access to the Ceph cluster and mounting Ceph FS:

1. Validate that the Ceph FUSE package is installed on the machine client-node1 (Ansible installs this as part of the client packages):

```
# rpm -qa |grep -i ceph-fuse
```

2. Validate that the Ceph FS keyring file is created client-node1 in /etc/ceph/ceph.client.cephfs.keyring, with the following contents (note your key will be different from the example):

```
[root@client-node1 ceph]# cat /etc/ceph/ceph.client.cephfs.keyring
[client.cephfs]
        key = AQAimbFZAFAVOBAAsKsSAO9rtD9+dVWoj0CDDA==
[root@client-node1 ceph]#
```

3. Mount Ceph FS using the FUSE client:

```
# ceph-fuse --keyring /etc/ceph/ceph.client.cephfs.keyring
            --name client.cephfs -m ceph-node1:6789 /mnt/cephfs
```

```
[root@client-node1 ceph]# ceph-fuse --keyring /etc/ceph/ceph.client.cephfs.keyring --nam
e client.cephfs -m ceph-node1:6789 /mnt/cephfs
ceph-fuse[4923]: starting ceph client
2017-09-07 23:18:46.778884 7fc873eedec0 -1 init, newargv = 0x7fc87f0f2a20 newargc=11
ceph-fuse[4923]: starting fuse
Aborted
[root@client-node1 ceph]# df -h /mnt/cephfs
Filesystem      Size  Used Avail Use% Mounted on
ceph-fuse       162G  4.1G  158G   3% /mnt/cephfs
[root@client-node1 ceph]#
```

4. To mount Ceph FS at OS boot, add the following lines to the /etc/fstab file on the client-node1:

```
# echo "id=cephfs,keyring=ceph.client.cephfs.keyring /mnt/cephfs
  fuse.ceph defaults 0 0 _netdev" >> /etc/fstab
# umount /mnt/cephfs
# mount /mnt/cephfs
```

```
[root@client-node1 ceph]# echo "id=cephfs,keyring=ceph.client.cephfs.keyring /mn
t/cephfs fuse.ceph defaults 0 0 _netdev" >> /etc/fstab
[root@client-node1 ceph]# umount /mnt/cephfs
[root@client-node1 ceph]# mount /mnt/cephfs
ceph-fuse[5062]: starting ceph client
2017-09-07 23:28:46.885160 7fe9fe11fec0 -1 init, newargv = 0x7fea09c4e1c0 newarg
c=13
ceph-fuse[5062]: starting fuse
[root@client-node1 ceph]# df -h /mnt/cephfs
Filesystem      Size  Used Avail Use% Mounted on
ceph-fuse       162G  4.1G  158G   3% /mnt/cephfs
[root@client-node1 ceph]#
```

Exporting the Ceph Filesystem as NFS

The **Network Filesystem (NFS)** is one of the most popular shareable filesystem protocols that can be used with every Unix-based system. Unix-based clients that do not understand the Ceph FS type can still access the Ceph Filesystem using NFS. To do this, we would require an NFS server in place that can re-export Ceph FS as an NFS share. NFS-Ganesha is an NFS server that runs in user space and supports the Ceph FS **File System Abstraction Layer (FSAL)** using libcephfs.

In this recipe, we will demonstrate creating `ceph-node1` as an NFS-Ganesha server and exporting Ceph FS as an NFS and mounting it on the `client-node1`.

How to do it...

Let's walk-through the steps to utilize `client-node1` as an NFS-Ganesha server to export Ceph FS as NFS:

1. On `ceph-node1`, install the packages required for `nfs-ganesha`:

   ```
   # sudo yum install -y nfs-utils nfs-ganesha
   ```

2. Since this is a test setup, disable the firewall. For the production setup, you might consider enabling the required ports over a firewall, which is generally `2049`:

   ```
   # systemctl stop firewalld; systemctl disable firewalld
   ```

3. Enable the `rpc` services required by NFS:

   ```
   # systemctl start rpcbind; systemctl enable rpcbind
   # systemctl start rpc-stat.d.service
   ```

4. Create the NFS-Ganesha configuration file, `/etc/ganesha.conf`, with the following content:

   ```
   [root@ceph-node1 ceph]# cat /etc/ganesha.conf
   EXPORT
   {
        Export_ID = 1;
        Path = "/";
        Pseudo = "/";
        Access_Type = RW;
        SecType = "none";
        NFS_Protocols = "3";
        Squash = No_Root_Squash;
        Transport_Protocols = TCP;

        FSAL {
                Name = CEPH;
        }
   }
   [root@ceph-node1 ceph]#
   ```

5. Finally, start the NFS Ganesha daemon by providing the `ganesha.conf` file that we created in the last step. You can verify the exported NFS share using the `showmount` command:

```
# ganesha.nfsd -f /etc/ganesha.conf -L /var/log/ganesha.log -N
NIV_DEBUG
# showmount -e
```

```
[root@ceph-node1 ceph]# ganesha.nfsd -f /etc/ganesha.conf -L /var/log/ganesha.log -N NIV_DEBU
G
[root@ceph-node1 ceph]# ps -ef |grep -i nfs
root       23674       1  0 23:50 ?        00:00:00 ganesha.nfsd -f /etc/ganesha.conf -L /var
/log/ganesha.log -N NIV_DEBUG
root       23705   22638  0 23:51 pts/1    00:00:00 grep --color=auto -i nfs
[root@ceph-node1 ceph]# 
```

Let's recall the steps that we have taken: `ceph-node2` has been configured as Ceph MDS, and `ceph-node1` has been configured as the NFS-Ganesha server. Next, in order to mount the NFS share on the client machines, we just need to install the NFS client packages and mount the share exported by `ceph-node1`, as shown next:

Install the NFS client packages on `client-node1` and `mount`:

```
root@client-node1 # yum install -y nfs-utils
                  # mkdir /mnt/cephfs
                  # mount -o rw,noatime 10.19.1.101:/ /mnt/cephfs
```

```
[root@client-node1 mnt]# mount -o rw,noatime 10.19.1.101:/ /mnt/cephfs
[root@client-node1 mnt]# df -h /mnt/cephfs
Filesystem       Size  Used Avail Use% Mounted on
10.19.1.101:/       0     0     0    - /mnt/cephfs
[root@client-node1 mnt]# 
```

Ceph FS – a drop-in replacement for HDFS

Hadoop is a programming framework that supports the processing and storage of large data sets in a distributed computing environment. The Hadoop core includes the analytics MapReduce engine and the distributed file system known as **Hadoop Distributed File System** (**HDFS**), which has several weaknesses that are listed as follows:

- It had a single point of failure until the recent versions of HDFS

- It isn't POSIX compliant

- It stores at least three copies of data

- It has a centralized name server resulting in scalability challenges

The Apache Hadoop project and other software vendors are working independently to fix these gaps in HDFS.

The Ceph community has done some development in this space, and it has a filesystem plugin for Hadoop that possibly overcomes the limitations of HDFS and can be used as a drop-in replacement for it. There are three requirements for using Ceph FS with HDFS; they are as follows:

- Running the Ceph cluster

- Running the Hadoop cluster

- Installing the Ceph FS Hadoop plugin

The Hadoop and HDFS implementation are beyond the scope of this book; however, in this section, we will superficially discuss how Ceph FS can be used in conjunction with HDFS. Hadoop clients can access Ceph FS through a Java-based plugin named `hadoop-cephfs.jar`. The two-java classes that follow are required to support Hadoop connectivity to Ceph FS.

- `libcephfs.jar`: This file should be placed in `/usr/share/java/`, and the path should be added to `HADOOP_CLASSPATH` in the `Hadoop_env.sh` file.

- `libcephfs_jni.so`: This file should be added to the `LD_LIBRARY_PATH` environment parameter and placed in `/usr/lib/hadoop/lib`. You should also soft link it to `/usr/lib/hadoop/lib/native/Linux-amd64-64/libcephfs_jni.so`.

In addition to this, the native Ceph FS client must be installed on each node of the Hadoop cluster. For more of the latest information on using Ceph FS for Hadoop, please visit the official Ceph documentation at `http://ceph.com/docs/master/cephfs/hadoop`, and Ceph GitHub at `https://github.com/ceph/cephfs-hadoop`.

Monitoring Ceph Clusters

7

In this chapter, we will cover the following recipes:

- Monitoring Ceph clusters – the classic way
- Introducing Ceph Metrics and Grafana
- Installing and configuring Ceph Metrics with the Grafana dashboard
- Monitoring Ceph Clusters with Ceph Metrics with the Grafana dashboard

Introduction

Whether you have a small, medium, or exascale cluster, monitoring is the most critical part of your infrastructure. As soon as you have done the designing, deployment, and production service implementation of your Ceph cluster, monitoring becomes the key responsibility of the storage administrator. In this chapter, we will learn multiple ways to monitor your Ceph cluster and its components. We will cover both the CLI and GUI monitoring of Ceph using its native CLI tools; we will also implement Ceph Metrics with Grafana which is an open source Ceph cluster monitoring dashboard.

Monitoring Ceph clusters – the classic way

As a storage administrator, you need to keep an eye on your Ceph storage cluster and find out what's going on at a given time. Regular and disciplined monitoring keeps you updated with your cluster health. Based on monitoring notifications, you get a bit more time to take necessary action before service outages.

Monitoring a Ceph cluster is an everyday task that includes the monitoring of MON, OSD, MDS, PG, as well as storage provisioning services, such as RBD, radosgw, Ceph FS, and Ceph clients. Ceph, by default, comes with a rich set of native command-line tools and APIs to perform monitoring on these components. In addition to this, there are also open source projects that are intentionally developed for monitoring Ceph clusters on a GUI one-view dashboard. In the following recipes, we will focus on Ceph CLI tools for cluster monitoring.

In this recipe, we will learn commands that are used to monitor the overall Ceph cluster.

How to do it...

Here is how we go about monitoring the Ceph cluster. The steps are explained topic-wise in the following sections.

Checking the cluster's health

To check the health of your cluster, use the `ceph` command followed by `health` as the command option:

```
# ceph health
```

The output of this command will be divided into several sections separated by a semicolon:

```
[root@ceph-node1 ~]# ceph health
HEALTH_WARN 64 pgs degraded; 1408 pgs stuck unclean; recovery 1/5744 objects degraded (0.017%)
[root@ceph-node1 ~]#
```

The first section of the output shows that your cluster is in the warning state, `HEALTH_WARN`, as `64 pgs degraded`. The second section represents that 1,408 PGs are not clean, and the third section of the output represents that cluster recovery is going on for 1 out of 5,744 objects and the cluster is 0.017% degraded. If your cluster is healthy, you will receive the output as `HEALTH_OK`.

To find out more details of your cluster health, use the `ceph health detail` command. This command will tell you all the PGs that are not active and clean, that is, all the PGs that are unclean, inconsistent, and degraded will be listed here with their details. If your cluster is healthy, you will receive the output as `HEALTH_OK`.

```
[root@ceph-node2 ceph]# ceph health detail
HEALTH_ERR 61 pgs degraded; 6 pgs inconsistent; 1312 pgs stuck unclean; recovery 3/5746 objects degraded (0.052%); 8 scrub errors
pg 9.76 is stuck unclean since forever, current state active+remapped, last acting [7,3,2]
pg 8.77 is stuck unclean since forever, current state active+remapped, last acting [4,6,8]
pg 7.78 is stuck unclean for 788849.714074, current state active+remapped, last acting [6,5,1]
pg 6.79 is stuck unclean since forever, current state active+remapped, last acting [4,7,8]
pg 5.7a is stuck unclean since forever, current state active+remapped, last acting [7,4,2]
pg 4.7b is stuck unclean since forever, current state active+remapped, last acting [7,3,1]
pg 11.74 is stuck unclean for 788413.925336, current state active+remapped, last acting [4,7,8]
pg 10.75 is stuck unclean for 788412.797947, current state active+remapped, last acting [7,3,0]
```

You can see in the previous image, we have PG states like active+remapped and with a given acting set. Here active means Ceph will process requests to the placement group and remapped means the placement group is temporarily mapped to a different set of OSDs from what CRUSH specified.

Monitoring cluster events

You can monitor cluster events using the ceph command with the -w option. This command will display all the cluster event's messages including information [INF], warning [WRN], and error [ERR] in real time. The output of this command will be continuous, live cluster changes; you can use *Ctrl + C* to get on to the shell:

```
# ceph -w
```

```
[root@ceph-node3 ~]#
[root@ceph-node3 ~]# ceph -w
    cluster 8e396f0b-81ba-4a79-8bf2-7d29be9de05b
     health HEALTH_ERR
            clock skew detected on mon.ceph-node2
            71 pgs are stuck inactive for more than 300 seconds
            71 pgs peering
            71 pgs stuck inactive
            71 pgs stuck unclean
            Monitor clock skew detected
     monmap e3: 3 mons at {ceph-node1=192.168.1.101:6789/0,ceph-node2=192.168.1.102:6789/0,ceph-node3=192.168.1.103:6789/0}
            election epoch 42, quorum 0,1,2 ceph-node1,ceph-node2,ceph-node3
     osdmap e100: 9 osds: 9 up, 9 in; 64 remapped pgs
            flags sortbitwise,require_jewel_osds
      pgmap v271: 128 pgs, 1 pools, 709 bytes data, 1 objects
            318 MB used, 161 GB / 161 GB avail
                  64 remapped+peering
                  57 active+clean
                   7 peering

2017-09-14 21:17:49.199614 mon.1 [WRN] message from mon.0 was stamped 0.095604s in the future, clocks not synchronized
2017-09-14 21:18:13.229524 mon.0 [WRN] mon.1 192.168.1.102:6789/0 clock skew 0.104511s > max 0.05s
2017-09-14 21:18:42.090731 mon.0 [INF] pgmap v272: 128 pgs: 57 active+clean, 64 remapped+peering, 7 peering; 709 bytes data, 318 MB used, 161 GB / 161 GB avail
^C[root@ceph-node3 ~]#
```

You can see in the preceding screenshot we have two types of event messages listed, WRN and INF, one for PG's recovery and another for monitor clock skew.

There are other options that can be used with the `ceph` command to gather different types of event details. They are as follows:

- `--watch-debug`: to watch debug events
- `--watch-info`: to watch info events
- `--watch-sec`: to watch security events
- `--watch-warn`: to watch warning events
- `--watch-error`: to watch error events

The cluster utilization statistics

To find out your cluster's space utilization statistics, use the `ceph` command with the `df` option. This command will show the total cluster size, the available size, the used size, and the percentage. This will also display the POOLS information, such as NAME, ID, utilization, and the number of objects in each pool:

```
# ceph df
```

The output is as follows:

```
[root@ceph-node1 ~]# ceph df
GLOBAL:
    SIZE      AVAIL     RAW USED     %RAW USED
    134G      127G      7440M          5.39
POOLS:
    NAME                    ID     USED      %USED     MAX AVAIL     OBJECTS
    rbd                     0      114M      0.08      42924M        2629
    images                  1      53002k    0.04      42924M        12
    volumes                 2      47        0         42924M        8
    vms                     3      208M      0.15      42924M        31
    .rgw.root               4      162       0         42924M        2
    .rgw.control            5      0         0         42924M        8
    .rgw                    6      2731      0         42924M        15
    .rgw.gc                 7      0         0         42924M        32
    .users.uid              8      736       0         42924M        4
    .users.email            9      8         0         42924M        1
    .users                  10     16        0         42924M        2
    .users.swift            11     8         0         42924M        1
    .rgw.buckets.index      12     0         0         42924M        9
    .rgw.buckets            13     1744      0         42924M        4
```

Ceph df command output for checking cluster usage

`ceph df` gives us details of USED, %USED, and OBJECTS in the cluster for each pool, we do have `ceph df detail` command. If you add the `detail switch` in the `ceph df` command, it will give you RAW USED, QUOTA OBJECTS details.

Checking the cluster's status

Checking the cluster's status is the most common and the most frequent operation when managing a Ceph cluster. You can check the status of your cluster using the `ceph` command and status as the option:

```
# ceph status
```

Instead of the status subcommand, you can also use a shorter version, `-s`, as an option:

```
# ceph -s
```

The following screenshot shows the status of our cluster:

```
[root@ceph-node2 ~]#
[root@ceph-node2 ~]# ceph -s
    cluster c3d8db32-808c-4f06-b585-d33c1d620846
     health HEALTH_OK
     monmap e1: 3 mons at {ceph-node1=192.168.1.101:6789/0,ceph-node2=192.168.1.102:6789/0,ceph-node3=192.168.1.103:6789/0}
            election epoch 14, quorum 0,1,2 ceph-node1,ceph-node2,ceph-node3
      fsmap e5: 1/1/1 up {0=ceph-node2=up:active}
     osdmap e102: 9 osds: 9 up, 9 in
            flags sortbitwise,require_jewel_osds
      pgmap v480: 224 pgs, 13 pools, 40166 kB data, 214 objects
            444 MB used, 161 GB / 161 GB avail
                 224 active+clean
[root@ceph-node2 ~]#
```

This command will dump a lot of useful information for your Ceph cluster:

- `cluster`: This command represents the Ceph unique cluster ID.
- `health`: This command shows the cluster health.
- `monmap`: This command represents the monitor map epoch version, monitor information, monitor election epoch version, and monitor quorum status.
- `fsmap`: This command represents the fsmap (mdsmap) epoch version and the fsmap (mdsmap) status.
- `osdmap`: This command represents the OSD map epoch, OSD total, up and in count.
- `pgmap`: This command shows the pgmap version, total number of PGs, pool count, capacity in use for a single copy, and total objects. It also displays information about cluster utilization including used size, free size, and total size. Finally, it will display the PG status.

In order to view the real-time cluster status, you can use `ceph status` with the Linux `watch` command to get the continuous output:

```
# watch ceph -s
```

The cluster authentication entries

Ceph works on an authentication system based on keys. All cluster components interact with each other once they undergo a key-based authentication system. You can use the `ceph` command with the `auth list` subcommand to get a list of all the keys:

```
# ceph auth list
```

To find out more about command operation, you can use help with the suboption. For instance, run # `ceph auth --help` and use the command as directed in the help.

Monitoring Ceph MON

Usually, a Ceph cluster is deployed with more than one MON instance for high availability. Since there is a large number of monitors, they should attain a quorum to make the cluster function properly.

How to do it...

We will now focus on Ceph commands for OSD monitoring. The steps will be explained topic-wise in the following sections.

Checking the MON status

To display the cluster's MON status and MON map, use the `ceph` command with either `mon stat` or the `mon dump` suboption:

```
# ceph mon stat
# ceph mon dump
```

The following screenshot displays the output of this command:

```
[root@ceph-node1 ~]# ceph mon stat
e3: 3 mons at {ceph-node1=192.168.1.101:6789/0,ceph-node2=192.168.1.102:6789/0,ceph-node3=192.168.1.103:6789/0}, election epoch 42, quorum 0,1,2 ceph-node1,ceph-node2,ceph-node3
[root@ceph-node1 ~]#
[root@ceph-node1 ~]# ceph mon dump
dumped monmap epoch 3
epoch 3
fsid 8e396f0b-81ba-4a79-8bf2-7d29be9de05b
last_changed 2017-08-06 07:05:54.148845
created 2017-08-06 06:41:37.688498
0: 192.168.1.101:6789/0 mon.ceph-node1
1: 192.168.1.102:6789/0 mon.ceph-node2
2: 192.168.1.103:6789/0 mon.ceph-node3
[root@ceph-node1 ~]#
```

Checking the MON quorum status

To maintain a quorum between Ceph MONs, the cluster should always have more than half of the available monitors in a Ceph cluster. Checking the quorum status of a cluster is very useful at the time of MON troubleshooting. You can check the quorum status by using the `ceph` command and the `quorum_status` subcommand:

```
# ceph quorum_status -f json-pretty
```

The following screenshot displays the output of this command:

```
[root@ceph-node1 ~]#
[root@ceph-node1 ~]# ceph quorum_status -f json-pretty
{
    "election_epoch": 42,
    "quorum": [
        0,
        1,
        2
    ],
    "quorum_names": [
        "ceph-node1",
        "ceph-node2",
        "ceph-node3"
    ],
    "quorum_leader_name": "ceph-node1",
    "monmap": {
        "epoch": 3,
        "fsid": "8e396f0b-81ba-4a79-8bf2-7d29be9de05b",
        "modified": "2017-08-06 07:05:54.148845",
        "created": "2017-08-06 06:41:37.688498",
        "mons": [
            {
                "rank": 0,
                "name": "ceph-node1",
                "addr": "192.168.1.101:6789\/0"
            },
            {
                "rank": 1,
                "name": "ceph-node2",
                "addr": "192.168.1.102:6789\/0"
            },
            {
                "rank": 2,
                "name": "ceph-node3",
                "addr": "192.168.1.103:6789\/0"
            }
        ]
    }
}
[root@ceph-node1 ~]#
```

The quorum status displays `election_epoch`, which is the election version number, and `quorum_leader_name`, which denotes the hostname of the quorum leader. It also displays the MON map epoch and cluster ID. Each cluster monitor is allocated with a rank. For I/O operations, clients first connect to the quorum lead monitor; if the leader MON is unavailable, the client then connects to the next rank monitor:

 To generate the formatted output for `ceph` commands, use the `-f json-pretty` option.

Monitoring Ceph OSDs

Monitoring OSDs is a crucial task and requires a lot of attention, as there are a lot of OSDs to monitor and take care of. The bigger your cluster, the more OSDs it will have and the more rigorous the monitoring it will require. Generally, Ceph clusters host a lot of disks, so the chances of facing an OSD failure are quite high.

How to do it...

We will now focus on `ceph` commands for OSD monitoring. The steps will be explained topic-wise in the following sections.

OSD tree view

The tree view in OSD is quite useful for knowing OSD statuses such as `in` or `out` and `up` or `down`. The tree view in OSD displays each node with all its OSDs and its location in the CRUSH map. You can check the tree view of OSD by using the following command:

```
# ceph osd tree
```

```
[root@ceph-node1 ~]#
[root@ceph-node1 ~]# ceph osd tree
ID WEIGHT   TYPE NAME              UP/DOWN REWEIGHT PRIMARY-AFFINITY
-1 0.15834 root default
-2 0.05278      host ceph-node1
 0 0.01759          osd.0            up    1.00000        1.00000
 1 0.01759          osd.1            up    1.00000        1.00000
 2 0.01759          osd.2            up    1.00000        1.00000
-3 0.05278      host ceph-node3
 3 0.01759          osd.3            up    1.00000        1.00000
 5 0.01759          osd.5            up    1.00000        1.00000
 7 0.01759          osd.7            up    1.00000        1.00000
-4 0.05278      host ceph-node2
 4 0.01759          osd.4            up    1.00000        1.00000
 6 0.01759          osd.6            up    1.00000        1.00000
 8 0.01759          osd.8            up    1.00000        1.00000
[root@ceph-node1 ~]#
```

This command displays various useful information for Ceph OSDs, such as WEIGHT, UP/DOWN status, and in/out status. The output will be beautifully formatted as per your Ceph CRUSH map. If you were maintaining a big cluster, this format would be beneficial to locating your OSDs and their hosting server from a long list.

OSD statistics

To check OSD statistics, use # ceph osd stat; this command will help you get the OSD map epoch, total OSD count, and their in and up statuses.

To get detailed information about the Ceph cluster and OSD, execute the following command:

```
# ceph osd dump
```

This is a very useful command that will output the OSD map epoch, pool details including pool ID, pool name, pool type, that is, replicated or erasure, CRUSH ruleset, replication size, min_size (minimum number of up/in OSD's in a PG to serve the IO), and PGs. This command will also display information for each OSD, such as the OSD ID, status, weight, last clean interval epoch, and so on. All this information is extremely helpful for cluster monitoring and troubleshooting.

You can also make an OSD blacklist to prevent it from connecting to other OSDs so that no heartbeat process can take place. It's mostly used to prevent a lagging Metadata Server from making bad changes to data on the OSD. Usually, blacklists are maintained by Ceph itself and shouldn't need manual intervention, but it's good to know.

To display blacklisted clients, execute the following command:

```
# ceph osd blacklist ls
```

Checking the CRUSH map

We can query the CRUSH map directly from the `ceph osd` commands. The CRUSH map command-line utility can save a lot of the system administrator's time as compared to the conventional way of viewing and editing it after the decompilation of the CRUSH map:

- To view the CRUSH map, execute the following command:

  ```
  # ceph osd crush dump
  ```

- To view the CRUSH map rules, execute the following command:

  ```
  # ceph osd crush rule list
  ```

- To view the detailed CRUSH rule, execute the following command:

  ```
  # ceph osd crush rule dump <crush_rule_name>
  ```

The following figure displays the output of our query CRUSH map:

```
[root@ceph-node1 ~]# ceph osd crush rule list
[
    "replicated_ruleset"
]
[root@ceph-node1 ~]# ceph osd crush rule dump replicated_ruleset
{
    "rule_id": 0,
    "rule_name": "replicated_ruleset",
    "ruleset": 0,
    "type": 1,
    "min_size": 1,
    "max_size": 10,
    "steps": [
        {
            "op": "take",
            "item": -1,
            "item_name": "default"
        },
        {
            "op": "chooseleaf_firstn",
            "num": 0,
            "type": "host"
        },
        {
            "op": "emit"
        }
    ]
}
[root@ceph-node1 ~]#
```

If you are managing a large Ceph cluster with several hundreds of OSDs, it's sometimes difficult to find the location of a specific OSD in the CRUSH map. It's also difficult if your CRUSH map contains a multiple bucket hierarchy. You can use ceph osd find to search for an OSD and its location in a CRUSH map:

```
# ceph osd find <Numeric_OSD_ID>
```

```
[root@ceph-node1 ~]#
[root@ceph-node1 ~]# ceph osd find 1
{
    "osd": 1,
    "ip": "192.168.1.101:6808\/8690",
    "crush_location": {
        "host": "ceph-node1",
        "root": "default"
    }
}
[root@ceph-node1 ~]#
```

Monitoring PGs

OSDs store PGs and each PG contains objects. The overall health of a cluster depends majorly on PGs. The cluster will remain in a HEALTH_OK status only if all the PGs are on the status, active+clean. If your Ceph cluster is not healthy, then there are chances that the PGs are not active+clean. Placement groups can exhibit multiple states and even combinations of states. The following are some states that a PG can be:

- **Creating**: The PG is being created.
- **Peering**: The process of bringing all of the OSDs that store PGs into agreement about the state of all objects including their metadata in that PG.
- **Active**: Once the peering operation is completed, Ceph lists the PG as active. Under the active state, the data in the PG data is available on the primary PG and its replica for the I/O operation.
- **Clean**: A clean state means that the primary and secondary OSDs have successfully peered and no PG moves away from their correct location. It also shows that PGs are replicated the correct number of times.
- **Down**: This means that the replica with the necessary data is down, so the PG is offline.
- **Degraded**: Once an OSD is down, Ceph changes the state of all the PGs that are assigned to that OSD to degraded. After the OSD comes up, it has to peer again to make the degraded PGs clean. If the OSD remains down and out for more than 300 seconds, Ceph recovers all the PGs that are degraded from their replica PGs to maintain the replication count. Clients can perform I/O even after PGs are in the degraded stage.
- **Recovering**: When an OSD goes down, the content of the PGs of that OSD fall behind the contents of the replica PGs on other OSDs. Once the OSD comes up, Ceph initiates a recovery operation on the PGs to keep them up to date with the replica PGs in other OSDs.
- **Backfilling**: As soon as a new OSD is added to the cluster, Ceph tries to rebalance the data by moving some PGs from other OSDs to this new OSD; this process is known as backfilling. Once the backfilling is completed for the PGs, the OSD can participate in the client I/O.
- **Remapped**: Whenever there is a change in the PG acting set, data migration happens from the old acting set OSD to the new acting set OSD. This operation might take some time depending on the data size that is being migrated to the new OSD. During this time, the old primary OSD of the old acting group serves to the client request. As soon as the data migration operation completes, Ceph uses new primary OSDs from the acting group.

An acting set refers to a group of OSDs responsible for PGs. The first OSD is known as the primary OSD from the acting set and is responsible for the peering and replication operations for each PG with its secondary OSDs. It also entertains I/O operations from clients. The OSD, which is up, remains in the acting set. Once the primary OSD is down, it is first removed from the up set; the secondary OSD is then promoted to be the primary OSD.

- **Stale**: Ceph OSD reports their statistics to the Ceph monitor every 0.5 seconds; by any chance, if the primary OSDs of the PG acting set fail to report their statistics to the monitors, or if other OSDs have reported the primary OSD down, the monitor will consider those PGs as stale.
- **Inconsistent:** Ceph detects inconsistencies in one or more replica OSD of an object or multiple objects in the placement group (for example, objects are the wrong size, objects are missing from one replica *after* recovery finished, and so on).
- **Undersized**: The placement group has fewer copies than the configured replication size.
- **Incomplete**: Ceph detects that a placement group has missing information about writes that may have occurred, or does not have any healthy copies.
- **Snaptrim**: The PGs are currently being trimmed.
- **Snaptrim_wait**: The PGs are waiting to be trimmed.

You can monitor PGs using the following commands:

- To get the PG status, run # `ceph pg stat`:

```
[root@ceph-node1 ~]# ceph pg stat
v20780: 1628 pgs: 1628 active+clean; 2422 MB data, 7440 MB used, 127 GB / 134 GB avail
[root@ceph-node1 ~]#
```

The output of the `pg stat` command will display a lot of information in a specific format: `vNNNN: X pgs: Y active+clean; R MB data, U MB used, F GB / T GB avail`.

Where the variables are defined as follows:

- vNNNN: This is the PG map version number
- X: The total number of PGs

- Y: The number of PGs that have an `active+clean` state
- R: The raw data stored
- U: The real data stored after replication
- F: The free capacity remaining
- T: The total capacity

- To get the PG list, execute the following command:

```
# ceph pg dump -f json-pretty
```

This command will generate a lot of essential information with respect to PGs, such as the PG map version, PG ID, PG state, acting set, acting set primary, and so on.
The output of this command can be huge depending on the number of PGs in your cluster and if you want, you can run with `json-pretty`; it will dump the output in plain text.

- To query a particular PG for detailed information, execute the following command, which has the syntax as `ceph pg <PG_ID> query`:

```
# ceph pg <pg_id> query
```

- To list stuck PGs, execute the following command that has the syntax as `ceph pg dump_stuck < unclean | Inactive | stale >`:

```
# ceph pg dump_stuck unclean
```

Monitoring Ceph MDS

Metadata Servers are used only for Ceph FS, which is not production-ready as of now. The Metadata Server has several states, such as `UP`, `DOWN`, `ACTIVE`, and `INACTIVE`. While performing the monitoring of MDS, you should make sure the state of MDS is `UP` and `ACTIVE`. The following commands will help you get information related to the Ceph MDS.

How to do it...

You can use the following commands to check the details of the Ceph Filesystem:

1. Check the Ceph FS Filesystem list:

```
# ceph fs ls
```

2. Check the MDS status:

    # **ceph mds stat**

The output is shown in the following screenshot:

```
[root@ceph-node2 ~]#
[root@ceph-node2 ~]# ceph fs ls
name: cephfs, metadata pool: cephfs_metadata, data pools: [cephfs_data ]
[root@ceph-node2 ~]#
[root@ceph-node2 ~]# ceph mds stat
e5: 1/1/1 up {0=ceph-node2=up:active}
[root@ceph-node2 ~]#
```

3. Display the details of the Metadata Server:

    # **ceph mds dump**

The output is shown in the following screenshot:

```
[root@ceph-node2 ~]#
[root@ceph-node2 ~]# ceph mds dump
dumped fsmap epoch 5
fs_name cephfs
epoch   5
flags   0
created 2017-09-16 00:19:15.167808
modified        2017-09-16 00:19:15.167808
tableserver     0
root    0
session_timeout 60
session_autoclose       300
max_file_size   1099511627776
last_failure    0
last_failure_osd_epoch  0
compat  compat={},rocompat={},incompat={1=base v0.20,2=client writeable ranges,3=default file layouts on dirs,
4=dir inode in separate object,5=mds uses versioned encoding,6=dirfrag is stored in omap,8=file layout v2}
max_mds 1
in      0
up      {0=44387}
failed
damaged
stopped
data_pools      11
metadata_pool   12
inline_data     disabled
44387:  192.168.1.102:6801/3079238059 'ceph-node2' mds.0.4 up:active seq 2
[root@ceph-node2 ~]#
```

Introducing Ceph Metrics and Grafana

Ceph Metrics is a tool that allows a user to visually monitor various metrics in a running Ceph cluster. It has two components collectd and Grafana.

collectd

collectd is a daemon which collects system and application performance metrics periodically and delivers a method to store the values in different ways. It collects metrics from various sources, for example, the operating system platform, user applications, system and user log files, and external devices, and accumulates this information or makes it available over the network.

In Ceph Metrics, the Ceph nodes will have collectd installed along with collector plugins from `cephmetrics-collectd`.

Grafana

Grafana is an open source, feature rich metrics dashboard and graph editor for Graphite, Elasticsearch, OpenTSDB, Prometheus, and InfluxDB. It has a tagline *The open platform for beautiful analytics and monitoring.*

In Ceph Metrics the dashboard host will have Grafana installed and configured to display various dashboards by querying data received from Ceph nodes through a Graphite-Web, Python-Carbon, and Python-Whisper stack: `https://github.com/ceph/cephmetrics`.

 GitHub link for Ceph Metrics project: `https://github.com/ceph/cephmetrics`.

Installing and configuring Ceph Metrics with the Grafana dashboard

You have used `ceph-ansible` to set up your cluster, and you can use the same `ceph-ansible` virtual machine to install `cephmetrics` to take advantage of the inventory file—`/etc/ansible/hosts`.

How to do it...

We will use the following commands for configuring Ceph Metrics in `ceph-node1`:

1. In this book, `ceph-ansible` virtual machine is `ceph-node1`. Perform the following steps in `ceph-node1`. This will install repositories which include the `cephmetrics` packages and its dependencies.

   ```
   sudo su -
   mkdir ~/cephmetrics
   curl -L -o /etc/yum.repos.d/cephmetrics.repo
   http://download.ceph.com/cephmetrics/rpm-
                              master/el7/cephmetrics.repo
   yum install cephmetrics-ansible -y
   ```

2. Edit the inventory file.

   You need to modify `/etc/ansible/hosts` to add Ceph Metrics node and in this book, we are using `ceph-node1` as Ceph Metrics node. If you are running `ansible-playbook` on a host mentioned in the inventory file, you will need to append `ansible_connection=local` to each line in the inventory file that mentions that host.

3. After adding the inventory, the file format looks like this:

   ```
   [ceph-grafana]
   ceph-node1 ansible_connection=local

   [mons]
   ceph-node1 ansible_connection=local
   ceph-node2
   ceph-node3

   [osds]
   ceph-node1 ansible_connection=local
   ceph-node2
   ceph-node3

   [rgws]
   rgw-node1
   ```

At the time of writing this book, Ceph Metrics was in development mode for CentOS and Ubuntu, and we had continuous enhancement going on for some of its limitations. Ceph Metrics limitations are listed in the following README screenshot.

This file is present in the `ceph-node1` VM path: `/usr/share/cephmetrics-ansible/README.md`:

```
[root@ceph-node1 cephmetrics-ansible]# cat README.md
# Deploying cephmetrics with ansible

This set of ansible roles, in combination with `playbook.yml`, provide a way to deploy cephmetrics to monitor a Ceph cluster.

## Prerequisites
- RHEL 7 is supported with `devel_mode` set to `True` or `False`. Ubuntu 16.04 and CentOS 7 are supported only when `devel_mode` is `True` at this point.
- Currently only RHEL 7 is supported for all hosts
- A functional [ceph](https://ceph.com/) cluster. [collectd](https://collectd.org/) will be used to collect metrics
- A separate host to receive data pushed by hosts in the Ceph cluster, and run the dashboard to display that data.
- An inventory file describing your cluster.
- A host on which to execute `ansible-playbook` to orchestrate the deployment. This can be the same as the dashboard host.
- Passwordless SSH access from the deploy host to the ceph hosts. The username should be the same for all hosts.
- Passwordless sudo access on the ceph and dashboard hosts
- All hosts must share the same DNS domain

## Roles
- [ceph-collectd](./roles/ceph-collectd/): Used for ceph cluster hosts
- [ceph-grafana](./roles/ceph-grafana/): Used for the dashboard host

## Variables
You may override certain variables by creating a `vars.yml` file:
- `ansible_ssh_user`: The user account use for SSH connections. This may also be set on a per-host basis in the inventory file.
- `cluster`: The name of the Ceph cluster. Default: ceph
- `firewalld_zone`: The `firewalld` zone to use when opening ports for Grafana and Carbon. Default: public
- `devel_mode`: Whether to perform a development-mode deployment vs. a production deployment. Default: true
- `whisper`: May be used to configure [whisper retention](http://graphite.readthedocs.io/en/latest/config-carbon.html#storage-schemas-conf) settings. Default:
    ```
    whisper:
      retention:
        - ['10s', '7d']
        - ['1m', '30d']
        - ['15m', '5y']
    ```
- `update_alerts`: Whether to update the alerts dashboard along with the rest. Removes any user-defined alerts. Default: false

These variables are only relevent when `devel_mode` is true:
- `use_epel`: Whether or not to use EPEL and grafana.com instead of ceph.com-sourced packages for dependencies. Default: false

## Current Limitations

- Currently, metrics are only *displayed* for `osd` and `rgw` hosts.
- Authentication for grafana and graphite is fixed and creates a user `admin` with password `admin`.
- Services are deployed on the dashboard host directly; there is not yet support for a containerized deployment.

## Usage
If you are not overriding any variables:
    ```
    ansible-playbook -v -i ./inventory
    ```
Or, if you are:
    ```
    ansible-playbook -v -i ./inventory -e '@vars.yml'
    ```
```

4. For CentOS installation, we need to change the `devel_mode` and the `use_epel` from `false` to `true` in `roles/cephmetrics-common/defaults/main.yml` file:

```
use_epel: true
devel_mode: true
```

```
[root@ceph-node1 cephmetrics-ansible]#
[root@ceph-node1 cephmetrics-ansible]# cat roles/cephmetrics-common/defaults/main.yml | egrep -i 'devel_mode|use_epel'
  use_epel: true
  devel_mode: true
[root@ceph-node1 cephmetrics-ansible]# _
```

5. Add the following lines at the top of the `roles/ceph-collectd/tasks/configure_collectd.yml` file because Ceph Metrics is still in development—this was a known issue so we need to do it by manually editing it:

```
- name: Set collectd_dir
  set_fact:
  collectd_dir: "/usr/lib{{ '64' if ansible_pkg_mgr == 'yum'
else '' }}/collectd"

- name: Set collectd_cephmetrics_dir
  set_fact:
  collectd_cephmetrics_dir: "{{ collectd_dir }}/cephmetrics"
```

6. Run the Ceph Metrics playbook:

```
ansible-playbook -v playbook.yml
```

```
[root@ceph-node1 ~]#
[root@ceph-node1 ~]# cd /usr/share/cephmetrics-ansible
[root@ceph-node1 cephmetrics-ansible]# ansible-playbook -v playbook.yml
Using /usr/share/cephmetrics-ansible/ansible.cfg as config file

PLAY [ceph-grafana] **************************************************************************

TASK [Gathering Facts] **********************************************************************
ok: [ceph-node1]
```

7. Once completed, you will have the following output having dashboard link and username and password:

```
PLAY [localhost] ****************************************************************************************

TASK [Print dashboard URL] *****************************************************************************
ok: [localhost] => {
    "msg": "All done! You may access your dashboard at http://ceph-node1:3000/ with user 'admin' and password 'admin'."
}

PLAY RECAP *********************************************************************************************
ceph-node1                 : ok=65    changed=35    unreachable=0    failed=0
ceph-node2                 : ok=27    changed=12    unreachable=0    failed=0
ceph-node3                 : ok=27    changed=12    unreachable=0    failed=0
localhost                  : ok=1     changed=0     unreachable=0    failed=0
rgw-node1                  : ok=27    changed=12    unreachable=0    failed=0

[root@ceph-node1 cephmetrics-ansible]#
```

Monitoring Ceph clusters with Ceph Metrics with the Grafana dashboard

In this recipe, you will see how to monitor a Ceph cluster with the help of Ceph Metrics with the Grafana dashboard. The dashboard has information about the major Ceph daemons and their performances.

How to do it ...

You should use the Grafana login page by using the link `ceph-node1:3000/login` and username and password as `admin`:

1. Log in to the dashboard with the help of the given link and username/password:

2. Once you log in, you will have the following dashboard:

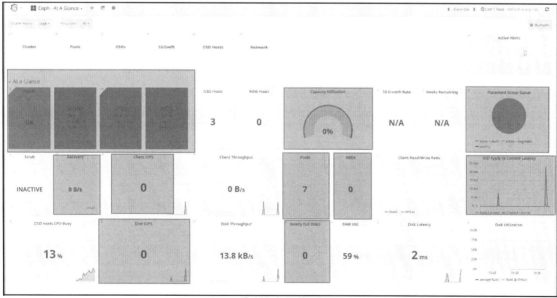

Ceph Metrics Dashboard

The first light green tab in the preceding dashboard screenshot is nothing but the cluster health which is HEALTH_OK and after that, the three dark green tabs are MON, OSD, and MDS and they are giving the total number of daemons:

- For MON, you can see we have three MONs and all three are in the quorum
- For OSD, you can see we have nine OSDs and all nine are up and in
- For MDS, we can see we do not have any MDS because we do not have a MDS daemon running

Following is the cluster status from the command line for the previous Ceph Metrics dashboard screenshot:

```
[root@ceph-node1 ~]# ceph -s
    cluster 69af1beb-6726-49eb-acdf-3841f42686db
     health HEALTH_OK
     monmap e1: 3 mons at {ceph-node1=192.168.1.101:6789/0,ceph-node2=192.168.1.102:6789/0,ceph-node3=192.168.1.103:6789/0}
            election epoch 84, quorum 0,1,2 ceph-node1,ceph-node2,ceph-node3
     osdmap e119: 9 osds: 9 up, 9 in
            flags sortbitwise,require_jewel_osds
      pgmap v31197: 112 pgs, 7 pools, 1702 bytes data, 175 objects
            382 MB used, 161 GB / 161 GB avail
                 112 active+clean
  client io 102 B/s rd, 0 op/s rd, 0 op/s wr
[root@ceph-node1 ~]#
```

The dashboard also has the following tabs:

- **Capacity Utilization**: Cluster capacity utilization
- **Placement Group Status**: Placement group states—active+clean (green color), active+degraded (yellow color), and peering (blue color)
- **Recovery**: Cluster data rebalance—recovery and backfill
- **Client IOPS**: The client IOPS
- **Pools**: Number of Pools
- **RBDs**: Number of RBD images
- **OSD Apply vs Commit Latency**: OSD Filestore apply vs commit latency, helps in tracking the OSD Filestore performance

The last row has Ceph cluster system resources:

- **Disk IOPS**: This is a tab which has information about cluster OSD node disk IOPS
- **Nearly Full Disks**: This covers the nearly full disks in the cluster

This dashboard screenshot has cluster health as HEALTH_WARN, because some of the placement groups were having three placement group states—peering (blue), active+degraded (yellow) and active+clean (green) and if all placement groups are not active+clean then the cluster health will be in the warning state:

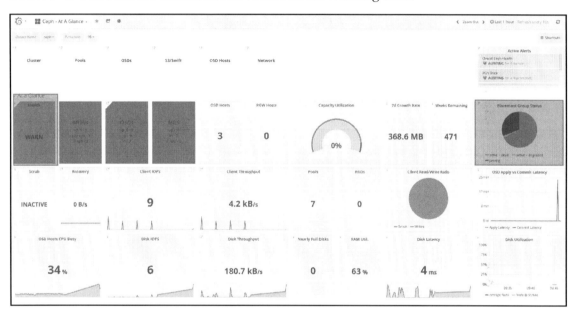

Ceph Metrics Dashboard in Health Warn with different PG states

 Most of the tabs in the dashboard take you to a new dashboard window which will have complete information about that tab.

For example, the **Health** tab in detail:

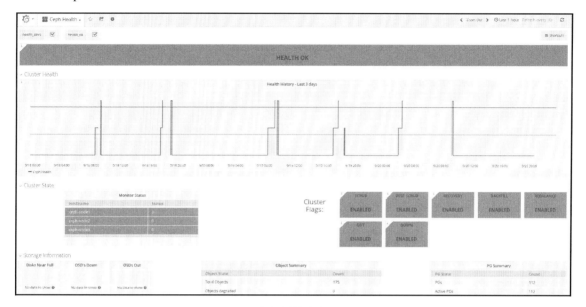

Ceph Health in detail

Third-row disk tabs:

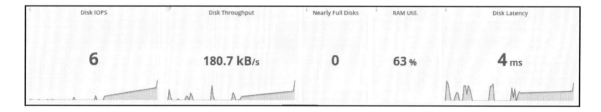

You will have the following dashboard if you click on any one of the tabs that are above the disk related tab:

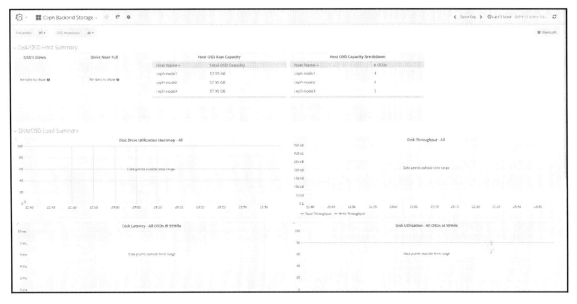

OSD disk tab in detail

Ceph Metrics can also report your RGW statistics and S3/SWIFT protocol details. You can see in the previous image, it has **RGW Hosts** and **S3/SWIFT** tabs.

8
Operating and Managing a Ceph Cluster

In this chapter, we will cover the following recipes:

- Understanding Ceph service management
- Managing the cluster configuration file
- Running Ceph with SYSTEMD
- Scale-up versus scale-out
- Scaling out your Ceph cluster
- Scaling down your Ceph cluster
- Replacing a failed disk in the Ceph cluster
- Upgrading your Ceph cluster
- Maintaining a Ceph cluster

Introduction

At this point, I'm sure you are pretty confident in Ceph cluster deployment, provisioning, as well as monitoring. In this chapter, we will cover standard topics such as Ceph service management. We will also cover advanced topics such as scaling up your cluster using ceph-ansible by adding OSD and MON nodes and finally, upgrading the Ceph cluster followed by some maintenance operations.

Understanding Ceph service management

Every component of Ceph, whether it's MON, OSD, MDS, or RGW, runs as a service on top of an underlying operating system. As a Ceph storage administrator, you should know about the Ceph services and how to operate them. As per Red Hat based distributions, Ceph daemons are managed as a traditional systemd manager service. Each time you start, restart, and stop Ceph daemons (or your entire cluster), you must specify at least one option and one command. You may also specify a daemon type or a daemon instance. The general syntax for this is as follows:

```
systemctl [options...] command [service name...]
```

The `systemctl` options include:

- `--help` or `-h`: Prints a short help text
- `--all` or `-a`: When listing units, show all loaded units, regardless of their state
- `--signal` or `-s`: When used will kill, choose which signal to send to the selected process
- `--force` or `-f`: When used with enable, overwrites any existing conflicting symlinks
- `--host` or `-h`: Execute an operation on a remote host

The `systemctl` commands include the following:

- `status`: Shows status of the daemon
- `start`: Starts the daemon
- `stop`: Stops the daemon

- `restart`: Stops and then starts the daemon
- `kill`: Kills the specified daemon
- `reload`: Reloads the config file without interrupting pending operations
- `list-units`: Lists known units managed by systemd
- `condrestart`: Restarts if the service is already running
- `enable`: Turns the service on for the next boot or other triggering event
- `disable`: Turns the service off for the next boot or other triggering event
- `is-enabled`: Used to check whether a service is configured to start or not in the current environment

`systemctl` can target the following Ceph service types:

- `ceph-mon`
- `ceph-osd`
- `ceph-mds`
- `ceph-radosgw`

Managing the cluster configuration file

If you are managing a large cluster, it's good practice to keep your cluster configuration file (`/etc/ceph/ceph.conf`) updated with information about cluster MONs, OSDs, MDSs, and RGW nodes. With these entries in place, you can manage all your cluster services from a single node.

How to do it...

`ceph-ansible` manages all aspects of the ceph configuration file that we will be using to update our cluster configuration. In order to achieve this, we will be updating the Ceph configuration file using the `ceph_conf_overrides` section of the `/etc/ansible/group_vars/all.yml` file and will be adding the details of all MON, OSD, and MDS nodes. Ansible supports the same sections as the Ceph configuration file: `[global]`, `[mon]`, `[osd]`, `[mds]`, `[rgw]`, and so on.

Adding monitor nodes to the Ceph configuration file

Since we have three monitor nodes, add their details to the `ceph_conf_overrides` section of the `all.yml` file:

1. In `ceph-node1` in the `/usr/share/ceph-ansible/group_vars` directory, edit the `ceph_conf_overrides` section of the `all.yml` to reflect the three monitors in the cluster:

```
##################
# CONFIG OVERRIDE #
##################

# Ceph configuration file override.
# This allows you to specify more configuration options
# using an INI style format.
# The following sections are supported: [global], [mon], [osd], [mds], [rgw]
#
# Example:
# ceph_conf_overrides:
#   global:
#     foo: 1234
#     bar: 5678
#
ceph_conf_overrides:
  mon:
    mon data: /var/lib/ceph/mon/$cluster-$id
  mon.ceph-node1:
    host: ceph-node1
    mon addr: ceph-node1:6789
  mon.ceph-node2:
    host: ceph-node2
    mon addr: ceph-node2:6789
  mon.ceph-node3:
    host: ceph-node3
    mon addr: ceph-node3:6789
```

2. Save the updated `all.yml` file and re-run the playbook from the `/usr/share/ceph-ansible` directory:

   ```
   # ansible-playbook site.yml
   ```

3. Validate that the Ceph configuration file has properly updated the monitor nodes in the cluster by viewing the `/etc/ceph/ceph.conf` file:

```
[mon]
        mon data = /var/lib/ceph/mon/$cluster-$id
[mon.ceph-node1]
        host = ceph-node1
        mon addr = ceph-node1:6789
[mon.ceph-node2]
        host = ceph-node2
        mon addr = ceph-node2:6789
[mon.ceph-node3]
        host = ceph-node3
        mon addr = ceph-node3:6789
```

 The spacing and format of the `all.yml` file needs to be exactly as seen in the screenshot and example or else when the ansible-playbook is run, it will error out due to improper format.

Adding an MDS node to the Ceph configuration file

As in the monitors, let's add MDS node details to the `/etc/ceph/ceph.conf` file from `ceph-node1` using Ansible:

1. On `ceph-node1` in the `/usr/share/ceph-ansible/group_vars` directory, edit the `ceph_conf_overrides` section of the `all.yml` to reflect the MDS nodes details. As with the monitors, please be careful with the formatting of the file or the running of the playbook will fail with a formatting error:

```
ceph_conf_overrides:
    mon:
        mon data: /var/lib/ceph/mon/$cluster-$id
    mon.ceph-node1:
        host: ceph-node1
        mon addr: ceph-node1:6789
    mon.ceph-node2:
        host: ceph-node2
        mon addr: ceph-node2:6789
    mon.ceph-node3:
        host: ceph-node3
        mon addr: ceph-node3:6789

    mds.ceph-node2:
        host: ceph-node2
```

2. Save the updated `all.yml` file and re-run the playbook from the `/usr/share/ceph-ansible` directory:

   ```
   # ansible-playbook site.yml
   ```

3. Validate that the Ceph configuration file updated the MDS node in the cluster by viewing the `/etc/ceph/ceph.conf` file:

```
[mds]

[mds.ceph-node2]
            host = ceph-node2
```

Adding OSD nodes to the Ceph configuration file

Now, let's add the OSD nodes details to the `/etc/ceph/ceph.conf` file from `ceph-node1` using Ansible:

1. On `ceph-node1` in the `/usr/share/ceph-ansible/group_vars` directory, edit the `ceph_conf_overrides` section of the `all.yml` to reflect the OSD nodes details. As with the monitors, please be careful with the formatting of the file or the running of the playbook will fail with a formatting error:

```
ceph_conf_overrides:
  mon:
    mon data: /var/lib/ceph/mon/$cluster-$id
  mon.ceph-node1:
    host: ceph-node1
    mon addr: ceph-node1:6789
  mon.ceph-node2:
    host: ceph-node2
    mon addr: ceph-node2:6789
  mon.ceph-node3:
    host: ceph-node3
    mon addr: ceph-node3:6789

  mds.ceph-node2:
    host: ceph-node2

  osd:
    osd data: /var/lib/ceph/osd/$cluster-$id
    osd journal: /var/lib/ceph/osd/$cluster-$id/journal
  osd.0:
    host: ceph-node1
  osd.1:
    host: ceph-node1
  osd.2:
    host: ceph-node1
  osd.3:
    host: ceph-node2
  osd.4:
    host: ceph-node2
  osd.5:
    host: ceph-node2
  osd.6:
    host: ceph-node3
  osd.7:
    host: ceph-node3
  osd.8:
    host: ceph-node3
```

2. Save the updated `all.yml` file and re-run the playbook from the `/usr/share/ceph-ansible` directory:

```
# ansible-playbook site.yml
```

3. Validate that the Ceph configuration file properly updated the OSD nodes in the cluster by viewing the `/etc/ceph/ceph.conf` file:

```
[osd]
        osd data = /var/lib/ceph/osd/$cluster-$id
        osd journal = /var/lib/ceph/osd/$cluster-$id/journal
[osd.0]
        host = ceph-node1
[osd.1]
        host = ceph-node1
[osd.2]
        host = ceph-node1
[osd.3]
        host = ceph-node2
[osd.4]
        host = ceph-node2
[osd.5]
        host = ceph-node2
[osd.6]
        host = ceph-node3
[osd.7]
        host = ceph-node3
[osd.8]
        host = ceph-node3
```

Running Ceph with systemd

Ceph process management is done through the systemd service. Systemd is a replacement for the UNIX System V systems (**SYSVINIT**). The general syntax for managing Ceph daemons using systemd is `systemctl [options] {command} {service/target}`.

How to do it...

Let's have a detailed look at managing Ceph daemons using systemd:

Starting and stopping all daemons

To start or stop all Ceph daemons, perform the following set of commands.

Let's see how to start and stop all Ceph daemons:

1. To start all Ceph services on a particular node, execute the systemd manager for the Ceph unit with the `start` command. This command will start all Ceph services that you have deployed for this node:

   ```
   # systemctl start ceph.target
   ```

2. To stop all Ceph services on one particular node, execute the systemd manager for the Ceph unit using the `stop` command. This command will stop all Ceph services that you have deployed for this node:

   ```
   # systemctl stop ceph\*.service ceph\*.target
   ```

3. To start/stop all Ceph services on a remote host, execute the systemd manager with the `-H` option (specifying the remote hostname) with the `start` or `stop` command on the Ceph unit.

4. To start all Ceph services for `ceph-node2` from `ceph-node1` use the following command:

   ```
   root@ceph-node1 # systemctl -H ceph-node2 start ceph.target
   ```

5. To stop all Ceph services for `ceph-node2` from `ceph-node1` use the following command:

   ```
   root@ceph-node1 # systemctl -H ceph-node2 stop ceph\*.service
   ceph\*.target
   ```

Since your `ceph.conf` file has all of your Ceph hosts defined and your current node can `ssh` to all those other nodes you can use the `-H` option to start and stop all Ceph services for a particular host from another remote host. The `ceph.conf` file should be identical in all the nodes.

Querying systemd units on a node

To list the Ceph systemd units on a Ceph node, perform the following set of commands.

Let's see how to determine which Ceph services are running on a particular node. This can be helpful to determine the location of which OSD or MON services are running on a certain node:

1. To list all the Ceph systemd units on a node, execute the systemd manager for the Ceph service/target using the `status` command. This command will display all active services/targets systemd has loaded:

    # **systemctl status ceph*.service ceph*.target**

2. To list the status on a particular Ceph service, execute the systemd manager for the specified Ceph service using the `status` command. To check the status of `mon.0` issue:

    root@ceph-node1 # systemctl status ceph-mon@ceph-node1

    To check the status of `osd.1` issue:

    root@ceph-node1 # systemctl status ceph-osd@1

3. To list all the systemd units on a particular node from a remote host, execute the systemd manager with the -H option (specifying the remote hostname) using the `status` command. This command will display all active services/targets systemd has loaded on a remote host. To check all systemd units on `ceph-node2` from `ceph-node1` issue:

    root@ceph-node1 # systemctl -H ceph-node2 status ceph*.service ceph*.target

4. To list the status on a particular Ceph service on a remote host, execute the systemd manager with the -H option (specifying the remote hostname), using the `status` command. To check the status of `mon.1` from `ceph-node1` issue:

    root@ceph-node1 # systemctl -H ceph-node2 status ceph-mon@ceph-node2

Starting and stopping all daemons by type

To start or stop all Ceph daemons by their types, perform the following set of commands:

Starting daemons by type:

1. To start the Ceph monitor daemons on localhost, execute the systemd manager with the `start` command followed by the daemon type:

   ```
   # systemctl start ceph-mon.target
   ```

2. To start the Ceph monitor daemon on a remote host, execute the same command with the `-H` option and the specified hostname. To start `mon.1` from `ceph-node1` issue:

   ```
   root@ceph-node1 # systemctl -H ceph-node2 start ceph-mon.target
   ```

3. Similarly, you can start daemons of other types, that is `osds`, `mds`, and `ceph-radosgw` by issuing:

   ```
   # systemctl start ceph-osd.target
   # systemctl start ceph-mds.target
   # systemctl start ceph-radosgw.target
   ```

Stopping daemons by type:

1. To stop the Ceph monitor daemons on a localhost, execute the systemd manager with the `stop` command followed by the daemon type:

   ```
   # systemctl stop ceph-mon.target
   ```

2. To stop the Ceph monitor daemon on a remote host, execute the same command with the `-H` option and the specified hostname. To stop `mon.1` from `ceph-node1` issue:

   ```
   root@ceph-node1 # systemctl -H ceph-node2 stop ceph.mon.target
   ```

3. Similarly, you can stop daemons of other types, that is `osds`, `mds`, and `ceph-radosgw` by issuing:

   ```
   # systemctl stop ceph-osd.target
   # systemctl stop ceph-mon.target
   # systemctl stop ceph-radosgw.target
   ```

Starting and stopping a specific daemon

To start or stop a specific Ceph daemon, perform the following set of commands:

Starting a specific daemon by instance:

To start a specific daemon on a local host, execute the systemd manager with the `start` command followed by the {daemon_type}@{id/hostname}, for example:

1. Start the mon.0 daemon:

```
root@ceph-node1 # systemctl start ceph-mon@ceph-node1
```

2. Similarly, you can start other daemons and their instances:

```
root@ceph-node1 # systemctl start ceph-osd@1
root@ceph-node1 # systemctl -H ceph-node2 start ceph-mon@ceph-node2
root@rgw-node1 # systemctl stop ceph-radosgw@rgw-node1
```

Stopping a specific daemon by instance:

To stop a specific daemon on the local host, execute the systemd manager with the `stop` command followed by the {daemon_type}@{id/hostname}, for example:

1. Stop the mon.0 daemon:

```
root@ceph-node1 # systemctl stop ceph-mon@ceph-node1
```

2. Similarly, you can stop other daemons and their instances:

```
root@ceph-node1 # systemctl stop ceph-osd@1
root@ceph-node1 # systemctl -H ceph-node2 stop ceph-mon@ceph-node2</kbd>
root@rgw-node1 # systemctl start ceph-radosgw@rgw-node1
```

Scale-up versus scale-out

When you are building up a storage infrastructure, scalability is one of the most important design aspects. The storage solution that you have chosen for your infrastructure should be scalable enough to accommodate your future data needs. Usually, a storage system starts with small to medium capacity and grows gradually into a large storage solution.

Traditional storage systems were based on scale-up design and were limited by a certain storage capacity. If you try to expand these storage systems over a certain limit, you might need to compromise the performance, reliability, and availability. The scale-up design methodology for storage involves adding disk resources to the existing controller systems, which becomes a bottleneck for performance, capacity, and manageability when it reaches a certain level.

On the other hand, scale-out design focuses on adding entire new devices containing disks, CPU, memory, and other resources to the existing storage cluster. With this type of design, you don't face the challenges that have been seen in scale-up design; it rather benefits from linear performance improvement. The following diagram explains the scale-up and scale-out design of a storage system:

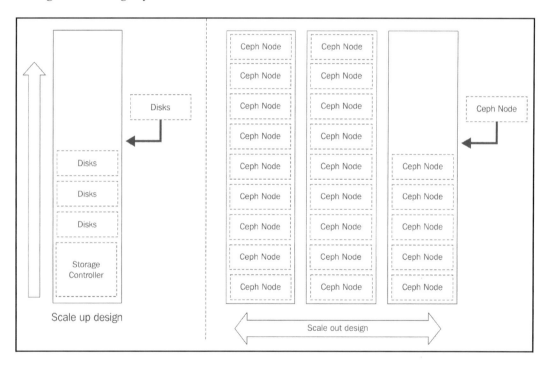

Ceph is a seamless scalable storage system based on scale-out design, where you can add a compute node with a bunch of disks to an existing Ceph cluster and extend your storage system to a larger storage capacity.

Scaling out your Ceph cluster

From the roots, Ceph has been designed to grow from a few nodes to several hundreds, and it's supposed to scale on the fly without any downtime. In this recipe, we will dive deep into the Ceph scale-out feature by adding MON, OSD, MDS, and RGW nodes.

How to do it...

Scaling out a Ceph cluster is important as the need for increased capacity in the cluster grows. Let's walk through expanding several areas of the Ceph cluster:

Adding the Ceph OSD

Adding an OSD node to the Ceph cluster is an online process. To demonstrate this, we require a new virtual machine named `ceph-node4` with three disks that will act as OSDs. This new node will then be added to our existing Ceph cluster.

Run the following commands from `ceph-node1` until otherwise specified from any other node:

1. Create a new node, `ceph-node4`, with three disks (OSD). You can follow the process of creating a new virtual machine with disks and the OS configuration, as mentioned in the *Setting up a virtual infrastructure* recipe in `Chapter 1`, *Ceph – Introduction and Beyond*, and make sure `ceph-node1` can ssh into `ceph-node4`. Before adding the new node to the Ceph cluster, let's check the current OSD tree. As shown in the following screenshot, the cluster has three nodes and a total of nine OSDs:

       # ceph osd tree

```
[root@ceph-node1 ~]# ceph osd tree
ID WEIGHT  TYPE NAME            UP/DOWN REWEIGHT PRIMARY-AFFINITY
-1 0.15834 root default
-2 0.05278     host ceph-node1
 0 0.01759         osd.0            up  1.00000          1.00000
 1 0.01759         osd.1            up  1.00000          1.00000
 2 0.01759         osd.2            up  1.00000          1.00000
-3 0.05278     host ceph-node3
 3 0.01759         osd.3            up  1.00000          1.00000
 4 0.01759         osd.4            up  1.00000          1.00000
 5 0.01759         osd.5            up  1.00000          1.00000
-4 0.05278     host ceph-node2
 6 0.01759         osd.6            up  1.00000          1.00000
 7 0.01759         osd.7            up  1.00000          1.00000
 8 0.01759         osd.8            up  1.00000          1.00000
```

2. Update the `/etc/ansible/hosts` file with `ceph-node4` under the `[osds]` section:

```
[mons]
ceph-node1
ceph-node2
ceph-node3

[osds]
ceph-node1
ceph-node2
ceph-node3
ceph-node4
```

3. Verify that Ansible can reach the newly added `ceph-node4` mentioned in `/etc/ansible/hosts`:

root@ceph-node1 # ansible all -m ping

```
[root@ceph-node1 ~]# ansible all -m ping
ceph-node2 | SUCCESS => {
    "changed": false,
    "ping": "pong"
}
ceph-node3 | SUCCESS => {
    "changed": false,
    "ping": "pong"
}
ceph-node4 | SUCCESS => {
    "changed": false,
    "ping": "pong"
}
ceph-node1 | SUCCESS => {
    "changed": false,
    "ping": "pong"
}
```

4. List the available devices of `ceph-node4` to be used as OSD's (`sdb`, `sdc`, and `sdd`):

root@ceph-node4 # lsblk

```
[root@ceph-node4 vagrant]# lsblk
NAME            MAJ:MIN RM  SIZE RO TYPE MOUNTPOINT
sda               8:0    0    8G  0 disk
├─sda1            8:1    0  500M  0 part /boot
└─sda2            8:2    0  7.5G  0 part
  ├─centos-swap 253:0    0  820M  0 lvm  [SWAP]
  └─centos-root 253:1    0  6.7G  0 lvm  /
sdb               8:16   0   20G  0 disk
sdc               8:32   0   20G  0 disk
sdd               8:48   0   20G  0 disk
sr0              11:0    1 1024M  0 rom
```

5. Review the `osds.yml` file on `ceph-node1` and validate that it lists the specified `devices` corresponding to the storage devices on the OSD node `ceph-node4` and that `journal_collocation` is set to `true`:

```
devices:
  - /dev/sdb
  - /dev/sdc
  - /dev/sdd
journal_collocation: true
```

6. Run the Ansible playbook to deploy the OSD node `ceph-node4` with three OSDs from the `/usr/share/ceph-ansible` directory:

```
root@ceph-node1 ceph-ansible # ansible-playbook site.yml
```

```
PLAY RECAP *************************************************************************
ceph-node1                 : ok=123   changed=2    unreachable=0    failed=0
ceph-node2                 : ok=117   changed=2    unreachable=0    failed=0
ceph-node3                 : ok=118   changed=2    unreachable=0    failed=0
ceph-node4                 : ok=60    changed=16   unreachable=0    failed=0
```

7. As soon as you add new OSDs to the Ceph cluster, you will notice that the Ceph cluster starts rebalancing the existing data to the new OSDs. You can monitor rebalancing using the following command; after a while, you will notice that your Ceph cluster becomes stable:

```
# watch ceph -s
```

```
Every 2.0s: ceph -s                                          Fri Aug 18 00:17:29 2017

    cluster f05098c5-b187-43ef-bd58-03c8567620d5
     health HEALTH_OK
     monmap e3: 3 mons at {ceph-node1=192.168.1.101:6789/0,ceph-node2=192.168.1.102:6789/0,ceph-node3=19
2.168.1.103:6789/0}
            election epoch 50, quorum 0,1,2 ceph-node1,ceph-node2,ceph-node3
     osdmap e180: 12 osds: 12 up, 12 in
            flags sortbitwise,require_jewel_osds
      pgmap v479: 128 pgs, 1 pools, 0 bytes data, 0 objects
            440 MB used, 215 GB / 215 GB avail
                 128 active+clean
```

8. Once the addition of the OSDs for `ceph-node4` completes successfully, you will notice the cluster's new storage capacity:

> `# rados df`

```
[root@ceph-node1 ceph-ansible]# rados df
pool name              KB      objects      clones      degraded      unfound        rd        rd
KB         wr      wr KB
rbd                     0           0           0           0           0           0           0
0           0           0
  total used         450992           0
  total avail      225906016
  total space      226357008
```

> `# ceph df`

```
[root@ceph-node1 ~]#
[root@ceph-node1 ~]# ceph df

GLOBAL:
    SIZE      AVAIL      RAW USED      %RAW USED
    161G      161G         317M          0.19
POOLS:
    NAME      ID      USED      %USED      MAX AVAIL      OBJECTS
    rbd       0        0          0         55155M          0
[root@ceph-node1 ~]#
```

9. Check the OSD tree; it will give you a better understanding of your cluster. You should notice the new OSDs under `ceph-node4`, which have been recently added:

> `# ceph osd tree`

```
[root@ceph-node1 ceph-ansible]# ceph osd tree
ID WEIGHT  TYPE NAME              UP/DOWN REWEIGHT PRIMARY-AFFINITY
-1 0.21112 root default
-2 0.05278     host ceph-node1
 0 0.01759         osd.0               up  1.00000          1.00000
 1 0.01759         osd.1               up  1.00000          1.00000
 2 0.01759         osd.2               up  1.00000          1.00000
-3 0.05278     host ceph-node3
 3 0.01759         osd.3               up  1.00000          1.00000
 4 0.01759         osd.4               up  1.00000          1.00000
 5 0.01759         osd.5               up  1.00000          1.00000
-4 0.05278     host ceph-node2
 6 0.01759         osd.6               up  1.00000          1.00000
 7 0.01759         osd.7               up  1.00000          1.00000
 8 0.01759         osd.8               up  1.00000          1.00000
-5 0.05278     host ceph-node4
 9 0.01759         osd.9               up  1.00000          1.00000
10 0.01759         osd.10              up  1.00000          1.00000
11 0.01759         osd.11              up  1.00000          1.00000
```

10. This command outputs some valuable information such as OSD weight, any reweight that may be set, primary affinity that is set, which Ceph node hosts which OSD, and the UP/DOWN status of an OSD.

Just now, we learned how to add a new node to the existing Ceph cluster. It's a good time to understand that as the number of OSDs increases, choosing the right value for the PG becomes more important because it has a significant influence on the behavior of the cluster. Increasing the PG count on a large cluster can be an expensive operation. I encourage you to take a look at `http://docs.ceph.com/docs/master/rados/operations/placement-groups/#choosing-the-number-of-placement-groups` for any updated information on **Placement Groups (PGs)**.

Adding the Ceph MON

In an environment where you have deployed a large Ceph cluster, you might want to increase your monitor count. Like in an OSD, adding new monitors to the Ceph cluster is an online process. In this recipe, we will configure `ceph-node4` as a monitor node.

Since this is a test Ceph cluster, we will add `ceph-node4` as the fourth monitor node. However, in the production setup, you should always have an *odd number* of monitor nodes in your Ceph cluster in order to form a quorum:

1. Update the `/etc/ansible/hosts` file with `ceph-node4` under the `[mons]` section:

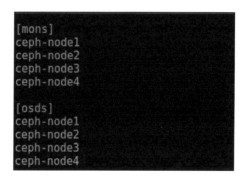

```
[mons]
ceph-node1
ceph-node2
ceph-node3
ceph-node4

[osds]
ceph-node1
ceph-node2
ceph-node3
ceph-node4
```

2. Run the Ansible playbook to deploy the new MON on `ceph-node4`:

root@ceph-node1 ceph-ansible # ansible-playbook site.yml

```
PLAY RECAP *********************************************************************************************************
ceph-node1                     : ok=127    changed=6     unreachable=0    failed=0
ceph-node2                     : ok=121    changed=6     unreachable=0    failed=0
ceph-node3                     : ok=121    changed=6     unreachable=0    failed=0
ceph-node4                     : ok=122    changed=13    unreachable=0    failed=0
```

3. Once `ceph-node4` is configured as a monitor node, check the ceph status to see the cluster status. Please note that `ceph-node4` is your new monitor node:

```
[root@ceph-node1 ceph-ansible]# ceph -s
    cluster f05098c5-b187-43ef-bd58-03c8567620d5
     health HEALTH_OK
     monmap e4: 4 mons at {ceph-node1=192.168.1.101:6789/0,ceph-node2=192.168.1.102:6789/0,ceph-node3=19
2.168.1.103:6789/0,ceph-node4=192.168.1.104:6789/0}
            election epoch 58, quorum 0,1,2,3 ceph-node1,ceph-node2,ceph-node3,ceph-node4
     osdmap e207: 12 osds: 12 up, 12 in
            flags sortbitwise,require_jewel_osds
      pgmap v565: 128 pgs, 1 pools, 0 bytes data, 0 objects
            448 MB used, 215 GB / 215 GB avail
                 128 active+clean
```

4. Check the Ceph monitor status and notice `ceph-node4` as the new Ceph monitor:

```
[root@ceph-node1 ceph-ansible]# ceph mon stat
e4: 4 mons at {ceph-node1=192.168.1.101:6789/0,ceph-node2=192.168.1.102:6789/0,ceph-node3=192.168.1.103:
6789/0,ceph-node4=192.168.1.104:6789/0}, election epoch 58, quorum 0,1,2,3 ceph-node1,ceph-node2,ceph-no
de3,ceph-node4
```

There's more...

For an object storage use case, you will have to deploy the Ceph RGW component using Ansible, and to make your object storage service highly available and performing, you should deploy more than one instance of the Ceph RGW. A Ceph object storage service can easily scale from one to several nodes of RGW using Ansible.

The following diagram shows how multiple RGW instances can be deployed and scaled to provide the **High-Availability (HA)** object storage service:

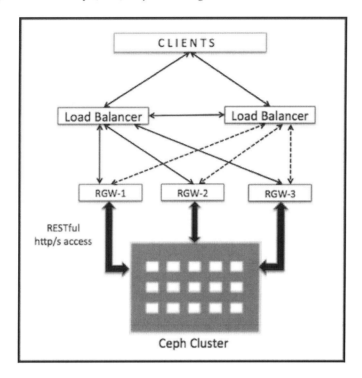

Scaling RGW is the same as adding additional RGW nodes with Ansible; please refer to the *Installing Rados Gateway* recipe in `Chapter 4`, *Working with Ceph Object Storage*, to add more RGW nodes to your Ceph environment.

Scaling down your Ceph cluster

One of the most important features of a storage system is its flexibility. A good storage solution should be flexible enough to support its expansion and reduction without causing any downtime to the services. Traditional storage systems have limited flexibility; the expansion and reduction of such systems is a tough job. Sometimes, you feel locked with storage capacity and that you cannot perform changes as per your needs.

Ceph is an absolutely flexible storage system that supports on-the-fly changes to storage capacity, whether expansion or reduction. In the last recipe, we learned how easy it is to scale out a Ceph cluster. In this recipe, we will scale down a Ceph cluster, without any impact on data accessibility, by removing `ceph-node4` from the Ceph cluster.

How to do it...

Since removing an OSD node is not currently supported in ceph-ansible, let's follow the next set of steps to do this manually.

Removing the Ceph OSD

Before proceeding with the cluster size reduction, scaling it down, or removing the OSD node, make sure that the cluster has enough free space to accommodate all the data present on the node you are planning to move out. The cluster should not be at its full ratio, which is the percentage of used disk space in an OSD. So, as best practice, do not remove the OSD or OSD node without considering the impact on the full ratio. At the current time of writing this book Ceph-Ansible does not support scaling down of the Ceph OSD nodes in a cluster and this must be done manually.

1. As we need to scale down the cluster, we will remove `ceph-node4` and all of its associated OSDs out of the cluster. Ceph OSDs should be set out so that Ceph can perform data recovery. From any of the Ceph nodes, take the OSDs out of the cluster:

    ```
    # ceph osd out osd.9
    # ceph osd out osd.10
    # ceph osd out osd.11
    ```

    ```
    [root@ceph-node1 ~]# ceph osd out osd.9
    marked out osd.9.
    [root@ceph-node1 ~]# ceph osd out osd.10
    marked out osd.10.
    [root@ceph-node1 ~]# ceph osd out osd.11
    marked out osd.11.
    [root@ceph-node1 ~]#
    ```

2. As soon as you mark an OSD out of the cluster, Ceph will start rebalancing the cluster by migrating the PGs out of the OSDs that were made out to other OSDs inside the cluster. Your cluster state will become unhealthy for some time, but it will be good for the server data to clients. Based on the number of OSDs removed, there might be some drop in cluster performance until the recovery time is complete. You can throttle the backfill and recovery as covered in this chapter in throttle backfill and recovery section.

Once the cluster is healthy again, it should perform as usual:

```
# ceph -s
```

```
root@ceph-node4 ~]# ceph -s
    cluster f05098c5-b187-43ef-bd58-03c8567620d5
     health HEALTH_WARN
            37 pgs peering
     monmap e4: 4 mons at {ceph-node1=192.168.1.101:6789/0,ceph-node2=192.168.1.102:6789/0,ceph-node3=192
168.1.103:6789/0,ceph-node4=192.168.1.104:6789/0}
            election epoch 60, quorum 0,1,2,3 ceph-node1,ceph-node2,ceph-node3,ceph-node4
     osdmap e255: 12 osds: 12 up, 9 in
            flags sortbitwise,require_jewel_osds
      pgmap v664: 128 pgs, 1 pools, 0 bytes data, 0 objects
            349 MB used, 161 GB / 161 GB avail
                  87 active+clean
                  32 peering
                   5 remapped+peering
                   4 activating
```

Here, you can see that the cluster is in the recovery mode but at the same time is serving data to clients. You can observe the recovery process using the following:

```
# ceph -w
```

```
2017-08-18 01:37:21.513877 mon.0 [INF] from='client.? 192.168.1.101:0/1982323814' entity='client.admin' c
md=[{"prefix": "osd out", "ids": ["osd.11"]}]: dispatch
2017-08-18 01:37:21.936129 mon.0 [INF] from='client.? 192.168.1.101:0/1982323814' entity='client.admin' c
md='[{"prefix": "osd out", "ids": ["osd.11"]}]': finished
2017-08-18 01:37:22.010637 mon.0 [INF] osdmap e268: 12 osds: 12 up, 9 in
2017-08-18 01:37:22.077412 mon.0 [INF] pgmap v802: 128 pgs: 18 remapped+peering, 29 peering, 81 active+cl
ean; 0 bytes data, 354 MB used, 161 GB / 161 GB avail
2017-08-18 01:37:22.199150 mon.0 [INF] osdmap e269: 12 osds: 12 up, 9 in
2017-08-18 01:37:22.221990 mon.0 [INF] pgmap v803: 128 pgs: 18 remapped+peering, 29 peering, 81 active+cl
ean; 0 bytes data, 354 MB used, 161 GB / 161 GB avail
```

3. As we have marked osd.9, osd.10, and osd.11 as out of the cluster, they will not participate in storing data, but their services are still running. Let's stop these OSDs:

```
root@ceph-node1 # systemctl -H ceph-node4 stop ceph-osd.target
```

Once the OSDs are down, check the OSD tree; you will observe that the OSDs are down and out:

```
# ceph osd tree
```

```
[root@ceph-node1 ~]# ceph osd tree
ID WEIGHT  TYPE NAME              UP/DOWN REWEIGHT PRIMARY-AFFINITY
-1 0.21112 root default
-2 0.05278     host ceph-node1
 0 0.01759         osd.0              up  1.00000          1.00000
 1 0.01759         osd.1              up  1.00000          1.00000
 2 0.01759         osd.2              up  1.00000          1.00000
-3 0.05278     host ceph-node3
 3 0.01759         osd.3              up  1.00000          1.00000
 4 0.01759         osd.4              up  1.00000          1.00000
 5 0.01759         osd.5              up  1.00000          1.00000
-4 0.05278     host ceph-node2
 6 0.01759         osd.6              up  1.00000          1.00000
 7 0.01759         osd.7              up  1.00000          1.00000
 8 0.01759         osd.8              up  1.00000          1.00000
-5 0.05278     host ceph-node4
 9 0.01759         osd.9            down     0             1.00000
10 0.01759         osd.10           down     0             1.00000
11 0.01759         osd.11           down     0             1.00000
```

4. Now that the OSDs are no longer part of the Ceph cluster, let's remove them from the CRUSH map:

```
# ceph osd crush remove osd.9
# ceph osd crush remove osd.10
# ceph osd crush remove osd.11
```

```
[root@ceph-node1 ~]# ceph osd crush remove osd.9
removed item id 9 name 'osd.9' from crush map
[root@ceph-node1 ~]# ceph osd crush remove osd.10
removed item id 10 name 'osd.10' from crush map
[root@ceph-node1 ~]# ceph osd crush remove osd.11
removed item id 11 name 'osd.11' from crush map
[root@ceph-node1 ~]#
```

5. As soon as the OSDs are removed from the CRUSH map, the Ceph cluster becomes healthy. You should also observe the OSD map; since we have not removed the OSDs, it will still show 12 OSDs, 9 UP, and 9 IN:

```
# ceph -s
```

```
[root@ceph-node1 ~]# ceph -s
    cluster f05098c5-b187-43ef-bd58-03c8567620d5
     health HEALTH_OK
     monmap e4: 4 mons at {ceph-node1=192.168.1.101:6789/0,ceph-node2=192.168.1.102:6789/0,ceph-node3=192
.168.1.103:6789/0,ceph-node4=192.168.1.104:6789/0}
            election epoch 64, quorum 0,1,2,3 ceph-node1,ceph-node2,ceph-node3,ceph-node4
     osdmap e293: 12 osds: 9 up, 9 in
            flags sortbitwise,require_jewel_osds
      pgmap v1052: 128 pgs, 1 pools, 0 bytes data, 0 objects
            361 MB used, 161 GB / 161 GB avail
                 128 active+clean
```

6. Remove the OSD authentication keys:

```
# ceph auth del osd.9
# ceph auth del osd.10
# ceph auth del osd.11
```

```
[root@ceph-node1 ~]# ceph auth del osd.9
updated
[root@ceph-node1 ~]# ceph auth del osd.10
updated
[root@ceph-node1 ~]# ceph auth del osd.11
updated
```

7. Finally, remove the OSD and check your cluster status; you should observe 9 OSDs, 9 UP, and 9 IN, and the cluster health should be OK:

```
# ceph osd rm osd.9
# ceph osd rm osd.10
# ceph osd rm osd.11
```

```
[root@ceph-node1 ~]# ceph osd rm osd.9
removed osd.9
[root@ceph-node1 ~]# ceph osd rm osd.10
removed osd.10
[root@ceph-node1 ~]# ceph osd rm osd.11
removed osd.11
[root@ceph-node1 ~]#
```

8. To keep your cluster clean, perform some housekeeping; as we have removed all the OSDs from the CRUSH map, `ceph-node4` does not hold any items. Remove `ceph-node4` from the CRUSH map; this will remove all the traces of this node from the Ceph cluster:

```
# ceph osd crush remove ceph-node4
```

```
[root@ceph-node1 ~]# ceph osd crush remove ceph-node4
removed item id -5 name 'ceph-node4' from crush map
```

9. Once the OSD node has been removed from the cluster and the CRUSH map, a final validation of the Ceph status should be done to verify HEALTH_OK:

```
# ceph -s
```

```
[root@ceph-node1 ~]# ceph -s
    cluster f05098c5-b187-43ef-bd58-03c8567620d5
     health HEALTH_OK
     monmap e4: 4 mons at {ceph-node1=192.168.1.101:6789/0,ceph-node2=192.168.1.102:6789/0,ceph-node3=192
.168.1.103:6789/0,ceph-node4=192.168.1.104:6789/0}
            election epoch 64, quorum 0,1,2,3 ceph-node1,ceph-node2,ceph-node3,ceph-node4
     osdmap e297: 9 osds: 9 up, 9 in
            flags sortbitwise,require_jewel_osds
      pgmap v1082: 128 pgs, 1 pools, 0 bytes data, 0 objects
            362 MB used, 161 GB / 161 GB avail
                 128 active+clean
```

10. To complete removal of `ceph-node4` from the cluster, update the `/etc/ansible/hosts` file on `ceph-node1` and remove `ceph-node4` from the `[osds]` section so the next time the playbook is run it will not redeploy `ceph-node4` as an OSD node:

```
[mons]
ceph-node1
ceph-node2
ceph-node3
ceph-node4

[osds]
ceph-node1
ceph-node2
ceph-node3
```

Removing the Ceph MON

Removing a Ceph MON is generally not a very frequently required task. When you remove monitors from a cluster, consider that Ceph monitors use the PAXOS algorithm to establish consensus about the master cluster map. You must have a sufficient number of monitors to establish a quorum for consensus on the cluster map. In this recipe, we will learn how to remove the `ceph-node4` monitor from the Ceph cluster. At the current time of writing this book, ceph-ansible does not support scaling down of Ceph MON nodes in a cluster and this must be done manually.

1. Check the monitor status:

    # ceph mon stat

```
[root@ceph-node1 ceph-ansible]# ceph mon stat
e4: 4 mons at {ceph-node1=192.168.1.101:6789/0,ceph-node2=192.168.1.102:6789/0,ceph-node3=192.168.1.103:6
789/0,ceph-node4=192.168.1.104:6789/0}, election epoch 64, quorum 0,1,2,3 ceph-node1,ceph-node2,ceph-node
3,ceph-node4
```

2. Stop the monitor service on `ceph-node4`:

    root@ceph-node1 # systemctl -H ceph-node4 stop ceph-mon.target

3. Remove the monitor from the cluster:

    # ceph mon remove ceph-node4

```
[root@ceph-node1 ceph-ansible]# ceph mon remove ceph-node4
removing mon.ceph-node4 at 192.168.1.104:6789/0, there will be 3 monitors
```

4. Check to see that your monitors have left the quorum:

```
# ceph quorum_status --format json-pretty
```

```
[root@ceph-node1 ceph-ansible]# ceph quorum_status --format json-pretty
{
    "election_epoch": 70,
    "quorum": [
        0,
        1,
        2
    ],
    "quorum_names": [
        "ceph-node1",
        "ceph-node2",
        "ceph-node3"
    ],
    "quorum_leader_name": "ceph-node1",
    "monmap": {
        "epoch": 5,
        "fsid": "f05098c5-b187-43ef-bd58-03c8567620d5",
        "modified": "2017-08-18 02:33:32.706251",
        "created": "2017-08-17 17:21:11.831589",
        "mons": [
            {
                "rank": 0,
                "name": "ceph-node1",
                "addr": "192.168.1.101:6789\/0"
            },
            {
                "rank": 1,
                "name": "ceph-node2",
                "addr": "192.168.1.102:6789\/0"
            },
            {
                "rank": 2,
                "name": "ceph-node3",
                "addr": "192.168.1.103:6789\/0"
            }
        ]
    }
}
```

5. Update the `/etc/ansible/hosts` file and remove `ceph-node4` from the
   `[mons]` section so `ceph-node4` is not redeployed as a mon and the `ceph.conf`
   file is properly updated:

6. You can choose to back up the monitor data on `ceph-node4` or remove it. To
   back it up, you can create a removed directory and move the data there:

   ```
   # mkdir /var/lib/ceph/mon/removed
   # mv /var/lib/ceph/mon/ceph-ceph-node4
   /var/lib/ceph/mon/removed/ceph-ceph-node4
   ```

7. If you choose not to back up the monitor data, then remove the monitor data on
   `ceph-node4`:

   ```
   # rm -r /var/lib/ceph/mon/ceph-ceph-node4
   ```

8. Re-run the Ansible playbook to update the `ceph.conf` on all the nodes in the
   cluster to complete the removal of monitor `ceph-node4`:

   ```
   root@ceph-node1 # ansible-playbook site.yml
   ```

9. Finally, check the monitor status; the cluster should have three monitors:

   ```
   [root@ceph-node1 ceph-ansible]# ceph mon stat
   e5: 3 mons at {ceph-node1=192.168.1.101:6789/0,ceph-node2=192.168.1.102:6789/0,ceph-node3=192.168.1.103:6
   789/0}, election epoch 70, quorum 0,1,2 ceph-node1,ceph-node2,ceph-node3
   ```

Replacing a failed disk in the Ceph cluster

A Ceph cluster can be made up of 10 to several thousand physical disks that provide storage capacity to the cluster. As the number of physical disks increases for your Ceph cluster, the frequency of disk failures also increases. Hence, replacing a failed disk drive might become a repetitive task for a Ceph storage administrator. In this recipe, we will learn about the disk replacement process for a Ceph cluster.

How to do it...

These steps will walk you through the proper replacement process of a Ceph OSD:

1. Let's verify cluster health; since this cluster does not have any failed disk status, it would be HEALTH_OK:

   ```
   # ceph status
   ```

   ```
   [root@ceph-node1 ceph-ansible]# ceph status
       cluster f05098c5-b187-43ef-bd58-03c8567620d5
        health HEALTH_OK
        monmap e5: 3 mons at {ceph-node1=192.168.1.101:6789/0,ceph-node2=192.168.1.102:6789/0,ceph-node3=192
   .168.1.103:6789/0}
               election epoch 70, quorum 0,1,2 ceph-node1,ceph-node2,ceph-node3
        osdmap e311: 9 osds: 9 up, 9 in
               flags sortbitwise,require_jewel_osds
         pgmap v1118: 128 pgs, 1 pools, 0 bytes data, 0 objects
               353 MB used, 161 GB / 161 GB avail
                    128 active+clean
   ```

2. Since we are demonstrating this exercise on virtual machines, we need to forcefully fail a disk by bringing `ceph-node1` down, detaching a disk, and powering up the VM. Execute the following commands from your HOST machine:

   ```
   # VBoxManage controlvm ceph-node1 poweroff
   # VBoxManage storageattach ceph-node1 --storagectl "SATA" --
   port 1 --device 0 --type hdd --medium none
   # VBoxManage startvm ceph-node1
   ```

The following screenshot will be your output:

```
teeri:ceph-cookbook ksingh$ VBoxManage  controlvm ceph-node1 poweroff
0%...10%...20%...30%...40%...50%...60%...70%...80%...90%...100%
teeri:ceph-cookbook ksingh$
teeri:ceph-cookbook ksingh$ VBoxManage storageattach ceph-node1 --storagectl "SATA" --port 1 --device 0 --type hdd --medium none
teeri:ceph-cookbook ksingh$ VBoxManage startvm ceph-node1
Waiting for VM "ceph-node1" to power on...
VM "ceph-node1" has been successfully started.
teeri:ceph-cookbook ksingh$
```

3. Now `ceph-node1` contains a failed disk, `osd.0`, which should be replaced:

    # ceph osd tree

```
[root@ceph-node1 ~]# ceph osd tree
ID WEIGHT  TYPE NAME          UP/DOWN REWEIGHT PRIMARY-AFFINITY
-1 0.15834 root default
-2 0.05278     host ceph-node1
 0 0.01759         osd.0         down  1.00000          1.00000
 1 0.01759         osd.1           up  1.00000          1.00000
 2 0.01759         osd.2           up  1.00000          1.00000
-3 0.05278     host ceph-node3
 3 0.01759         osd.3           up  1.00000          1.00000
 4 0.01759         osd.4           up  1.00000          1.00000
 5 0.01759         osd.5           up  1.00000          1.00000
-4 0.05278     host ceph-node2
 6 0.01759         osd.6           up  1.00000          1.00000
 7 0.01759         osd.7           up  1.00000          1.00000
 8 0.01759         osd.8           up  1.00000          1.00000
```

    # ceph -s

```
[root@ceph-node1 ~]# ceph -s
    cluster f05098c5-b187-43ef-bd58-03c8567620d5
     health HEALTH_WARN
            50 pgs stuck unclean
            1/9 in osds are down
     monmap e5: 3 mons at {ceph-node1=192.168.1.101:6789/0,ceph-node2=192.168.1.102:6789/0,ceph-node3=192
.168.1.103:6789/0}
            election epoch 78, quorum 0,1,2 ceph-node1,ceph-node2,ceph-node3
     osdmap e336: 9 osds: 8 up, 9 in; 50 remapped pgs
            flags sortbitwise,require_jewel_osds
      pgmap v1209: 128 pgs, 1 pools, 0 bytes data, 0 objects
            321 MB used, 143 GB / 143 GB avail
                  78 active+clean
                  41 active+remapped
                   9 active
```

You will also notice that `osd.0` is DOWN. However, in the `ceph osd tree` it's still showing a weight of 1.00000 meaning it is still marked as IN. As long as its status is marked IN, the Ceph cluster will not trigger data recovery for this drive. A further look into the `ceph -s` shows us an `osdmap` of `9 osds: 8 up, 9 in.` By default, the Ceph cluster takes 300 seconds to mark a down disk as OUT and then triggers data recovery. The reason for this timeout is to avoid unnecessary data movements due to short-term outages, for example, server reboot. One can increase or even decrease this timeout value if you prefer.

4. You should wait 300 seconds to trigger data recovery, or else you can manually mark the failed OSD as OUT:

    ```
    # ceph osd out osd.0
    ```

5. As soon as the OSD is marked OUT, the Ceph cluster will initiate a recovery operation for the PGs that were hosted on the failed disk. You can watch the recovery operation using the following command:

    ```
    # ceph status
    ```

6. Let's now remove the failed disk OSD from the Ceph CRUSH map:

    ```
    # ceph osd crush rm osd.0
    ```

7. Delete the Ceph authentication keys for the OSD:

    ```
    # ceph auth del osd.0
    ```

8. Finally, remove the OSD from the Ceph cluster:

    ```
    # ceph osd rm osd.0
    ```

    ```
    [root@ceph-node1 ~]# ceph osd crush rm osd.0
    removed item id 0 name 'osd.0' from crush map
    [root@ceph-node1 ~]# ceph auth del osd.0
    updated
    [root@ceph-node1 ~]# ceph osd rm osd.0
    removed osd.0
    [root@ceph-node1 ~]#
    ```

9. Since one of your OSDs is unavailable, the cluster health will not be OK, and the cluster will be performing recovery. Nothing to worry about here; this is a normal Ceph operation. Once the recovery operation is complete, your cluster will attain HEALTH_OK:

```
# ceph -s
# ceph osd stat
```

```
[root@ceph-node1 ~]# ceph -s
    cluster f05098c5-b187-43ef-bd58-03c8567620d5
     health HEALTH_OK
     monmap e5: 3 mons at {ceph-node1=192.168.1.101:6789/0,ceph-node2=192.168.1.102:6789/0,ceph-node3=192
.168.1.103:6789/0}
            election epoch 78, quorum 0,1,2 ceph-node1,ceph-node2,ceph-node3
     osdmap e343: 8 osds: 8 up, 8 in
            flags sortbitwise,require_jewel_osds
      pgmap v1238: 128 pgs, 1 pools, 0 bytes data, 0 objects
            324 MB used, 143 GB / 143 GB avail
                 128 active+clean
[root@ceph-node1 ~]# ceph osd stat
     osdmap e343: 8 osds: 8 up, 8 in
            flags sortbitwise,require_jewel_osds
[root@ceph-node1 ~]#
```

10. At this point, you should physically replace the failed disk with the new disk on your Ceph node. These days, almost all the servers and server OS support disk hot swapping, so you will not require any downtime for disk replacement.

11. Since we are simulating this on a virtual machine, we need to power off the VM, add a new disk, and restart the VM. Once the disk is inserted, make a note of its OS device ID:

```
# VBoxManage controlvm ceph-node1 poweroff
# VBoxManage storageattach ceph-node1 --storagectl "SATA" --
port 1 --device 0 --type hdd --medium ceph-node1_disk2.vdi
# VBoxManage startvm ceph-node1
```

12. Before adding the new disk back into the cluster, we will zap the disk to validate it is in a clean state:

```
root@ceph-node1 # ceph-disk zap /dev/sdb
```

13. View the device to validate that partitions were cleared with zap:

```
# lsblk
```

```
[root@ceph-node1 ceph-ansible]# lsblk
NAME                MAJ:MIN RM  SIZE RO TYPE MOUNTPOINT
sda                    8:0    0    8G  0 disk
├─sda1                 8:1    0  500M  0 part /boot
└─sda2                 8:2    0  7.5G  0 part
  ├─centos-swap      253:0    0  820M  0 lvm  [SWAP]
  └─centos-root      253:1    0  6.7G  0 lvm  /
sdb                    8:16   0   20G  0 disk
sdc                    8:32   0   20G  0 disk
├─sdc1                 8:33   0   18G  0 part /var/lib/ceph/osd/ceph-1
└─sdc2                 8:34   0    2G  0 part
sdd                    8:48   0   20G  0 disk
├─sdd1                 8:49   0   18G  0 part /var/lib/ceph/osd/ceph-2
└─sdd2                 8:50   0    2G  0 part
sr0                   11:0    1 1024M  0 rom
```

14. Add the new disk into the cluster using the `ceph-disk prepare` command:

```
root@ceph-node1 # ceph-disk --setuser ceph --setgroup ceph
prepare --fs-type xfs /dev/sdb
```

The `ceph-disk` prepare command does all the manual work of creating the OSD, the OSD key, authentication, placing the OSD in the CRUSH map, and so on:

```
[root@ceph-node1 ceph-ansible]# ceph-disk --setuser ceph --setgroup ceph prepare --fs-type xfs /dev/sdb
The operation has completed successfully.
The operation has completed successfully.
meta-data=/dev/sdb1              isize=2048   agcount=4, agsize=1179583 blks
         =                       sectsz=512   attr=2, projid32bit=1
         =                       crc=1        finobt=0, sparse=0
data     =                       bsize=4096   blocks=4718331, imaxpct=25
         =                       sunit=0      swidth=0 blks
naming   =version 2              bsize=4096   ascii-ci=0 ftype=1
log      =internal log           bsize=4096   blocks=2560, version=2
         =                       sectsz=512   sunit=0 blks, lazy-count=1
realtime =none                   extsz=4096   blocks=0, rtextents=0
Warning: The kernel is still using the old partition table.
The new table will be used at the next reboot.
The operation has completed successfully.
```

15. Check the device after the prepare completes to validate that the OSD directory is mounted:

    ```
    # lsblk
    ```

```
[root@ceph-node1 ceph-ansible]# lsblk
NAME             MAJ:MIN RM  SIZE RO TYPE MOUNTPOINT
sda                8:0    0    8G  0 disk
├─sda1             8:1    0  500M  0 part /boot
└─sda2             8:2    0  7.5G  0 part
  ├─centos-swap  253:0    0  820M  0 lvm  [SWAP]
  └─centos-root  253:1    0  6.7G  0 lvm  /
sdb                8:16   0   20G  0 disk
├─sdb1             8:17   0   18G  0 part /var/lib/ceph/osd/ceph-0
└─sdb2             8:18   0    2G  0 part
sdc                8:32   0   20G  0 disk
├─sdc1             8:33   0   18G  0 part /var/lib/ceph/osd/ceph-1
└─sdc2             8:34   0    2G  0 part
sdd                8:48   0   20G  0 disk
├─sdd1             8:49   0   18G  0 part /var/lib/ceph/osd/ceph-2
└─sdd2             8:50   0    2G  0 part
sr0               11:0    1 1024M  0 rom
```

16. Once the `ceph-disk prepare` command completes, the OSD will be added to the cluster successfully and Ceph will perform a backfilling operation and will start moving PGs from secondary OSDs to the new OSD. The recovery operation might take a while, but after it, your Ceph cluster will be HEALTH_OK again:

    ```
    # ceph -s
    # ceph osd stat
    ```

```
[root@ceph-node1 ceph-ansible]# ceph -s
    cluster f05098c5-b187-43ef-bd58-03c8567620d5
     health HEALTH_OK
     monmap e5: 3 mons at {ceph-node1=192.168.1.101:6789/0,ceph-node2=192.168.1.102:6789/0,ceph-node3=192
.168.1.103:6789/0}
            election epoch 86, quorum 0,1,2 ceph-node1,ceph-node2,ceph-node3
     osdmap e368: 9 osds: 9 up, 9 in
            flags sortbitwise,require_jewel_osds
      pgmap v1317: 128 pgs, 1 pools, 0 bytes data, 0 objects
            378 MB used, 161 GB / 161 GB avail
                 128 active+clean
[root@ceph-node1 ceph-ansible]# ceph osd stat
     osdmap e368: 9 osds: 9 up, 9 in
            flags sortbitwise,require_jewel_osds
```

Upgrading your Ceph cluster

One of the several reasons for the greatness of Ceph is that almost all the operations on a Ceph cluster can be performed online, which means that your Ceph cluster is in production and serving clients, and you can perform administrative tasks on the cluster without downtime. One of these operations is upgrading the Ceph cluster version.

Since the first chapter, we have been using the Jewel release of Ceph. We will be demonstrating upgrading the Ceph cluster version from Jewel to Kraken using the Ansible `rolling_update.yml` playbook located in the `/usr/share/ceph-ansible/infrastructure playbooks` directory. The `rolling_update.yml` playbook fully automates the Ceph cluster upgrade process.

Ansible upgrades the Ceph nodes in the following order, one at a time:

- Monitor nodes
- OSD nodes
- MDS nodes
- Ceph RadosGW nodes
- All other Ceph client nodes

During the upgrade, Ansible will also set the `noout`, `noscrub`, and `nodeep-scrub` flags on the cluster to prevent any unnecessary data movement on the cluster and overhead from scrubbing. Ansible also has built-in checks during the upgrade which will check cluster PG states and will not move forward if the cluster encounters an issue.

> Once you upgrade a Ceph daemon, you cannot downgrade it. It's very much recommended to refer to the release-specific sections at `http://docs.ceph.com/docs/master/release-notes/` to identify release-specific procedures for upgrading the Ceph cluster.

How to do it...

In this recipe, we will upgrade our Ceph cluster, which is running on the Jewel release (10.2.9), to the latest stable Kraken (11.2.1) release:

1. On `ceph-node1` navigate to the `/usr/share/ceph-ansible/group_vars/all.yml` file and change the `ceph_stable_release` from Jewel to Kraken:

```
# COMMUNITY VERSION
ceph_stable: true # use ceph stable branch
#ceph_mirror: http://download.ceph.com
#ceph_stable_key: https://download.ceph.com/keys/release.asc
ceph_stable_release: kraken # ceph stable release
#ceph_stable_repo: "{{ ceph_mirror }}/debian-{{ ceph_stable_release }}"
```

2. On `ceph-node1` navigate to the `/usr/share/ceph-ansible/group_vars/all.yml` file and uncomment and change the `upgrade_ceph_packages` from `False` to `True`:

```
# This variable determines if ceph packages can be updated.  If False, the
# package resources will use "state=present".  If True, they will use
# "state=latest".
upgrade_ceph_packages: True
```

3. Copy the `rolling_update.yml` from the infrastructure-playbooks directory to the `/usr/share/ceph-ansible` directory:

```
# cp /usr/share/ceph-ansible/infrastructure-
playbooks/rolling_update.yml /usr/share/ceph-ansible
```

4. Run the `rolling_update.yml` playbook:

```
# ansible-playbook rolling_update.yml
```

5. Once the playbook completes, validate the new running Ceph version on our Ceph nodes using `ceph tell`:

```
# ceph tell mon.* version
# ceph tell osd.* version
```

```
[root@ceph-node1 ceph]# ceph tell mon.* version
mon.ceph-node1: ceph version 11.2.1 (e0354f9d3b1eea1d75a7dd487ba8098311be38a7)
mon.ceph-node2: ceph version 11.2.1 (e0354f9d3b1eea1d75a7dd487ba8098311be38a7)
mon.ceph-node3: ceph version 11.2.1 (e0354f9d3b1eea1d75a7dd487ba8098311be38a7)
[root@ceph-node1 ceph]# ceph tell osd.* version
osd.0: {
    "version": "ceph version 11.2.1 (e0354f9d3b1eea1d75a7dd487ba8098311be38a7)"
}
osd.1: {
    "version": "ceph version 11.2.1 (e0354f9d3b1eea1d75a7dd487ba8098311be38a7)"
}
osd.2: {
    "version": "ceph version 11.2.1 (e0354f9d3b1eea1d75a7dd487ba8098311be38a7)"
}
osd.3: {
    "version": "ceph version 11.2.1 (e0354f9d3b1eea1d75a7dd487ba8098311be38a7)"
}
osd.4: {
    "version": "ceph version 11.2.1 (e0354f9d3b1eea1d75a7dd487ba8098311be38a7)"
}
osd.5: {
    "version": "ceph version 11.2.1 (e0354f9d3b1eea1d75a7dd487ba8098311be38a7)"
}
osd.6: {
    "version": "ceph version 11.2.1 (e0354f9d3b1eea1d75a7dd487ba8098311be38a7)"
}
osd.7: {
    "version": "ceph version 11.2.1 (e0354f9d3b1eea1d75a7dd487ba8098311be38a7)"
}
osd.8: {
    "version": "ceph version 11.2.1 (e0354f9d3b1eea1d75a7dd487ba8098311be38a7)"
}
```

6. Running `ceph -v` will also show the newly upgraded Kraken (11.2.1) running on the Ceph cluster:

```
# ceph -v
```

```
[root@ceph-node1 ceph]# ceph -v
ceph version 11.2.1 (e0354f9d3b1eea1d75a7dd487ba8098311be38a7)
```

Running the `rolling_update.yml` playbook will prompt a question: *Are you sure you want to upgrade the cluster?*. Once a *Yes* reply is entered, Ansible will kick off the upgrade; this is your last chance to abort the upgrade!

Maintaining a Ceph cluster

Being a Ceph storage admin, maintaining your Ceph cluster will be one of your top priorities. Ceph is a distributed system that is designed to grow from tens of OSDs to several thousands of them. One of the key things required to maintain a Ceph cluster is to manage its OSDs. In this recipe, we will cover Ceph sub commands for OSDs and PGs that will help you during cluster maintenance and troubleshooting.

How to do it...

To understand the need for these commands better, let's assume a scenario where you want to add a new node to your production Ceph cluster. One way is to simply add the new node with several disks to the Ceph cluster, and the cluster will start backfilling and shuffling the data on to the new node. This is fine for a test cluster.

However, the situation becomes very critical when it comes to a production setup, where you should use some of the `ceph osd` subcommands/flags, which are mentioned as follows, before adding a new node to the cluster, such as `noin`, `nobackfill`, and so on. This is done so that your cluster does not immediately start the backfilling process when the new node comes in. You can then unset these flags during non-peak hours, and the cluster will take its time to rebalance:

1. The usages of these flags are as simple as set and unset. For example, to set a flag, use the following command lines:

```
# ceph osd set <flag_name>
# ceph osd set noout
# ceph osd set nodown
# ceph osd set norecover
```

2. Now to unset the same flags, use the following command lines:

```
# ceph osd unset <flag_name>
# ceph osd unset noout
# ceph osd unset nodown
# ceph osd unset norecover
```

How it works...

We will now learn what these flags are and why they are used:

- `noout`: This forces the Ceph cluster to not mark any OSD as out of the cluster, irrespective of its status. It makes sure all the OSDs remain inside the cluster.
- `nodown`: This forces the Ceph cluster to not mark any OSD down, irrespective of its status. It makes sure all the OSDs remain UP and none of them DOWN.
- `noup`: This forces the Ceph cluster to not mark any down OSD as UP. So, any OSD that is marked DOWN can only come UP after this flag is unset. This also applies to new OSDs that are joining the cluster.
- `noin`: This forces the Ceph cluster to not allow any new OSD to join the cluster. This is quite useful if you are adding several OSDs at once and don't want them to join the cluster automatically.
- `norecover`: This forces the Ceph cluster to not perform cluster recovery.
- `nobackfill`: This forces the Ceph cluster to not perform backfilling. This is quite useful when you are adding several OSDs at once and don't want Ceph to perform automatic data placement on the new node.
- `norebalance`: This forces the Ceph cluster to not perform cluster rebalancing.
- `noscrub`: This forces Ceph to not perform OSD scrubbing.
- `nodeep-scrub`: This forces Ceph to not perform OSD deep scrubbing.

Throttle the backfill and recovery:

If you want to add the new OSD node in production peak hours or non-peak hours and you want to have the least impact in client IO as compared to Ceph data rebalance - recovery and backfill IO due to new OSD new. You can throttle the backfill and recovery with the help of following commands:

- Set `osd_max_backfills` = 1 option to throttle the backfill threads. You can add this in ceph.conf [osd] section and you can also set it dynamically with the following command:

  - `# ceph tell osd.* injectargs '--osd_max_backfills 1'`

- Set `osd_recovery_max_active` = 1 option to throttle the recovery threads. You can add this in ceph.conf [osd] section and you can also set it dynamically with the following command:

  - `# ceph tell osd.* injectargs '--osd_recovery_max_active 1'`

- Set `osd_recovery_op_priority` = 1 option to lower the recovery priority. You can add this in ceph.conf [osd] section and you can also set it dynamically with the following command:

  - `# ceph tell osd.* injectargs '--osd_recovery_op_priority 1'`

With the Jewel release of Ceph, there are two additional flags that are enabled by default when a Ceph cluster is installed at Jewel. If the cluster was upgraded from a version prior to Jewel (Hammer for example) these flags can be enabled:

- `sortbitwise`: The `sortbitwise` flag indicates that objects are sorted in a bitwise fashion. The old sort order `nibblewise`, was an historical artifact of filestore that is simply inefficient with the current version of Ceph. Bitwise sort order makes operations that require listing objects, like backfill and scrubbing, a bit more efficient:

  ```
  # ceph osd set sortbitwise
  ```

- `require_jewel_osds`: This flag prevents any pre-Jewel OSDs from joining the Ceph cluster. The purpose of this flag is to prevent an OSD from joining the cluster that will not support features that the Jewel code supports leading to possible OSD flapping and cluster issues:

  ```
  # ceph osd set require_jewel_osds
  ```

Setting the `sortbitwise` flag is a disruptive change as each PG must go through peering and each client must re-send inflight requests. There is no data movement in the cluster from setting this flag. Also note that ALL OSD's in the cluster must be running Jewel prior to setting this flag.

In addition to these flags, you can also use the following commands to repair OSDs and PGs:

- `ceph osd repair`: This performs repairing on a specified OSD.
- `ceph pg repair`: This performs repairing on a specified PG. Use this command with caution; based on your cluster state, this command can impact user data if not used carefully.
- `ceph pg scrub`: This performs scrubbing on a specified PG.
- `ceph deep-scrub`: This performs deep-scrubbing on specified PGs.

The Ceph CLI is quite powerful for end-to-end cluster management. You can get more information at `http://docs.ceph.com/docs/master/rados/man/`.

d manager service. Each time you start, restart, and stop Ceph daemons (or your entire cluster), you must specify at least one option and one command. You may also specify a daemon type or a daemon instance. The general syntax for this is as follows:

```
systemctl [options...] command [service name...]
```

The `systemctl` options include:

- `--help` or `-h`: Prints a short help text
- `--all` or `-a`: When listing units, show all loaded units, regardless of their state
- `--signal` or `-s`: When used will kill, choose which signal to send to the selected process
- `--force` or `-f`: When used with enable, overwrite any existing conflicting symlinks
- `--host` or `-h`: Execute an operation on a remote host

The `systemctl` commands include the following:

- `status`: Shows status of the daemon
- `start`: Starts the daemon
- `stop`: Stops the daemon
- `restart`: Stops and then starts the daemon
- `kill`: Kills the specified daemon

- `reload`: Reloads the config file without interrupting pending operations
- `list-units`: List known units managed by systemd
- `condrestart`: Restarts if the service is already running
- `enable`: Turns the service on for the next boot or other triggering event
- `disable`: Turns the service off for the next boot or other triggering event
- `is-enabled`: Used to check whether a service is configured to start or not in the current environment

`systemctl` can target the following Ceph service types:

- `ceph-mon`
- `ceph-osd`
- `ceph-mds`
- `ceph-radosgw`

9
Ceph under the Hood

In this chapter, we will cover the following recipes:

- Ceph scalability and high availability
- Understanding the CRUSH mechanism
- CRUSH map internals
- CRUSH tunables
- Ceph cluster map
- High availability monitors
- Ceph authentication and authorization
- I/O path from a Ceph client to a Ceph cluster
- Ceph placement group
- Placement group states
- Creating Ceph pools on specific OSDs

Introduction

In this chapter, we will take a deep dive into the internal workings of Ceph by understanding its features such as scalability, high availability, authentication, and authorization. We will also cover CRUSH map, which is one of the most important parts of the Ceph cluster. Finally, we will go through dynamic cluster management and the custom CRUSH map settings for Ceph pools.

Ceph scalability and high availability

To understand Ceph scalability and high availability, let's first talk about the architecture of traditional storage systems. Under this architecture, to store or retrieve data, clients talk to a centralized component known as a controller or gateway. These storage controllers act as a single point of contact for a client's request. The following diagram illustrates this situation:

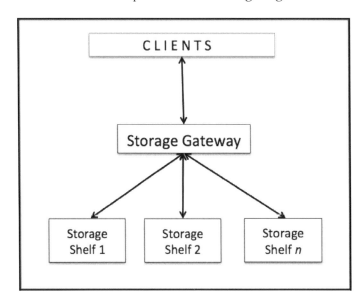

This storage gateway, which acts as a single point of entry to storage systems, also becomes the single point of failure. This also imposes a limit on scalability and performance while a single point of failure is being introduced, such that the whole system goes down if the centralized component goes down.

Ceph does not follow this traditional storage architecture; it has been totally reinvented for the next-generation of storage. Ceph eliminates the centralized gateway by enabling the clients to interact with the Ceph OSD daemons directly. The following diagram illustrates how clients connect to the Ceph cluster:

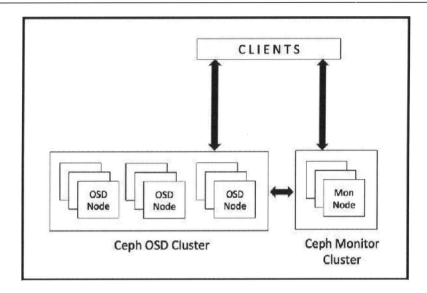

The Ceph OSD daemons create objects and their replicas on other Ceph nodes to ensure data safety and high availability. A cluster of monitors is used by Ceph to eliminate centralization and to ensure high availability. Ceph uses an algorithm called **Controlled Replication Under Scalable Hashing** (**CRUSH**). With the help of CRUSH, a client on demand calculates where the data should be written to or read from. In the following recipe, we will examine the details of the Ceph CRUSH algorithm.

Understanding the CRUSH mechanism

When it comes to data storage and management, Ceph uses the CRUSH algorithm, which is an intelligent data distribution mechanism of Ceph. As we discussed in the last recipe, traditional storage systems use a central metadata/index table to know where the user's data is stored. Ceph, on the other hand, uses the CRUSH algorithm to deterministically compute where the data should be written to or read from. Instead of storing metadata, CRUSH computes metadata on demand, thus removing the need for a centralized server/gateway or broker. It empowers Ceph clients to compute metadata, also known as *CRUSH lookup*, and communicates with OSDs directly.

For a read/write operation to Ceph clusters, clients first contact a Ceph monitor and retrieve a copy of the cluster map, which is inclusive of five maps, namely the monitor, OSD, MDS, and CRUSH and PG maps; we will cover these maps later in this chapter. These cluster maps help clients know the state and configuration of the Ceph cluster. Next, the data is converted to objects using an object name and pool names/IDs. This object is then hashed with the number of PGs to generate a final PG within the required Ceph pool. This calculated PG then goes through a CRUSH lookup function to determine the primary, secondary, and tertiary OSD locations to store or retrieve data.

Once the client gets the exact OSD ID, it contacts the OSDs directly and stores the data. All of these compute operations are performed by the clients; hence, they do not affect the cluster performance. The following diagram illustrates the entire process:

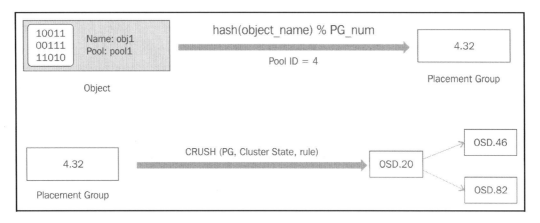

CRUSH map internals

To know what is inside a CRUSH map, and for easy editing, we need to extract and decompile it to convert it into a human-readable form. The following diagram illustrates this process:

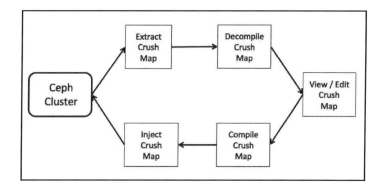

The change to the Ceph cluster by the CRUSH map is dynamic, that is, once the new CRUSH map is injected into the Ceph cluster, all the changes will come into effect immediately, on the fly.

How to do it...

We will now take a look at the CRUSH map of our Ceph cluster:

1. Extract the CRUSH map from any of the monitor nodes:

    ```
    # ceph osd getcrushmap -o crushmap_compiled_file
    ```

2. Once you have the CRUSH map, decompile it to convert it into a human-readable/editable form:

    ```
    # crushtool -d crushmap_compiled_file
                -o crushmap_decompiled_file
    ```

    At this point, the output file, `crushmap_decompiled_file`, can be viewed/edited in your favorite editor. In the next recipe, we will learn how to perform changes to the CRUSH map.

3. Once the changes are done, you should compile these changes:

    ```
    # crushtool -c crushmap_decompiled_file -o newcrushmap
    ```

4. Finally, inject the newly compiled CRUSH map into the Ceph cluster:

    ```
    # ceph osd setcrushmap -i newcrushmap
    ```

How it works...

Now that we know how to edit the Ceph CRUSH map, let's understand what's inside the CRUSH map. A CRUSH map file contains four main sections; they are as follows:

- **Devices**: This section of the CRUSH map keeps a list of all the OSD devices in your cluster. The OSD is a physical disk corresponding to the `ceph-osd` daemon. To map the PG to the OSD device, CRUSH requires a list of OSD devices. This list of devices appears in the beginning of the CRUSH map to declare the device in the CRUSH map. The following is the sample device list:

```
# devices
device 0 osd.0
device 1 osd.1
device 2 osd.2
device 3 osd.3
device 4 osd.4
device 5 osd.5
device 6 osd.6
device 7 osd.7
device 8 osd.8
```

- **Bucket types**: This defines the types of buckets used in your CRUSH hierarchy. Buckets consist of a hierarchical aggregation of physical locations (for example, rows, racks, chassis, hosts, and so on) and their assigned weights. They facilitate a hierarchy of nodes and leaves, where the node bucket represents a physical location and can aggregate other nodes and leaves buckets under the hierarchy. The leaf bucket represents the `ceph-osd` daemon and its underlying physical device. The following table lists the default bucket types:

Number	CRUSH Bucket	Description
0	**OSD**	An OSD daemon (for example, osd.1, osd.2, and so on).
1	**Host**	A host name containing one or more OSDs.
2	**Rack**	A computer rack containing one or more hosts.
3	**Row**	A row in a series of racks.
4	**Room**	A room containing racks and rows of hosts.
5	**Data Center**	A physical data center containing rooms.
6	**Root**	This is the beginning of the bucket hierarchy.

CRUSH also supports custom bucket type creation. These default bucket types can be deleted and new types can be introduced as per your needs.

- **Bucket instances**: Once you define bucket types, you must declare bucket instances for your hosts. A bucket instance requires the bucket type, a unique name (string), a unique ID expressed as a negative integer, a weight relative to the total capacity of its item, a bucket algorithm (straw, by default), and the hash (0, by default, reflecting the CRUSH hash rjenkins1). A bucket may have one or more items, and these items may consist of other buckets or OSDs. The item should have a weight that reflects the relative weight of the item. The general syntax of a bucket type looks as follows:

```
[bucket-type] [bucket-name] {
id [a unique negative numeric ID]
weight [the relative capacity the item]
alg [ the bucket type: uniform | list | tree | straw |straw2]
hash [the hash type: 0 by default]
item [item-name] weight [weight]
}
```

We will now briefly cover the parameters used by the CRUSH bucket instance:

- bucket-type: It's the type of bucket, where we must specify the OSD's location in the CRUSH hierarchy.
- bucket-name: A unique bucket name.
- id: The unique ID, expressed as a negative integer.

- `weight`: Ceph writes data evenly across the cluster disks, which helps in performance and better data distribution. This forces all the disks to participate in the cluster and make sure that all cluster disks are equally utilized, irrespective of their capacity. To do so, Ceph uses a weighting mechanism. CRUSH allocates weights to each OSD. The higher the weight of an OSD, the more physical storage capacity it will have. A weight is a relative difference between device capacities. We recommend using 1.00 as the relative weight for a 1 TB storage device. Similarly, a weight of 0.5 would represent approximately 500 GB, and a weight of 3.00 would represent approximately 3 TB.

- `alg`: Ceph supports multiple algorithm bucket types for your selection. These algorithms differ from each other on the basis of performance and reorganizational efficiency. Let's briefly cover these bucket types:

  - `uniform`: The `uniform` bucket can be used if the storage devices have exactly the same weight. For non-uniform weights, this bucket type should not be used. The addition or removal of devices in this bucket type requires the complete reshuffling of data, which makes this bucket type less efficient.

  - `list`: The `list` buckets aggregate their contents as linked lists and can contain storage devices with arbitrary weights. In the case of cluster expansion, new storage devices can be added to the head of a linked list with minimum data migration. However, storage device removal requires a significant amount of data movement. So, this bucket type is suitable for scenarios under which the addition of new devices to the cluster is extremely rare or non-existent. In addition, `list` buckets are efficient for small sets of items, but they may not be appropriate for large sets.

- `tree`: The `tree` buckets store their items in a binary tree. It is more efficient than list buckets because a bucket contains a larger set of items. Tree buckets are structured as a weighted binary search tree with items at the leaves. Each interior node knows the total weight of its left and right subtrees and is labeled according to a fixed strategy. The `tree` buckets are an all-around boon, providing excellent performance and decent reorganization efficiency.

- `straw`: To select an item using `list` and `tree` buckets, a limited number of hash values need to be calculated and compared by weight. They use a divide and conquer strategy, which gives precedence to certain items (for example, those at the beginning of a list). This improves the performance of the replica placement process, but it introduces moderate reorganization when bucket contents change due to addition, removal, or re-weighting.

The `straw` bucket type allows all items to compete fairly against each other for replica placement. In a scenario where removal is expected and reorganization efficiency is critical, `straw` buckets provide optimal migration behavior between subtrees. This bucket type allows all items to fairly compete against each other for replica placement through a process analogous to a draw of straws.

- `straw2`: This is an improved `straw` bucket that correctly avoids any data movement between items A and B, when neither A's nor B's weights are changed. In other words, if we adjust the weight of item C by adding a new device to it, or by removing it completely, the data movement will take place to or from C, never between other items in the bucket. Thus, the `straw2` bucket algorithm reduces the amount of data migration required when changes are made to the cluster.

- `hash`: Each bucket uses a hash algorithm. Currently, Ceph supports `rjenkins1`. Enter 0 as your hash setting to select `rjenkins1`.
- `item`: A bucket may have one or more items. These items may consist of node buckets or leaves. Items may have a weight that reflects the relative weight of the item.

The following screenshot illustrates the CRUSH bucket instance. Here, we have three host bucket instances. These host bucket instances consist of OSDs buckets:

```
# buckets
host ceph-node1 {
        id -2           # do not change unnecessarily
        # weight 0.053
        alg straw
        hash 0  # rjenkins1
        item osd.0 weight 0.018
        item osd.1 weight 0.018
        item osd.2 weight 0.018
}
host ceph-node3 {
        id -3           # do not change unnecessarily
        # weight 0.053
        alg straw
        hash 0  # rjenkins1
        item osd.3 weight 0.018
        item osd.5 weight 0.018
        item osd.7 weight 0.018
}
host ceph-node2 {
        id -4           # do not change unnecessarily
        # weight 0.053
        alg straw
        hash 0  # rjenkins1
        item osd.4 weight 0.018
        item osd.6 weight 0.018
        item osd.8 weight 0.018
}
root default {
        id -1           # do not change unnecessarily
        # weight 0.158
        alg straw
        hash 0  # rjenkins1
        item ceph-node1 weight 0.053
        item ceph-node3 weight 0.053
        item ceph-node2 weight 0.053
}
```

- **Rules**: The CRUSH maps contain CRUSH rules that determine the data placement for pools. As the name suggests, these are the rules that define the pool properties and the way data gets stored in the pools. They define the replication and placement policy that allows CRUSH to store objects in a Ceph cluster. The default CRUSH map contains a rule for default pools, that is, `rbd`. The general syntax of a CRUSH rule looks as follows:

```
rule <rulename>
{
ruleset <ruleset>
type [ replicated | erasure ]
min_size <min-size>
max_size <max-size>
step take <bucket-type>
step [choose|chooseleaf] [firstn] <num> <bucket-type>
step emit
}
```

We will now briefly cover these parameters used by the CRUSH rule:

- `ruleset`: An integer value; it classifies a rule as belonging to a set of rules.
- `type`: A string value; it's the type of pool that is either replicated or erasure coded.
- `min_size`: An integer value; if a pool makes fewer replicas than this number, CRUSH will not select this rule.
- `max_size`: An integer value; if a pool makes more replicas than this number, CRUSH will not select this rule.
- `step take`: This takes a bucket name and begins iterating down the tree.
- `step choose firstn <num> type <bucket-type>`: This selects the number (N) of buckets of a given type, where the number (N) is usually the number of replicas in the pool (that is, pool size):
  - If `num == 0`, select N buckets
  - If `num > 0 && < N`, select num buckets
  - If `num < 0`, select N − num buckets

For example: `step choose firstn 1 type row`

In this example, `num=1`, and let's suppose the pool size is 3, then CRUSH will evaluate this condition as `1 > 0 && < 3`. Hence, it will select 1 row type bucket.

- `step chooseleaf firstn <num> type <bucket-type>`: This first selects a set of buckets of a bucket type, and then chooses the leaf node from the subtree of each bucket in the set of buckets. The number of buckets in the set (`N`) is usually the number of replicas in the pool:
  - If `num == 0`, select `N` buckets
  - If `num > 0 && < N`, select `num` buckets
  - If `num < 0`, select `N - num` buckets

For example: `step chooseleaf firstn 0 type row`

In this example, `num=0`, and let's suppose the pool size is 3, then CRUSH will evaluate this condition as `0 == 0`, and then select a row type bucket set, such that the set contains three buckets. Then it will choose the leaf node from the subtree of each bucket. In this way, CRUSH will select three leaf nodes.

- `step emit`: This first outputs the current value and empties the stack. This is typically used at the end of a rule, but it may also be used to form different trees in the same rule.

CRUSH tunables

In Ceph, developers calculate the placement of data by making an enhancement to the CRUSH algorithm. Developers have introduced a series of CRUSH tunable options to support the change in behavior. These options control the improved variation or legacy of the algorithm that is used. Both Ceph servers and clients must support the new version of CRUSH for using new tunables.

Hence, Ceph developers have named CRUSH tunable profiles in the name of the Ceph version in which they were introduced. For example, the Firefly release supports the firefly tunables that will not work with the older clients. The `ceph-osd` and `ceph-mon` will prevent older clients from connecting to the cluster, as soon as a given set of tunables are changed from the legacy default behavior. These old clients do not support the new CRUSH features.

For more information, please visit `http://docs.ceph.com/docs/jewel/rados/operations/crush-map/#tunables`.

The evolution of CRUSH tunables

In the following section, we will explain the evolution of the CRUSH tunables.

Argonaut – legacy

Using the legacy CRUSH tunable Argonaut is fine behavior for some clusters as long as a large amount of OSD's have not been marked out of the cluster as this can cause issues with properly rebalancing data when OSD's are marked out.

Bobtail – CRUSH_TUNABLES2

The Bobtail profile fixes several CRUSH issues:

- In CRUSH hierarchies with a smaller number of devices in buckets, such as a host leaf bucket with one OSDs - three OSDs under it, the PGs may get mapped to less than the desired number of replica
- In larger Ceph clusters with several hierarchy layers (`row`, `rack`, `host`, `osd`) it is possible that a small amount of PGs could get mapped to less than the desired amount of OSDs
- If an OSD gets marked out in Bobtail, the data usually gets rebalanced to nearby OSDs in the bucket instead of across the entire CRUSH hierarchy

The following are the new tunables:

- `choose_local_tries`: The number of local retries is given by this tunable. The legacy and optimal values are 2 and 0, respectively.
- `choose_local_fallback_tries`: The legacy and optimal values are 5 and 0, respectively.
- `choose_total_tries`: The total number of attempts required for an item to be chosen. Legacy value was 19. Further testing has shown that this is too low of a value and the more appropriate value for a typical cluster is 50. For very large clusters, a bigger value might be necessary to properly choose an item.

- `chooseleaf_descend_once`: Either a recursive `chooseleaf` attempt will retry, or will only try once and allow the original placement to retry. The default and optimal values of legacy are `0` and `1`, respectively:
  - **Migration impact**: A moderate amount of data movement is triggered if we move from Argonaut version to Bobtail version. We will have to be cautious on a cluster that is already populated with data.

Firefly – CRUSH_TUNABLES3

The Firefly profile resolves an issue where the `chooseleaf` CRUSH rule behavior, which is responsible for PG mappings, will come up with too few results when too many OSDs have been marked out of the cluster and will not be able to map the PG.

The following are the new tunables:

- `chooseleaf_vary_r`: If a recursive `chooseleaf` attempt starts with a non-zero value of `r`, based on the number of attempts parent has already made. The default value of legacy is `0`, but with such a value, CRUSH is sometimes not able to find a mapping, which can lead to PGs in an unmapped state. The optimal value (in terms of computational cost and correctness) is `1`:
  - **Migration impact**: For the existing clusters that have lots of existing data, changing from `0` to `1` will cause a lot of data to move; a value of `4` or `5` will allow CRUSH to find a valid mapping, but it will make less data move.
- `straw_calc_version`: This tunable resolves an issue when there were items in the CRUSH map with a weight of `0` or a mix of different weights in `straw` buckets. This would lead CRUSH to distribute data incorrectly throughout the cluster. Old is preserved by the value `0`, broken internal weight calculation; behavior is fixed by the value `1`:
  - **Migration impact**: Move to the `straw_calc_version 1` tunable and then adjust a `straw` bucket (add, remove, or reweight an item, or use the `reweight-all` command) triggers a small to moderate amount of data movement if the cluster has hit one of the problematic conditions. This tunable option is special because it has absolutely no impact concerning the required kernel version in the client side.

Hammer – CRUSH_V4

The Hammer tunable profile does not affect the mapping of existing CRUSH maps simply by changing the profile and requires manual manipulation of the CRUSH map by enabling a new `straw` bucket type on CRUSH buckets:

- `straw2`: The `straw2` bucket resolves several initial limitations of the original `straw` bucket algorithm. The major change is that with the initial `straw` buckets, changing the weight of a bucket item would lead to multiple PG mapping changes of other bucket items outside the item that was actually reweighted. `straw2` will allow only changing mappings to or from the bucket that was actually reweighted:
  - **Migration impact**: Changing a bucket type from `straw` to `straw2` will result in a fairly small amount of data movement, depending on how much the bucket item weights vary from each other. When all the weights are same, no data will move, and when item weights vary considerably there will be more movement.

Jewel – CRUSH_TUNABLES5

The Jewel profile will improve CRUSH's overall behavior by limiting the number PG mapping changes when an OSD is marked out of the cluster.

The following is the new tunable:

- `chooseleaf_stable`: A recursive `chooseleaf` attempt will use a better value for an inner loop that greatly reduces the number of mapping changes when an OSD is marked out. The legacy value is `0`, while the new value of `1` uses the new approach:
  - `Migration impact`: Changing this value on an existing cluster will result in a very large amount of data movement as almost every PG mapping is likely to change

Ceph and kernel versions that support given tunables

Following are the Ceph and kernel versions that support given tunables:

Tunables	Ceph and kernel versions that support given tunables
CRUSH_TUNABLES	Argonaut series, v0.48.1 or recent version v0.49 or greater Linux kernel version v3.6 or recent (for the file system and RBD kernel clients)
CRUSH_TUNABLES2	v0.55 or recent, including Bobtail series (v0.56.x) Linux kernel version v3.9 or recent (for the filesystem and RBD kernel clients)
CRUSH_TUNABLES3	v0.78 (Firefly) or recent version CentOS 7.1, Linux kernel version v3.15 or recent (for the filesystem and RBD kernel clients)
CRUSH_V4	v0.94 (Hammer) or recent CentOS 7.1, Linux kernel version v4.1 or recent (for the filesystem and RBD kernel clients)
CRUSH_TUNABLES5	v10.2.0 (Jewel) or recent CentOS 7.3, Linux kernel version v4.5 or recent (for the filesystem and RBD kernel clients)

Warning when tunables are non-optimal

Ceph clusters will issue a health warning if the current running CRUSH tunables are not optimal for the current running Ceph version starting at v0.74.

In order to remove this warning from the Ceph cluster you can adjust the tunables on the existing cluster. Adjusting the CRUSH tunables will result in some data movement (possibly as much as 10% of the data on the cluster). This is the obviously preferred route to take, but care should be taken on a production cluster as any movement of data may affect the current cluster performance.
You can enable optimal tunables with:

```
ceph osd crush tunables optimal
```

If you begin to see issues with performance due to the load from the data movement on the cluster caused by the rebalance from the tunables change or if you run into a client compatibility issue (old kernel `cephfs` or `rbd` clients, or prebobtail `librados` clients) you can switch back to legacy tunables with:

```
ceph osd crush tunables legacy
```

A few important points

An adjustment to a CRUSH tunable will result in the shift of some PGs between storage nodes. If the Ceph cluster contains a large amount of data already, be prepared that there may be a good amount of PG movement with a CRUSH tunable change.

Monitor and OSD daemons will start and each daemon will require the new enabled CRUSH features of each new connection as they receive the updated maps. Any client that is already connected to the cluster will be grandfathered in; this will lead to unwanted behaviors if the clients (kernel version, Ceph version) do not support the newly enabled features. If you choose to set your CRUSH tunables to optimal, please verify that all Ceph nodes and clients are running the same version:

- If your CRUSH tunables are set to a value that is not legacy, then reverted back to default value the OSD daemons will not be required to support the feature. Please note that the OSD peering process does require reviewing and comprehending old maps, so you should not run old versions of Ceph if the cluster had previously used a non-legacy CRUSH tunable, even if the latest maps were reverted to legacy default values. It is very important to validate that all OSDs are running the same Ceph version.
  The simplest way to adjust the CRUSH tunables is by changing to a known profile. Those are:
  - `legacy`: The `legacy` profile gives the legacy behavior from Argonaut and previous versions
  - `argonaut`: The `argonaut` profile gives the legacy values that are supported by the original Argonaut release
  - `bobtail`: The values that are supported by the Bobtail release are given by the `bobtail` profile
  - `firefly`: The values that are supported by Firefly release are given by the `firefly` profile
  - `hammer`: The values that are supported by the Hammer release are given by the `hammer` profile

- `jewel`: The values that are supported by the Jewel release are given by the `jewel` profile
- `optimal`: The `optimal` profile gives the best/optimal values of the current Ceph version
- `default`: The default values of a new cluster is given by `default` profile

You can select a profile on a running cluster with the following command:

```
ceph osd crush tunables {PROFILE}
```

Note that this may result in some data movement.

You can check the current profile on a running cluster with the following command:

```
ceph osd crush show-tunables
```

```
[vagrant@ceph-node3 ~]$
[vagrant@ceph-node3 ~]$ sudo ceph osd crush tunables optimal
adjusted tunables profile to optimal
[vagrant@ceph-node3 ~]$ sudo ceph osd crush show-tunables
{
    "choose_local_tries": 0,
    "choose_local_fallback_tries": 0,
    "choose_total_tries": 50,
    "chooseleaf_descend_once": 1,
    "chooseleaf_vary_r": 1,
    "chooseleaf_stable": 1,
    "straw_calc_version": 1,
    "allowed_bucket_algs": 54,
    "profile": "jewel",
    "optimal_tunables": 1,
    "legacy_tunables": 0,
    "minimum_required_version": "jewel",
    "require_feature_tunables": 1,
    "require_feature_tunables2": 1,
    "has_v2_rules": 0,
    "require_feature_tunables3": 1,
    "has_v3_rules": 0,
    "has_v4_buckets": 0,
    "require_feature_tunables5": 1,
    "has_v5_rules": 0
}
[vagrant@ceph-node3 ~]$
```

Ceph cluster map

Ceph monitors are responsible for monitoring the health of the entire cluster as well as maintaining the cluster membership state, state of peer nodes, and cluster configuration information. The Ceph monitor performs these tasks by maintaining a master copy of the cluster map. The cluster map includes monitor maps, OSD maps, the PG map, the CRUSH map, and the MDS map. All these maps are collectively known as *cluster maps*. Let's take a quick look at the functionality of each map:

- **Monitor map**: It holds end-to-end information about the monitor node, which includes the Ceph cluster ID, monitor hostname, and IP address with the port number. It also stores the current epoch for map creation and last changed time too. You can check your cluster's monitor map by executing the following:

  ```
  # ceph mon dump
  ```

- **OSD map**: It stores some common fields, such as cluster ID, epoch for OSD map creation and last changed, and information related to pools, such as pool names, pool ID, type, replication level, and PGs. It also stores OSD information such as count, state, weight, last clean interval, and OSD host information. You can check your cluster's OSD maps by executing the following:

  ```
  # ceph osd dump
  ```

- **PG map**: It holds the PG version, timestamp, last OSD map epoch, full ratio, and near full ratio information. It also keeps track of each PG ID, object count, state, state stamp, up and acting OSD sets, and finally, the scrub details. To check your cluster PG map, execute the following:

  ```
  # ceph pg dump
  ```

- **CRUSH map**: It holds information on your clusters devices, buckets, failure domain hierarchy, and the rules defined for the failure domain when storing data. To check your cluster CRUSH map, execute the following:

  ```
  # ceph osd crush dump
  ```

- **MDS map**: This stores information on the current MDS map epoch, map creation and modification time, data and metadata pool ID, cluster MDS count, and the MDS state. To check your cluster MDS map, execute the following:

  ```
  # ceph mds dump
  ```

High availability monitors

The Ceph monitor does not store and serve data to clients; it serves updated cluster maps to clients as well as to other cluster nodes. Clients and other cluster nodes periodically check with monitors for the most recent copies of cluster maps. The Ceph monitor must be contacted by Ceph clients for obtaining the most recent copy of the cluster map before they can read or write data.

A Ceph storage cluster can operate with a single monitor, however, this introduces the risk of a single point of failure to the cluster; that is, if the monitor node goes down, Ceph clients cannot read or write data. To overcome this, a typical Ceph cluster consists of a cluster of Ceph monitors. A multi-monitored Ceph architecture develops quorum and provides consensus for distributed decision-making in clusters by using the Paxos algorithm. The monitor count in your cluster should be an odd number; the bare minimum requirement is one monitor node, and the recommended count is three. Since a monitor operates in the quorum, more than half of the total monitor nodes should always be available to prevent split-brain problems. Out of all the cluster monitors, one of them operates as the leader. The other monitor nodes are entitled to become leaders if the leader monitor is unavailable. A production cluster must have at least three monitor nodes to provide high availability.

Ceph authentication and authorization

In this recipe, we will cover the authentication and authorization mechanism used by Ceph. Users are either individuals or system actors such as applications, which use Ceph clients to interact with the Ceph storage cluster daemons. The following diagram illustrates this flow:

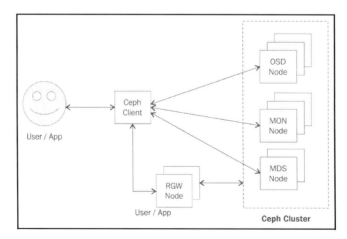

Ceph provides two authentication modes. They are as follows:

- `none`: With this mode, any user can access the Ceph cluster without authentication. This mode is disabled by default. Cryptographic authentication, which includes encrypting and decrypting user keys, has some computational costs. You can disable the Ceph authentication if you are very sure that your network infrastructure is secure, the clients/Ceph cluster nodes have established trust, and you want to save some computation by disabling authentication. However, this is not recommended, and you might be at risk of a man-in-the-middle attack. Still, if you are interested in disabling the Ceph authentication, you can do it by adding the following parameters in the global section of your Ceph configuration file on all the nodes, followed by the Ceph service restart:

  ```
  auth cluster required = none
  auth service required = none
  auth client required = none
  ```

- `cephx`: Ceph provides its Cephx authentication system to authenticate users and daemons in order to identify users and protect against man-in-the-middle attacks. The Cephx protocol works similar to Kerberos to some extent and allows clients to access the Ceph cluster. It's worth knowing that the Cephx protocol does not do data encryption. In a Ceph cluster, the Cephx protocol is enabled by default. If you have disabled Cephx by adding the preceding `auth` options to your cluster configuration file, then you can enable Cephx in two ways. One is to simply remove all `auth` entries from the cluster configuration file, which are `none`, or you can explicitly enable Cephx by adding the following options in the cluster configuration file and restarting the Ceph services:

  ```
  auth cluster required = cephx
  auth service required = cephx
  auth client required = cephx
  ```

Now that we have covered the different authentication modes of Ceph, let's understand how authentication and authorization works within Ceph.

Ceph authentication

To access the Ceph cluster, an actor/user/application invokes the Ceph client to contact the cluster's monitor node. Usually, a Ceph cluster has more than one monitor, and a Ceph client can connect to any monitor node to initiate the authentication process. This multimonitor architecture of Ceph removes a single point of failure situation during the authentication process.

To use Cephx, an administrator, that is, `client.admin`, must create a user account on the Ceph cluster. To create a user account, the `client.admin` user invokes the `ceph auth get-or-create key` command. The Ceph authentication subsystem generates a username and a secret key, stores this information on the Ceph monitor, and returns the user's secret key to the `client.admin` user that has invoked the user creation command. The Ceph sysadmin should share this username and secret key with the Ceph client that wants to use the Ceph storage service in a secure manner. The following diagram visualizes this entire process:

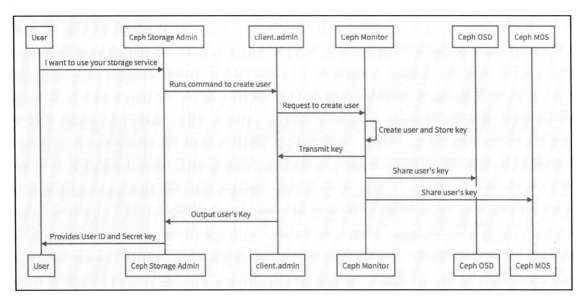

In the last recipe, we learned the process of user creation and how a user's secret keys are stored across all the cluster nodes. We will now examine how users are authenticated by Ceph and allowed access to cluster nodes.

In order to access the Ceph cluster, the client first contacts the Ceph monitor node and passes only its username. The Cephx protocol works in such a way that both parties are able to prove to each other that they have a copy of the key without actually revealing it. This is the reason that a client only sends its username, but not its secret key.

The session key for the user is generated by the monitor is encrypted with the secret key associated with that user. The encrypted session key is transmitted by the monitor back to the client. The client then decrypts the payload with its key to retrieve the session key. This session key remains valid for that user for the current session.

Using the session key, the client requests for a ticket from the Ceph monitor. The Ceph monitor verifies the session key and then generates a ticket, encrypted with the user's secret key, and transmits this to the user. The client decrypts the ticket and uses it to sign requests to OSDs and metadata servers throughout the cluster.

The ongoing communications between the Ceph nodes and the client are authenticated by the Cephx protocol. Each message sent between the Ceph nodes and the client, post the initial authentication, is signed using a ticket that the metadata nodes, OSDs, and monitors verify with their shared secret key. Cephx tickets do expire, so an attacker cannot use an expired ticket or session key to gain access to the Ceph cluster. The following diagram illustrates the entire authentication process that has been explained here:

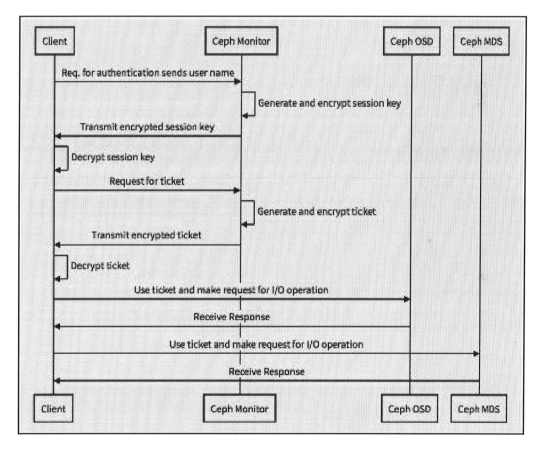

Ceph authorization

In the last recipe, we covered the authentication process used by Ceph. In this recipe, we will examine its authorization process. Once a user is authenticated, he is authorized for different types of access, activities, or roles. Ceph uses the term capabilities, which is abbreviated to caps. Capabilities are the rights a user gets that define the level of access they have to operate the cluster. The capability syntax looks as follows:

```
{daemon-type} 'allow {capability}' [{daemon-type} 'allow {capability}']
```

A detailed explanation of capability syntax is as follows:

- **Monitor caps**: Includes the r, w, x, parameters, and allow profiles {cap}. For example:

    ```
    mon 'allow rwx' or mon 'allow profile osd'
    ```

- **OSD caps**: Includes r, w, x, class-read, class-write, and profile OSD. For example:

    ```
    osd 'allow rwx' or osd 'allow class-read, allow rwx pool=rbd'
    ```

- **MDS caps**: Only requires allow. For example:

    ```
    mds 'allow'
    ```

Let's understand each capability:

- allow: This implies rw only for MDS.
- r: This gives the user read access, which is required with the monitor to read CRUSH maps.
- w: This gives the user write access to objects.
- x: This gives the user the ability to call class methods, including read and write, and also, the rights to perform auth operations on monitors.

 Ceph can be extended by creating shared object classes called Ceph classes. Ceph can load .so classes stored in the OSD class dir. For a class, you can create new object methods that have the ability to call native methods in the Ceph object store, for example, the objects that you have defined in your class can call native Ceph methods such as read and write.

- `class-read`: This is a subset of x that allows users to call class read methods.
- `class-write`: This is a subset of x that allows users to call class write methods.
- `*`: This gives users full permission (r, w, and x) on a specific pool as well as to execute admin commands.
- `profile osd`: This allows users to connect as an OSD to other OSDs or monitors. Used for the OSD heartbeat traffic and status reporting.
- `profile mds`: This allows users to connect as an MDS to other MDSs.
- `profile bootstrap-osd`: This allows users to bootstrap an OSD. For example, `ceph-deploy` and `ceph-disk` tools use the client.bootstrap-osd user, which has permission to add keys and bootstrap an OSD.
- `profile bootstrap-mds`: This allows the user to bootstrap the metadata server. For example, the `ceph-deploy` tool uses the `client.bootstrap-mds` user to add keys and bootstrap the metadata server.

A user can be the individual user of an application, such as cinder/nova in the case of OpenStack. Creating users allows you to control what can access your Ceph storage cluster, its pools, and the data within the pools. In Ceph, a user should have a type, which is always client, and an ID, which can be any name. So, a valid username syntax in Ceph is `TYPE.ID`, that is, `client.<name>`, for example, `client.admin` or `client.cinder`.

How to do it...

In the following recipe, we will discuss more Ceph user management by running some commands:

1. To list the users in your cluster, execute the following command:

   ```
   # ceph auth list
   ```

   The output of this command shows that for each daemon type, Ceph creates a user with different capabilities. It also lists the `client.admin` user, which is the cluster admin user.

2. To retrieve a specific user, for example, `client.admin`, execute the following:

```
# ceph auth get client.admin
```

```
[vagrant@ceph-node3 ~]$
[vagrant@ceph-node3 ~]$ sudo ceph auth get client.admin
exported keyring for client.admin
[client.admin]
        key = AQDyj4ZZZBISKhAAnOlJYPyttbcDUBde0pIvfg==
        caps mds = "allow *"
        caps mon = "allow *"
        caps osd = "allow *"
[vagrant@ceph-node3 ~]$
```

3. Create a user, `client.rbd`:

```
# ceph auth get-or-create client.rbd
```

```
[vagrant@ceph-node3 ~]$
[vagrant@ceph-node3 ~]$ sudo ceph auth get-or-create client.rbd
[client.rbd]
        key = AQCabZhZusKJMxAAAHh4TP+XDVzy48T7ulxnhw==
[vagrant@ceph-node3 ~]$
```

This will create the user, `client.rbd`, with no capabilities, and a user with no caps is of no use.

4. Add capabilities to the `client.rbd` user and list the user's capabilities:

```
[vagrant@ceph-node3 ~]$
[vagrant@ceph-node3 ~]$ sudo ceph auth caps client.rbd mon 'allow r' osd 'allow rwx pool=rbd'
updated caps for client.rbd
[vagrant@ceph-node3 ~]$ sudo ceph auth get client.rbd
exported keyring for client.rbd
[client.rbd]
        key = AQCabZhZusKJMxAAAHh4TP+XDVzy48T7ulxnhw==
        caps mon = "allow r"
        caps osd = "allow rwx pool=rbd"
[vagrant@ceph-node3 ~]$
```

I/O path from a Ceph client to a Ceph cluster

Let's have a quick recap of how clients access the Ceph cluster. To perform a write operation with the Ceph cluster, the client gets the latest copy of the cluster map from the Ceph monitor (if they do not have it already). The cluster map provides information about the Ceph cluster layout. Then the client writes/reads the object, which is stored on a Ceph pool. The pool selects OSDs based on the CRUSH ruleset for that pool. The following diagram illustrates this entire process:

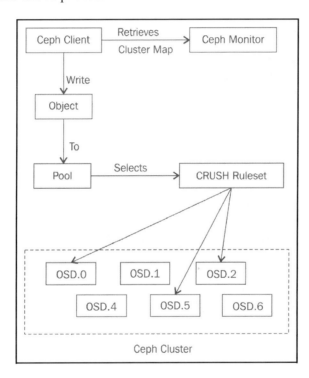

Now, let's understand the process of data storage inside the Ceph cluster. Ceph stores data in logical partitions known as pools. These pools hold multiple PGs, which in turn hold objects. Ceph is a true distributed storage system in which each object is replicated and stored across different OSDs each time. This mechanism has been explained with the help of the following diagram, in which we have tried to present how objects get stored in the Ceph cluster:

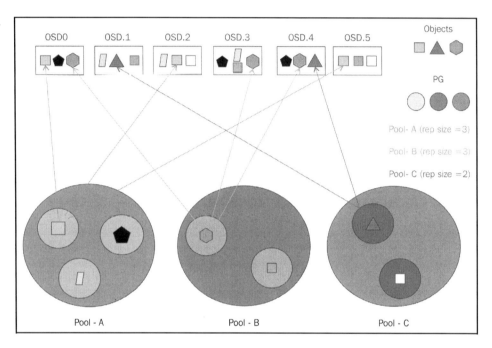

Ceph Placement Group

A **Placement Group** (**PG**) is a logical collection of objects that are replicated on OSDs to provide reliability in a storage system. Depending on the replication level of a Ceph pool, each PG is replicated and distributed on more than one OSD of a Ceph cluster. You can consider a PG as a logical container holding multiple objects, such that this logical container is mapped to multiple OSDs:

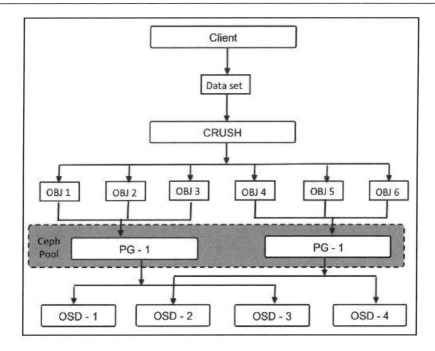

The PGs are essential for the scalability and performance of a Ceph storage system. Without PGs, it will be difficult to manage and track tens of millions of objects that are replicated and spread over hundreds of OSDs. The management of these objects without a PG will also result in a computational penalty. Instead of managing every object individually, a system has to manage the PGs with numerous objects. This makes Ceph a more manageable and less complex system.

Each PG requires some system resources, as they have to manage multiple objects. The number of PGs in a cluster should be meticulously calculated, and this is discussed later in this book. Usually, increasing the number of PGs in your cluster rebalances the OSD load. A recommended number of PGs per OSD is 50 to 100, to avoid high resource utilization on the OSD node. As the amount of data on a Ceph cluster increases, you might need to tune the cluster by adjusting the PG counts. When devices are added to or removed from a cluster, CRUSH manages the relocation of PGs in the most optimized way.

Now, we have understood that a Ceph PG stores its data on multiple OSDs for reliability and high availability. These OSDs are referred to as primary, secondary, tertiary, and so on, and they belong to a set known as the acting set for that PG. For each PG acting set, the first OSD is primary and the latter are secondary and tertiary.

How to do it…

To understand this better, let's find out the acting set for a PG from our Ceph cluster:

1. Add a temporary object with name `hosts` to a pool `rbd`:

   ```
   # rados put -p rbd hosts /etc/hosts
   ```

2. Check the PG name for object `hosts`:

   ```
   # ceph osd map rbd hosts
   ```

```
[vagrant@ceph-node3 ~]$
[vagrant@ceph-node3 ~]$ sudo rados put -p rbd hosts /etc/hosts
[vagrant@ceph-node3 ~]$ sudo ceph osd map rbd hosts
osdmap e67 pool 'rbd' (0) object 'hosts' -> pg 0.ea1b298e (0.e) -> up ([2,4,3], p2) acting ([2,4,3], p2)
[vagrant@ceph-node3 ~]$
```

If you observe the output, Placement Group (`0.e`) has an up set `[2,4,3]` and an acting set `[2,4,3]`. So, here `osd.2` is the primary OSD, and `osd.4` and `osd.3` are secondary and tertiary OSDs. The primary OSD is the only OSD that entertains write operations from clients. When it comes to read, by default it also comes from the primary OSD; however, we can change this behavior by setting up read affinity.

The OSD's that are up remains in the up set, as well as the acting set. Once the primary OSD is down, it is first removed from the up set and then from the acting set. The secondary OSD is then promoted to become the primary OSD. Ceph recovers PGs of the failed OSD to a new OSD and then adds it to the up and acting sets to ensure high availability. In a Ceph cluster, an OSD can be the primary OSD for some PGs, while at the same time, it can be the secondary or tertiary OSD for other PGs.

Placement Group states

Ceph PGs may exhibit several states based on what's happening inside the cluster at that point in time. To know the state of a PG, you can see the output of the command `ceph status`. In this recipe, we will cover these different states of PGs and understand what each state actually means:

- **Creating**: The PG is being created. This generally happens when pools are being created or when PGs are increased for a pool.
- **Active**: All PGs are active, and requests to the PG will be processed.

- **Clean**: All objects in the PG are replicated the correct number of times.
- **Down**: A replica with necessary data is down, so the PG is offline (down).
- **Replay**: The PG is waiting for clients to replay operations after an OSD has crashed.
- **Splitting**: The PG is being split into multiple PGs. Usually, a PG attains this state when PGs are increased for an existing pool. For example, if you increase the PGs of a pool rbd from 64 to 128, the existing PGs will split, and some of their objects will be moved to new PGs.
- **Scrubbing**: The PG is being checked for inconsistencies.
- **Degraded**: Some objects in the PG are not replicated as many times as they are supposed to be.
- **Inconsistent**: The PG replica is not consistent. For example, there is the wrong size of object, or objects are missing from one replica after recovery is finished.
- **Peering**: The PG is undergoing the peering process, in which it's trying to bring the OSDs that store the replicas of the PG into agreement about the state of the objects and metadata in the PG.
- **Repair**: The PG is being checked, and any inconsistencies found will be repaired (if possible).
- **Recovering**: Objects are being migrated/synchronized with replicas. When an OSD goes down, its contents may fall behind the current state of other replicas in the PGs. So, the PG goes into a recovering state and objects will be migrated/synchronized with replicas.
- **Backfill**: When a new OSD joins the cluster, CRUSH will reassign PGs from existing OSDs in the cluster to the newly added OSD. Once the backfilling is complete, the new OSD will begin serving requests when it is ready.
- **Backfill-wait**: The PG is waiting in line to start backfill.
- **Incomplete**: A PG is missing a necessary period of history from its log. This generally occurs when an OSD that contains needed information fails or is unavailable.
- **Stale**: The PG is in an unknown state—the monitors have not received an update for it since the PG mapping changed. When you start your cluster, it is common to see the stale state until the peering process completes.
- **Remapped**: When the acting set that services a PG changes, the data migrates from the old acting set to the new acting set. It may take some time for a new primary OSD to service requests. So, it may ask the old primary OSD to continue to service requests until the PG migration is complete. Once data migration completes, the mapping uses the primary OSD of the new acting set.

The following are two more new PG states that were added in jewel release for the snapshot trimming feature:

- `snaptrim`: The PGs are currently being trimmed
- `snaptrim_wait`: The PGs are waiting to be trimmed

Creating Ceph pools on specific OSDs

A Ceph cluster typically consists of several nodes having multiple disk drives. And, these disk drives can be of mixed types. For example, your Ceph nodes might contain disks of the types SATA, NL-SAS, SAS, SSD, or even PCIe, and so on. Ceph provides you with the flexibility to create pools on specific drive types. For example, you can create a high performing SSD pool from a set of SSD disks, or you can create a high capacity, low-cost pool using the SATA disk drives.

In this recipe, we will understand how to create a pool named `ssd-pool` backed by SSD disks, and another pool named `sata-pool`, which is backed by SATA disks. To achieve this, we will edit CRUSH maps and make the necessary configurations.

The Ceph cluster that we deployed and have played around with in this book is hosted on virtual machines and does not have real SSD disks backing it. Hence, we will be assuming we have a few virtual disks as SSD disks for learning purposes. There will be no change if you are performing this exercise on a real SSD disk-based Ceph cluster.

For the following demonstration, let's assume that `osd.0`, `osd.3`, and `osd.6` are SSD disks, and we would be creating an SSD pool on these disks. Similarly, let's assume `osd.1`, `osd.5`, and `osd.7` are SATA disks, which would be hosting the SATA pool.

How to do it...

Let's begin the configuration:

1. Get the current CRUSH map and decompile it:

```
# ceph osd getcrushmap -o crushmapdump
# crushtool -d crushmapdump -o crushmapdump-decompiled
```

```
[vagrant@ceph-node3 ~]$
[vagrant@ceph-node3 ~]$ sudo ceph osd getcrushmap -o crushmapdump
got crush map from osdmap epoch 67
[vagrant@ceph-node3 ~]$ sudo crushtool -d crushmapdump -o crushmapdump-decompiled
[vagrant@ceph-node3 ~]$ ls -l crushmapdump-decompiled
-rw-r--r-- 1 root root 1476 Aug 19 20:35 crushmapdump-decompiled
[vagrant@ceph-node3 ~]$
```

2. Edit the `crushmapdump-decompiled` CRUSH map file and add the following section after the `root` default section:

```
root ssd {
        id -5
        alg straw
        hash 0
        item osd.0 weight 0.010
        item osd.3 weight 0.010
        item osd.6 weight 0.010
}

root sata {
        id -6
        alg straw
        hash 0
        item osd.1 weight 0.010
        item osd.4 weight 0.010
        item osd.7 weight 0.010
}
```

3. Create the CRUSH rule by adding the following rules under the `rule` section of the CRUSH map, and then save and exit the file:

```
rule ssd-pool {
        ruleset 1
        type replicated
        min_size 1
        max_size 10
        step take ssd
        step chooseleaf firstn 0 type osd
        step emit
}

rule sata-pool {
        ruleset 2
        type replicated
        min_size 1
        max_size 10
        step take sata
        step chooseleaf firstn 0 type osd
        step emit
}
```

4. Compile and inject the new CRUSH map in the Ceph cluster:

```
# crushtool -c crushmapdump-decompiled -o crushmapdump-compiled
```

```
# ceph osd setcrushmap -i crushmapdump-compiled
```

Add the `osd_crush_update_on_start=false` option in either the `[global]` or `[osd]` section of `ceph.conf` in all the OSD nodes so in future if any OSD nodes or OSD's will be restarted they will use custom CRUSH map and will not update it back to default.

5. Once the new CRUSH map has been applied to the Ceph cluster, check the OSD tree view for the new arrangement, and notice the `ssd` and `sata` root buckets:

```
# ceph osd tree
```

```
[root@ceph-node1 ~]# ceph osd tree
ID WEIGHT  TYPE NAME               UP/DOWN REWEIGHT PRIMARY-AFFINITY
-6 0.02998 root sata
 1 0.00999     osd.1                up    1.00000         1.00000
 4 0.00999     osd.4                up    1.00000         1.00000
 7 0.00999     osd.7                up    1.00000         1.00000
-5 0.02998 root ssd
 0 0.00999     osd.0                up    1.00000         1.00000
 3 0.00999     osd.3                up    1.00000         1.00000
 6 0.00999     osd.6                up    1.00000         1.00000
-1 0.09000 root default
-3 0.03000     host ceph-node2
 3 0.00999         osd.3            up    1.00000         1.00000
 4 0.00999         osd.4            up    1.00000         1.00000
 5 0.00999         osd.5            up    1.00000         1.00000
-4 0.03000     host ceph-node3
 6 0.00999         osd.6            up    1.00000         1.00000
 7 0.00999         osd.7            up    1.00000         1.00000
 8 0.00999         osd.8            up    1.00000         1.00000
-2 0.03000     host ceph-node1
 1 0.00999         osd.1            up    1.00000         1.00000
 2 0.00999         osd.2            up    1.00000         1.00000
 0 0.00999         osd.0            up    1.00000         1.00000
[root@ceph-node1 ~]#
```

6. Create and verify the `ssd-pool`.

 Since this is a small cluster hosted on virtual machines, we will create these pools with a few PGs.

1. Create the `ssd-pool`:

   ```
   # ceph osd pool create ssd-pool 8 8
   ```

2. Verify the `ssd-pool`; notice that the `crush_ruleset` is 0, which is by default:

   ```
   # ceph osd dump | grep -i ssd
   ```

```
[root@ceph-node1 ~]# ceph osd pool create ssd-pool 8 8
pool 'ssd-pool' created
[root@ceph-node1 ~]# ceph osd dump | grep -i ssd
pool 45 'ssd-pool' replicated size 3 min_size 2 crush_ruleset 0 object_hash rjenkins pg_num 8 pgp_num 8
last_change 4446 flags hashpspool stripe_width 0
[root@ceph-node1 ~]#
```

3. Let's change the `crush_ruleset` to 1 so that the new pool gets created on the SSD disks:

```
# ceph osd pool set ssd-pool crush_ruleset 1
```

4. Verify the pool and notice the change in `crush_ruleset`:

```
# ceph osd dump | grep -i ssd
```

```
[root@ceph-node1 ~]# ceph osd pool set ssd-pool crush_ruleset 1
set pool 45 crush_ruleset to 1
[root@ceph-node1 ~]# ceph osd dump | grep -i ssd
pool 45 'ssd-pool' replicated size 3 min_size 2 crush_ruleset 1 object_hash rjenkins pg_num 8 pgp_num 8
last_change 4448 flags hashpspool stripe_width 0
[root@ceph-node1 ~]# _
```

7. Similarly, create and verify `sata-pool`:

```
[root@ceph-node1 ~]# ceph osd pool create sata-pool 8 8
pool 'sata-pool' created
[root@ceph-node1 ~]# ceph osd dump | grep -i sata
pool 46 'sata-pool' replicated size 3 min_size 2 crush_ruleset 0 object_hash rjenkins
pg_num 8 pgp_num 8 last_change 4450 flags hashpspool stripe_width 0
[root@ceph-node1 ~]#
[root@ceph-node1 ~]# ceph osd pool set sata-pool crush_ruleset 2
set pool 46 crush_ruleset to 1
[root@ceph-node1 ~]#
[root@ceph-node1 ~]# ceph osd dump | grep -i sata
pool 46 'sata-pool' replicated size 3 min_size 2 crush_ruleset 2 object_hash rjenkins
pg_num 8 pgp_num 8 last_change 4452 flags hashpspool stripe_width 0
[root@ceph-node1 ~]#
```

8. Let's add some objects to these pools:

1. Since these pools are new, they should not contain any objects, but let's verify this by using the `rados` list command:

```
# rados -p ssd-pool ls
```

```
# rados -p sata-pool ls
```

2. We will now add an object to these pools using the `rados put` command. The syntax would be `rados -p <pool_name> put <object_name> <file_name>`:

```
# rados -p ssd-pool put dummy_object1 /etc/hosts
# rados -p sata-pool put dummy_object1 /etc/hosts
```

3. Using the `rados` list command, list these pools. You should get the object names that we stored in the last step:

```
# rados -p ssd-pool ls
# rados -p sata-pool ls
```

```
[root@ceph-node1 ~]# rados -p ssd-pool ls
[root@ceph-node1 ~]# rados -p sata-pool ls
[root@ceph-node1 ~]#
[root@ceph-node1 ~]# rados -p ssd-pool put dummy_object1 /etc/hosts
[root@ceph-node1 ~]# rados -p sata-pool put dummy_object1 /etc/hosts
[root@ceph-node1 ~]#
[root@ceph-node1 ~]# rados -p ssd-pool ls
dummy_object1
[root@ceph-node1 ~]# rados -p sata-pool ls
dummy_object1
[root@ceph-node1 ~]#
```

9. Now, the interesting part of this entire section is to verify that the objects are getting stored on the correct set of OSDs:

1. For the `ssd-pool`, we have used the OSDs 0, 3, and 6. Check the `osd map` for `ssd-pool` using the syntax `ceph osd map <pool_name> <object_name>`:

   ```
   # ceph osd map ssd-pool dummy_object1
   ```

2. Similarly, check the object from sata-pool:

   ```
   # ceph osd map sata-pool dummy_object1
   ```

```
[root@ceph-node1 ~]# ceph osd map ssd-pool dummy_object1
osdmap e4455 pool 'ssd-pool' (45) object 'dummy_object1' -> pg 45.71968e96 (45.6) -> up ([3,0,6], p3) acting ([3,0,6], p3)
[root@ceph-node1 ~]#
[root@ceph-node1 ~]# ceph osd map sata-pool dummy_object1
osdmap e4455 pool 'sata-pool' (46) object 'dummy_object1' -> pg 46.71968e96 (46.6) -> up ([1,7,4], p1) acting ([1,7,4], p1)
[root@ceph-node1 ~]#
```

As shown in the preceding screenshot, the object that is created on `ssd-pool` is actually stored on the OSDs set [3,0,6], and the object that is created on `sata-pool` gets stored on the OSDs set [1,7,4]. This output was expected, and it verifies that the pool that we created uses the correct set of OSDs as we requested. This type of configuration can be very useful in a production setup, where you would like to create a fast pool based on SSDs only, and a medium/slower performing pool based on spinning disks.

10
Production Planning and Performance Tuning for Ceph

In this chapter, we will cover the following recipes:

- The dynamics of capacity, performance, and cost
- Choosing hardware and software components for Ceph
- Ceph recommendations and performance tuning
- Ceph erasure-coding
- Creating an erasure-coded pool
- Ceph cache tiering
- Creating a pool for cache tiering
- Creating a cache tier
- Configuring a cache tier
- Testing a cache tier
- Cache tiering – possible dangers in production environments

Introduction

In this chapter, we will learn some very interesting topics with regards to Ceph. These will include hardware/software recommendations, performance tuning for Ceph components (that is, Ceph MON and OSD), and clients, including OS tuning. Finally, we will understand Ceph erasure-coding and cache tiering, covering different techniques for both.

The dynamics of capacity, performance, and cost

Ceph is a software-defined storage solution that is designed to run on commodity hardware. This ability makes it a flexible and economic solution that is tailored for your needs. Since all the intelligence of Ceph resides in its software, it requires a good set of hardware to make it an overall package that is a great storage solution.

Ceph hardware selection requires meticulous planning based on your storage needs and the use case that you have. Organizations need optimized hardware configurations that allow them to start small and scale up to several petabytes. The following diagram represents a few factors that are used to determine an optimal configuration for a Ceph cluster:

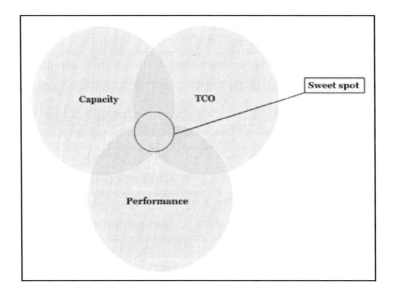

Different organizations have different storage workloads that generally require a middle-ground shared by the performance, capacity, and TCO. Ceph is unified storage, that is, it can provision file, block, and object storage from the same cluster. Ceph is also able to provision different types of storage pools within the same cluster that are targeted at different workloads. This ability allows an organization to tailor its storage infrastructure as per its needs. There are multiple ways to define your storage needs; the following diagram shows one way of doing this:

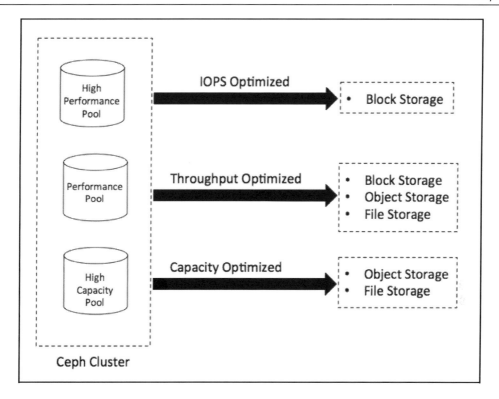

Other methods are as follows:

- **IOPS optimized**: The highlight of this type of configuration is that it has the highest **IOPS (I/O operations per second)** with low **TCO (Total Cost of Ownership)** per I/O. It is typically implemented using high-performance nodes containing faster SSD disks, PCIe SSD, NVMe, and so on, for data storage. It is generally used for block storage, however, you can use it for other workloads that require a high IOPS. These deployments are suitable for cloud computing applications such as MySQL or MariaDB instances as virtual machines running on OpenStack.

- **Throughput optimized**: Its highlights include the highest throughput and a low cost per throughput. It is typically implemented using SSD disks and PCIe SSD for OSD journals, with a high bandwidth, physically-separated dual network. It is mostly used for block storage. If your use case requires a high-performance object or file storage, then you should consider this. These deployments are suitable for serving up large amounts of data, such as graphics, audio, and video content.

- **Capacity optimized**: Its highlights include a low cost per TB and a low cost per rack unit of physical space in the data center. It is also known as economic storage, cheap storage, and archival/long-term storage, and is typically implemented using dense servers full of spinning disks, usually 36 to 72, with 4 TB to 6 TB of physical disk space per server. It is generally used for low cost, large storage capacity objects or filesystem storage. It is a good candidate for using erasure-coding to maximize the usable capacity. These deployments are suitable for storing backup data for a long amount of time.

Choosing hardware and software components for Ceph

As mentioned earlier, Ceph hardware selection requires meticulous planning based on your environment and storage needs. The type of hardware component, network infrastructure, and cluster design are some critical factors you should consider during the initial phase of Ceph storage planning. There is no golden rule for Ceph hardware selection as it depends on various factors such as budget, performance versus capacity (or both), fault tolerance level, and the use case.

Ceph is hardware agnostic; organizations are free to select any hardware of their choice based on budget, performance or capacity requirements, or use case. They have full control over their storage cluster and the underlying infrastructure. Also, one of the advantages of Ceph is that it supports heterogeneous hardware. You can mix hardware brands while creating your Ceph cluster infrastructure. For example, while building your Ceph cluster, you can mix hardware from different manufacturers such as HP, Dell, Supermicro, and so on, and even off-the-shelf hardware that can lead to significant cost savings.

You should keep in mind that hardware selection for Ceph is driven by the workload that you are planning to put on your storage cluster, the environment, and the features you will be using. In this recipe, we will learn some general practices for selecting hardware for your Ceph cluster.

Processor

The Ceph monitor daemon maintains the cluster maps and does not serve any data to the client, hence it is lightweight and does not have very strict processor requirements. In most cases, an average single core server processor will do the job for the Ceph monitor. On the other hand, the Ceph MDS is a bit more resource hungry. It requires significantly higher CPU processing power with quad core or better. For a small Ceph cluster or proof of concept environment, you can co-locate Ceph monitors with other Ceph components such as the OSD, RADOS Gateway, or even the Ceph MDS. For a medium-to-large-scale environment, instead of being shared, Ceph Monitors should be hosted on dedicated machines.

A Ceph OSD daemon requires a fair amount of processing power as it serves data to clients. To estimate the CPU requirement for the Ceph OSD, it's important to know how many OSDs the server will be hosting. It's generally recommended that each OSD daemon should have a minimum of one CPU core GHz. You can use the following formula to estimate the OSD CPU requirement:

((CPU sockets*CPU cores per socket*CPU clock speed in GHz) / No. Of OSD) >=1

For example, a server with a single socket, six-core, 2.5 GHz CPU should be good enough for 12 Ceph OSDs, and each OSD will get roughly 1.25 GHz of computing power:

((1*6*2.5)/12)= 1.25

Here are a few more examples of processors for the Ceph OSD node:

- **Intel® Xeon® Processor E5-2620 v4 (2.10 GHz, 8 cores)**:
  1*8*2.10 = 16.8 implies this is good for a Ceph node with up to 16 OSDs

- **Intel® Xeon® Processor E5-2680 v4 (2.40 GHz, 14 cores)**:
  1*14*2.40 = 33.6 implies this is good for a Ceph node with up to 33 OSDs

If you are planning to use the Ceph erasure-coding feature, then it would be more beneficial to get a more powerful CPU, as erasure-coding operations require more processing power. When settling on a CPU when using Ceph erasure-coding, it would be best to overestimate the processing power required as opposed to underestimating it.

If you were planning to use the Ceph erasure-coded pool, then it would be useful to get a more powerful CPU, as Ceph OSDs that host erasure-coded pools will use more of the CPU than Ceph OSDs that host replicated pools.

Memory

Monitor and MDS daemons need to serve their data rapidly, hence they should have enough memory for faster processing. The rule of thumb is to have 2 GB or more memory per daemon instance—this should be good for Ceph MDS and monitors in smaller Ceph clusters. Larger Ceph clusters should look to increase this amount. Ceph MDS depends on a lot on data caching; as they need to serve data quickly, they require plenty of RAM. The higher the RAM for Ceph MDS, the better the performance of Ceph FS will be.

OSDs generally require a fair amount of physical memory. For an average workload, 1 GB of memory per OSD daemon instance should suffice. However, from a performance point of view, 2 GB per OSD daemon is a good choice, and having more memory also helps during recovery and improves caching. This recommendation assumes that you are using one OSD daemon for one physical disk. If you use more than one physical disk per OSD, your memory requirements will grow as well. Generally, more physical memory is good, because during cluster recovery, memory consumption increases significantly. It's worth knowing that OSD memory consumption will increase if you consider the RAW capacity of the underlying physical disk. So, the OSD requirements for a 6 TB disk would be more than those of a 4 TB disk. You should make this decision wisely, such that memory will not become a bottleneck in your cluster's performance.

It is usually cost-effective to over-allocate CPU and memory at an earlier stage of your cluster planning, as you can add more physical disks in a JBOD style to the same host anytime—if it has enough system resources—rather than purchasing an entirely new node, which is a bit costly.

Network

Ceph is a distributed storage system and it relies heavily on the underlying network infrastructure. If you want your Ceph cluster to be reliable and performant, make sure that you have your network designed for it. It's recommended that all cluster nodes have two redundant separate networks for cluster and client traffic.

Set up cluster and client networks on separate NICs.

For a small proof of concept, or to test the Ceph cluster of a few nodes, a 1 GBps network speed should work well. If you have a mid-to-large sized cluster (a few tens of nodes), you should think about using 10 GBps or more network bandwidth. At the time of recovery/re-balancing, the network plays a vital role. If you have a good 10 GBps or more in terms of your bandwidth network connection, your cluster will recover quickly, or else it might take some time. So, from a performance point of view, a 10 GBps or more dual network will be a good option. A well-designed Ceph cluster makes use of two physically separated networks: one for the **Cluster Network** (internal network), and another for the **Client Network** (external network). Both these networks should be physically separated right from the server to the network switch, and everything in-between, as shown in the following diagram:

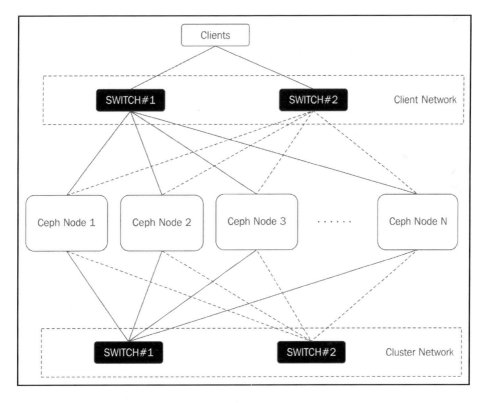

With respect to the network, another topic of debate is whether to use an Ethernet network or InfiniBand network or more precisely a 10 G network or a 40 G or higher bandwidth network. It depends on several factors such as workload, the size of your Ceph cluster, the density and number of Ceph OSD nodes, and so on. In several deployments, I have seen customers using both 10 G and 40 G networks with Ceph. In this case, the Ceph cluster ranges to several PB and a few hundred nodes, in which they are using the client network as 10 G, and the internal cluster network as high bandwidth, low latency 40 G. Nevertheless, the price of the Ethernet network is going down; based on your use case, you can decide on the network type that you would like to have.

For network optimization, you can choose to use jumbo frames for a better CP/bandwidth ratio. If jumbo frames are to be utilized, please remember to validate that all interconnecting network gear is configured to handle jumbo frames. Enabling jumbo frames will be discussed in a recipe later in this chapter.

> A 1 GBps network is not suitable for production clusters. For example, in the case of drive failure, replicating 1 TB of data across a 1 GBps network takes 3 hours, and 3 TB (a typical drive configuration) takes 9 hours. With a 10 GBps network, the replication times would be 20 minutes for 1 TB and 1 hour for 3 TB.

Disk

Performance and economics for the Ceph clusters both depend heavily on an effective choice of storage media. You should understand your workload and possible performance requirements before selecting the storage media for your Ceph cluster. Ceph uses storage media in two ways: the OSD journal part and the OSD data part. As explained in earlier chapters, every write operation in Ceph is currently a two-step process. When an OSD receives a request to write an object, it first writes that object to the journal part of the OSDs in the acting set, and sends a write acknowledgment to the clients. Soon after, the journal data is synced to the data partition. It's worth knowing that replication is also an important factor during write performances. The replication factor is usually a trade-off between reliability, performance, and TCO. In this way, all the cluster performance revolves around the OSD journal and data partition.

Partitioning the Ceph OSD journal

If your workload is performance-centric, then it's recommended you use SSDs. By using an SSD, you can achieve significant throughput improvement by reducing the access time and write latency. To use SSDs as journals, we create multiple logical partitions on each physical SSD, such that each SSD logical partition (journal) is mapped to one OSD data partition. In this case, the OSD data partition is located on a spinning disk and has its journal on the faster SSD partition. The following diagram illustrates this configuration:

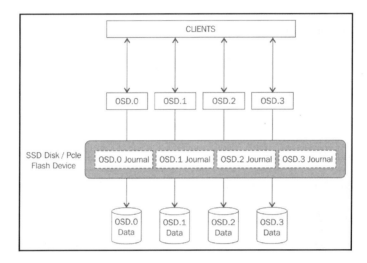

In this type of setup, you should keep in mind not to overload SSDs by storing multiple journals beyond their limits. Usually, 10 GB to 20 GB journal size should be good enough for most cases, however, if you have a larger SSD, you can create a larger journal device; in this case, don't forget to increase the filestore maximum and minimum synchronization time intervals for OSD.

The two most common types of non-volatile fast storage that are used with Ceph are SATA or SAS SSDs, and PCIe or NVMe SSDs. To achieve good performance from your SATA/SAS SSDs, your SSD to OSD ratio should be 1:4, that is, one SSD shared with four OSD data disks. In the case of PCIe or NVMe flash devices, depending on device performance the SSD to OSD ratio can vary from 1:12 to 1:18, that is, one flash device shared with 12 to 18 OSD data disks.

The SSD to OSD ratio mentioned here is very general and works well in most cases. However, I would encourage you to test your SSD/PCIe against your specific workloads and environment to get the best out of it.

The dark side of using a single SSD for multiple journals is that if you lose your SSD, hosting multiple journals, all the OSDs associated with this SSD will fail and you might lose your data. However, you can overcome this situation by using RAID one for journals, but this will increase your storage cost. Also, the SSD cost per GB is nearly ten times more when compared to HDD. So, if you are building a cluster with SSDs, it will increase the cost per GB for your Ceph cluster. However, if you are looking for significant performance improvements out of your Ceph cluster, it's worth investing in SSD for journals.

We have learned a lot about SSD journals and understood that they can contribute to improving write performance. However, if you are not concerned about extreme performance, and the cost per TB is a deciding factor for you, then you should consider configuring the journal and data partition on the same hard disk drive. This means that, out of your large spinning disk, you will allocate a few GBs for the OSD journal and use the remaining capacity of the same drive with the OSD data. This kind of setup might not be as performant as the SSD journal-based one, but the TCO of price per TB of storage would be fairly less.

In general, the established formula for the OSD-to-journal ratio is:

Journal number = (SSD seq write speed) / (spinning disk seq write speed)

The preceding formula usually yields around four to five spinning drives to an SSD journal disk. This means that a single SSD disk can be used to carry a journal of around four to five OSDs, as per the preceding formula.

Partitioning Ceph OSD data

OSDs are the real workhorses that store all the data. In a production environment, you should use an enterprise, cloud, or archive class hard disk drive with your Ceph cluster. Typically, desktop class HDDs are not well suited to a production Ceph cluster. The reason being that in a Ceph cluster, several hundreds of rotating HDDs are installed in close proximity, and the combined rotational vibration can become a challenge with desktop-class HDDs. This increases the disk failure rate and can hinder the overall performance. The enterprise-class HDDs are purposely built to handle vibrations, and they themselves generate very little rotational vibration. Also, their **Median Time Between Failure (MTBF)** is significantly higher than desktop class HDDs.

Another thing to consider for the Ceph OSD data disk is its interface, that is, SATA or SAS. The NL-SAS HDDs have dual SAS 12 GBps ports, and they are generally more high performing than single ported 6 GBps SATA interface HDDs. Also, dual SAS ports provide redundancy and can also allow for simultaneous reading and writing. Another aspect of SAS devices is that they have lower **unrecoverable read errors (URE)** when compared to SATA drives. The lower the URE, the fewer scrubbing errors and placement group repair operations.

The density of your Ceph OSD node is also an important factor for cluster performance, usable capacity, and TCO. Generally, it's better to have a larger number of smaller nodes than a few large capacity nodes, but this is always open for debate. You should select the density of your Ceph OSD node such that one node should be less than 10% of the total cluster size.

For example, in a 1 PB Ceph cluster, you should avoid using 4 x 250 TB OSD nodes, in which each node constitutes 25% of the cluster capacity. Instead, you can have 13 x 80 TB OSD nodes, in which each node size is less than 10% of the cluster capacity. However, this might increase your TCO and can affect several other factors in terms of your cluster planning.

Planning Ceph OSD node density properly can prevent elongated cluster recovery times during OSD node failures. A cluster can recover much quicker from a failure of an OSD node housing 10% of the cluster data than a node hosting 25% of the cluster data!

Operating system

Ceph is a software-defined system that runs on top of a Linux-based operating system. Ceph supports most of the major Linux distributions. As of now, the valid operating system choices to run Ceph clusters are RHEL, CentOS, Fedora, Debian, Ubuntu, openSUSE, and SLES. For the Linux kernel version, it's recommended that you deploy Ceph on newer releases of the Linux kernel. We also recommend deploying it on release with **long-term support** (**LTS**). At the time of writing this book, the Linux kernel v3.16.3, or a later version, is recommended and is a good starting point. It's a good idea to keep an eye on `http://docs.ceph.com/docs/master/start/os-recommendations`. According to documentation, CentOS 7 and Ubuntu 14.04 are tier-1 distributions for which comprehensive functional, regression, and stress test suites are run on a continuous basis, and with no doubt, RHEL 7 is the best choice if you are using the enterprise Red Hat Ceph Storage product.

OSD filesystem

The Ceph OSD daemon runs on top of a filesystem that can be XFS, EXT, or even Btrfs. However, selecting the right filesystem for the Ceph OSD is a critical factor as OSD daemons rely heavily on the stability and performance of the underlying filesystem. Apart from stability and performance, the filesystem also provides **extended attributes** (**XATTRs**) that Ceph OSD daemons take advantage of. The XATTR provides internal information on the object state, snapshot, metadata, and ACL to the Ceph OSD daemon, which helps in data management.

That's why the underlying filesystem should provide sufficient capacity for XATTRs. Btrfs provides significantly larger XATTR metadata, which is stored within a file. XFS has a relatively large limit (64 KB) that most deployments won't encounter, but ext4 is too small to be usable. If you are using the ext4 filesystem for your Ceph OSD, you should always add `filestore xattr use omap = true` to the following setting to the `[OSD]` section of your `ceph.conf` file. Filesystem selection is quite important for a production workload, and with regards to Ceph, these filesystems differ from each other in various ways, as follows:

- **XFS**: XFS is a reliable, mature, and very stable filesystem, which is recommended for production usage of Ceph clusters. However, XFS stands lower when compared to Btrfs. XFS has small performance issues in terms of metadata scaling. Also, XFS is a journaling filesystem, that is, each time a client sends data to write to a Ceph cluster, it is first written to a journaling space and then to an XFS filesystem. This increases the overhead of writing the same data twice, and thus makes the XFS perform slower when compared to Btrfs, which does not use journals. XFS is the currently *recommended* OSD filesystem for production Ceph workloads.

- **Btrfs**: The OSD, with the Btrfs filesystem underneath, delivers the best performance when compared to XFS and ext4 filesystem-based OSDs. One of the major advantages of using Btrfs is that it supports copy-on-write and writable snapshots. With the Btrfs filesystem, Ceph uses parallel journaling, that is, Ceph writes to the OSD journal and OSD data in parallel, which boosts write performance. It also supports transparent compression and pervasive checksums, and it incorporates multi-device management in a filesystem. It has an attractive feature: online FSCK. However, despite these new features, Btrfs is currently not production-ready, but it remains a good candidate for test deployments.

- **Ext4**: The fourth extended filesystem (ext4) is also a journaling filesystem that is production-ready for Ceph OSD. However, we don't recommend using ext4 due to limitations in terms of the size of the XATTRs it can store, and the problems this will cause with the way Ceph handles long RADOS object names. These issues will generally not surface with Ceph clusters using only short object names (RBD for example), but other client users like RGW that make use of long object names will have issues. Starting with Jewel, the `ceph-osd` daemon will not start if the configured max object name cannot be safely stored on ext4. If the cluster is planned to be used only with short object names (RBD usage only), then you can set the following configuration options to continue using ext4:

```
osd max object name len = 256
osd max object namespace len = 64
```

 Don't get confused between Ceph journaling and filesystem journaling (XFS, ext4); they are both different. Ceph does its journaling while writing to the filesystem, and then the filesystem does its journaling while writing data to underlying disks.

Ceph recommendations and performance tuning

In this recipe, we will learn some performance tuning parameters for the Ceph cluster. These cluster-wide configuration parameters are defined in the Ceph configuration file so that each time any Ceph daemon starts, it will respect the defined settings. By default, the configuration file name is `ceph.conf`, which is located in the `/etc/ceph` directory. This configuration file has a global section as well as several sections for each service type. Whenever a Ceph service type starts, it applies the configuration defined under the `[global]` section as well as the daemon specific section. A Ceph configuration file has multiple sections, as shown in the following screenshot:

```
[global]
      fsid                          = {UUID}
      public network                = 192.168.0.0/24
      cluster network               = 192.168.0.0/24
      osd pool default pg num       = 128
[mon]
[mon.alpha]
      host                          = alpha
      mon addr                      = 192.168.0.10:6789
[mds]
[mds.alpha]
      host                          = alpha
[osd]
      osd recovery max active        = 3
      osd max backfills              = 5
[osd.0]
      host                           = delta
[osd.1]
      host                           = epsilon
[client]
      rbd cache                      = true
[client.radosgw.gateway]
      host                           = ceph-radosgw
```

We will now discuss the role of each section of the configuration file:

- **Global section**: The global section of the cluster configuration file begins with the [global] keyword. All the settings defined under this section apply to all the daemons of the Ceph cluster. The following is an example of a parameter defined in the [global] section:

      public network = 192.168.0.0/24

- **Monitor section**: The settings defined under the [mon] section of the configuration file are applied to all the Ceph monitor daemons in the cluster. The parameter defined under this section overrides the parameters defined under the [global] section. The following is an example of a parameter usually defined under the [mon] section:

      mon initial members = ceph-mon1

- **OSD section**: The settings defined in the [osd] section are applied to all the Ceph OSD daemons in the Ceph cluster. The configuration defined under this section overrides the same setting defined under the [global] section. The following is an example of the settings in this section:

      osd mkfs type = xfs

- **MDS section**: The settings defined in the [mds] section are applied to all the Ceph MDS daemons in the Ceph cluster. The configuration defined under this section overrides the same setting defined under the [global] section. The following is an example of the settings in this section:

      mds cache size = 250000

- **Client section**: The settings defined under the [client] section are applied to all the Ceph clients. The configuration defined under this section overrides the same setting defined under the [global] section. The following is an example of the settings in this section:

      rbd cache size = 67108864

If utilizing Ansible as a deployment tool for Ceph, then Ansible will manage the `ceph.conf` file for the cluster. Be sure to include any custom configuration settings applied to specific sections, and that they are properly updated on the Ansible management node in the `/usr/share/ceph-ansible/group_vars/all.yml` file, under the `ceph_conf_overrides` section as discussed in previous chapters. If this is not done, any management done using Ansible will wipe out the custom configuration settings in your `ceph.conf` file!

In the next recipe, we will learn some tips for performance tuning the Ceph cluster. Performance tuning is a vast topic that requires an understanding of Ceph, as well as other components of your storage stack. There is no silver bullet for performance tuning. It depends a lot on the underlying infrastructure and your environment.

Tuning global clusters

The global parameters should be defined under the `[global]` section of your Ceph cluster configuration file, as follows:

- **Network**: It's recommended that you use two physically separated networks for your Ceph cluster, which are referred to as public and cluster networks respectively. Earlier in this chapter, we covered the need for two different networks. Let's now understand how we can define them in a Ceph configuration:
    - `public network`: Use this syntax to define the public network `public network = {public network / netmask}`:

    `public network = 192.168.100.0/24`

    - `cluster network`: Use this syntax to define the cluster network `cluster network = {cluster network / netmask}`:

    `cluster network = 192.168.1.0/24`

- `max open files`: If this parameter is in place and the Ceph cluster starts, it sets the maximum open file descriptors at the OS level. This keeps OSD daemons from running out of the file descriptors. The default value of this parameter is zero, but you can set it as up to a 64 bit integer:

    `max open files = 131072`

- `osd pool default min size`: This is the replication level in a degraded state, which should be set lower than the `osd pool default size` value. It sets the minimum number of replicas for the objects in pool in order to acknowledge a write operation from clients when the cluster is degraded. If the minimum size does not match, Ceph will not acknowledge it or write to the client. In production environments where data consistency is vital, this is recommended to be 2. The default value is 0:

```
osd pool default min size = 2
```

- `osd pool default pg` / `osd pool default pgp`: Make sure that the cluster has a realistic number of placement groups. The recommended value of placement groups per OSD is 100. Use this formula to calculate the PG count: *(Total number of OSD * 100)/number of replicas.*
  For 10 OSDs and a replica size of three, the PG count should be under *(10*100)/3 = 333*:

```
osd pool default pg num = 128
osd pool default pgp num = 128
```

As explained earlier, the PG and PGP number should be kept the same. The PG and PGP values vary a lot depending on the cluster size. The previously mentioned configurations should not harm your cluster, but you may want to think before applying these values. You should know that these parameters do not change the PG and PGP numbers for existing pools; they are applied when you create a new pool without specifying the PG and PGP values.

- `osd pool default crush rule`: The default CRUSH ruleset to use when creating a pool:

```
osd pool default crush rule = 0
```

- **Disable in memory logs**: Each Ceph subsystem has a logging level for its output logs, and it logs in-memory. We can set different values for each of these subsystems by setting a log file level and a memory level for debug logging on a scale of 1 to 20, where 1 is terse and 20 is verbose. The first setting is the log level and the second setting is the memory level. You must separate them with a forward slash as follows:

```
debug <subsystem> = <log-level>/<memory-level>
```

The default logging level is good enough for your cluster, unless you see that the memory level logs are impacting your performance or memory consumption. In such a case, you can try to disable the in-memory logging. To disable the default values of in-memory logs, add the following parameters:

```
debug_default = 0/0
debug_lockdep = 0/0
debug_context = 0/0
debug_crush = 0/0
debug_mds = 0/0
debug_mds_balancer = 0/0
debug_mds_locker = 0/0
debug_mds_log = 0/0
debug_mds_log_expire = 0/0
debug_mds_migrator = 0/0
debug_buffer = 0/0
debug_timer = 0/0
debug_filer = 0/0
debug_objecter = 0/0
debug_rados = 0/0
debug_rbd = 0/0
debug_journaler = 0/0
debug_objectcatcher = 0/0
debug_client = 0/0
debug_osd = 0/0
debug_optracker = 0/0
debug_objclass = 0/0
debug_filestore = 0/0
debug_journal = 0/0
debug_ms = 0/0
debug_monc = 0/0
debug_tp = 0/0
debug_auth = 0/0
debug_finisher = 0/0
debug_heartbeatmap = 0/0
debug_perfcounter = 0/0
debug_asok = 0/0
debug_throttle = 0/0
debug_mon = 0/0
debug_paxos = 0/0
debug_rgw = 0/0
debug_javaclient = 0/0
```

Tuning Monitor

The monitor tuning parameters should be defined under the `[mon]` section of your Ceph cluster configuration file as follows:

- `mon_osd_down_out_interval`: This is the number of seconds Ceph waits before marking a Ceph OSD daemon as *down* and *out* if it doesn't respond. This option comes in handy when your OSD nodes crash and reboot by themselves or after some short glitch in the network. You don't want your cluster to start rebalancing as soon as the problem comes, rather, for it to wait for a few minutes and see if the problem gets fixed (default 300):

  ```
  mon_osd_down_out_interval = 600
  ```

- `mon_allow_pool_delete`: To avoid the accidental deletion of the Ceph pool, set this parameter as false. This can be useful if you have many administrators managing the Ceph cluster, and you do not want to take any risks with client data (default true):

  ```
  mon_allow_pool_delete = false
  ```

- `mon_osd_min_down_reporters`: The Ceph OSD daemon can report to MON about its peer OSDs if they are down, by default this value is two. With this option, you can change the minimum number of Ceph OSD daemons required to report a down Ceph OSD to the Ceph monitor. In a large cluster, it's recommended that you have this value larger than the default; three should be a good number:

  ```
  mon_osd_min_down_reporters = 3
  ```

OSD tuning

In this recipe, we will understand the general OSD tuning parameters that should be defined under the `[osd]` section of your Ceph cluster configuration file.

OSD general settings

The following settings allow the Ceph OSD daemon to determine the filesystem type, mount options, as well as some other useful settings:

- `osd_mkfs_options_xfs`: At the time of OSD creation, Ceph will use these `xfs` options to create the OSD filesystem:

  ```
  osd_mkfs_options_xfs = "-f -i size=2048
  ```

- `osd_mount_options_xfs`: It supplies the `xfs` filesystem mount options to OSD. When Ceph is mounting an OSD, it will use the following options for OSD filesystem mounting:

  ```
  osd_mount_options_xfs = "rw,noatime,largeio,
  inode64,swalloc,logbufs=8,logbsize=256k,delaylog,allocsize=4M"
  ```

- `osd_max_write_size`: The maximum size in MB an OSD can write at a time:

  ```
  osd_max_write_size = 256
  ```

- `osd_client_message_size_cap`: The largest client data message in bytes that is allowed in memory:

  ```
  osd_client_message_size_cap = 1073741824
  ```

- `osd_map_dedup`: Remove duplicate entires in the OSD map:

  ```
  osd_map_dedup = true
  ```

- `osd_op_threads`: The number of threads to service the Ceph OSD daemon operations. Set it to zero to disable it. Increasing the number may increase the request processing rate:

  ```
  osd_op_threads = 16
  ```

- `osd_disk_threads`: The number of disk threads that are used to perform background disk intensive OSD operations such as scrubbing and snap trimming:

  ```
  osd_disk_threads = 1
  ```

- `osd_disk_thread_ioprio_class`: It is used in conjunction with `osd_disk_thread_ioprio_priority`. This tunable can change the I/O scheduling class of the disk thread, and it only works with the Linux kernel CFQ scheduler. The possible values are `idle`, `be`, or `rt`:
  - `idle`: The disk thread will have a lower priority than any other thread in the OSD. It is useful when you want to slow down the scrubbing on an OSD that is busy handling client requests.
  - `be`: The disk threads have the same priority as other threads in the OSD.
  - `rt`: The disk thread will have more priority than all the other threads. This is useful when scrubbing is much needed, and it can be prioritized at the expense of client operations:

    ```
    osd_disk_thread_ioprio_class = idle
    ```

- `osd_disk_thread_ioprio_priority`: It's used in conjunction with `osd_disk_thread_ioprio_class`. This tunable can change the I/O scheduling priority of the disk thread ranging from 0 (highest) to 7 (lowest). If all OSDs on a given host are in class idle and are competing for I/O and not doing many operations, this parameter can be used to lower the disk thread priority of one OSD to 7 so that another OSD with a priority of zero can potentially scrub faster. Like the `osd_disk_thread_ioprio_class`, this also works with the Linux kernel CFQ scheduler:

  ```
  osd_disk_thread_ioprio_priority = 0
  ```

 The OSD disk thread `ioprio_class` and the osd disk thread `ioprio_priority` will only be effective if the scheduler is CFQ. The schedulers can be changed at runtime without affecting the I/O operations. This will be discussed in a recipe later in the chapter.

```
[root@ceph-node1 ~]# cat /sys/block/sda/queue/scheduler
noop [deadline] cfq
[root@ceph-node1 ~]# echo cfq > /sys/block/sda/queue/scheduler
[root@ceph-node1 ~]# cat /sys/block/sda/queue/scheduler
noop deadline [cfq]
```

OSD journal settings

Ceph OSD daemons support the following journal configurations:

- `osd journal size`: Ceph's default OSD journal size value is zero; you should use the `osd_journal_size` parameter to set the journal size. The journal size should be at least twice the product of the expected drive speed and filestore max sync interval. If you are using SSD journals, it's usually good to create journals larger than 10 GB and increase the filestore minimum/maximum sync intervals:

  ```
  osd_journal_size = 20480
  ```

- `journal_max_write_bytes`: The maximum number of bytes the journal can write at once:

  ```
  journal_max_write_bytes = 1073714824
  ```

- `journal_max_write_entries`: The maximum number of entries the journal can write at once:

  ```
  journal_max_write_entries = 10000
  ```

- `journal queue max ops`: The maximum number of operations allowed in the journal queue at a given time:

  ```
  journal queue max ops = 50000
  ```

- `journal queue max bytes`: The maximum number of bytes allowed in the journal queue at a given time:

  ```
  journal queue max bytes = 10485760000
  ```

- `journal_dio`: This enables direct I/O to the journal. It requires `journal block align` to be set to `true`:

  ```
  jorunal_dio = true
  ```

- `journal_aio`: This enables the use of `libaio` for asynchronous writes to the journal. It requires `journal_aio` to be set to `true`:

  ```
  journal_aio = true
  ```

- `journal block align`: This block aligns *write* operations. It's required for *dio* and *aio*.

OSD filestore settings

These are a few filestore settings that can be configured for Ceph OSD daemons:

- `filestore merge threshold`: This is the minimum number of subdirectories before merging them into a parent directory. A negative value can be set here to disable subdirectory merging:

  ```
  filestore merge threshold = 50
  ```

- `filestore_split_multiple`: The maximum number of files in a subdirectory before splitting it into child directories:

  ```
  filestore_split_multiple = 12
  ```

- `filestore xattr useomap`: Uses the object map for XATTRs. Needs to be set to `true` for the ext4 filesystems:

  ```
  filestore xattr useomap = true
  ```

- `filestore sync interval`: In order to create a consistent commit point, the filestore needs to quiesce write operations and do a `syncfs()` operation, which syncs data from the journal to the data partition and thus frees the journal. A more frequently performed sync operation reduces the amount of data that is stored in a journal. In such cases, the journal becomes underutilized. Configuring less frequent syncs allows the filesystem to coalesce small writes better, and we might get improved performance. The following parameters define the minimum and maximum time period between two syncs:

  ```
  file_store_min_sync_interval = 10
  file_store_max_sync_interval = 15
  ```

- `filestore_queue_max_ops`: The maximum number of operations that a filestore can accept before blocking new operations from joining the queue:

  ```
  filestore_queue_max_ops = 2500
  ```

- `filestore_max_queue_bytes`: The maximum number of bytes in an operation:

  ```
  filestore_max_queue_bytes = 10485760
  ```

- `filestore_queue_commiting_max_ops`: The maximum number of operations the filestore can commit:

  ```
  filestore_queue_commiting_max_ops = 5000
  ```

- `filestore_queue_commiting_max_bytes`: The maximum number of bytes the filestore can commit:

```
filestore_ queue_commiting_max_bytes = 10485760000
```

OSD recovery settings

These settings should be used when you want performance over-recovery or vice versa. If your Ceph cluster is unhealthy and is under recovery, you might not get its usual performance, as the OSDs will be busy with recovery. If you still prefer performance over recovery, you can reduce the recovery priority to keep OSDs less occupied with recovery. You can also set these values if you want a quick recovery for your cluster, helping the OSDs to perform recovery faster:

- `osd_recovery_max_active`: The number of active recovery requests per OSD at a given moment:

```
osd_recovery_max_active = 1
```

- `osd_recovery_max_single_start`: This is used in conjunction with `osd_recovery_max_active`. To understand this, let's assume `osd_recovery_max_single_start` is equal to 1, and `osd_recovery_max_active` is equal to three. In this case, it means that the OSD will start a maximum of one recovery operation at a time, out of a total of three operations active at that time:

```
osd_recovery_max_single_start = 1
```

- `osd_recovery_op_priority`: This is the priority set for the recovery operation. This is relative to `osd client op priority`. The higher the number, the higher the recovery priority:

```
osd_recovery_op_priority = 1
```

- `osd client op priority`: This is the priority set for client operation. The higher the number, the higher the client operation priority:

```
osd client op priority = 63
```

- `osd_recovery_max_chunk`: The maximum size of a recovered chuck of data in bytes:

```
osd_recovery_max_chunk = 1048576
```

- `osd_recovery_threads`: The number of threads needed for recovering data:

      osd_recovery_threads = 1

OSD backfilling settings

OSD backfilling settings allow Ceph to set backfilling operations at a lower priority than requests to read and write:

- `osd_max_backfills`: The maximum number of backfills allowed to or from a single OSD:

      osd_max_backfills = 2

- `osd_backfill_scan_min`: The minimum number of objects per backfill scan:

      osd_backfill_scan_min = 8

- `osd_backfill_scan_max`: The maximum number of objects per backfill scan:

      osd_backfill_scan_max = 64

OSD scrubbing settings

OSD scrubbing is important for maintaining data integrity, but it can reduce performance. You can adjust the following settings to increase or decrease scrubbing operations:

- `osd_max_scrubs`: The maximum number of simultaneous scrub operations for a Ceph OSD daemon:

      osd_max_scrubs = 1

- `osd_scrub_sleep`: The time in seconds that scrubbing sleeps between two consecutive scrubs:

      osd_scrub_sleep = .1

- `osd_scrub_chunk_min`: The minimum number of data chunks an OSD should perform scrubbing on:

      osd_scrub_chunk_min = 1

- `osd_scrub_chunk_max`: The maximum number of data chunks an OSD should perform scrubbing on:

  ```
  osd_scrub-chunk_max = 5
  ```

- `osd_deep_scrub_stride`: The read size in bytes while doing a deep scrub:

  ```
  osd_deep_scrub_stride = 1048576
  ```

- `osd_scrub_begin_hour`: The earliest hour that scrubbing can begin. This is used in conjunction with `osd_scrub_end_hour` to define a scrubbing time window:

  ```
  osd_scrub_begin_hour = 19
  ```

- `osd_scrub_end_hour`: This is the upper bound when the scrubbing can be performed. This works in conjunction with `osd_scrub_begin_hour` to define a scrubbing time window:

  ```
  osd_scrub_end_hour = 7
  ```

> A scrub/deep scrub that is initiated prior to the `osd_scrub_end_hour` may run through the intended end hour. The end hour is just a stop time for initiating new scrubs on the cluster.

Tuning the client

The client tuning parameters should be defined under the `[client]` section of your Ceph configuration file. Usually, this `[client]` section should also be present in the Ceph configuration file hosted on the client node. The parameters are as follows:

- `rbd_cache`: Enables caching for the **RADOS Block Device (RBD)**:

  ```
  rbd_cache = true
  ```

- `rbd_cache_writethrough_until_flush`: Starts out in write-through mode, and switches to writeback after the first flush request is received:

  ```
  rbd_cache_writethrough_until_flush = true
  ```

- `rbd_concurrent_management_ops`: The number of concurrent management operations that can be performed on `rbd`:

```
rbd_concurrent_management_ops = 10
```

- `rbd_cache_size`: The rbd cache size in bytes:

```
rbd_cache_size = 67108864 #64M
```

- `rbd_cache_max_dirty`: The limit in bytes at which the cache should trigger a writeback. It should be less than `rbd_cache_size`:

```
rbd_cache_max_dirty = 50331648 #48M
```

- `rbd_cache_target_dirty`: The dirty target before the cache begins writing data to the backing store:

```
rbd_cache_target_dirty = 33554432 #32M
```

- `rbd_cache_max_dirty_age`: The number of seconds that the dirty data is in the cache before writeback starts:

```
rbd_cache_max_dirty_age = 2
```

- `rbd_default_format`: This uses the second RBD format, which is supported by librbd and the Linux kernel (since version 3.11). This adds support for cloning and is more easily extensible, allowing for more features in the future:

```
rbd_default_format = 2
```

Tuning the operating system

In the last recipe, we covered the tuning parameters for Ceph MON, OSD, and clients. In this recipe, we will cover a few general tuning parameters which can be applied to the operating system, which are as follows:

- `kernel.pid_max`: This is a Linux kernel parameter that is responsible for the maximum number of threads and process IDs. By default, the Linux kernel has a relatively small `kernel.pid_max` value. You should configure this parameter with a higher value on Ceph nodes hosting several OSDs, typically more than 20 OSDs. This setting helps spawn multiple threads for faster recovery and rebalancing. To use this parameter, execute the following command from the root user:

```
# echo 4194303 > /proc/sys/kernel/pid_max
```

- `file-max`: This is the maximum number of open files on a Linux system. It's generally a good idea to have a larger value for this parameter:

```
# echo 26234859 > /proc/sys/fs/file-max
```

- `disk read_ahead`: The `read_ahead` parameter speeds up the disk read operation by fetching data beforehand and loading it in the random access memory. It sets up up a relatively higher value for `read_ahead` and will benefit clients performing sequential read operations.
  Let's assume that the disk `vda` is an RBD that is mounted on a client node. Use the following command to check its `read_ahead` value, which is the default in most cases:

```
# cat /sys/block/vda/queue/read_ahead_kb
```

To set `read_ahead` to a higher value, that is, 8 MB for vda RBD, execute the following command:

```
# echo "8192" > /sys/block/vda/queue/read_ahead_kb
```

The `read_ahead` settings are used on Ceph clients that use the mount's RBD. To get a read performance boost, you can set it to several MB, depending on your hardware and on all your RBD devices.

- **Virtual memory**: Due to the heavily I/O-focused profile, swap usage can result in the entire server becoming unresponsive. A low swappiness value is recommended for high I/O workload. Set `vm.swappiness` to `0` in `/etc/sysctl.conf` to prevent this:

```
# echo "vm.swappiness=0" >> /etc/sysctl.conf
```

- `min_free_kbytes`: This provides the minimum number of KB to keep free across the system. You can keep 1 % to 3% of the total system memory free with `min_free_kbytes` by running the following command:

```
# echo 262144 > /proc/sys/vm/min_free_kbytes
```

- `zone_reclaim_mode`: This allows someone to set more or less aggressive approaches to reclaim memory when a zone runs out of memory. If it is set to 0, then no zone reclaim occurs. Allocations will be satisfied from other zones in the system. Set this with the following command:

  ```
  # echo 0 > /proc/sys/vm/zone_reclaim_mode
  ```

- `vfs_cache_pressure`: This percentage value controls the tendency of the kernel to reclaim the memory which is used for caching directory and inode objects. Set this with the following command:

  ```
  # echo 50 /proc/sys/vm/vfs_cache_pressure
  ```

- **I/O scheduler**: Linux gives us the option to select the I/O scheduler, and this can be changed without rebooting, too. It provides three options for I/O schedulers, which are as follows:

  - **Deadline**: The deadline I/O scheduler replaces CFQ as the default I/O scheduler in Red Hat Enterprise Linux 7 and its derivatives, as well as in Ubuntu Trusty. The deadline scheduler favors read over writes via the use of separate I/O queues for each. This scheduler is suitable for most use cases, but particularly for those in which read operations occur more often than write operations. Queued I/O requests are sorted into a read or write batch and then scheduled for execution in increasing LBA order. The read batches take precedence over the write batches by default, as applications are more likely to block on reading the I/O. For Ceph OSD workloads deadlines, the I/O scheduler looks promising.

  - **CFQ**: The **Completely Fair Queuing** (**CFQ**) scheduler was the default scheduler in Red Hat Enterprise Linux (4, 5, and 6) and its derivatives. The default scheduler is only for devices identified as SATA disks. The CFQ scheduler divides processes into three separate classes: real-time, best effort, and idle. Processes in the real-time class are always performed before processes in the best effort class, which are always performed before processes in the idle class. This means that processes in the real-time class can starve both the best effort and idle processes of the processor time. Processes are assigned to the best effort class by default.

- **Noop**: The Noop I/O scheduler implements a simple **first-in first-out (FIFO)** scheduling algorithm. Requests are merged at the generic block layer through a simple last-hit cache. This can be the best scheduler for CPU-bound systems using fast storage. For an SSD, the NOOP I/O scheduler can reduce I/O latency and increase throughput as well as eliminate the CPU time spent reordering I/O requests. This scheduler typically works well with SSDs, virtual machines, and even with NVMe cards. Thus, the Noop I/O scheduler should be a good choice for SSD disks used for Ceph journals.

  Execute the following command to check the default I/O scheduler for the disk device `sda` (the default scheduler should appear inside square brackets):

```
# cat /sys/block/sda/queue/scheduler
```

Change the default I/O scheduler for the `sda` disk to `deadline`:

```
# echo deadline > /sys/block/sda/queue/scheduler
```

Change the default I/O scheduler for the disk to `noop`:

```
# echo noop > /sys/block/sda/queue/scheduler
```

You must repeat these commands to change the default schedulers to either `deadline` or `noop`, based on your requirements for all the disks. Also, to make this change permanent, you need to update the grub boot loader with the required elevator option.

- **I/O scheduler queue**: The default I/O scheduler queue size is 128. The scheduler queue sorts and writes in an attempt to optimize for sequential I/O and to reduce the seek time. Changing the depth of the scheduler queue to 1024 can increase the proportion of sequential I/O that disks perform and improve the overall throughput.

  To check the scheduler depth for the `sda` block device, use the following command:

```
# cat /sys/block/sda/queue/nr_requests
```

To increase the scheduler depth to 1024, use the following command:

```
# echo 1024 > /sys/block/sda/queue/nr_request
```

Tuning the net

The Ethernet frames th   re known as **jumbo frames**. Enabling jumb   h is using for both the cluster and client netwc   nd overall network performance.

Jumbo frames should b   k switch side, otherwise, a mismatch   nable jumbo frames on the interface eth0, exec

```
# ifconfig eth0 r
```

Similarly, you should do this for other interfaces that are participating in the Ceph networks. To make this change permanent, you should add this configuration in the interface configuration file.

Sample tuning profile for OSD nodes

Some various sysctl parameters that you can implement—which are known to have a positive impact on Ceph OSD network node performance—follow. If intending to use these parameters in production, please test and verify prior to implementing.

How to do it...

Proper tuning can lead to great performance improvements in your cluster during everyday I/O workloads and recovery/rebalance scenarios. Let's look at setting a recommended tuning profile for your OSD nodes:

1. Create a file: /etc/sysctl.d/ceph-tuning.conf.

   An example is shown in the following screenshot:

```
[root@ceph-node1 vagrant]# vim /etc/sysctl.d/ceph-tuning.conf
```

2. Update with the following parameters:

```
### Network tuning ###
net.core.rmem_max = 56623104
net.core.wmem_max = 56623104
net.core.rmem_default = 56623104
net.core.wmem_default = 56623104
```

```
net.core.optmem_max = 40960
net.ipv4.tcp_rmem = 4096 87380 56623104
net.ipv4.tcp_wmem = 4096 65536 56623104
net.core.somaxconn = 1024
net.core.netdev_max_backlog = 50000
net.ipv4.tcp_max_syn_backlog = 30000
net.ipv4.tcp_max_tw_buckets = 2000000
net.ipv4.tcp_tw_reuse = 1
net.ipv4.tcp_fin_timeout = 10
net.ipv4.tcp_slow_start_after_idle = 0
net.ipv4.conf.all.send_redirects = 0
net.ipv4.conf.all.accept_redirects = 0
net.ipv4.conf.all.accept_source_route = 0
net.ipv4.tcp_mtu_probing = 1
net.ipv4.tcp_timestamps = 0
```

The following screenshot shows an example:

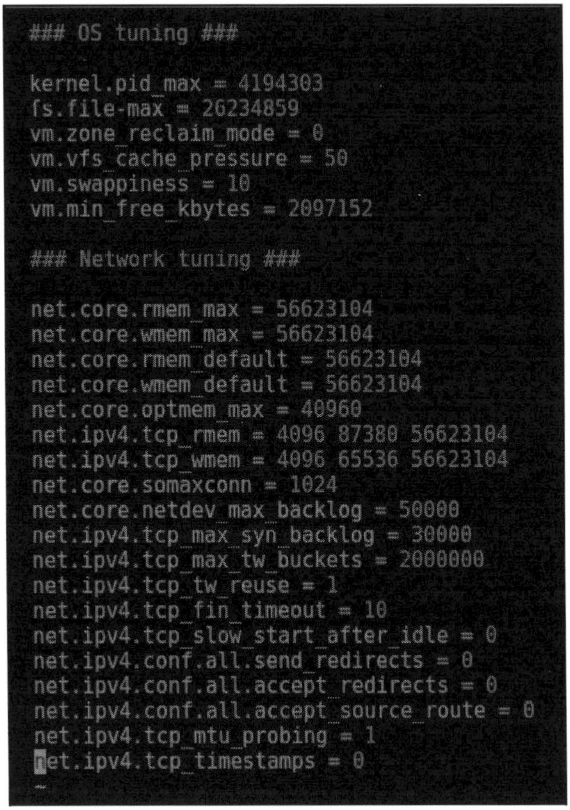

3. Load the values:

```
# systcl -p /etc/sysctl.d/ceph-tuning.conf
```

For further information on these values, please see: https://www.kernel.org/doc/Documentation/sysctl/.

 Do not use this profile on your VirtualBox lab as the VMs cannot handle these values and will crash.

Ceph erasure-coding

The default data protection mechanism in Ceph is replication. It's proven and is one of the most popular methods of data protection. However, the downside of replication is that it requires double the amount of storage space to provide redundancy. For instance, if you were planning to build a storage solution with 1 PB of usable capacity with a replication factor of three, you would require 3 PB of raw storage capacity for 1 PB of usable capacity, that is, 200% or more. In this way, with the replication mechanism, the cost per GB of the storage system increases significantly. For a small cluster, you might ignore the replication overhead, but for large environments, it becomes significant.

The Firefly release of Ceph introduced another method for data protection known as **erasure-coding**. This method of data protection is absolutely different from the replication method. It guarantees data protection by dividing each object into smaller chunks known as data chunks, encoding them with coding chunks, and finally storing all these chunks across the different failure zones of a Ceph cluster. The concept of erasure-coding revolves around the equation $n = k + m$. This is explained in the following list:

- **k**: This is the number of chunks the original object is divided into; it is also known as **data chunks**.
- **m**: This is the extra code added to the original data chunks to provide data protection; it is also known as **coding chunks**. For ease of understanding, you can consider it as the reliability level.
- **n**: This is the total number of chunks created after the erasure-coding process.

Based on the preceding equation, every object in an erasure-coded Ceph pool will be stored as *k+m* chunks, and each chunk is stored in a unique OSD with an acting set. In this way, all the chunks of an object are spread across the entire Ceph cluster, providing a higher degree of reliability. Now, let's discuss some useful terms with regards to erasure-coding:

- **Recovery:** At the time of recovery, we will require any *k* chunks out of *n* chunks to recover the data.
- **Reliability level:** With erasure-coding, Ceph can tolerate failure up to *m* chunks.
- **Encoding Rate (r):** This can be calculated using the formula $r = k / n$, where r is less than 1 storage required. This is calculated using the formula $1/r$.

To understand these terms better, let's consider an example. A Ceph pool is created with five OSDs based on the erasure code *(3, 2)* rule. Every object that is stored inside this pool will be divided into sets of data and coding chunks as given by this formula: $n = k + m$.

Consider $5 = 3 + 2$, then n = 5, $k = 3$ and $m = 2$. Every object will be divided into three data chunks, and two extra erasure-coded chunks will be added to it, making a total of five chunks that will be stored and distributed on five OSDs of an erasure-coded pool in a Ceph cluster. In the event of failure, to construct the original file we need (*k* chunks), three chunks out of (*n* chunks), and five chunks to recover it. Thus, we can sustain the failure of any (*m*) two OSDs as the data can be recovered using three OSDs:

- *Encoding rate (r)* = 3 / 5 = 0.6 < 1
- *Storage Required* = 1/r = 1 / 0.6 = 1.6 times of original file

Let's suppose that there is a data file of the size 1 GB. To store this file in a Ceph cluster on an erasure-coded *(3, 5)* pool, you will need 1.6 GB of storage space, which will provide to you with file storage with the sustainability of two OSD failures.

In contrast to the replication method, if the same file is stored on a replicated pool, then in order to sustain the failure of two OSDs, Ceph will need a pool of replica size three, which eventually requires 3 GB of storage space to reliably store 1 GB of the file. In this way, you can reduce storage costs by approximately 40% by using the erasure-coding feature of Ceph and getting the same reliability as with replication.

Erasure-coded pools require less storage space compared to replicated pools, however, this storage saving element comes at the cost of performance because the erasure-coding process divides every object into multiple smaller data chunks, and a few newer coding chunks are mixed in with these data chunks. Finally, all these chunks are stored in the different failure zones of a Ceph cluster. This entire mechanism requires a bit more computational power from the OSD nodes. Moreover, at the time of recovery, decoding the data chunks also requires a lot of computing. So, you might find the erasure-coding mechanism for storing data somewhat slower than the replication mechanism. Erasure-coding is mainly use-case dependent, and you can get the most out of erasure-coding based on your data storage requirements.

Erasure code plugin

Ceph gives us options to choose the erasure code plugin while creating the erasure code profile. One can create multiple erasure code profiles with different plugins each time. Choosing the right profile is important because it cannot be modified after the pool is created. In order to change a profile, a new pool with a different profile needs to be created, and all objects from the previous pool moved to the new pool. Ceph supports the following plugins for erasure-coding:

- **Jerasure erasure code plugin**: The Jerasure plugin is the most generic and flexible plugin. It is also the default for Ceph erasure-coded pools. The Jerasure plugin encapsulates the Jerasure library. Jerasure uses the Reed Solomon Code technique. The following diagram illustrates Jerasure code *(3, 2)*. As explained, data is first divided into three data chunks, and an additional two coded chunks are added, and they finally get stored in the unique failure zone of the Ceph cluster, as shown in the following diagram:

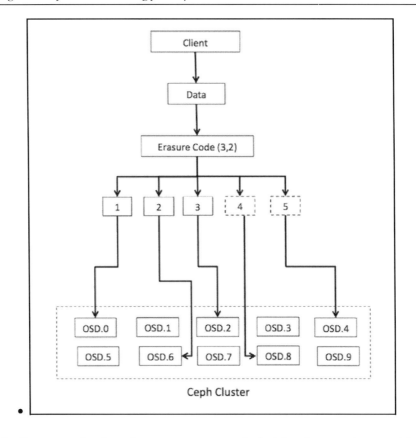

With the Jerasure plugin, when an erasure-coded object is stored on multiple OSDs, recovering from the loss of one OSD requires reading from all the others. For instance, if Jerasure is configured with $k=3$ and $m=2$, losing one OSD requires reading from all five OSDs to repair, which is not very efficient during recovery.

- **Locally repairable erasure code plugin**: Since Jerasure erasure code (Reed Solomon) was not recovery efficient, it was improved by the local parity method, and the new method is known as **Locally Repairable erasure Code** (**LRC**). The LRC plugin creates local parity chunks that are able to recover using less OSD, which makes it recovery-efficient. To understand this better, let's assume that LRC is configured with $k=8$, $m=4$, and $l=4$ (locality). It will create an additional parity chunk for every four OSDs. When a single OSD is lost, it can be recovered with only four OSDs instead of 11, which is the case with Jerasure. See the following diagram:

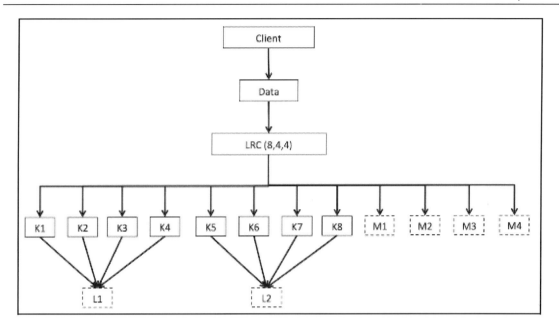

LRCs are designed to lower the bandwidth when recovering from the loss of a single OSD. As illustrated previously, a local parity chunk (L) is generated for every four data chunks (K). When **K3** is lost, instead of recovering from all *[(K+M)-K3]* chunks, that is, 11 chunks, with LRC, it's enough to recover from the **K1**, **K2**, **K4**, and **L1** chunks.

- **Shingled erasure code plugin**: The locally repairable codes are optimized for single OSD failure. For multiple OSD failures, the recovery overhead is large with LRC because it has to use global parity (M) for recovery. Let's reconsider the previous scenario and assume that multiple data chunks, **K3** and **K4**, are lost. To recover the lost chunks using LRC, it needs to recover from **K1**, **K2**, **L1** (the local parity chunk), and **M1** (the global parity chunk). Thus, LRC involves overhead with multi-disk failure.

To address this problem, **Shingled Erasure Code** (SHEC) has been introduced. The SHEC plugin encapsulates multiple SHEC libraries and allows Ceph to recover data more efficiently than Jerasure and LRC. The goal of the SHEC method is to efficiently handle multiple disk failure. Under this method, the calculation range for local parities has been shifted, and will parity the overlap between them (like shingles on a roof) to maintain durability.

- Let's understand this by the example SHEC (10,6,5) where *K=10* (data chunks), *m=6* (parity chunks), and *l=5* (calculation range). In this case, the diagrammatic representation of SHEC looks as follows:

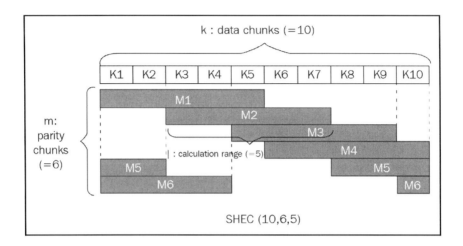

Recovery efficiency is one of the biggest features of SHEC. It minimizes the amount of data read from the disk during recovery. If chunks *K6* and *K9* are lost, SHEC will use the *M3* and *M4* parity chunks, and the **K5**, **K7**, **K8**, and **K10** data chunks for recovery. The same has been illustrated in the following diagram:

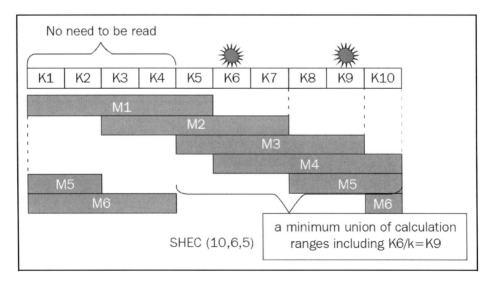

For multi-disk failure, SHEC is expected to recover more efficiently than other methods. SHEC's recovery time was 18.6% faster than the Solomon code in the case of a double disk failure.

- **ISA-I erasure code plugin**: The **Intelligent Storage Acceleration (ISA)** plugin encapsulates the ISA library. ISA-I was optimized for Intel platforms using some platform-specific instructions, and thus runs only on Intel architecture. ISA can be used in either of the two forms of Reed Solomon, that is, Vandermonde or Cauchy.

Creating an erasure-coded pool

Erasure code is implemented by creating a Ceph pool of the type erasure. This pool is based on an erasure code profile that defines erasure-coding characteristics. We will first create an erasure code profile, and then we will create an erasure-coded pool based on this profile.

How to do it...

The following steps will show you how to create an EC profile and then apply that profile to an EC pool.

1. The command mentioned in this recipe will create an erasure code profile with the name EC-profile, which will have characteristics of $k=3$ and $m=2$, which are the numbers of data and coding chunks respectively. So, every object that is stored in the erasure-coded pool will be divided into 3 (k) data chunks, and 2 (m) additional coding chunks are added to them, making a total of 5 $(k + m)$ chunks. Finally, these 5 $(k + m)$ chunks are spread across different OSD failure zones:

   1. Create the erasure code profile:

      ```
      # ceph osd erasure-code-profile set EC-profile
        ruleset-failure-domain=osd k=3 m=2
      ```

   2. List the profile:

      ```
      # ceph osd erasure-code-profile ls
      ```

   3. Get the contents of your erasure code profile:

      ```
      # ceph osd erasure-code-profile get EC-profile
      ```

This is shown in the following screenshot:

```
[root@ceph-node1 ~]# ceph osd erasure-code-profile set EC-profile ruleset-failure-domain=osd k=3 m=2
[root@ceph-node1 ~]# ceph osd erasure-code-profile ls
EC-profile
default
[root@ceph-node1 ~]# ceph osd erasure-code-profile get EC-profile
jerasure-per-chunk-alignment=false
k=3
m=2
plugin=jerasure
ruleset-failure-domain=osd
ruleset-root=default
technique=reed_sol_van
w=8
[root@ceph-node1 ~]#
```

2. Create a Ceph pool of the `erasure` type, which is based on the erasure code profile that we created in *step 1*:

    ```
    # ceph osd pool create EC-pool 16 16 erasure EC-profile
    ```

    Check the status of your newly created pool; you should find that the size of the pool is *5 (k + m)*, that is, the erasure size. Hence, data will be written to five different OSDs, as shown in the following screenshot:

```
[root@ceph-node1 ~]# ceph osd pool create EC-pool 16 16 erasure EC-profile
pool 'EC-pool' created
[root@ceph-node1 ~]# ceph osd dump | grep -i EC-pool
pool 1 'EC-pool' erasure size 5 min_size 3 crush_ruleset 1 object_hash rjenkins pg_num 16 pgp_num 16 last_change 42 flags hashpspool stripe_width 4128
```

3. Let's now add some data to this newly created Ceph pool. To do this, we will create a dummy file, `hello.txt`, and add this file to the `EC-pool` as shown in the following screenshot:

```
[root@ceph-node1 ~]# echo "Hello Ceph" >> hello.txt
[root@ceph-node1 ~]# cat hello.txt
Hello Ceph
[root@ceph-node1 ~]# rados -p EC-pool ls
[root@ceph-node1 ~]# rados -p EC-pool put object1 hello.txt
[root@ceph-node1 ~]# rados -p EC-pool ls
object1
[root@ceph-node1 ~]#
```

4. To verify if the erasure-coded pool is working correctly, we will check the OSD map for the `EC-pool` and `object1` as shown in the following screenshot:

```
[root@ceph-node1 ~]# ceph osd map EC-pool object1
osdmap e53 pool 'EC-pool' (2) object 'object1' -> pg 2.bac5debc (2.c) -> up ([2,8,0,7,6], p2) acting ([2,8,0,7,6], p2)
```

If you observe the output, you will notice that `object1` is stored in the placement group `2.c`, which in turn is stored in the `EC-pool`. You will also notice that the placement group is stored on five OSDs, that is, `osd.2`, `osd.8`, `osd.0`, `osd.7`, and `osd.6`. If you go back to step 1, you will see that we created the erasure-coded profile of *(3,2)*. This is why `object1` is stored on five OSDs.

At this stage, we have completed the setting up of an erasure pool in a Ceph cluster. Now, we will deliberately try to break OSDs to see how the erasure pool behaves when OSDs are unavailable.

5. We will now try to bring down `osd.2` and `osd.8`, one by one.

These are optional steps and you should not be performing this on your production Ceph cluster. Also, the OSD numbers might change for your cluster; replace them wherever necessary.

Bring down `osd.2` and check the OSD map for `EC-pool` and `object1`. You should notice that `osd.2` is replaced by the word NONE, which means that *osd.2* is no longer available for this pool:

```
root@ceph-node2 # systemctl stop ceph-osd@2
              # ceph osd map EC-pool object1
```

This is shown in the following screenshot:

```
[root@ceph-node2 vagrant]# systemctl stop ceph-osd@2
[root@ceph-node2 vagrant]# ceph osd map EC-pool object1
osdmap e59 pool 'EC-pool' (2) object 'object1' -> pg 2.bac5debc (2.c) -> up ([NONE,8,0,7,6], p8) acting
([NONE,8,0,7,6], p8)
```

6. Similarly, break one or more OSD, that is, `osd.8`, and notice the OSD map for the `EC-pool` and `object1`. You will notice that, like `osd.2`, `osd.8` also gets replaced by the word NONE, which means that `osd.8` is also no longer available for this `EC-pool`:

```
root@ceph-node1 # ststemctl stop ceph-osd@8
                 # ceph osd map EC-pool object1
```

This is shown in the following screenshot:

```
[root@ceph-node1 ~]# systemctl stop ceph-osd@8
[root@ceph-node1 ~]# ceph osd map EC-pool object1
osdmap e61 pool 'EC-pool' (2) object 'object1' -> pg 2.bac5debc (2.c) -> up ([NONE,NONE,0,7,6], p0) acting ([NONE,NONE,0,7,6], p0)
```

Now, the `EC-pool` is running on three OSDs, which is the minimum requirement for setting up the erasure pool. As discussed earlier, the `EC-pool` will require any three chunks out of five in order to read the data. Now, we have only three chunks left, which are on `osd.0`, `osd.7`, and `osd.6`, and we can still access the data. Let's verify the data reading:

```
# rados -p EC-pool ls
# rados -p EC-pool get object1 /tmp/object1
# cat /tmp/object1
```

```
[root@ceph-node1 ~]# rados -p EC-pool ls
object1
[root@ceph-node1 ~]# rados -p EC-pool get object1 /tmp/object1
[root@ceph-node1 ~]# cat /tmp/object1
Hello Ceph
[root@ceph-node1 ~]#
```

The erasure code feature is greatly benefited by Ceph's robust architecture. When Ceph detects the unavailability of any failure zone, it starts its basic operation of recovery. During the recovery operation, erasure pools rebuild themselves by decoding failed chunks onto new OSDs, and after that, they make all the chunks available automatically.

In the last two steps mentioned, we intentionally broke `osd.2` and `osd.8`. After a while, Ceph will start recovery and will regenerate missing chunks onto different OSDs. Once the recovery operation is complete, you should check the OSD map for the `EC-pool` and `object1`. You will be amazed to see the new OSD IDs as `osd.1` and `osd.3`. And thus, an erasure pool becomes healthy without administrative input, as shown in the following screenshot:

```
[root@ceph-node1 ~]# ceph osd stat
    osdmap e67: 9 osds: 7 up, 7 in
         flags sortbitwise,require_jewel_osds
[root@ceph-node1 ~]# ceph osd map EC-pool object1
osdmap e67 pool 'EC-pool' (2) object 'object1' -> pg 2.bac5debc (2.c) -> up ([1,3,0,7,6], p1) acting ([1,3,0,7,6], p1)
```

Ceph cache tiering

Like erasure-coding, the cache tiering feature has also been introduced in the Ceph Firefly release. A cache tier provides Ceph clients with better I/O performance for a subset of the data stored in a cache tier. A cache tiering creates a Ceph pool on top of faster disks, typically SSDs. This cache pool should be placed in front of a regular, replicated erasure pool such that all the client I/O operations are handled by the cache pool first; later, the data is flushed to existing data pools. The clients enjoy high-performance from the cache pool, while their data is written to regular pools transparently. The following diagram illustrates Ceph cache tiering:

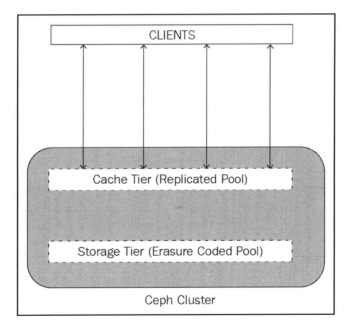

A cache tier is constructed on top of an expensive, faster SSD/NVMe, thus it provides clients with better I/O performance. The cache tier is backed up by a storage tier, which is made up of HDDs with the type replicated or erasure. The entire client I/O request goes to the cache tier and gets a faster response, whether it's read or write; the faster cache tier serves the client request. Based on the policy that we created for the cache tier, it flushes all its data to the backing storage tier so that it can cache new requests from clients. All the data migration between the cache and storage tiers happens automatically and is transparent to clients. The cache tiering agent handles the migration of data between the cache tier and the storage tier. Administrators have the ability to configure how this migration takes place. There are two main scenarios, which we will discuss in the following sections.

Writeback mode

When Ceph cache tiering is configured as a writeback mode, a Ceph client writes the data to the cache tier pool, that is, to the faster pool, and hence receives acknowledgment instantly. Based on the flushing/evicting policy that you have set for your cache tier, data is migrated from the cache tier to the storage tier, and eventually removed from the cache tier by a cache-tiering agent. During a read operation by the client, data is first transferred from the storage tier to the cache tier by the cache-tiering agent, and it is then served to clients. The data remains in the cache tier until it becomes inactive or cold. The cache tier with the writeback mode is ideal for mutable data such as photo or video editing, transactional data, and so on. The writeback mode is ideal for mutable data.

Read-only mode

When Ceph cache tiering is configured as a read-only mode, it works only for the client's read operations. The write operations are not handled in this mode and they are stored in the storage tier. When any client performs read operations, the cache-tiering agent copies the requested data from the storage tier to the cache tier. Based on the policy that you have configured for the cache tier, stale objects are removed from the cache tier. This approach is ideal when multiple clients need to read large amounts of similar data, for example, social media content. Immutable data is a good candidate for the read-only cache tier.

There is a lot of talk in the upstream Ceph community about the stability and actual performance improvements of utilizing cache tiering with Ceph. It is recommended that you fully research this feature prior to deploying it in a production environment!

Creating a pool for cache tiering

To get the best out of the cache tiering feature of Ceph, you should use faster disks such as SSDs and make a fast cache pool on top of slower/regular pools made up of HDDs. In `Chapter 9`, *Ceph Under the Hood*, we covered the process of creating Ceph pools on specific OSDs by modifying the CRUSH map. To set up the cache tier in your environment, you need to first modify your crush map and create a ruleset for the SSD disk. Since we have already covered this in `Chapter 9`, *Ceph Under the Hood, Creating Ceph Pools on Specific OSDs* recipe we will use the same ruleset for SSD, which is based on `osd.0`, `osd.3`, and `osd.6`. As this is a test setup, and we do not have real SSDs, we will assume that OSDs zero, three, and six are SSDs and will create a cache pool on top of them, as illustrated in this diagram:

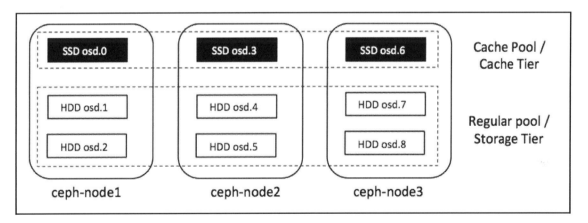

Let's check the CRUSH layout using the command `ceph osd crush rule ls`, as shown in the following screenshot. We already have the `ssd-pool` CRUSH rule that we created in `Chapter 9`, *Ceph Under the Hood, Creating Ceph Pools on Specific OSDs* recipe. You can get more information on this CRUSH rule by running the `ceph osd crush rule dump ssd-pool` command:

```
[root@ceph-node1 ~]# ceph osd crush rule ls
[
    "replicated_ruleset",
    "ssd-pool",
    "sata-pool",
    "EC-pool"
]
```

How to do it...

We will now create a pool that we will use for cache tiering:

1. Create a new pool with the name `cache-pool` and set `crush_ruleset` as 1 so that the new pool gets created on SSD disks:

   ```
   # ceph osd pool create cache-pool 16 16
   # ceph osd pool set cache-pool crush_ruleset 1
   ```

   This is shown in the following screenshot:

```
[root@ceph-node1 ~]# ceph osd pool create cache-pool 16 16
pool 'cache-pool' created
[root@ceph-node1 ~]# ceph osd pool set cache-pool crush_ruleset 1
set pool 4 crush_ruleset to 1
[root@ceph-node1 ~]#
```

2. Make sure that your pool is created correctly, which means that it should always store all the objects on osd.0, osd.3, and osd.6.

3. List the cache-pool for contents; since it's a new pool, it should not have any content:

   ```
   # rados -p cache-pool ls
   ```

4. Add a temporary object to the cache-pool to make sure it's storing the object on the correct OSDs:

   ```
   # rados -p cache-pool put object1 /etc/hosts
   # rados -p cache-pool ls
   ```

5. Verify the OSD map for the cache-pool and object1; it should get stored on osd.0, osd.3, and osd.6:

   ```
   # ceph osd map cache-pool object1
   ```

6. Finally, remove the object:

   ```
   # rados -p cache-pool rm object1
   ```

```
[root@ceph-node1 ~]# rados -p cache-pool ls
[root@ceph-node1 ~]# rados -p cache-pool put object1 /etc/hosts
[root@ceph-node1 ~]# rados -p cache-pool ls
object1
[root@ceph-node1 ~]# ceph osd map cache-pool object1
osdmap e84 pool 'cache-pool' (4) object 'object1' -> pg 4.bac5debc (4.c) -> up ([0,3,6], p0) acting ([0,3,6], p0)
[root@ceph-node1 ~]#
[root@ceph-node1 ~]# rados -p cache-pool rm object1
[root@ceph-node1 ~]# rados -p cache-pool ls
```

See also

- Refer to the *Creating a cache tier* recipe in this chapter.

Creating a cache tier

In the last recipe, we created a pool, `cache-pool`, based on SSDs. We will now use this pool as a cache tier for the erasure-coded pool, `EC-pool`, that we created earlier in this chapter:

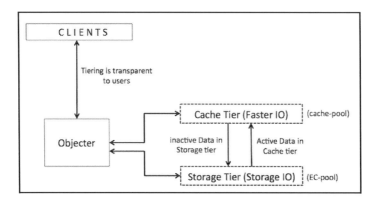

The upcoming instructions will guide you through the creation of a cache tier with the writeback mode and how to set the overlay with an EC-pool.

How to do it...

Following this set of steps, we will create a cache tier for our erasure-coded pool:

1. Create a cache tier that will associate storage-pools with cache-pools. The syntax is `ceph osd tier add <storage_pool> <cache_pool>`:

   ```
   # ceph osd tier add EC-pool cache-pool
   ```

2. Set the cache mode as either writeback or read-only. In this demonstration, we will use writeback, and the syntax is `ceph osd tier cache-mode <cache_pool> writeback`:

   ```
   # ceph osd tier cache-mode cache-pool writeback
   ```

3. To direct all the client requests from the standard pool to the cache pool, set the pool overlay using the syntax `ceph osd tier set-overlay <storage_pool> <cache_pool>`:

   ```
   # ceph osd tier set-overlay EC-pool cache-pool
   ```

4. On checking the pool details, you will notice that the EC-pool has `tier`, `read_tier`, and `write_tier` set as 4, which is the pool ID for the `cache-pool`. Similarly, for `cache-pool`, the settings will be `tier_of` set to 5 and `cache_mode` as `writeback`. All these settings imply that the cache pool is configured correctly:

```
# ceph osd dump | egrep -i "EC-pool|cache-pool"
```

Output of Ceph osd dump command

Configuring a cache tier

A cache tier has several configuration options that define the cache tier policy. This cache tier policy is required to flush data from the cache tier to the storage tier in case of a writeback. In the case of the read-only cache tier, it moves the data from the storage tier to the cache tier. In this recipe, I have tried to demonstrate the cache tier with the writeback mode. These are some settings that you should configure for your production environment, with different values based on your requirements.

How to do it...

Now that we have a cache tier configured, we need to set some recommended configuration options for the cache pool:

1. If looking to use a cache-tier in a production deployment, you should use the bloom filters data structure after careful review of the cache-tier considerations:

```
# ceph osd pool set cache-pool hit_set_type bloom
```

2. `hit_set_count` defines how much time in seconds each hit set should cover, and `hit_set_period` defines how many such hit sets are to be persisted:

```
# ceph osd pool set cache-pool hit_set_count 1
# ceph osd pool set cache-pool hit_set_period = 300
```

3. `target_max_bytes` is the maximum number of bytes after the cache-tiering agent starts flushing/evicting objects from a cache pool. `target_max_objects` is the maximum number of objects after which a cache-tiering agent starts flushing/evicting objects from a cache pool:

```
# ceph osd pool set cache-pool target_max_bytes 1000000
# ceph osd pool set cache-pool target_max_objects 10000
```

This is shown in the following screenshot:

```
[root@ceph-node1 ~]# ceph osd pool set cache-pool hit_set_type bloom
set pool 4 hit_set_type to bloom
[root@ceph-node1 ~]# ceph osd pool set cache-pool hit_set_count 1
set pool 4 hit_set_count to 1
[root@ceph-node1 ~]# ceph osd pool set cache-pool hit_set_period 300
set pool 4 hit_set_period to 300
[root@ceph-node1 ~]# ceph osd pool set cache-pool target_max_bytes 1000000
set pool 4 target_max_bytes to 1000000
[root@ceph-node1 ~]# ceph osd pool set cache-pool target_max_objects 10000
set pool 4 target_max_objects to 10000
```

4. Enable `cache_min_flush_age` and `cache_min_evict_age`, which are the times in seconds that a cache-tiering agent takes to flush and evict objects from a cache tier to a storage tier:

```
# ceph osd pool set cache-pool cache_min_flush_age 300
# ceph osd pool set cache-pool cache_min_evict_age 300
```

This is shown in the following screenshot:

```
[root@ceph-node1 ~]# ceph osd pool set cache-pool cache_min_flush_age 300
set pool 4 cache_min_flush_age to 300
[root@ceph-node1 ~]# ceph osd pool set cache-pool cache_min_evict_age 300
set pool 4 cache_min_evict_age to 300
```

5. Enable `cache_target_dirty_ratio`, which is the percentage of the cache pool containing dirty (modified) objects before the cache-tiering agent flushes them to the storage tier:

```
# ceph osd pool set cache-pool cache_target_dirty_ratio .01
```

6. Enable `cache_target_full_ratio`, which is the percentage of the cache pool containing unmodified objects before the cache-tiering agent flushes them to the storage tier:

```
ceph osd pool set cache-pool cache_target_full_ratio .02
```

This is shown in the following screenshot:

```
[root@ceph-node1 ~]# ceph osd pool set cache-pool cache_target_dirty_ratio .01
set pool 4 cache_target_dirty_ratio to .01
[root@ceph-node1 ~]# ceph osd pool set cache-pool cache_target_full_ratio .02
set pool 4 cache_target_full_ratio to .02
```

Once you have completed these steps, the Ceph cache tiering setup should complete, and you can start adding your workload to it.

7. Create a temporary file of 500 MB that we will use to write to the EC-pool, and which will eventually be written to a cache-pool:

```
# dd if=/dev/zero of=/tmp/file1 bs=1M count=500
```

This is shown in the following screenshot:

```
[root@ceph-node1 ~]# dd if=/dev/zero of=/tmp/file1 bs=1M count=500
500+0 records in
500+0 records out
524288000 bytes (524 MB) copied, 2.43794 s, 215 MB/s
```

Testing a cache tier

Since our cache tier is ready, during the *write* operation, clients will see what is being written to their regular pools, but actually, it's being written on cache-pools first and then, based on the cache tier policy data, it will be flushed to the storage tier. This data migration is transparent to the client.

How to do it...

1. In the previous recipe, we created a 500 MB test file named /tmp/file1; we will now put this file in an EC-pool:

   ```
   # rados -p EC-pool put object1 /tmp/file1
   ```

2. Since an EC-pool is tiered with a cache-pool, the named file1 will get written to the EC-pool as object metadata, but the actual object will get written into the cache-pool. To verify this, list each pool to get the object names:

   ```
   # rados -p EC-pool ls
   # rados -p cache-pool ls
   ```

   This is shown in the following screenshot:

   ```
   [root@ceph-node1 ~]# rados -p EC-pool put object1 /tmp/file1
   [root@ceph-node1 ~]# rados -p EC-pool ls
   object1
   [root@ceph-node1 ~]# rados -p cache-pool ls
   object1
   ```

3. When viewing rados df, we can see the actual space the object is taking up in each of the pools and where it truly resides:

   ```
   # rados df
   ```

   This is shown in the following screenshot:

4. After 300 seconds (as we have configured the cache_min_evict_age to 300 seconds), the cache tiering agent will migrate the object from the cache-pool to the EC-pool, and object1 will be removed from the cache-pool:

   ```
   # rados df
   ```

This is shown in the following screenshot:

```
[root@ceph-node1 ~]# rados df
pool name            KB     objects    clones   degraded    unfound       rd     rd KB       wr      wr KB
EC-pool          512000           1         0          0          0        1         0        4     516101
cache-pool            0           0         0          0          0        1         0      125     507928
rbd                   0           0         0          0          0        0         0        0          0
  total used      1200020           1
  total avail   168567736
  total space   169767756
```

```
# rados -p EC-pool ls
# rados -p cache-pool ls
```

```
[root@ceph-node1 ~]# rados -p EC-pool ls
object1
[root@ceph-node1 ~]# rados -p cache-pool ls
[root@ceph-node1 ~]#
```

If you take a closer look at steps 3 and 4, you will notice that data has migrated from the `cache-pool` to the `EC-pool` after a certain amount of time, which is totally transparent to the users.

Cache tiering – possible dangers in production environments

Prior to deploying cache tiering in any type of production use-case proper thorough testing should be done to validate no outlying performances issues due to the cache tiering feature. Cache tiering has been known to deteriorate read/write performance in most client workloads and should be used *only* with extreme caution:

- **Workload dependent**: The use of cache tiering to improve cluster performance is dependent on the type of work the cluster will be doing. The promoting and demotion of objects in and out of the cache can only be effective if there is large commonality in the data access pattern and client requests reach a smaller number of objects. When designing the cache pool, it is important that it is large enough to capture your planned working set for the defined workload to avoid any type of cache thrashing.

- **Difficult to benchmark**: Any common benchmarking methods used on the Ceph cluster will report terrible performance with the use of cache tiering. This is because most performance benchmarking tools are not geared toward writing/reading a small object set, therefore it can take a longer time for the cache tier to heat up and show it's usefulness. The time it takes for the tier to heat up can be costly.

- **Usually slower**: Workloads that span large numbers of objects and are not cache-tireing friendly can show much lower performance then a normal RADOS pool not utilizing a cache tier.

- **Complexity**: Deciding to utilize cache-tiering can lead to further configuration and management complexity within your Ceph cluster. The use of cache tiering may put you in a position where you encounter an issue that no other Ceph user has encountered; this may put your cluster at risk.

Known good workloads

Cache tiering can be useful when using RGW and the RGW workload contains a majority of reading operations against objects that are recently written or constantly accessed. Cache tiering in this use case—that holds the object in a faster tier for a configurable period of time—may actually improve performance.

Known bad workloads

Following are the known bad workloads:

RBD with a replicated cache and erasure-coded base: A workload that is properly skewed will still send writes to cold objects time and time again. Since small writes are still not supported by a cache tier, the entire 4 MB object must be promoted into the cache tier in order to satisfy smaller writes. A very small number of users have deployed this configuration and it is only successful because their use case is backup data that remains cold and is not sensitive to performance.

RBD with a replicated cache and base: When using RBD with a replicated base, the tier can perform better when the base is erasure-coded, but this is still highly determined by the skew present in the workload and can be incredibly difficult to determine. This use case requires an extremely good understanding of the workload and cache tiering must be tuned and configured properly and carefully.

11
The Virtual Storage Manager for Ceph

In this chapter, we will cover the following recipes:

- Understanding the VSM architecture
- Setting up the VSM environment
- Getting ready for VSM
- Installing VSM
- Creating a Ceph cluster using VSM
- Exploring the VSM dashboard
- Upgrading the Ceph cluster using VSM
- VSM roadmap
- VSM resources

Introductionc

The **Virtual Storage Manager** (**VSM**) is software originally initiated and developed by Intel for Ceph cluster management; it was later open sourced by Intel under the Apache 2.0 License. Ceph comes with the `ceph-deploy` CLI tool for cluster deployment, and it also provides a rich CLI for cluster management. VSM, on the other hand, provides a web-based user interface to simplify the creation and management of Ceph clusters. By using the VSM GUI Ceph cluster, the operator can monitor overall cluster health, manage cluster hardware and storage capacity, as well as attach the Ceph storage pools to the OpenStack Cinder.

VSM is developed in Python using OpenStack Horizon as its base for the application framework. It has the familiar look and feel of OpenStack Horizon for both software developers and OpenStack administrators. Some of the key features of VSM include the following:

- A web-based user interface for easy administration of the Ceph cluster
- It better organizes and manages the server and storage devices
- It aids the Ceph cluster's deployment and scale up by adding the MON, OSD, and MDS nodes
- It aids the Ceph cluster component and capacity monitoring
- It is beneficial to the overall cluster and individual node performance monitoring
- It allows the creation of erasure coded and cache tier pools
- It assists in creating and attaching pools to the OpenStack Cinder
- It brings the multiuser management interface to Ceph cluster
- It allows for the upgrading of the Ceph cluster

Understanding the VSM architecture

In this recipe, we will quickly go through the architecture of VSM, which consists of the following components:

The VSM controller

VSM is a web-based application that is typically hosted on a controller machine, which is referred to as a VSM controller node. You can use a dedicated physical or virtual server that can act as a VSM controller node. The VSM controller software is the core component of VSM that connects to the Ceph cluster through VSM agents. The VSM controller gathers all the data coming from VSM agents and monitors the Ceph cluster. For operations such as cluster creation, pool creation, and so on, the VSM controller sends instructions to VSM agents to perform the required operation. As shown in the following diagram, Ceph administrators/operators connect to the VSM controller node via HTTPs or APIs, and they can use VSM software. The VSM controller node also connects to the OpenStack controller to configure OpenStack to use Ceph. In addition to the web user interface service, the VSM controller also hosts MariaDB and RabbitMQ.

The VSM agent

The VSM agent is a process that runs on all Ceph cluster nodes. The job of the VSM agent is to send server configuration, cluster health/status information, as well as performance data to the VSM controller. The VSM agent uses the server manifest file to identify the VSM controller node, authenticate against it, and determine server configuration.

The following diagram illustrates the interaction of different VSM components with each other as well as with the OpenStack infrastructure and VSM operators:

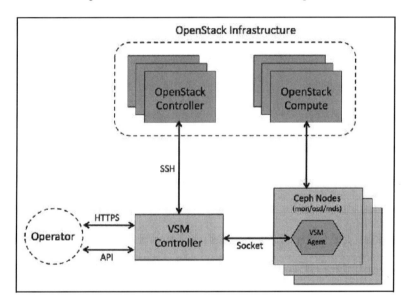

Setting up the VSM environment

In order to use VSM, you are required to build the Ceph cluster using VSM. VSM version 2.2.0 can control or manage the existing Ceph cluster (import the existing Ceph cluster). In this recipe, we will use Vagrant to launch four virtual machines named `vsm-controller`, `vsm-node1`, `vsm-node2`, and `vsm-node3`. The `vsm-controller` virtual machine will act as the VSM controller node and `vsm-node1`, `vsm-node2`, and `vsm-node3` will act as VSM agent nodes running the Ceph cluster.

How to do it...

Perform the following steps for setting up the VSM environment:

1. The `Vagrantfile` for launching the VSM virtual machines is available on the `Ceph-Cookbook-Second-Edition` GitHub repository. Clone this repository, if you have not already done so:

    ```
    $ git clone git@github.com:PacktPublishing/Ceph-Cookbook-
      Second-Edition.git
    ```

2. `Vagrantfile` for launching the VSM nodes is located on the `vsm` directory:

    ```
    $ cd vsm
    ```

3. Launch the virtual machines:

    ```
    $ vagrant up vsm-controller vsm-node1 vsm-node2 vsm-node3
    ```

4. Once the virtual machines are launched, you should have four virtual machines running with proper networking in place:

```
[vumrao@ceph-jewel vsm]$
[vumrao@ceph-jewel vsm]$ vagrant status
Current machine states:

vsm-node1                 running (virtualbox)
vsm-node2                 running (virtualbox)
vsm-node3                 running (virtualbox)
vsm-controller            running (virtualbox)

This environment represents multiple VMs. The VMs are all listed
above with their current state. For more information about a specific
VM, run `vagrant status NAME`.
[vumrao@ceph-jewel vsm]$
```

To log in to these VMs, use `cephuser` as both the username and password. For a root login, the password is `vagrant`. Vagrant automates the networking between these VMs with the following details:

```
192.168.123.100 vsm-controller
192.168.123.101 vsm-node1
192.168.123.102 vsm-node2
192.168.123.103 vsm-node3
```

Getting ready for VSM

In the last recipe, we preconfigured virtual machines using Vagrant; they are to be used with VSM. In this recipe, we will learn about the preflight configuration that is needed on these VMs so that it can be used with VSM.

Please note that by using Vagrant, we have done most of this preflight configuration using the shell script file, `Ceph-Cookbook-Second-Edition/vsm/post-deploy.sh`, present in the GitHub repository that we cloned in the last recipe. You might not want to repeat these first four steps as Vagrant already performed them. We are explaining these steps here so that you can learn what Vagrant did in the background.

How to do it...

Use the following steps to configure the VSM environment:

1. Create the user, `cephuser`, on all the nodes that will be used for VSM deployment. For simplicity, we will set the password of this user as `cephuser`. You can always use a username of your choice. Also, provide `sudo` rights to this user:

   ```
   # useradd cephuser
   # echo 'cephuser:cephuser' | chpasswd
   # echo "cephuser ALL=(ALL) NOPASSWD: ALL" >>
    /etc/sudoers
   ```

2. Ensure that the NTP is configured:

   ```
   # systemctl stop ntpd
   # systemctl stop ntpdate
   # ntpdate 0.centos.pool.ntp.org > /dev/null 2> /dev/null
   # systemctl start ntpdate
   # systemctl start ntpd
   ```

3. Install `tree` (optional), `git`, and the `epel` packages:

   ```
   # yum install -y tree git epel-release
   ```

4. Add host information to the `/etc/hosts` file:

   ```
   192.168.123.100 vsm-controller
   192.168.123.101 vsm-node1
   192.168.123.102 vsm-node2
   192.168.123.103 vsm-node3
   ```

These are some steps that we have automated using Vagrant, which uses the `post-deploy.sh` script. If you are using the specified GitHub `Ceph-Cookbook-Second-Edition` repository that we have created for VSM, then you do not need to perform these four steps.

The following steps must be performed on the nodes as specified:

1. Log in to the `vsm-controller` node, and generate and share the SSH keys with other VSM nodes. During this step, you will need to input the `cephuser` password, which is `cephuser`:

   ```
   # ssh cephuser@192.168.123.100
   $ mkdir .ssh;ssh-keygen -f .ssh/id_rsa -t rsa -N ''
   $ ssh-copy-id vsm-node1
   $ ssh-copy-id vsm-node2
   $ ssh-copy-id vsm-node3
   ```

2. Using Vagrant, we have attached three VirtualBox virtual disks on each `vsm-node1`, `vsm-node2`, `vsm-node3`, which will be used as Ceph OSD disks. We need to partition these disks manually for the Ceph OSD and Journal so that VSM can use them with Ceph. Execute the following commands on `vsm-node1`, `vsm-node2`, `vsm-node3`:

   ```
   $ sudo parted /dev/sdb -- mklabel gpt
   $ sudo parted -a optimal /dev/sdb -- mkpart primary 10% 100%
   $ sudo parted -a optimal /dev/sdb -- mkpart primary 0 10%
   $ sudo parted /dev/sdc -- mklabel gpt
   $ sudo parted -a optimal /dev/sdc -- mkpart primary 10% 100%
   $ sudo parted -a optimal /dev/sdc -- mkpart primary 0 10%
   $ sudo parted /dev/sdd -- mklabel gpt
   $ sudo parted -a optimal /dev/sdd -- mkpart primary 0 10%
   $ sudo parted -a optimal /dev/sdd -- mkpart primary 10% 100%
   ```

```
[cephuser@vsm-node1 ~]$
[cephuser@vsm-node1 ~]$  sudo parted /dev/sdb -- mklabel gpt
Information: You may need to update /etc/fstab.

[cephuser@vsm-node1 ~]$ sudo parted -a optimal /dev/sdb -- mkpart primary 10% 100%
Information: You may need to update /etc/fstab.

[cephuser@vsm-node1 ~]$ sudo parted -a optimal /dev/sdb -- mkpart primary 0 10%
Warning: The resulting partition is not properly aligned for best performance.
Ignore/Cancel? Ignore
Information: You may need to update /etc/fstab.

[cephuser@vsm-node1 ~]$
```

3. Once you have created partitions on all disks, list block devices on these nodes to verify that the partitions look as shown here:

```
[cephuser@vsm-node1 ~]$
[cephuser@vsm-node1 ~]$ lsblk
NAME             MAJ:MIN RM   SIZE RO TYPE MOUNTPOINT
sda                  8:0   0    8G  0 disk
├─sda1               8:1   0  500M  0 part /boot
└─sda2               8:2   0  7.5G  0 part
  ├─centos-swap    253:0   0  820M  0 lvm  [SWAP]
  └─centos-root    253:1   0  6.7G  0 lvm  /
sdb                 8:16   0   20G  0 disk
├─sdb1              8:17   0   18G  0 part
└─sdb2              8:18   0    2G  0 part
sdc                 8:32   0   20G  0 disk
├─sdc1              8:33   0   18G  0 part
└─sdc2              8:34   0    2G  0 part
sdd                 8:48   0   20G  0 disk
├─sdd1              8:49   0   18G  0 part
└─sdd2              8:50   0    2G  0 part
sr0                 11:0   1 1024M  0 rom
[cephuser@vsm-node1 ~]$
```

4. At this stage, we have completed the prerequisites required for VSM:

```
[vumrao@ceph-jewel vsm]$
[vumrao@ceph-jewel vsm]$ for i in controller node1 node2 node3 ; do VBoxManage snapshot vsm-$i take good-state ; done
0%...10%...20%...30%...40%...50%...60%...70%...80%...90%...100%
Snapshot taken. UUID: ece2b285-6468-4897-9787-e37027e65d10
0%...10%...20%...30%...40%...50%...60%...70%...80%...90%...100%
Snapshot taken. UUID: 28abc511-357a-4333-94c3-e01a048a8ae5
0%...10%...20%...30%...40%...50%...60%...70%...80%...90%...100%
Snapshot taken. UUID: b24bffb5-50d6-4375-880a-4b9b9a323a3e
0%...10%...20%...30%...40%...50%...60%...70%...80%...90%...100%
Snapshot taken. UUID: 20469eef-ad7e-4bc8-b092-8b4b1793aa6a
[vumrao@ceph-jewel vsm]$
```

Installing VSM

In the last recipe, we made all the preparations required for deploying VSM. In this recipe, we will learn how to automatically deploy VSM on all the nodes.

How to do it...

We will be using the following steps to install the VSM software:

1. Before proceeding with VSM installation, let us upgrade all four VMs to the latest CentOS 7 packages and configuration:

   ```
   $ sudo yum update -y
   $ sudo reboot
   ```

2. Log in to all four VSM VMs and configure Ceph Jewel version repositories:

   ```
   sudo yum install -y http://download.ceph.com/rpm-jewel/el7/noarch/
                       ceph-release-1-1.el7.noarch.rpm
   ```

3. In this demonstration, we will use CentOS 7 as the base operating system; let's download the VSM repository for CentOS 7. Log in to the vsm-controller node as cephuser and get the VSM version 2.2.0:

   ```
   ssh cephuser@192.168.123.100
   $ wget https://github.com/01org/virtual-storage-
     manager/releases/download/v2.2.0/2.2.0-521-centos7.tar.gz
   ```

4. VSM is also available for the Ubuntu OS and can be downloaded from `https://github.com/01org/virtual-storage-manager`.

5. Extract VSM:

```
$ tar -xvf 2.2.0-521-centos7.tar.gz
$ cd  2.2.0-521
```

```
[cephuser@vsm-controller ~]$ cd 2.2.0-521
[cephuser@vsm-controller 2.2.0-521]$ ls -la
total 600
drwxr-xr-x 4 cephuser cephuser   4096 Jul 29  2016 .
drwx------ 4 cephuser cephuser    137 Aug  9 04:31 ..
-rw-r--r-- 1 cephuser cephuser  49343 Jul 29  2016 CHANGELOG.md
-rw-r--r-- 1 cephuser cephuser 195591 Jul 29  2016 CHANGELOG.pdf
-rwxr-xr-x 1 cephuser cephuser     94 Jul 29  2016 get_pass.sh
-rw-r--r-- 1 cephuser cephuser  30605 Jul 29  2016 INSTALL.md
-rw-r--r-- 1 cephuser cephuser 252953 Jul 29  2016 INSTALL.pdf
-rw-r--r-- 1 cephuser cephuser    739 Jul 29  2016 installrc
-rwxr-xr-x 1 cephuser cephuser  24629 Jul 29  2016 install.sh
-rw-r--r-- 1 cephuser cephuser    580 Jul 29  2016 LICENSE
drwxr-xr-x 2 cephuser cephuser     65 Jul 29  2016 manifest
-rw-r--r-- 1 cephuser cephuser    320 Jul 29  2016 NOTICE
-rwxr-xr-x 1 cephuser cephuser   1155 Jul 29  2016 prov_node.sh
-rw-r--r-- 1 cephuser cephuser   3121 Jul 29  2016 README.md
-rw-r--r-- 1 cephuser cephuser      4 Jul 29  2016 RELEASE
-rw-r--r-- 1 cephuser cephuser   1176 Jul 29  2016 rpms.lst
-rwxr-xr-x 1 cephuser cephuser   2569 Jul 29  2016 uninstall.sh
-rw-r--r-- 1 cephuser cephuser      6 Jul 29  2016 VERSION
drwxr-xr-x 3 cephuser cephuser   4096 Jul 29  2016 vsmrepo
[cephuser@vsm-controller 2.2.0-521]$
```

6. Set the controller node and agent node's address; add the following lines to the `installrc` file:

```
AGENT_ADDRESS_LIST="192.168.123.101 192.168.123.102
                    192.168.123.103"
CONTROLLER_ADDRESS="192.168.123.100"
```

7. Verify the `installrc` file:

```
$ cat installrc | egrep -v "#|^$"
```

```
[cephuser@vsm-controller 2.2.0-521]$
[cephuser@vsm-controller 2.2.0-521]$ cat installrc | egrep -v "#|^$"
AGENT_ADDRESS_LIST="192.168.123.101 192.168.123.102 192.168.123.103"
CONTROLLER_ADDRESS="192.168.123.100"
[cephuser@vsm-controller 2.2.0-521]$
```

8. In the `manifest` folder, create directories using the name of the management IP of the `vsm-controller` and `vsm-nodes`:

```
$ cd manifest
$ mkdir 192.168.123.100 192.168.123.101 192.168.123.102
        192.168.123.103
```

9. Copy the sample cluster manifest file to `192.168.123.100/cluster.manifest`, which is the `vsm-controller` node:

```
$ cp cluster.manifest.sample 192.168.123.100/cluster.manifest
```

10. Edit the `cluster.manifest` file that we added in the last step with the following changes:

```
[management_addr]
192.168.123.0/24

[ceph_public_addr]
192.168.123.0/24

[ceph_cluster_addr]
192.168.123.0/24
```

You should know that in a production environment, it's recommended that you have separate networks for Ceph management, Ceph public, and Ceph cluster traffic. Using the `cluster.manifest` file, VSM can be instructed to use these different networks for your Ceph cluster.

11. Edit the `manifest/server.manifest.sample` file and make the following changes:

1. Add the VSM controller IP, `192.168.123.100`, under the `[vsm_controller_ip]` section.

2. Add a disk device name for `[sata_device]` and `[journal_device]`, as shown in the following screenshot. Make sure that the `sata_device` and `journal_device` names are separated by a space:

`vim server.manifest.sample`

```
[vsm_controller_ip]
192.168.123.100

[role]
#role can be storage, monitor, mds and rgw
storage
monitor

[auth_key]
token-tenant

[ssd]
#format [ssd_device]  [journal_device]

[7200_rpm_sata]
#format [sata_device]   [journal_device]
/dev/sdb1 /dev/sdb2
/dev/sdc1 /dev/sdc2
/dev/sdd1 /dev/sdd2

[10krpm_sas]
#format [sas_device]  [journal_device]
#%osd-by-path-1%    %journal-by-path-1%
#%osd-by-path-2%    %journal-by-path-2%
#%osd-by-path-3%    %journal-by-path-3%
#%osd-by-path-4%    %journal-by-path-4%
#%osd-by-path-5%    %journal-by-path-5%
#%osd-by-path-6%    %journal-by-path-6%
#%osd-by-path-7%    %journal-by-path-7%

[ssd_cached_7200rpm_sata]
#format [intel_cache_device]   [journal_device]

[ssd_cached_10krpm_sas]
#format [intel_cache_device]   [journal_device]
```

The `server.manifest` file provides several configuration options for different types of disks. In a production environment, it's recommended that you use the correct disk type based on your hardware.

12. Once you have made changes to the `manifest/server.manifest.sample` file, verify all the changes:

```
$ cat server.manifest.sample | egrep -v "#|^$"
```

```
[cephuser@vsm-controller manifest]$
[cephuser@vsm-controller manifest]$ cat server.manifest.sample | egrep -v "#|^$"
[vsm_controller_ip]
192.168.123.100
[role]
storage
monitor
[auth_key]
token-tenant
[ssd]
[7200_rpm_sata]
/dev/sdb1 /dev/sdb2
/dev/sdc1 /dev/sdc2
/dev/sdd1 /dev/sdd2
[10krpm_sas]
[ssd_cached_7200rpm_sata]
[ssd_cached_10krpm_sas]
[cephuser@vsm-controller manifest]$
```

13. Copy the `manifest/server.manifest.sample` file that we edited in the previous steps to all the VSM nodes, that is, `vsm-node1`, `vsm-node2`, and `vsm-node3`:

```
$ cp server.manifest.sample 192.168.123.101/server.manifest
$ cp server.manifest.sample 192.168.123.102/server.manifest
$ cp server.manifest.sample 192.168.123.103/server.manifest
```

14. Verify the manifest directory structure:

```
$ tree
```

```
[cephuser@vsm-controller manifest]$
[cephuser@vsm-controller manifest]$ tree
.
├── 192.168.123.100
│   └── cluster.manifest
├── 192.168.123.101
│   └── server.manifest
├── 192.168.123.102
│   └── server.manifest
├── 192.168.123.103
│   └── server.manifest
├── cluster.manifest.sample
└── server.manifest.sample

4 directories, 6 files
[cephuser@vsm-controller manifest]$
```

15. To begin the VSM installation, add the execute permission to the `install.sh` file:

    ```
    $ cd ..
    $ chmod +x install.sh
    ```

16. Finally, install VSM by running the `install.sh` file with the `--check-dependence-package` parameter, which downloads packages that are necessary for the VSM installation from `https//github.com/01org/vsm-dependencies`:

    ```
    $ ./install.sh -u cephuser -v 2.1 --check-dependence-package
    ```

    We need to use the version as 2.1 in the command line for resolving the dependencies. But the installed version will be 2.2.0. This book is targeted for Ceph version Jewel and VSM 2.2.0 is still in beta and has not released 2.2 dependencies, we need to use 2.1 released dependencies. VSM 2.2.0 beta is the only version which supports Jewel.

    The VSM installation will take several minutes. The installer process might require you to input the `cephuser` password for the `vsm-controller` node. In that case, please input `cephuser` as the password. In case you encounter any errors and wish to restart the VSM installation, it is recommended that you clean your system before you retry it. Execute the `uninstall.sh` script file for a system cleanup.

Once the installation is finished, you will have the following messages as shown in the screenshot:

```
Warning: Permanently added '192.168.123.103' (ECDSA) to the list of known hosts.
Restarting diamond (via systemctl):                        [  OK  ]
Connection to 192.168.123.103 closed.
+ ssh -t cephuser@192.168.123.103 'cd /etc/yum.repos.d; if [[ -d /tmp/backup ]]; then sudo -E mv /tmp/backup/* .; sudo -E rm -rf /tmp/backup; fi'
Warning: Permanently added '192.168.123.103' (ECDSA) to the list of known hosts.
Connection to 192.168.123.103 closed.
+ _scp_vsm_conf_to_agent_from_controller 192.168.123.103
+ [[ -n '' ]]
+ echo Finished.
Finished.
+ set +o xtrace
[cephuser@vsm-controller 2.2.0-521]$
```

17. Once the VSM installation is finished, extract the password for the admin user by executing `get_pass.sh` on the `vsm-controller` node:

    ```
    $ ./get_pass.sh
    ```

    ```
    [cephuser@vsm-controller 2.2.0-521]$
    [cephuser@vsm-controller 2.2.0-521]$ ./get_pass.sh
    9f80e475f1e3f31dd442
    [cephuser@vsm-controller 2.2.0-521]$
    ```

18. Finally, log in to the VSM dashboard, `https://192.168.123.100/dashboard/vsm`, with the user, `admin`, and password that we extracted in the last step.

Creating a Ceph cluster using VSM

In the last recipe, we just installed VSM; we do not yet have a Ceph cluster. In this recipe, we will create the Ceph cluster using VSM so that VSM can manage this cluster later. You will find that deploying the Ceph cluster is extremely easy with VSM.

How to do it...

To create the Ceph cluster from the VSM dashboard, navigate to **Cluster Management | Create Cluster**, and then click on the **Create Cluster** button.

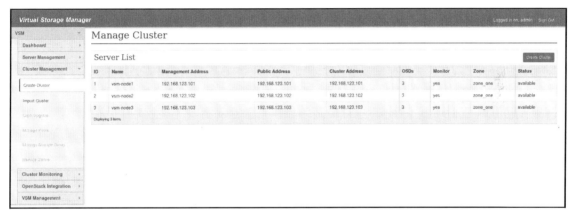

VSM Dashboard create cluster section

If you check preceding screenshot, version 2.2.0 has the **Import Cluster** tab. As 2.20 is still in beta, we need to use a couple of hacks:

1. Disable MDSs and RGWs and restart `vsm-api`.

   Open file `/usr/lib/python2.7/site-packages/vsm/api/v1/clusters.py`.

   The file can be found at `https://github.com/01org/virtual-storage-manager/blob/master/source/vsm/vsm/api/v1/clusters.py`.

RGW is already disabled, we need to do it for MDS also:

```
"""

# only and should only one mds
mds_count = 0
for server in server_list:
    if server['is_mds'] == False:
    #if server['is_mds'] == True:
        mds_count = mds_count + 1
if mds_count > 1:
    raise exc.HTTPBadRequest("More than one mds.")

"""

# RGW with simple configuration(one rgw instance)
# RGW with federated configuration(multiple rgw instances)

"""
# only and should only one rgw
rgw_count = 0
for server in server_list:
    if server['is_rgw'] == True:
        rgw_count = rgw_count + 1
if rgw_count > 1:
    raise exc.HTTPBadRequest("More than one rgw.")
"""
```

```
/etc/init.d/vsm-api restart
```

2. Disable MDSs and RGWs and restart `vsm-scheduler`:

Open file `/usr/lib/python2.7/site-packages/vsm/scheduler/manager.py`.

```
for ser in server_list:
    if ser['is_monitor'] == True:
        count += 1
    #if ser['is_mds'] == True:
    #    mds_node = ser
    #if ser['is_rgw'] == True:
    #    rgw_node.append(ser)
```

/etc/init.d/vsm-scheduler restart

3. Select all the nodes by clicking on the checkbox next to the ID, and finally, click on the **Create Cluster** button:

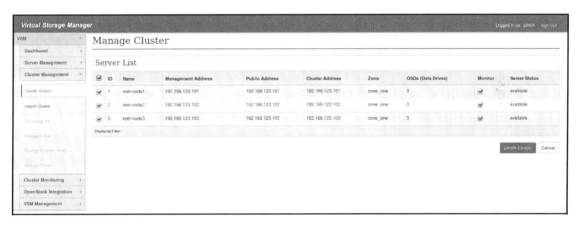

VSM Dashboard create cluster section after clicking on create cluster tab

The Ceph cluster's creation will take a few minutes. VSM will display very briefly what it's doing in the background under the status field of the dashboard as shown next:

Monitor	Zone	Status
yes	zone_one	///// Cleaning
yes	zone_one	///// Cleaning
yes	zone_one	///// Cleaning

After cleaning, it will mount disks, as shown under the status field of the dashboard in the following screenshot:

Monitor	Zone	Status
yes	zone_one	Mount disks
yes	zone_one	Mount disks
yes	zone_one	Mount disks

Once the Ceph cluster deployment is completed, VSM will display the node status as **Active**. But only monitor daemons will be up and OSDs will not be started. VSM creates the OSD data path as `/var/lib/ceph/osd/osd$id` but Ceph Jewel version expects the OSD's data path as `/var/lib/ceph/osd/$cluster-$id`:

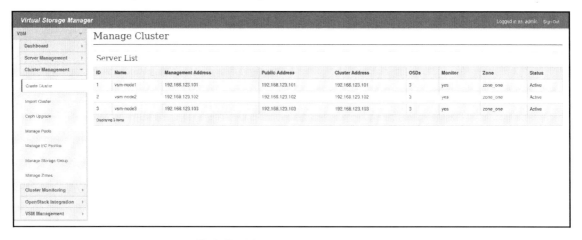

VSM Dashboard after cluster got created with status as active

4. We need to apply the following patch `/usr/lib/ceph/ceph-osd-prestart.sh` in all three VMs:

```
data="/var/lib/ceph/osd/${cluster:-ceph}-$id"
data="/var/lib/ceph/osd/osd$id"
```

5. Start the OSD's in all the three VM's one by one with the following command:

```
$ systemctl start ceph-osd@$id
```

This will bring all the OSDs up and in.

6. If PG's are stuck while creating, you might want to remove the default pool and recreate it:

```
[cephuser@vsm-node1 ~]$
[cephuser@vsm-node1 ~]$ ceph -s
    cluster 406d2572-7caf-11e7-9402-080027c5464e
     health HEALTH_OK
     monmap e1: 3 mons at {0=192.168.123.101:6789/0,1=192.168.123.102:6789/0,2=192.168.123.103:6789/0}
            election epoch 4, quorum 0,1,2 0,1,2
     osdmap e91: 9 osds: 9 up, 9 in
            flags sortbitwise,require_jewel_osds
      pgmap v246: 128 pgs, 1 pools, 0 bytes data, 0 objects
            306 MB used, 161 GB / 161 GB avail
                 128 active+clean
[cephuser@vsm-node1 ~]$ ceph osd tree
ID  WEIGHT  TYPE NAME                                   UP/DOWN REWEIGHT PRIMARY-AFFINITY
-16 9.00000 root vsm
-15 9.00000     storage_group capacity
-12 9.00000         zone zone_one_capacity
 -3 3.00000             host vsm-node1_capacity_zone_one
  0 1.00000                 osd.0                           up  1.00000          1.00000
  1 1.00000                 osd.1                           up  1.00000          1.00000
  2 1.00000                 osd.2                           up  1.00000          1.00000
 -6 3.00000             host vsm-node2_capacity_zone_one
  3 1.00000                 osd.3                           up  1.00000          1.00000
  4 1.00000                 osd.4                           up  1.00000          1.00000
  5 1.00000                 osd.5                           up  1.00000          1.00000
 -9 3.00000             host vsm-node3_capacity_zone_one
  6 1.00000                 osd.6                           up  1.00000          1.00000
  7 1.00000                 osd.7                           up  1.00000          1.00000
  8 1.00000                 osd.8                           up  1.00000          1.00000
[cephuser@vsm-node1 ~]$
```

Installed Ceph Jewel version:

```
[root@vsm-node1 ~]#
[root@vsm-node1 ~]# ceph -v
ceph version 10.2.9 (2ee413f77150c0f375ff6f10edd6c8f9c7d060d0)
[root@vsm-node1 ~]# ceph daemon osd.0 version
{"version":"10.2.9"}
[root@vsm-node1 ~]#
```

7. Finally, check the cluster status from **Dashboard** | **Cluster Status**:

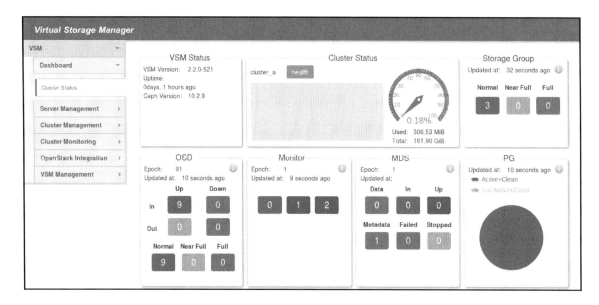

IOPS, **Latency**, **Bandwidth**, and **CPU** details are also available in the dashboard:

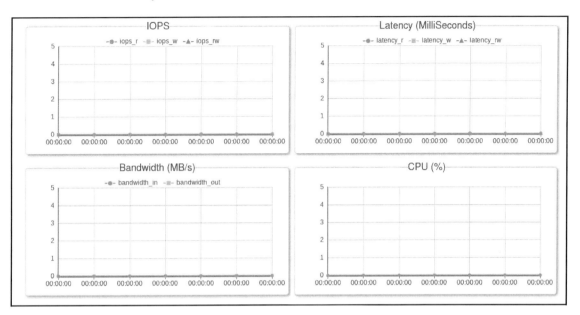

Exploring the VSM dashboard

The VSM dashboard makes most of the operations around the Ceph cluster extremely easy, whether it's deployment, server management, cluster management/monitoring, or even OpenStack integration. The VSM dashboard is very user-friendly and you can explore most of its features by yourself. The VSM dashboard provides the following options:

- **Dashboard**: This provides the complete status of the system including the following:
  - **VSM Status**: This gives you the VSM version, uptime, Ceph version, and so on
  - **Cluster Summary**: This gives you the Ceph cluster status, similar to the `ceph -s` command output
  - **Summary**: **OSD**, **Monitor**, **MDS**, and **PG** summary gives performance metrics such as **IOPS**, **Latency**, **Bandwidth**, and **CPU** utilization for all Ceph nodes

- **Server Management**: This includes the following:
    - **Manage Servers**: The functions are described as follows:
        - It provides lists of all servers with information such as **Management Address**, **Cluster Address** and **Public Address**, **Ceph Version**, **Status**, and so on
        - It provides options to `Add Servers` or `Remove Servers`, **Add Monitors**, and **Start Servers** or **Stop Servers**:

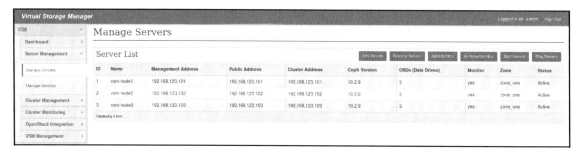

VSM Dashboard Manage Server section - server list tab

- **Manage Devices**: The functions are described as follows:
    - This gives the list of all Ceph OSDs including their status, weight, server they are hosted on, as well as storage class
    - This allows the creation of new OSDs as well as the restarting, removing, and restoring of OSDs

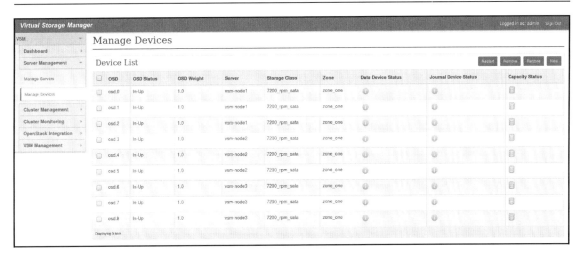

VSM Dashboard Manage Device section - device list tab

- **Cluster Management**: This section of the VSM dashboard provides several options to manage the Ceph cluster:
  - **Create Cluster**, **Upgrade Cluster**, and **Manage Pools** helps you to create replicated/erasure coded pools, add/remove cache tier, and so on
  - **Manage Storage Group** adds new storage groups
- **Cluster Monitoring**: This section of the VSM dashboard provides complete cluster monitoring, including all of its components:
  - **Storage Group Status**
  - **Pool Status**
  - **OSD Status**
  - **Monitor Status**
  - **MDS Status**
  - **PG Status**
  - **RBD Status**

The components can be seen in the following screenshot:

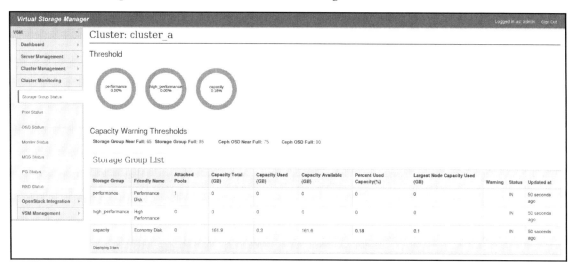

VSM Dashboad cluster storage group status

- **OpenStack Integration**: This section of the VSM dashboard allows us to integrate Ceph storage to the OpenStack by adding OpenStack endpoints and presenting RBD pools to OpenStack:

    - **Manage RBD Pools**: Presents RBD Pools to OpenStack
    - **OpenStack Access**: Adds the OpenStack endpoint

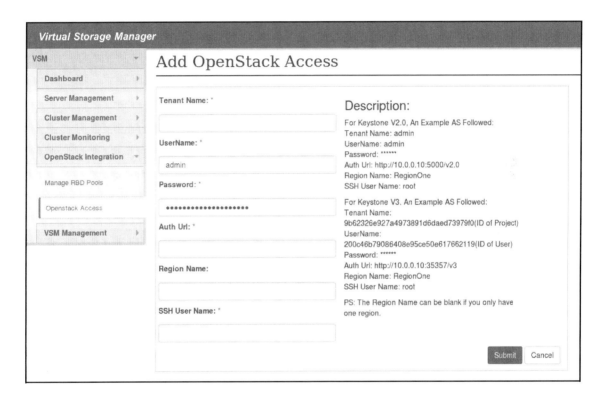

- **VSM Management**: This section of the VSM dashboard allows us to manage settings related to the VSM dashboard itself:
    - **Add/Remove User**: Create or remove a user and change the password
    - **Settings**: Various settings related to Ceph

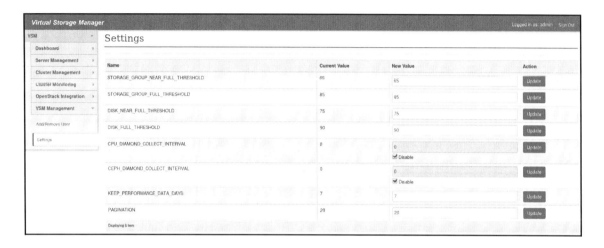

Upgrading the Ceph cluster using VSM

You are now quite familiar with VSM and know that it provides a nice dashboard that makes complicated Ceph related operations, such as Cluster creation, extremely easy. Another important aspect of VSM is that it automates the Ceph cluster upgrade process and simplifies it but as 2.2.0 is the latest beta release and it at the most, supports version Jewel and this Jewel version is already installed so we are not covering the upgrade to Kraken or Luminous release in this upgrade section.

VSM roadmap

The current stable version of VSM at the time of writing this book is 2.1. This is not the same version that we demonstrated in this chapter. In this chapter, we used 2.2 beta version because this is the version which supports Jewel. 2.2 supports cluster import and Ceph version Jewel.

VSM resources

In this chapter, we covered most of the important aspects of VSM. If you were planning to use VSM in your environment, I would recommend that you check out the following resources to get more information on VSM:

- The official source code repository can be found at: `https://github.com/01org/virtual-storage-manager`
- VSM Wiki can be found at: `https://github.com/01org/virtual-storage-manager/wiki`
- The VSM issue, development, and roadmap tracking can be found at: `https://01.org/jira/browse/VSM`
- The VSM mailing list can be found at: `http://vsm-discuss.33411.n7.nabble.com/`

As you already know that VSM is an open source project, it's worth mentioning that VSM's development efforts are being led by Intel with the help of its community.

We would like to thank Dan Ferber and Yaguang Wang from Intel, as well as the entire VSM community, for delivering to us a nice piece of software for deploying and managing the Ceph cluster. To help VSM develop further, please become an active member of the community and consider giving back by making meaningful contributions.

12
More on Ceph

In this chapter, we will cover the following recipes:

- Disk performance baseline
- Baseline network performance
- Ceph rados bench
- RADOS load-gen
- Benchmarking the Ceph Block Device
- Benchmarking Ceph RBD using FIO
- Ceph admin socket
- Using the ceph tell command
- Ceph REST API
- Profiling Ceph memory
- The ceph-objectstore-tool
- Using ceph-medic
- Deploying the experimental Ceph BlueStore

Introduction

In the previous chapters, we covered different ways to deploy, provision, and administer Ceph. In this chapter, we will cover benchmarking the Ceph cluster, which is a must-do thing before moving to production. We will also cover advanced methods of Ceph administration and troubleshooting using the admin socket, REST API, and the `ceph-objectstore-tool`. Finally, we will learn about Ceph memory profiling.

Benchmarking your Ceph cluster before using it for the production workload should be a priority. Benchmarking gives you approximate results on how your cluster will perform during read, write, latency, and other workloads.

Before doing the real benchmarking, it's a good idea to establish a baseline for the expected maximum performance by measuring the performance of the hardware connected to the cluster node, such as the disk and network.

Disk performance baseline

The disk performance baseline test will be done in two steps. First, we will measure the performance of a single disk, and after that, we will measure the performance of all the disks connected to one Ceph OSD node simultaneously.

> To get realistic results, I am running the benchmarking tests described in this recipe against a Ceph cluster deployed on physical hardware. We can also run these tests on the Ceph cluster, hosted on a virtual machine, but we might not get appealing results.

Single disk write performance

To get the disk read and write performance, we will use the dd command with oflag set to direct in order to bypass disk cache for realistic results.

How to do it...

Let's benchmark single disk write performance:

1. Drop caches:

   ```
   # echo 3 > /proc/sys/vm/drop_caches
   ```

2. Use dd to write a file named deleteme of the size 10G, filled with zeros /dev/zero as the input file to the directory where Ceph OSD is mounted, that is, /var/lib/ceph/osd/ceph-0/:

   ```
   # dd if=/dev/zero of=/var/lib/ceph/osd/ceph-0/deleteme
     bs=10G count=1
     oflag=direct
   ```

Ideally, you should repeat step 1 and step 2 a few times and take the average value. In our case, the average value for write operations comes to be *121 MB/s*, as shown in the following screenshot:

```
[root@ceph4 ~]# dd if=/dev/zero of=/var/lib/ceph/osd/ceph-0/deleteme bs=10G count=1 oflag=
direct
0+1 records in
0+1 records out
2147479552 bytes (2.1 GB) copied, 17.81 s, 121 MB/s
[root@ceph4 ~]# dd if=/dev/zero of=/var/lib/ceph/osd/ceph-0/deleteme bs=10G count=1 oflag=
direct
0+1 records in
0+1 records out
2147479552 bytes (2.1 GB) copied, 17.7427 s, 121 MB/s
[root@ceph4 ~]# dd if=/dev/zero of=/var/lib/ceph/osd/ceph-0/deleteme bs=10G count=1 oflag=
direct
0+1 records in
0+1 records out
2147479552 bytes (2.1 GB) copied, 17.7595 s, 121 MB/s
[root@ceph4 ~]# dd if=/dev/zero of=/var/lib/ceph/osd/ceph-0/deleteme bs=10G count=1 oflag=
direct
0+1 records in
0+1 records out
2147479552 bytes (2.1 GB) copied, 17.8519 s, 120 MB/s
[root@ceph4 ~]# dd if=/dev/zero of=/var/lib/ceph/osd/ceph-0/deleteme bs=10G count=1 oflag=
direct
0+1 records in
0+1 records out
2147479552 bytes (2.1 GB) copied, 17.8278 s, 120 MB/s
[root@ceph4 ~]#
```

Multiple disk write performance

As the next step, we will run `dd` on all the OSD disks used by Ceph on the node, `ceph-node1`, to get the aggregated disk write performance out of a single node.

How to do it...

Let's benchmark multiple disk write performance:

1. Get the total number of disks in use with the Ceph OSD; in my case, it's three disks:

   ```
   # mount | grep -i osd | wc -l
   ```

2. Drop caches:

```
# echo 3 > /proc/sys/vm/drop_caches
```

3. The following command will execute the dd command on all the Ceph OSD disks:

```
# for i in `mount | grep osd | awk '{print $3}'`;
  do (dd if=/dev/zero
  of=$i/deleteme bs=10G count=1 oflag=direct &) ; done
```

To get the aggregated disk write performance, take the average of all the write speeds. In my case, the average comes out to be *127 MB/s*:

```
[root@ceph4 ~]# for i in `mount | grep osd | awk '{print $3}'`; do (dd if=/dev/zero of=$i/
deleteme bs=10G count=1 oflag=direct &) ; done
[root@ceph4 ~]# 0+1 records in
0+1 records out
2147479552 bytes (2.1 GB) copied, 16.5385 s, 130 MB/s
0+1 records in
0+1 records out
2147479552 bytes (2.1 GB) copied, 16.8428 s, 128 MB/s
0+1 records in
0+1 records out
2147479552 bytes (2.1 GB) copied, 17.3382 s, 124 MB/s
```

Single disk read performance

To get the single disk read performance, we will again use the dd command.

How to do it...

Let's benchmark single disk read performance:

1. Drop caches:

```
# echo 3 > /proc/sys/vm/drop_caches
```

2. Use dd to read from the file <span></span> ated during the write test. We wil <span></span> read the <span></span> file to /dev/null with flag set to direct:

```
# d<span></span>f=/dev/null bs=10G
  co<span></span>
```

Ideally, <span></span> es and take the average value. I <span></span> ns comes to be *133 MB/s*, as shown <span></span>

Multiple disk read performance

Similar to the single disk read performance, we will use dd to get the aggregated multiple disk read performance.

How to do it...

Let's benchmark multiple disk read performance:

1. Get the total number of disks in use with the Ceph OSD; in my case, it's three disks:

```
# mount | grep -i osd | wc -l
```

2. Drop caches:

```
# echo 3 > /proc/sys/vm/drop_caches
```

3. The following command will execute the `dd` command on all the Ceph OSD disks:

```
# for i in `mount | grep osd | awk '{print $3}'`;
do (dd if=$i/deleteme
 of=/dev/null bs=10G count=1 iflag=direct &); done
```

To get the aggregated disk read performance, take the average of all the read speeds. In my case, the average comes out to be *137 MB/s*:

```
[root@ceph4 ~]# dd if=/var/lib/ceph/osd/ceph-0/deleteme of=/dev/null bs=10G count=1 iflag=
direct
0+1 records in
0+1 records out
2147479552 bytes (2.1 GB) copied, 16.0875 s, 133 MB/s
[root@ceph4 ~]# dd if=/var/lib/ceph/osd/ceph-0/deleteme of=/dev/null bs=10G count=1 iflag=
direct
0+1 records in
0+1 records out
2147479552 bytes (2.1 GB) copied, 16.0845 s, 134 MB/s
[root@ceph4 ~]# dd if=/var/lib/ceph/osd/ceph-0/deleteme of=/dev/null bs=10G count=1 iflag=
direct
0+1 records in
0+1 records out
2147479552 bytes (2.1 GB) copied, 16.0866 s, 133 MB/s
```

Results

Based on the tests that we performed, the results will look like this. These results vary a lot from environment to environment; the hardware that you are using and the number of disks on the OSD node can play a big part:

Operation	Per Disk	Aggregate
Read	133 MB/s	137 MB/s
Write	121 MB/s	127 MB/s

Baseline network performance

In this recipe, we will perform tests to discover the baseline performance of the network between the Ceph OSD nodes. For this, we will be using the `iperf` utility. Make sure that the `iperf` package is installed on the Ceph nodes. `iperf` is a simple, point-to-point network bandwidth tester that works on the client-server model.

To start network benchmarking, execute `iperf` with the server option on the first Ceph node and with the client option on the second Ceph node.

How to do it...

Using `iperf`, let's get a baseline for our clusters' network performance:

1. Install `iperf` on the `ceph-node1` and `ceph-node2`:

   ```
   # sudo yum install iperf -y
   ```

2. On `ceph-node1`, execute `iperf` with `-s` for the server, and `-p` to listen on a specific port:

   ```
   # iperf -s -p 6900
   ```

```
[root@ceph-node1 vagrant]# iperf -s -p 6900
------------------------------------------------------------
Server listening on TCP port 6900
TCP window size: 85.3 KByte (default)
------------------------------------------------------------
[  4] local 10.19.1.101 port 6900 connected with 10.19.1.102
port 44198
[ ID] Interval       Transfer     Bandwidth
[  4]  0.0-10.0 sec  2.51 GBytes  2.15 Gbits/sec
```

You can skip the –p option if the TPC port `5201` is open, or you can choose any other port that is open and not in use.

3. On `ceph-node2`, execute `iperf` with the client option, `-c`:

```
# iperf -c ceph-node1 -p 6900
```

```
[root@ceph-node2 vagrant]# iperf -c ceph-node1 -p 6900
------------------------------------------------------------
Client connecting to ceph-node1, TCP port 6900
TCP window size: 85.0 KByte (default)
------------------------------------------------------------
[  3] local 10.19.1.102 port 44198 connected with 10.19.1.101
port 6900
[ ID] Interval       Transfer     Bandwidth
[  3]  0.0-10.0 sec  2.51 GBytes  2.15 Gbits/sec
```

You can also use the –p option with the `iperf` command to determine the number of parallel stream connections to make with the server. It will return a realistic result if you have a channel-bonding technique such as **LACP**.

This shows that we have a network connectivity of ~2.15 Gbits/s between the Ceph nodes. Similarly, you can perform a network bandwidth check for the other nodes of your Ceph cluster. The network bandwidth really depends on the network infrastructure you are using between your Ceph nodes.

See also

- `Chapter 10`, *Production Planning and Performance Tuning for Ceph,* where you can find more information related to Ceph networking.

Ceph rados bench

Ceph ships with an inbuilt benchmarking tool known as the `rados bench`, which can be used to measure the performance of a Ceph cluster at the pool level. The `rados bench` tool supports write, sequential read, and random read benchmarking tests, and it also allows the cleaning of temporary benchmarking data, which is quite neat.

How to do it...

Let's try to run some tests using the `rados bench`:

1. To run a 10 second write test to the pool RDB without cleanup, use the following command:

```
# rados bench -p rbd 10 write --no-cleanup
```

We get the following screenshot after executing the command:

```
[root@ceph-node1 vagrant]# rados bench -p rbd 10 write --no-cleanup
Maintaining 16 concurrent writes of 4194304 bytes to objects of size 4194304 for up to 10 seconds or 0 o
bjects
Object prefix: benchmark_data_ceph-node1_4602
  sec  Cur ops   started  finished  avg MB/s  cur MB/s  last lat(s)  avg lat(s)
    0       16        16         0         0         0            -           0
    1       16        16         0         0         0            -           0
    2       16        17         1   1.99799         2      1.48653     1.48653
    3       16        17         1   1.33238         0            -     1.48653
    4       16        22         6   5.99659        10      3.90358     3.21756
    5       16        24         8   6.39683         8      4.95659     3.61188
    6       16        26        10   6.66373         8      5.70409     3.96487
    7       16        30        14   7.99683        16      6.57053     4.62909
    8       16        33        17   8.49691        12      7.83897     5.07123
    9       16        34        18   7.99733         4      5.43368     5.09136
   10       16        34        18   7.19775         0            -     5.09136
   11       16        35        19   6.90705         2        6.455     5.16313
   12       15        35        20   6.66479         4      8.45558     5.32776
   13       14        35        21   6.45977         4      7.69405     5.44044
   14       14        35        21   5.99841         0            -     5.44044
   15       14        35        21   5.59856         0            -     5.44044
   16       14        35        21    5.2487         0            -     5.44044
   17        1        35        34   7.99808        13      8.64804     7.25059
Total time run:          17.098624
Total writes made:       35
Write size:              4194304
Object size:             4194304
Bandwidth (MB/sec):      8.18779
Stddev Bandwidth:        5.29011
Max bandwidth (MB/sec):  16
Min bandwidth (MB/sec):  0
Average IOPS:            2
Stddev IOPS:             1
Max IOPS:                4
Min IOPS:                0
Average Latency(s):      7.24247
Stddev Latency(s):       2.82164
Max latency(s):          12.7414
Min latency(s):          1.48653
```

You will notice my test actually ran for a total time of 17 seconds, this is due to running the test on VM's and extended time required to complete the write OPS for the test.

2. Similarly, to run a 10 second sequential read test on the RBD pool, run the following:

```
[root@ceph-node1 vagrant]# rados bench -p rbd 10 seq
  sec Cur ops   started  finished   avg MB/s  cur MB/s last lat(s)  avg lat(s)
    0      16        16         0        0        0         0           -           0
Total time run:        0.486342
Total reads made:      35
Read size:             4194304
Object size:           4194304
Bandwidth (MB/sec):    287.863
Average IOPS           71
Stddev IOPS:           0
Max IOPS:              0
Min IOPS:              2147483647
Average Latency(s):    0.210983
Max latency(s):        0.482909
Min latency(s):        0.00569763
[root@ceph-node1 vagrant]#
```

It might be interesting to know, in this case, why the read test finished in a few seconds, or why it didn't execute for the specified 10 seconds. It's because the read speed is faster than the write speed, and `rados bench` had finished reading all the data generated during the write test. However, this behavior depends highly on your hardware and software infrastructure.

3. Similar to running a random read test with the `rados bench`, execute the following:

```
# rados bench -p rbd 10 rand
```

```
[root@ceph-node1 vagrant]# rados bench -p rbd 10 rand
  sec Cur ops   started   finished   avg MB/s   cur MB/s last lat(s)   avg lat(s)
    0      16        16          0          0          0          -            0
    1      16        90         74    295.084        296   0.599054     0.163539
    2      16       167        151    301.505        308 0.00830807     0.174942
    3      16       256        240    319.497        356  0.0125922     0.178822
    4      16       339        323    322.601        332   0.985727     0.178563
    5      16       413        397    317.281        296   0.059229     0.189206
    6      16       492        476    317.058        316 0.00984665     0.191377
    7      16       575        559    319.178        332   0.729541     0.192266
    8      16       653        637    318.271        312   0.419988     0.195358
    9      16       741        725    321.953        352  0.0135654     0.192576
   10      16       824        808    322.952        332 0.00603637     0.192886
Total time run:         10.440927
Total reads made:       825
Read size:              4194304
Object size:            4194304
Bandwidth (MB/sec):     316.064
Average IOPS:           79
Stddev IOPS:            5
Max IOPS:               89
Min IOPS:               74
Average Latency(s):     0.200897
Max latency(s):         1.10138
Min latency(s):         0.00461121
[root@ceph-node1 vagrant]#
```

How it works...

The syntax for the `rados bench` is as follows:

```
# rados bench -p <pool_name> <seconds> <write|seq|rand> -b <block size> -t
--no-cleanup
```

The syntax can be explained as follows:

- `-p`: `-p` or `--pool` specifies the pool name.
- `<seconds>`: Tests the time in seconds.
- `<write|seq|rand>`: Is the type of test, for example, write, sequential read, or random read.
- `-b`: For the block size; by default, it's `4M`.
- `-t`: Is the number of concurrent threads; the default is `16`.
- `--no-cleanup`: Is the temporary data that is written to the pool by the `rados bench` that should not be cleaned. This data will be used for read operations when they are used with sequential reads or random reads. The default is cleaned up.

 Please note that I ran these tests on the Vagrant cluster which we deployed in this book. You can definitely run these commands against your physical cluster and will receive much better results than I have against the virtual machines!

The `rados bench` is a pretty handy tool to quickly measure the raw performance of your Ceph cluster, and you can creatively design your test cases based on write, read, and random read profiles.

RADOS load-gen

A bit similar to the `rados bench`, RADOS `load-gen` is another interesting tool provided by Ceph, which runs out-of-the-box. As the name suggests, the RADOS `load-gen` tool can be used to generate load on a Ceph cluster and can be useful to simulate high load scenarios.

How to do it...

1. Let's try to generate some load on our Ceph cluster with the following command:

```
# rados -p rbd load-gen --num-objects 50 --min-object-size 4M
--max-object-size 4M --max-ops 16 --min-op-len 4M --max-op-len 4M
--percent 5 --target-throughput 2000 --run-length 60
```

How it works...

The syntax for RADOS load-gen is as follows:

```
# rados -p <pool-name> load-gen
```

Following is the detailed explanation of preceding command:

- --num-objects: The total number of objects
- --min-object-size: The minimum object size in bytes
- --max-object-size: The maximum object size in bytes
- --min-ops: The minimum number of operations
- --max-ops: The maximum number of operations
- --min-op-len: The minimum operation length
- --max-op-len: The maximum operation length
- --max-backlog: The maximum backlog (in MB)
- --percent: The percentage of read operations
- --target-throughput: The target throughput (in MB)
- --run-length: The total run time in seconds

This command will generate load on the Ceph cluster by writing 50 objects to the RBD pool. Each of these objects and operation lengths is 4 MB in size, with 5% of the read, and test runtime as 60 seconds:

```
run length 60 seconds
preparing 50 objects
load-gen will run 60 seconds
     1: throughput=0MB/sec pending data=0
WRITE : oid=obj-SqfntMlPcrX_W_y off=0 len=4194304
READ : oid=obj-jmZb2a7EqJe6qlo off=0 len=4194304
READ : oid=obj-gxoKhvVN1K4VmnS off=0 len=4194304
op 2 completed, throughput=3.81MB/sec
READ : oid=obj-jmZb2a7EqJe6qlo off=0 len=4194304
op 1 completed, throughput=7.49MB/sec
WRITE : oid=obj-a0Lw9l0omUmuCZG off=0 len=4194304
op 4 completed, throughput=10.1MB/sec
READ : oid=obj-NeakTvz7c-zK08V off=0 len=4194304
op 3 completed, throughput=13.4MB/sec
READ : oid=obj-IkIfJv8PmKrhdge off=0 len=4194304
op 6 completed, throughput=16.3MB/sec
READ : oid=obj-IkIfJv8PmKrhdge off=0 len=4194304
op 5 completed, throughput=19.1MB/sec
op 0 completed, throughput=22.3MB/sec
READ : oid=obj-hJWFhQhGCbw3-sZ off=0 len=4194304
READ : oid=obj-PzmOkKBWXHslN1A off=0 len=4194304
op 9 completed, throughput=25.4MB/sec
READ : oid=obj-uz6SrFQ-u35jFSU off=0 len=4194304
op 7 completed, throughput=28.3MB/sec
```

The output has been trimmed for brevity's sake. Once the `load-gen` command finishes, it cleans all the objects it has created during the test and shows the operation throughput:

```
WRITE : oid=obj-IkIfJv8PmKrhdge off=0 len=4194304
op 2195 completed, throughput=147MB/sec
READ : oid=obj-sEr26ImSkp19do9 off=0 len=4194304
op 2199 completed, throughput=147MB/sec
READ : oid=obj-L5-GOQshs9IdyaY off=0 len=4194304
op 2200 completed, throughput=147MB/sec
waiting for all operations to complete
op 2197 completed, throughput=147MB/sec
cleaning up objects
op 2198 completed, throughput=147MB/sec
```

There's more...

You can also monitor your cluster status for the read and write speed/operation using the watch `ceph -s` command or `ceph -w`; meanwhile, RADOS `load-gen` will be running, just to see how it goes.

Benchmarking the Ceph Block Device

The tools, `rados bench`, and RADOS `load-gen`, which we discussed in the last recipe, are used to benchmark the Ceph cluster pool. In this recipe, we will focus on benchmarking the Ceph Block Device with the `rbd bench-write` tool. The `ceph rbd` command-line interface provides an option known as `bench-write`, which is a tool to perform write benchmarking operations on the Ceph Rados Block Device.

How to do it...

To benchmark the Ceph Block Device, we need to create a block device and map it to the Ceph client node:

1. Create a Ceph Block Device named `block-device1`, of size 10 G, and map it:

```
# rbd create block-device1 --size 10240 --image-feature layering
# rbd info --image block-device1
# rbd map block-device1
# rbd showmapped
```

```
[root@client-node1 ceph]# rbd create block-device1 --size 10240 --image-feature layering
[root@client-node1 ceph]# rbd info --image block-device1
rbd image 'block-device1':
        size 10240 MB in 2560 objects
        order 22 (4096 kB objects)
        block_name_prefix: rbd_data.d3982ae8944a
        format: 2
        features: layering
        flags:
[root@client-node1 ceph]# rbd map block-device1
/dev/rbd1
[root@client-node1 ceph]# rbd showmapped
id pool image          snap device
0  rbd  rbd1           -    /dev/rbd0
1  rbd  block-device1  -    /dev/rbd1
[root@client-node1 ceph]#
```

2. Create a filesystem on the block device and mount it:

```
# mkfs.xfs /dev/rbd1
# mkdir -p /mnt/ceph-block-device1
# mount /dev/rbd1 /mnt/ceph-block-device1
# df -h /mnt/ceph-block-device1
```

```
[root@client-node1 ceph]# mkfs.xfs /dev/rbd1
meta-data=/dev/rbd1              isize=512    agcount=17, agsize=162816 blks
         =                       sectsz=512   attr=2, projid32bit=1
         =                       crc=1        finobt=0, sparse=0
data     =                       bsize=4096   blocks=2621440, imaxpct=25
         =                       sunit=1024   swidth=1024 blks
naming   =version 2              bsize=4096   ascii-ci=0 ftype=1
log      =internal log           bsize=4096   blocks=2560, version=2
         =                       sectsz=512   sunit=8 blks, lazy-count=1
realtime =none                   extsz=4096   blocks=0, rtextents=0
[root@client-node1 ceph]# mkdir -p /mnt/ceph-block-device1
[root@client-node1 ceph]# mount /dev/rbd1 /mnt/ceph-block-device1
[root@client-node1 ceph]# df -h /mnt/ceph-block-device1
Filesystem      Size  Used Avail Use% Mounted on
/dev/rbd1        10G   33M   10G   1% /mnt/ceph-block-device1
[root@client-node1 ceph]#
```

3. To benchmark `block-device1` for 5 GB of total write length, execute the following command:

```
# rbd bench-write block-device1 --io-total 5368709200
```

```
[root@client-node1 ceph]# rbd bench-write block-device1 --io-total 5368709200
bench-write  io_size 4096 io_threads 16 bytes 5368709200 pattern sequential
  SEC      OPS   OPS/SEC    BYTES/SEC
    1     7712   7146.39   29271607.00
    2    10400   4772.22   19546995.12
    3    11984   3859.78   15809663.09
    4    13232   3208.56   13142247.04
    5    14304   2749.05   11260097.30
    6    16192   1713.59    7018868.12
    7    18000   1486.58    6089039.05
    8    19760   1584.64    6490679.38
    9    21920   1756.58    7194957.91
   10    22880   1788.79    7326901.81
   11    25776   1884.37    7718399.08
   12    28320   2168.06    8880367.34
   13    31536   2272.50    9308154.70
   14    32816   2212.22    9061271.50
   15    34288   2114.19    8659737.38
   16    35200   1707.37    6993367.68
   17    36624   1543.51    6322235.38
   18    37952   1316.11    5390785.79
   19    38400   1110.44    4548372.98
```

As you can see, the `rbd bench-write` outputs nicely formatted results.

How it works...

The syntax for the `rbd bench-write` looks like the following:

```
# rbd bench-write <RBD image name>
```

Following is the detailed explanation of preceding syntax:

- `--io-size`: The write size in bytes; the default is 4M
- `--io-threads`: The number of threads; the default is 16
- `--io-total`: The total bytes to write; the default is 1024M
- `--io-pattern <seq|rand>`: This is the write pattern, the default is seq

You can use different options with the `rbd bench-write` tool to adjust the block size, number of threads, and IO pattern.

See also

- `Chapter 2`, *Working with Ceph Block Device*, where we covered the creation of the Ceph Block Device in detail.

Benchmarking Ceph RBD using FIO

Flexible I/O (**FIO**); it's one of the most popular tools for generating I/O workload and benchmarking. FIO has recently added native support for RBD. FIO is highly customizable and can be used to simulate and benchmark almost all kinds of workloads. In this recipe, we will learn how FIO can be used to benchmark the Ceph RBD.

How to do it...

To benchmark the Ceph Block Device, we need to create a block device and map that to the Ceph client node:

1. Install the FIO package on the node where you mapped the Ceph RBD image. In our case, it's the `ceph-client1` node:

   ```
   # yum install fio -y
   ```

   Since FIO supports RBD ioengine, we do not need to mount the RBD image as a filesystem. To benchmark RBD, we simply need to provide the RBD image name, pool, and Ceph user that will be used to connect to the Ceph cluster. Create the FIO profile with the following content:

   ```
   [write-4M]
   description="write test with block size of 4M"
   ioengine=rbd
   clientname=admin
   pool=rbd
   rbdname=block-device1
   iodepth=32
   runtime=120
   rw=write
   bs=4M
   ```

```
[root@client-node1 ~]# vim write.fio
[root@client-node1 ~]# cat write.fio
[write-4M]
description="write test with block size of 4M"
ioengine=rbd
clientname=admin
pool=rbd
rbdname=block-device1
iodepth=32
runtime=120
rw=write
bs=4M
[root@client-node1 ~]#
```

2. To start FIO benchmarking, execute the following FIO command by providing the FIO profile file as an argument:

```
# fio write.fio
```

On completion, FIO generates a lot of useful information that should be carefully observed. However, at first glance, you might be interested mostly in IOPS and the aggregated bandwidth, which are both highlighted in the previous screenshot.

See Also

Chapter 2, *Working with Ceph Block Device*, where we covered the creation of the Ceph Block Device in detail.

For more information on FIO, visit https://github.com/axboe/fio.

Ceph admin socket

Ceph components are daemons and Unix-domain sockets. Ceph allows us to use these sockets to query its daemons. The Ceph admin socket is a powerful tool to get and set the Ceph daemon configurations at runtime. With this tool, changing the daemon configuration values becomes a lot easier, rather than changing the Ceph configuration file, which requires the daemon to restart.

To do this, you should log in to the node running the Ceph daemons and execute the ceph daemon commands.

How to do it...

There are two ways to access the admin socket:

1. Using the Ceph daemon-name:

   ```
   $ sudo ceph daemon {daemon-name} {option}
   ```

2. The default location is /var/run/ceph. Using the absolute path of the socket file:

   ```
   $ sudo ceph daemon {absolute path to socket file} {option}
   ```

We will now try to access the Ceph daemon using the admin socket:

1. List all the available admin socket commands for the OSD:

   ```
   # ceph daemon osd.0 help
   ```

2. Similarly, list all the available socket commands for MON:

   ```
   # ceph daemon mon.ceph-node1 help
   ```

3. Check the OSD configuration settings for `osd.0`:

```
# ceph daemon osd.0 config show
```

4. Check the MON configuration settings for `mon.ceph-node1`:

```
# ceph daemon mon.ceph-node1 config show
```

 The Ceph admin daemon allows you to change the daemon configuration settings at runtime. However, these changes are temporary. To permanently change the Ceph daemon configuration, update the Ceph configuration file.

5. To get the current config value for `osd`, use the `_recover_max_chunk` parameter for the `osd.0` daemon:

```
# ceph daemon osd.0 config get osd_recovery_max_chunk
```

6. To change the `osd_recovery_max_chunk` value for `osd.0`, execute the following command:

```
# ceph daemon osd.0 config set osd_recovery_max_chunk 1000000
```

```
[root@ceph-node3 ~]# ceph daemon osd.0 config get osd_recovery_max_chunk
{
    "osd_recovery_max_chunk": "8388608"
}

[root@ceph-node3 ~]#
[root@ceph-node3 ~]# ceph daemon osd.0 config set osd_recovery_max_chunk 1000000
{
    "success": "osd_recovery_max_chunk = '1000000' (unchangeable) "
}

[root@ceph-node3 ~]# ceph daemon osd.0 config get osd_recovery_max_chunk
{
    "osd_recovery_max_chunk": "1000000"
}

[root@ceph-node3 ~]#
```

Using the ceph tell command

Another efficient way to change the runtime configuration for the Ceph daemon without the overhead of logging in to that node is to use the `ceph tell` command.

How to do it...

The `ceph tell` command saves you the effort of logging into the node where the daemon is running. This command goes through the monitor node, so you can execute it from any node in the cluster:

1. The syntax for the `ceph tell` command is as follows:

   ```
   # ceph tell {daemon-type}.{id or *} injectargs
     --{config_setting_name} {value}
   ```

2. To change the `osd_recovery_threads` setting from `osd.0`, execute the following:

   ```
   # ceph tell osd.0 injectargs '--osd_recovery_threads=2'
   ```

3. To change the same setting for all the OSDs across the cluster, execute the following:

   ```
   # ceph tell osd.* injectargs '--osd_recovery_threads=2'
   ```

4. You can also change multiple settings as a one liner:

   ```
   # ceph tell osd.* injectargs '--osd_recovery_max_active=1
     --osd_recovery_max_single_start=1 --osd_recovery_op_priority=50'
   ```

Ceph REST API

Ceph comes with powerful REST API interface access, which allows you to administer your cluster programmatically. It can run as a WSGI application or as a standalone server, listening on the default port `5000`. It provides a similar kind of functionality to that of the Ceph command-line tool through an HTTP-accessible interface. Commands are submitted as HTTP GET and PUT requests, and the results can be returned in the JSON, XML, and text formats. In this recipe, I will quickly show you how to set up the Ceph REST API and interact with it.

How to do it...

Let's configure and use the Ceph REST API to check some cluster states:

1. Create a user, `client.restapi`, on the Ceph cluster with appropriate access to `mon`, `osd`, and `mds`:

   ```
   # ceph auth get-or-create client.restapi
       mds 'allow *' osd 'allow *'
   mon 'allow *' > /etc/ceph/ceph.client.restapi.keyring
   ```

2. Add the following section to the `ceph.conf` file:

   ```
   [client.restapi]
   log file = /var/log/ceph/ceph.restapi.log
   keyring = /etc/ceph/ceph.client.restapi.keyring
   ```

3. Execute the following command to start the `ceph-rest-api` as a standalone web server in the background:

   ```
   # nohup ceph-rest-api > /var/log/ceph-rest-api &> /var/log/
   ceph-rest-api-error.log &
   ```

   You can also run the `ceph-rest-api` without `nohup`, suppressing it to the background.

4. The `ceph-rest-api` should now be listening on `0.0.0.0:5000`; use `curl` to query the `ceph-rest-api` for the cluster health:

   ```
   # curl localhost:5000/api/v0.1/health
   ```

5. Similarly, check the `osd` and `mon` status via `rest-api`:

   ```
   # curl localhost:5000/api/v0.1/osd/stat
   # curl localhost:5000/api/v0.1/mon/stat
   ```

```
[root@ceph-node1 ceph-ansible]# curl localhost:5000/api/v0.1/health
HEALTH_OK
[root@ceph-node1 ceph-ansible]# curl localhost:5000/api/v0.1/osd/stat
    osdmap e140: 9 osds: 9 up, 9 in
            flags sortbitwise,require_jewel_osds
[root@ceph-node1 ceph-ansible]# curl localhost:5000/api/v0.1/mon/stat
e1: 3 mons at {ceph-node1=10.19.1.101:6789/0,ceph-node2=10.19.1.102:6789/0,ceph-node3=10.19.1.103:6789/0}, election
epoch 20, quorum 0,1,2 ceph-node1,ceph-node2,ceph-node3
[root@ceph-node1 ceph-ansible]#
```

6. The `ceph-rest-`   amands. To check
    the list of availab   llowing:

    ```
    # curl local
    ```

This commar   ood if you visit
`localhost:`   r the HTML for
easier readab

This is a basic implementat   uction
environment, it's a good id   a WSGI
application wrapped with   ncers. The `ceph-rest-api` is a scalable, lightweight service that allows you to administer your Ceph cluster like a pro.

Profiling Ceph memory

Memory profiling is the process of dynamic program analysis using *TCMalloc* to determine a program's memory consumption and identify ways to optimize it. In this recipe, we discuss how you can use memory profilers on the Ceph daemons for memory investigation.

How to do it...

Let's see how to profile memory use for the Ceph daemons running on our nodes:

1. Start the memory profiler on a specific daemon:

    ```
    # ceph tell osd.2 heap start_profiler
    ```

To auto-start the profiler as soon as the Ceph `osd` daemon starts, set the environment variable as `CEPH_HEAP_PROFILER_INIT=true`.

It's a good idea to keep the profiler running for a few hours so that it can collect as much information related to the memory footprint as possible. At the same time, you can also generate some load on the cluster.

2. Next, print heap statistics about the memory footprint that the profiler has collected:

```
# ceph tell osd.2 heap stats
```

```
[root@ceph-node1 group_vars]# ceph tell osd.2 heap start_profiler
osd.2 started profiler
[root@ceph-node1 group_vars]#
[root@ceph-node1 group_vars]# ceph tell osd.2 heap stats
osd.2 tcmalloc heap stats:------------------------------------------------
MALLOC:       12410568 (    11.8 MiB) Bytes in use by application
MALLOC: +            0 (     0.0 MiB) Bytes in page heap freelist
MALLOC: +      1626984 (     1.6 MiB) Bytes in central cache freelist
MALLOC: +       129536 (     0.1 MiB) Bytes in transfer cache freelist
MALLOC: +      5362640 (     5.1 MiB) Bytes in thread cache freelists
MALLOC: +      1421472 (     1.4 MiB) Bytes in malloc metadata
MALLOC:   ------------
MALLOC: =     20951200 (    20.0 MiB) Actual memory used (physical + swap)
MALLOC: +       393216 (     0.4 MiB) Bytes released to OS (aka unmapped)
MALLOC:   ------------
MALLOC: =     21344416 (    20.4 MiB) Virtual address space used
MALLOC:
MALLOC:           1080              Spans in use
MALLOC:            121              Thread heaps in use
MALLOC:           8192              Tcmalloc page size
------------------------------------------------
Call ReleaseFreeMemory() to release freelist memory to the OS (via madvise()).
Bytes released to the OS take up virtual address space but no physical memory.
[root@ceph-node1 group_vars]# 
```

3. You can also dump heap stats on a file that can be used later; by default, it will create the dump file as `/var/log/ceph/osd.2.profile.0001.heap`:

```
# ceph tell osd.2 heap dump
```

```
[root@ceph-node1 group_vars]# ceph tell osd.2 heap dump
osd.2 dumping heap profile now.
------------------------------------------------
MALLOC:       12407576 (    11.8 MiB) Bytes in use by application
MALLOC: +            0 (     0.0 MiB) Bytes in page heap freelist
MALLOC: +      1686952 (     1.6 MiB) Bytes in central cache freelist
MALLOC: +       129536 (     0.1 MiB) Bytes in transfer cache freelist
MALLOC: +      5354816 (     5.1 MiB) Bytes in thread cache freelists
MALLOC: +      1421472 (     1.4 MiB) Bytes in malloc metadata
MALLOC:   ------------
MALLOC: =     21000352 (    20.0 MiB) Actual memory used (physical + swap)
MALLOC: +       344064 (     0.3 MiB) Bytes released to OS (aka unmapped)
MALLOC:   ------------
MALLOC: =     21344416 (    20.4 MiB) Virtual address space used
MALLOC:
MALLOC:           1083              Spans in use
MALLOC:            121              Thread heaps in use
MALLOC:           8192              Tcmalloc page size
------------------------------------------------
Call ReleaseFreeMemory() to release freelist memory to the OS (via madvise()).
Bytes released to the OS take up virtual address space but no physical memory.
[root@ceph-node1 group_vars]#
```

4. To read this dump file, you will require google-perftools:

```
# yum install -y google-perftools
```

 Refer to http://goog-perftools.sourceforge.net/doc/heap_profiler.
html for additional details.

5. To view the profiler logs:

```
# pprof --text {path-to-daemon} {log-path/filename}
# pprof --text /usr/bin/ceph-osd
                /var/log/ceph/osd.2.profile.0001.heap
```

6. For granule comparison, generate several profile dump files for the same daemon, and use the Google profiler tool to compare it:

```
# pprof --text --base /var/log/ceph/osd.0.profile.0001.heap
  /usr/bin/
  ceph-osd /var/log/ceph/osd.2.profile.0002.heap
```

7. Release memory that TCMalloc has allocated but is not being used by Ceph:

```
# ceph tell osd.2 heap release
```

8. Once you are done, stop the profiler as you do not want to leave this running in a production cluster:

```
# ceph tell osd.2 heap stop_profiler
```

The Ceph daemons process has matured much, and you might not really need memory profilers for analysis unless you encounter a bug that's causing memory leaks. You can use the previously discussed procedure to figure out memory issues with the Ceph daemons.

The ceph-objectstore-tool

One of the key features of Ceph is its self-repairing and self-healing qualities. Ceph does this by keeping multiple copies of placement groups across different *OSDs* and ensures very high probability that you will not lose your data. In very rare cases, you may see the failure of multiple *OSDs*, where one or more PG replicas are on a failed *OSD*, and the PG state becomes incomplete, which leads to errors in the cluster health. For granular recovery, Ceph provides a low-level PG and object data recovery tool known as `ceph-objectstore-tool`.

 The `ceph-objectstore-tool` can be a risky operation, and the command needs to be run either as root or sudo. **Do not attempt this on a production cluster without engaging the Red Hat Ceph Storage Support**, unless you are sure of what you are doing. It can cause irreversible data loss in your cluster.

How to do it...

Let's run through some example uses for the `ceph-objectstore-tool`:

1. Find incomplete PGs on your Ceph cluster. Using this command, you can get the PG ID and its acting set:

   ```
   # ceph health detail | grep incomplete
   ```

2. Using the acting set, you can locate the OSD host:

   ```
   # ceph osd find <osd_number>
   ```

3. Log in to the OSD node and stop the OSD that you intend to work on:

   ```
   # systemctl stop ceph-osd@<id>
   ```

The following sections describe the OSD and placement group functions that you can use with the `ceph-objectstore-tool`:

1. To identify the objects within an OSD, execute the following. The tool will output all objects, irrespective of their placement groups:

```
# ceph-objectstore-tool --data-path </path/to/osd>
--journal-path </path/to/journal> --op list
```

2. To identify the objects within a placement group, execute the following:

```
# ceph-objectstore-tool --data-path </path/to/osd>
--journal-path </path/to/journal> --pgid <pgid> --op list
```

3. To list the placement groups stored on an OSD, execute the following:

```
# ceph-objectstore-tool --data-path </path/to/osd>
--journal-path </path/to/journal> --op list-pgs
```

4. If you know the object ID that you are looking for, specify it to find the PG ID:

```
# ceph-objectstore-tool --data-path </path/to/osd>
--journal-path </path/to/journal> --op list <object-id>
```

5. Retrieve information about a particular placement group:

```
# ceph-objectstore-tool --data-path </path/to/osd>
--journal-path </path/to/journal> --pgid <pg-id> --op info
```

6. Retrieve a log of operations on a placement group:

```
# ceph-objectstore-tool --data-path </path/to/osd>
--journal-path </path/to/journal> --pgid <pg-id> --op log
```

Removing a placement group is a risky operation and may cause data loss; use this feature with caution. If you have a corrupt placement group on an OSD that prevents the peering or starting of the OSD service, before removing the placement group, ensure that you have a valid copy of the placement group on another OSD. As a precaution, before removing the PG, you can also take a backup of the PG by exporting it to a file:

1. To remove a placement group, execute the following command:

```
# ceph-objectstore-tool --data-path </path/to/osd>
--journal-path </path/to/journal> --pgid <pg-id> --op remove
```

2. To export a placement group to a file, execute the following:

```
# ceph-objectstore-tool --data-path </path/to/osd>
--journal-path </path/to/journal> --pgid <pg-id>
--file /path/to/file --op export
```

3. To import a placement group from a file, execute the following:

```
# ceph-objectstore-tool --data-path </path/to/osd>
--journal-path </path/to/journal> --file </path/to/file>
--op import
```

4. An OSD may have objects marked as lost. To list the lost or unfound objects, execute the following:

```
# ceph-objectstore-tool --data-path </path/to/osd>
--journal-path </path/to/journal> --op list-lost
```

5. To find objects marked as lost for a single placement group, specify pgid:

```
# ceph-objectstore-tool --data-path </path/to/osd>
--journal-path </path/to/journal> --pgid <pgid> --op list-lost
```

6. The ceph-objectstore-tool is purposely used to fix the PG's lost objects. An OSD may have objects marked lost. To remove the lost setting for the lost objects of a placement group, execute the following:

```
# ceph-objectstore-tool --data-path </path/to/osd>
--journal-path </path/to/journal> --op fix-lost
```

7. To fix lost objects for a particular placement group, specify pgid:

```
# ceph-objectstore-tool --data-path </path/to/osd>
--journal-path </path/to/journal> --pgid <pg-id> --op fix-lost
```

8. If you know the identity of the lost object you want to fix, specify the object ID:

```
# ceph-objectstore-tool --data-path </path/to/osd>
--journal-path </path/to/journal> --op fix-lost <object-id>
```

How it works...

The syntax for `ceph-objectstore-tool` is:

```
ceph-objectstore-tool <options>
```

The values for `<options>` can be as follows:

- `--data-path`: The path to the OSD
- `--journal-path`: The path to the journal
- `--op`: The operation
- `--pgid`: The placement group ID
- `--skip-journal-replay`: Use this when the journal is corrupted
- `--skip-mount-omap`: Use this when the LevelDB data store is corrupted and unable to mount
- `--file`: The path to the file, used with the import/export operation

To understand this tool better, let's take an example: a pool makes two copies of an object, and PGs are located on `osd.1` and `osd.2`. At this point, if failure happens, the following sequence will occur:

1. `osd.1` goes down.
2. `osd.2` handles all the write operations in a degraded state.
3. `osd.1` comes up and peers with `osd.2` for data replication.
4. Suddenly, `osd.2` goes down before replicating all the objects to `osd.1`.
5. At this point, you have data on `osd.1`, but it's stale.

After troubleshooting, you will find that you can read the `osd.2` data from the filesystem, but its `osd` service is not getting started. In such a situation, one should use the `ceph-objectstore-tool` to export/retrieve data from the failed `osd`. The `ceph-objectstore-tool` provides you with enough capability to examine, modify, and retrieve object data and metadata.

You should avoid using Linux tools such as `cp` and `rsync` for recovering data from a failed OSD, as these tools do not take all the necessary metadata into account, and the recovered object might be unusable!

Using ceph-medic

Since it's inception Ceph has lacked an overall health-check tool which would easily highlight an issue inside the Ceph cluster. The `ceph status` and `ceph health detail` commands exist and are good for providing overall cluster health details but do not point the user in any concrete direction if there is a more complex issue. The creation of the `ceph-medic` project enables running a single command to poll multiple predefined checks on a Ceph cluster. These checks range from best practice recommendations to validation of keyrings and directory ownership. The `ceph-medic` project continues to develop at a fast pace and new checks are added often.

 At the time of writing this book, only rpm repos built for centOS 7 are supported.

How to do it...

We will use the following steps to install and use `ceph-medic`:

1. Install the latest RPM repo:

   ```
   # wget http://download.ceph.com/ceph-medic/latest/rpm/el7/
         ceph-medic.repo
    -O /etc/yum.repos.d/ceph-medic.repo
   ```

2. Install `epel-release`:

   ```
   # yum install epel-release
   ```

3. Install the GPG key for `ceph-medic`:

   ```
   # wget https://download.ceph.com/keys/release.asc
   # rpm --import release.asc
   ```

4. Install `ceph-medic`:

   ```
   # yum install ceph-medic
   ```

5. Validate the install:

   ```
   # ceph-medic --help
   ```

6. Run `ceph-medic check` on your cluster:

```
# ceph-medic check
```

```
[root@ceph-node1 ~]# ceph-medic check
Host: ceph-node2              connection: [connected  ]
Host: client-node1            connection: [connected  ]
Host: ceph-node1              connection: [connected  ]
Host: ceph-node2              connection: [connected  ]
Host: ceph-node3              connection: [connected  ]
Host: ceph-node1              connection: [connected  ]
Host: ceph-node2              connection: [connected  ]
Host: ceph-node3              connection: [connected  ]
Collection completed!


==================== Starting remote check session ====================
Version: 1.0.2    Cluster Name: "ceph"
Total hosts: [8]
OSDs:    3    MONs:    3    Clients:    1
MDSs:    1    RGWs:    0    MGRs:       0


========================================================================


----------- clients -----------
 client-node1

----------- osds -----------
 ceph-node1
 ceph-node3
 ceph-node2

----------- mons -----------
 ceph-node1
   WMON2: collocated OSDs found: ceph-5,ceph-7,ceph-2
 ceph-node3
   WMON2: collocated OSDs found: ceph-4,ceph-8,ceph-0
 ceph-node2
   WMON2: collocated OSDs found: ceph-6,ceph-1,ceph-3

-------------mdss-------------
 ceph-node2

49 passed, 3 failed, on 8 hosts
[root@ceph-node1 ~]#
```

`ceph-medic` will output a complete log file to the current working directory where the command was issued. This log is much more verbose than the output the command sends to the terminal. This log location can be modified by utilizing the `--log-path` option in `~/.cephmedic.conf`.

How it works...

Since `ceph-medic` performs checks against the entire cluster it needs to know the nodes that exist in your cluster as well as have password-less SSH access to the nodes in your cluster. If your cluster is deployed via `ceph-ansible` then your nodes are already configured and this will not be required, if not, then you will need to point `ceph-medic` towards an inventory file and SSH config file.

The syntax for the `ceph-medic` command is as follows:

```
# ceph-medic --inventory /path/to/hosts
--ssh-config /path/to/ssh_config check
```

The `inventory` file is a typical Ansible `inventory` file and can be created in the current working directory where the `ceph-medic check` is run. The file must be called `hosts` and the following standard host groups are supported: `mons`, `osds`, `rgws`, `mdss`, `mgrs`, and clients. An example hosts file would look as follows:

```
[mons]
ceph-node1
ceph-node2
ceph-node3

[osds]
ceph-node1
ceph-node2
ceph-node3

[mdss]
ceph-node2
```

The SSH config file allows non-interactive SSH access to specific accounts that can sudo without a password prompt. This file can be created in the working directory where the `ceph-medic check` is run. An example SSH config file on a cluster of Vagrant VMs would look as follows:

```
Host ceph-node1
    HostName 127.0.0.1
```

```
    User vagrant
    Port 2200
    UserKnownHostsFile /dev/null
    StrictHostKeyChecking no
    PasswordAuthentication no
    IdentityFile /Users/andrewschoen/.vagrant.d/insecure_private_key
    IdentitiesOnly yes
    LogLevel FATAL

Host ceph-node2
    HostName 127.0.0.1
    User vagrant
    Port 2201
    UserKnownHostsFile /dev/null
    StrictHostKeyChecking no
    PasswordAuthentication no
    IdentityFile /Users/andrewschoen/.vagrant.d/insecure_private_key
    IdentitiesOnly yes
    LogLevel FATAL
```

See also

- The upstream project page has details of the `ceph-medic` tool and it's various checks and is a good source of information as this tool develops further: `https://github.com/ceph/ceph-medic`.

Deploying the experimental Ceph BlueStore

BlueStore is a new backend for the Ceph OSD daemons. Its highlights are better performance (roughly 2x for writes), full data checksumming, and built-in compression. Compared to the currently used FileStore backend, BlueStore allows for storing objects directly on the Ceph Block Device without requiring any filesystem interface. BlueStore is the new default storage backend for the Luminous (12.2.z) release and will be used by default when provisioning new OSDs. BlueStore is *not* considered production ready in Jewel and it is not recommended to run any production Jewel clusters with BlueStore as a backend.

Some of BlueStore's features and enhancements are:

- **RocksDB backend**: Metadata is stored in a RocksDB backend as opposed to FileStore's current LevelDB. RocksDB is a multithreaded backend and is much more performant than the current LevelDB backend.
- **Multi-device support**: BlueStore can use multiple block devices for storing different data.
- **No large double-writes**: BlueStore will only fall back to typical write-ahead journaling scheme if write size is below a certain configurable threshold.
- **Efficient block device usage**: BlueStore doesn't use a filesystem so it minimizes the need to clear the storage device cache.
- **Flexible allocator**: BlueStore can implement different policies for different types of storage devices. Basically setting different behaviors between SSDs and HDDs.

How to do it...

OSD's can be deployed with the BlueStore backend via `ceph-ansible` and I encourage you to deploy a second Ceph cluster or an OSD node in your existing cluster with the BlueStore backend and compare the benchmark tests described earlier in this chapter on the Ceph cluster or OSD node backed by BlueStore, you will see a significant improvement on `rados bench` testing!

To install `ceph-node4` as an OSD node with BlueStore backend via `ceph-ansible`, you can do the following:

1. Add `ceph-node4` to the `/etc/ansible/hosts` file under `[osds]`:

```
##########ceph-cookbook##############
[mons]
ceph-node1
ceph-node2
ceph-node3

[osds]
ceph-node1
ceph-node2
ceph-node3
ceph-node4
```

2. In the `group_vars/all.yml` file on the `ceph-ansible` management node, `ceph-node1,` update the config overrides and `osd_objectsotre` settings:

```
osd_objectstore: bluestore

ceph_conf_overrides:
         global:
                         enable experimental unrecoverable data
                                                         corrupting
                 features: 'bluestore rocksdb'
```

```
ceph_conf_overrides:
  global:
    enable experimental unrecoverable data corrupting features: 'bluestore rocksdb'


osd_objectstore: bluestore
```

3. In the `group_vars/osds.yml` file on the `ceph-ansible` management node, `ceph-node1,` update the following settings:

```
bluestore: true
 # journal colocation: true
```

```
#journal_collocation: true

bluestore: true
```

4. Rerun the Ansible playbook on `ceph-node1`:

```
root@ceph-node1 ceph-ansible # ansible-playbook site.yml
```

5. Check `ceph -s` command and note the new flags enabled in the cluster for the BlueStore experimental feature:

```
[root@ceph-node1 ceph-ansible]# ceph -s
2017-09-23 23:52:53.933048 7f93e1007700 -1 WARNING: the following dangerous and experimental features are enabled:
bluestore,rocksdb
2017-09-23 23:52:53.954601 7f93e1007700 -1 WARNING: the following dangerous and experimental features are enabled:
bluestore,rocksdb
    cluster d0195896-eb15-4ddc-8f6f-9387d381a886
     health HEALTH_OK
     monmap e1: 3 mons at {ceph-node1=10.19.1.101:6789/0,ceph-node2=10.19.1.102:6789/0,ceph-node3=10.19.1.103:6789/
0}
            election epoch 22, quorum 0,1,2 ceph-node1,ceph-node2,ceph-node3
      fsmap e25: 1/1/1 up {0=ceph-node2=up:active}
     osdmap e165: 12 osds: 12 up, 12 in
            flags sortbitwise,require_jewel_osds
      pgmap v7878: 144 pgs, 3 pools, 3193 MB data, 864 objects
            12902 MB used, 209 GB / 221 GB avail
                 144 active+clean
```

6. Check the OSD data directory on one of the newly deployed OSDs backed by BlueStore and compared to a FileStore backed OSD. You can see the link directly on the block device on the BlueStore OSD. The output for FileStore is as follows:

```
[root@ceph-node3 ceph-0]# ll
total 56
-rw-r--r--   1 root root   496 Sep 15 20:18 activate.monmap
-rw-r--r--   1 ceph ceph     3 Sep 15 20:18 active
-rw-r--r--   1 ceph ceph    37 Sep 15 20:18 ceph_fsid
drwxr-xr-x 120 ceph ceph  4096 Sep 20 21:00 current
-rw-r--r--   1 ceph ceph    37 Sep 15 20:18 fsid
lrwxrwxrwx   1 ceph ceph    58 Sep 15 20:18 journal -> /dev/disk/by-partuuid/b1aec159-80ca-4f95-9d33-fbd535d09b89
-rw-r--r--   1 ceph ceph    37 Sep 15 20:18 journal_uuid
-rw-------   1 ceph ceph    56 Sep 15 20:18 keyring
-rw-r--r--   1 ceph ceph    21 Sep 15 20:18 magic
-rw-r--r--   1 ceph ceph     6 Sep 15 20:18 ready
-rw-r--r--   1 ceph ceph     4 Sep 15 20:18 store_version
-rw-r--r--   1 ceph ceph    53 Sep 15 20:18 superblock
-rw-r--r--   1 ceph ceph     0 Sep 23 17:38 systemd
-rw-r--r--   1 ceph ceph    10 Sep 15 20:18 type
-rw-r--r--   1 ceph ceph     2 Sep 15 20:18 whoami
[root@ceph-node3 ceph-0]#
```

The output for BlueStore is as follows:

```
[vagrant@ceph-node4 ceph-10]$ ll
total 52
-rw-r--r-- 1 root root 496 Sep 23 23:46 activate.monmap
-rw-r--r-- 1 ceph ceph   3 Sep 23 23:46 active
lrwxrwxrwx 1 ceph ceph  58 Sep 23 23:46 block -> /dev/disk/by-partuuid/494f2e6e-3630-4326-9319-
ad1e6dece2c7
-rw-r--r-- 1 ceph ceph  37 Sep 23 23:46 block_uuid
-rw-r--r-- 1 ceph ceph   2 Sep 23 23:46 bluefs
-rw-r--r-- 1 ceph ceph  37 Sep 23 23:46 ceph_fsid
-rw-r--r-- 1 ceph ceph  37 Sep 23 23:46 fsid
-rw------- 1 ceph ceph  57 Sep 23 23:46 keyring
-rw-r--r-- 1 ceph ceph   8 Sep 23 23:46 kv_backend
-rw-r--r-- 1 ceph ceph  21 Sep 23 23:46 magic
-rw-r--r-- 1 ceph ceph   4 Sep 23 23:46 mkfs_done
-rw-r--r-- 1 ceph ceph   6 Sep 23 23:46 ready
-rw-r--r-- 1 ceph ceph   0 Sep 23 23:46 systemd
-rw-r--r-- 1 ceph ceph  10 Sep 23 23:46 type
-rw-r--r-- 1 ceph ceph   3 Sep 23 23:46 whoami
[vagrant@ceph-node4 ceph-10]$
```

`Ceph-node4` has now been successfully deployed with three OSDs with a BlueStore backend. The rest of the OSDs in the cluster remain with the Jewel default FileStore backend. Feel free to test performance comparisons between the BlueStore backend and FileStore backend with the tools provided in this chapter!

See Also

- For further details on Ceph BlueStore please see the recent upstream blog detailing this feature: `http://ceph.com/community/new-luminous-bluestore/`.

13
An Introduction to Troubleshooting Ceph

In this chapter, we will cover the following recipes:

- Initial troubleshooting and logging
- Troubleshooting network issues
- Troubleshooting monitors
- Troubleshooting OSDs
- Troubleshooting placement groups

Introduction

The previous recipes in this book have taught you how to deploy and manage a Ceph cluster as well as configure different clients to access the Ceph object store, but what do you do if an error appears on your cluster? The hardware backing a Ceph cluster is subject to failure as time passes, and troubleshooting Ceph does not have to be a frightening ordeal if you understand what the errors mean and what to look for in order to narrow down where the actual issue is. In this chapter, we will take look at some recipes that will enable you to become comfortable with troubleshooting various issues on your Ceph cluster and show you that with a proper understanding of some common error messages, Ceph troubleshooting is actually not that difficult!

Initial troubleshooting and logging

When you start troubleshooting issues with Ceph, you will first need to determine which Ceph component is causing the issue. This component can sometimes be clearly labeled in a `ceph health detail` output or a `status` command, but other times, it will require some further investigation to discover the actual issue. Verifying a high-level cluster's status can also help you determine whether there is just a single failure or an entire node failure. It's also wise to validate that something in your configuration could possibly be attributed to the issue, such as a configuration that is not recommended or a piece of hardware in the environment that is misconfigured. Various recipes in this chapter will help narrow these issues down, but let's begin by looking at a high-level overview of our cluster and what these commands can tell us.

How to do it...

Let's review some initial cluster state commands to help determine where we need to being our troubleshooting:

1. Validate the overall health of the Ceph storage cluster :

   ```
   # ceph health detail
   ```

   ```
   [root@ceph-node1 ceph-ansible]# ceph health detail
   HEALTH_OK
   ```

2. If the cluster is in a `HEALTH_OK` state, this command really does not tell you much. But if there are PGs or OSDs in the error state, this command can provide further details about the state of the cluster. Let's stop one of our OSD processes on `ceph-node2` and then rerun the `ceph health detail` to see what it reports:

   ```
   root@ceph-node2 # systemctl stop ceph-osd@<id>
                   # ceph health detail
   ```

```
[root@ceph-node1 ceph-ansible]# ceph health detail
HEALTH_WARN 53 pgs degraded; 52 pgs stuck unclean; 53 pgs undersized; recovery 296/2592 objects degraded (
11.420%); 1/9 in osds are down
pg 0.6 is stuck unclean for 118617.297247, current state active+undersized+degraded, last acting [7,8]
pg 2.4 is stuck unclean for 622.233778, current state active+undersized+degraded, last acting [4,2]
pg 0.5e is stuck unclean for 117625.282248, current state active+undersized+degraded, last acting [8,5]
pg 0.5d is stuck unclean for 118673.483082, current state active+undersized+degraded, last acting [8,5]
pg 0.5c is stuck unclean for 117554.556511, current state active+undersized+degraded, last acting [0,2]
pg 0.5b is stuck unclean for 118554.225229, current state active+undersized+degraded, last acting [0,7]
pg 0.2a is stuck unclean for 657.516159, current state active+undersized+degraded, last acting [2,0]
pg 0.2d is stuck unclean for 622.295727, current state active+undersized+degraded, last acting [0,5]
pg 0.36 is stuck unclean for 657.327802, current state active+undersized+degraded, last acting [0,2]
pg 0.7 is stuck unclean for 117605.533097, current state active+undersized+degraded, last acting [7,8]
```

3. With an OSD process stopped, you can see that the ceph health detail is much more verbose in its reporting, and I have trimmed this log. It shows the actual number of degraded objects due to the down OSD and that the PGs backed by the OSD that was stopped on ceph node2 are unclean and undersized as they have not yet been backfilled to another OSD.

4. Check the current status of your Ceph cluster:

```
# ceph status
```

```
[root@ceph-node1 ceph-ansible]# ceph -s
    cluster d0195896-eb15-4ddc-8f6f-9387d381a886
     health HEALTH_OK
     monmap e1: 3 mons at {ceph-node1=10.19.1.101:6789/0,ceph-node2=10.19.1.102
:6789/0,ceph-node3=10.19.1.103:6789/0}
            election epoch 28, quorum 0,1,2 ceph-node1,ceph-node2,ceph-node3
      fsmap e30: 1/1/1 up {0=ceph-node2=up:active}
     osdmap e217: 9 osds: 9 up, 9 in
            flags sortbitwise,require_jewel_osds
      pgmap v8155: 144 pgs, 3 pools, 3193 MB data, 864 objects
            9772 MB used, 152 GB / 161 GB avail
                 144 active+clean
```

ceph status (or ceph -s) provides more information than ceph health detail but is not as verbose if there is an issue in the cluster. Let's stop one of our OSD processes on ceph-node2 again and then rerun the ceph status to see what it reports:

```
[root@ceph-node1 ceph-ansible]# ceph -s
    cluster d0195896-eb15-4ddc-8f6f-9387d381a886
     health HEALTH_WARN
            53 pgs degraded
            53 pgs stuck unclean
            53 pgs undersized
            recovery 296/2592 objects degraded (11.420%)
            1/9 in osds are down
     monmap e1: 3 mons at {ceph-node1=10.19.1.101:6789/0,ceph-node2=10.19.1.102:6789/0,ceph-node3=10.19.1.103:6789/0}
            election epoch 28, quorum 0,1,2 ceph-node1,ceph-node2,ceph-node3
      fsmap e30: 1/1/1 up {0=ceph-node2=up:active}
     osdmap e229: 9 osds: 8 up, 9 in; 53 remapped pgs
            flags sortbitwise,require_jewel_osds
      pgmap v8245: 144 pgs, 3 pools, 3193 MB data, 864 objects
            9799 MB used, 152 GB / 161 GB avail
            296/2592 objects degraded (11.420%)
                  91 active+clean
                  53 active+undersized+degraded
  client io 264 MB/s rd, 88912 kB/s wr, 66 op/s rd, 76 op/s wr
[root@ceph-node1 ceph-ansible]#
```

Chapter 7, *Monitoring Ceph Clusters*, covers these commands in further detail. Either of these commands can assist you in narrowing down a component to begin troubleshooting a failure at the component level or the node level.

Troubleshooting network issues

Ceph storage depends highly upon the underlying network configuration and having a dedicated and reliable network connection. The network is one of the most important pieces in the cluster and is used by Ceph nodes in order to communicate with each other. An issue with the networking infrastructure can cause numerous issues on the Ceph cluster, from flapping OSDs (OSDs going down and up) to monitoring clock skew errors. Additionally, networking errors, such as packet loss or high latency, can cause stability and performance issues throughout the cluster.

How to do it...

If a cluster communication issue is suspected, here are some initial checks that can be undertaken:

1. Verify that the `ceph.conf` file has the IP address values set for `cluster_network` and `public_network`.

2. Verify that the networking interface on the nodes is up. You can use a Linux utility, such as `ifconfig` or `ip address`, to view the state of the configured networking interfaces:

```
[root@ceph-node2 vagrant]# ip address
1: lo: <LOOPBACK,UP,LOWER_UP> mtu 65536 qdisc noqueue state UNKNOWN qlen 1
    link/loopback 00:00:00:00:00:00 brd 00:00:00:00:00:00
    inet 127.0.0.1/8 scope host lo
       valid_lft forever preferred_lft forever
    inet6 ::1/128 scope host
       valid_lft forever preferred_lft forever
2: enp0s3: <BROADCAST,MULTICAST,UP,LOWER_UP> mtu 1500 qdisc pfifo_fast state UP qlen 1000
    link/ether 08:00:27:c5:46:4e brd ff:ff:ff:ff:ff:ff
    inet 10.0.2.15/24 brd 10.0.2.255 scope global dynamic enp0s3
       valid_lft 82032sec preferred_lft 82032sec
    inet6 fe80::a00:27ff:fec5:464e/64 scope link
       valid_lft forever preferred_lft forever
3: enp0s8: <BROADCAST,MULTICAST,UP,LOWER_UP> mtu 1500 qdisc pfifo_fast state UP qlen 1000
    link/ether 08:00:27:5e:f6:da brd ff:ff:ff:ff:ff:ff
    inet 10.19.1.102/24 brd 10.19.1.255 scope global enp0s8
       valid_lft forever preferred_lft forever
    inet6 fe80::a00:27ff:fe5e:f6da/64 scope link
       valid_lft forever preferred_lft forever
[root@ceph-node2 vagrant]# 
```

3. Validate that all Ceph nodes are able to communicate via short hostnames. You can validate that the `/etc/hosts` file on each node is properly updated.

4. Validate that the proper firewall ports are open for each component in the Ceph cluster. You can utilize the `firewall-cmd` utility to validate the port status. The proper firewall ports for each component are discussed in `Chapter 1`, *Ceph - Introduction and Beyond*:

```
# firewall-cmd --info-zone=public
```

```
[root@ceph-node2 vagrant]# firewall-cmd --info-zone=public
public (active)
  target: default
  icmp-block-inversion: no
  interfaces: enp0s3 enp0s8
  sources:
  services: dhcpv6-client ssh
  ports: 6789/tcp 6800-7100/tcp
  protocols:
  masquerade: no
  forward-ports:
  source-ports:
  icmp-blocks:
  rich rules:

[root@ceph-node2 vagrant]#
```

Port `6789` and port `6800` to port `7100` are open on interfaces `enp0s3` and `enp0s8`, as this node hosts a monitor and OSDs.

5. Validate that the network interfaces have no errors and that there is no latency between nodes. The Linux utilities `ethtool` and `ping` can be used to validate:

```
# ethtool -S <interface>
```

```
[root@ceph-node2 vagrant]# ethtool -S enp0s3
NIC statistics:
     rx_packets: 2845
     tx_packets: 2530
     rx_bytes: 355568
     tx_bytes: 224507
     rx_broadcast: 3
     tx_broadcast: 4
     rx_multicast: 0
     tx_multicast: 28
     rx_errors: 0
     tx_errors: 0
     tx_dropped: 0
     multicast: 0
     collisions: 0
     rx_length_errors: 0
     rx_over_errors: 0
     rx_crc_errors: 0
     rx_frame_errors: 0
     rx_no_buffer_count: 0
     rx_missed_errors: 0
     tx_aborted_errors: 0
     tx_carrier_errors: 0
     tx_fifo_errors: 0
     tx_heartbeat_errors: 0
     tx_window_errors: 0
     tx_abort_late_coll: 0
     tx_deferred_ok: 0
     tx_single_coll_ok: 0
     tx_multi_coll_ok: 0
     tx_timeout_count: 0
     tx_restart_queue: 0
     rx_long_length_errors: 0
     rx_short_length_errors: 0
     rx_align_errors: 0
     tx_tcp_seg_good: 0
     tx_tcp_seg_failed: 0
     rx_flow_control_xon: 0
     rx_flow_control_xoff: 0
     tx_flow_control_xon: 0
     tx_flow_control_xoff: 0
     rx_long_byte_count: 355568
     rx_csum_offload_good: 0
     rx_csum_offload_errors: 0
     alloc_rx_buff_failed: 0
     tx_smbus: 0
     rx_smbus: 0
     dropped_smbus: 0
[root@ceph-node2 vagrant]#
```

```
# ping <ceph node>
```

```
[root@ceph-node2 vagrant]# ping ceph-node1
PING ceph-node1 (10.19.1.101) 56(84) bytes of data.
64 bytes from ceph-node1 (10.19.1.101): icmp_seq=1 ttl=64 time=0.206 ms
64 bytes from ceph-node1 (10.19.1.101): icmp_seq=2 ttl=64 time=0.561 ms
64 bytes from ceph-node1 (10.19.1.101): icmp_seq=3 ttl=64 time=0.687 ms
64 bytes from ceph-node1 (10.19.1.101): icmp_seq=4 ttl=64 time=0.715 ms
64 bytes from ceph-node1 (10.19.1.101): icmp_seq=5 ttl=64 time=0.753 ms
^C
--- ceph-node1 ping statistics ---
5 packets transmitted, 5 received, 0% packet loss, time 4000ms
rtt min/avg/max/mdev = 0.206/0.584/0.753/0.201 ms
[root@ceph-node2 vagrant]#
```

6. If network performance is suspect, then the `iperf` utility can be utilized. This tool was discussed in detail in `Chapter 12`, *More on Ceph*.

7. Verify that NTP is set up and running on each of the Ceph nodes in the cluster:

```
# systemctl status ntpd
# ntpq -p
```

```
[root@ceph-node2 vagrant]# systemctl status ntpd
● ntpd.service - Network Time Service
   Loaded: loaded (/usr/lib/systemd/system/ntpd.service; enabled; vendor preset: disabled)
   Active: active (running) since Mon 2017-09-25 04:35:59 EEST; 1h 41min ago
 Main PID: 3772 (ntpd)
   CGroup: /system.slice/ntpd.service
           └─3772 /usr/sbin/ntpd -u ntp:ntp -g

Sep 25 04:35:59 ceph-node2 ntpd[3772]: Listen normally on 2 lo 127.0.0.1 UDP 123
Sep 25 04:35:59 ceph-node2 ntpd[3772]: Listen normally on 3 enp0s3 10.0.2.15 UDP 123
Sep 25 04:35:59 ceph-node2 ntpd[3772]: Listen normally on 4 enp0s8 10.19.1.102 UDP 123
Sep 25 04:35:59 ceph-node2 ntpd[3772]: Listen normally on 5 enp0s8 fe80::a00:27ff:fe5e:f6da UDP 123
Sep 25 04:35:59 ceph-node2 ntpd[3772]: Listen normally on 6 lo ::1 UDP 123
Sep 25 04:35:59 ceph-node2 ntpd[3772]: Listen normally on 7 enp0s3 fe80::a00:27ff:fec5:464e UDP 123
Sep 25 04:35:59 ceph-node2 ntpd[3772]: Listening on routing socket on fd #24 for interface updates
Sep 25 04:35:59 ceph-node2 ntpd[3772]: 0.0.0.0 c016 06 restart
Sep 25 04:35:59 ceph-node2 ntpd[3772]: 0.0.0.0 c012 02 freq_set kernel -5.984 PPM
Sep 25 04:36:07 ceph-node2 ntpd[3772]: 0.0.0.0 c615 05 clock_sync
[root@ceph-node2 vagrant]# ntpq -p
     remote           refid      st t when poll reach   delay   offset  jitter
==============================================================================
*time-b.nist.gov .NIST.          1 u  682  128  200   22.262   -0.837   0.159
+108.61.194.85.v 132.163.4.101    2 u    8  128  377   80.158   -0.605   0.835
+199-188-64-12.c 192.168.111.1    3 u   20  128  377   45.607   -2.353   0.792
-four0.fairy.mat 204.9.54.119     2 u   93  128  377   72.547  -15.518  30.169
[root@ceph-node2 vagrant]#
```

8. Lastly, you can verify that all Ceph nodes in the cluster have identical network configurations, as a single slow node can weigh down the entire Ceph cluster. This includes verifying that all nodes have identical MTU settings, bonding, and speed. The `ip address` and `ethtool` utilities can be used in validating this.

Troubleshooting monitors

Ceph monitor issues can usually be seen in the `ceph status` or `ceph health detail` command outputs, and they identify which monitor is reporting the issue. Ceph monitor logs are located at `/var/log/ceph/ceph-mon.<node-name>.log`, and this log can be investigated to determine the root cause of monitor failures or errors. The upcoming recipes will cover some common issues that can be seen in your Ceph cluster with monitors.

How to do it...

Let's take a look at some of the most common monitor errors and some steps on how to resolve these issues:

1. Ceph monitor is reporting a *clock skew*:
    - Clock skew can be reported in the monitor log file as well as in the `ceph status` command.
    - This error indicates that the monitor reporting the clock skew error has a clock that is not synchronized with the rest of the monitors in the cluster.
    - This error is usually due to improper NTP configuration or no NTP server running on the monitor node.
    - Network issues can also lead to clock skew errors. Follow the recipe in the previous section for proper NTP investigation and network troubleshooting.

2. Ceph monitor is reported as *out of quorum*:
    - Out of quorum can be reported in the monitor log file as well as in the `ceph status` command.
    - This error indicates that one or more MONs is marked as *down* but the other monitors in the cluster are able to form a quorum:
        - If the monitor is stuck in a *probing* state, then you would want to validate the network connectivity between the monitor and the other nodes in the cluster. You can follow the previous section on network troubleshooting.

- If the monitor is stuck in a state of *electing*, then you would want to check for a clock skew.
- If the monitor sets itself as a leader but is not in quorum with the rest of the monitors, then the monitors may have a clock skew issue. If the monitor process is running but MON is marked as down, you can check the current status of the monitor by utilizing the *admin socket* on MON:

```
# ceph daemon mon.<nodename> mon_status
```

- If the monitor process is not running, you can attempt to start the monitor:

```
# systemctl start ceph-mon@<node name>
# systemctl status ceph-mon@<node name>
```

- If the monitor fails to start and then review the monitor log file `/var/log/ceph/ceph-mon.<node-name>.log` for a failure.
- If the monitor log contains the *corruption error in the middle of record* error, then the monitor likely has a corrupted `mon_store`. To resolve this issue, replace the Ceph monitor, as covered in `Chapter 8`, *Operating and managing a Ceph cluster*.
- If the monitor log contains the **Caught signal (Bus error)** error, then the monitors `/var` partition is likely full. You will need to delete any unused data from the `/var` partition, but *do not* delete any data from the monitor directory manually. You can manually compact the monitor store database using the following command or configuring to compact at start in the `ceph.conf` file under the `[mons]` section and restarting the monitor:

```
# ceph tell mon.<node name> compact
  mon_compact_on_start = true
```

3. Ceph monitor is reporting *store is getting too big!*:

  - The Ceph MON store is a `level.db` database and stores key-value pairs. The monitor can actually be delayed in responding to client requests if the `store.db` is too big, as it takes a longer time to query a large `level.db`.
  - This error will log prior to the `/var` partition on the monitor becoming full.
  - Validate the current size of the Ceph monitor store:

```
# du -sch /var/lib/ceph/mon/<cluster name>-
  <node name>/store.db
```

    - Compact the monitor store as required and as discussed.

4. How to inject a valid monitor map if the monitor has a corrupted or outdated map:

  - A Ceph monitor cannot gain a quorum if its map is outdated or corrupted. If two or more monitors are in quorum, the safest option is to obtain a valid `monmap` and inject it into the monitor that is unable to gain quorum:

    - On a monitor that is in quorum, pull the valid `monmap`:

```
# ceph mon getmap -o /tmp/monmap
```

    - Stop the monitor with the corrupted `monmap`, copy the valid `monmap` from a good monitor, and inject the `monmap` into the bad monitor:

```
# systemctl stop ceph-mon@<node-name>
# scp /tmp/monmap root@<nodename>:/tmp/monmap
# ceph-mon -i <id> --inject-monmap /tmp/monmap
```

    - Start the monitor with the corrupted `monmap`:

```
# systemctl start ceph-mon@<node-name>
```

- If the all monitors are unable to gain quorum, for example, you only have one monitor with a valid `monmap`, then the recovery scenario would differ from a valid quorum.

  - On a monitor that has a valid `monmap`, stop the monitor:

```
# systemctl stop ceph-mon@<node-name>
```

  - Pull the valid `monmap` from the stopped monitor:

```
# ceph mon getmap -o /tmp/monmap
```

  - Stop one of the monitors with a corrupted `monmap`:

```
# systemctl stop ceph-mon@<node-name>
```

  - Copy the good `monmap` to the monitor with the corrupted map:

```
# scp /tmp/monmap root@<nodename>:/tmp/monmap
```

  - Inject the `monmap` from the good monitor:

```
# ceph-mon -i <id> --inject-monmap /tmp/monmap
```

  - Start the monitor and check the `mon_status` to validate the quorum:

```
# systemctl start ceph-mon@<node-name>
# ceph daemon mon.<nodename> mon_status
```

- Let's see an example where `ceph-node1` has a good copy of the `monmap` and `ceph-node2` has a corrupted `monmap`:

  - Copy the good `monmap` from `ceph-node1`:

```
[root@ceph-node1 ~]# systemctl stop ceph-mon@ceph-node1
[root@ceph-node1 ~]# ceph mon getmap -o /tmp/monmap
2017-09-25 19:15:28.834861 7fba6c23d700  0 -- :/2713192057 >> 10.19.1.101:6789/0 pipe(0x7fba6805d820 sd=
3 :0 s=1 pgs=0 cs=0 l=1 c=0x7fba6805eae0).fault
got monmap epoch 1
[root@ceph-node1 ~]# scp /tmp/monmap root@ceph-node2:/tmp/monmap
monmap                                                  100%  496   570.5KB/s   00:00
[root@ceph-node1 ~]# systemctl start ceph-mon@ceph-node1
```

- Inject the `monmap` to `ceph-node2` and check
  `mon_status`:

```
[root@ceph-node2 mon]# systemctl stop ceph-mon@ceph-node2
[root@ceph-node2 mon]# ceph-mon -i ceph-node2 --inject-monmap /tmp/monmap
[root@ceph-node2 mon]# systemctl start ceph-mon@ceph-node2
[root@ceph-node2 mon]# ceph daemon mon.ceph-node2 mon_status
{
    "name": "ceph-node2",
    "rank": 1,
    "state": "peon",
    "election_epoch": 42,
    "quorum": [
        0,
        1,
        2
    ],
    "outside_quorum": [],
    "extra_probe_peers": [],
    "sync_provider": [],
    "monmap": {
        "epoch": 3,
        "fsid": "d0195896-eb15-4ddc-8f6f-9387d381a886",
        "modified": "2017-09-15 20:16:47.970977",
        "created": "2017-09-15 20:16:47.970977",
        "mons": [
            {
                "rank": 0,
                "name": "ceph-node1",
                "addr": "10.19.1.101:6789\/0"
            },
            {
                "rank": 1,
                "name": "ceph-node2",
                "addr": "10.19.1.102:6789\/0"
            },
            {
                "rank": 2,
                "name": "ceph-node3",
                "addr": "10.19.1.103:6789\/0"
            }
        ]
    }
}
[root@ceph-node2 mon]# 
```

Troubleshooting OSDs

As with Ceph monitor issues, Ceph OSD issues will usually first be seen in the `ceph health detail` or `status` commands. This will generally give you some idea as to where to start looking for the actual issue. For example, is a single OSD down or is a block of OSDs corresponding to a specific host down. Ceph OSD logs are located at `/var/log/ceph/ceph-osd.<id>.log` in the node hosting the specific OSD process and are the first area to begin looking when troubleshooting OSD issues. The upcoming recipes will show you how to troubleshoot some of the more common Ceph OSD issues you may come across in your Ceph cluster.

How to do it...

Before you begin troubleshooting OSDs, it's a good idea to validate your cluster and public network between the Ceph nodes, as OSD down issues can usually be caused by communication issues between peer OSDs and MONs:

1. How to handle a full OSD flag on your Ceph cluster:
    - Running a `ceph health detail` will provide you with the OSD ID that is currently flagged as full by the cluster:

      ```
      # ceph health detail
      ```

    - A full flag is indicated by the Ceph config option `mon_osd_full_ratio`; by default, this is 95%. Note that this config setting applies *only* to a situation when the flag gets set on the cluster and does not apply to the actual PGs.
    - Ceph will prevent client I/O from writing to a PG that resides on an OSD that has the full flag set to prevent any chance of data loss to the PGs on the full OSD.
    - We would want to validate the percentage of RAW capacity used to determine what safe recovery methods to take and whether we have cluster-free space for the recovery. If the capacity used by RAW is less than 75%, it is considered safe for recovery actions:

      ```
      # ceph df
      ```

```
[root@ceph-node1 ceph]# ceph df
GLOBAL:
    SIZE      AVAIL     RAW USED     %RAW USED
    161G      152G      9806M        5.91
POOLS:
    NAME              ID    USED     %USED    MAX AVAIL    OBJECTS
    rbd               0     3193M    5.91     50845M       844
    cephfs_data       1     0        0        50845M       0
    cephfs_metadata   2     2068     0        50845M       20
[root@ceph-node1 ceph]#
```

- Deleting unneeded data from the cluster would be the easiest method of recovery, but for any type of delete actions, we would need to increase the full ratio on the PGs as a delete is a write operation and writes are blocked to PGs on an OSD that's over 95% utilized with the full flag. In order to proceed, we must set the PG full ratio on the cluster higher than 95% in order to allow the delete operation to be successful:

    # ceph pg set_full_ratio 0.98

- Adding additional OSDs or OSD nodes is also a method to increase the RAW capacity in the cluster if you are just running out of space.

2. How to handle a near full OSD flag on your Ceph cluster:
    - As with the full flag, the near full flag can also be seen in the ceph health detail command and will provide the OSD ID that is flagged:

    # ceph health detail

    - A near full flag is indicated by the Ceph config option mon_osd_nearfull_ratio; by default, this is 85%. Note that this config setting applies *only* when the flag gets set on the cluster and does not apply to the actual PGs.
    - Typical causes and remedies for near full OSDs are as follows:
        - Improper imbalance of OSD count per node throughout the cluster. Look into the proper cluster balance.

- Improper balance of OSD weights in the CRUSH map throughout the cluster. Look into proper cluster balance or implement OSD weights by utilization. This will reweigh OSDs automatically based upon OSD utilization average (threshold) throughout the cluster. You can test this prior to implementation as well:

```
# ceph osd test-reweight-by-utilization
  [threshold] [weight change amount]
    [number of osds]
# ceph osd reweight-by-utilization [threshold]
  [weight change amount] [number of osds]
```

- Improper PG count setting per OSD count in the cluster. Utilize the Ceph PG calculator (http://ceph.com/ pgcalc/) tool to verify a proper PG count per OSD count in the Ceph cluster.
- Old CRUSH tunables being run on the cluster (optimal is recommended). Set CRUSH tunables to optimal in the cluster. Verify that any running clients support the version of tunables being set on the Ceph cluster. Kernel clients must support the running tunable, or issues will arise. Tunables and their features are detailed at http:// docs.ceph.com/docs/master/rados/operations/crush-map/?highlight=crush%20tunables#tunables:

```
# ceph osd crush tunables optimal
```

- Just putting too much data into the cluster than the backing hardware can support. Look into adding additional OSDs or OSD nodes to the Ceph cluster.

3. Ceph cluster reports that one or more OSDs are down:
    - If a single OSD is down, this error is typically due to a hardware failure on the backing disk.
    - If multiple OSDs are down, this error is typically due to communication issues between the peer OSDs or the OSDs and the monitors.

- In order to determine a direction to go for troubleshooting down OSDs, you need to determine which OSDs are actually down. The `ceph health detail` command provides these details:

    # ceph health detail

```
osd.1 is down since epoch 259, last address 10.19.1.102:6805/3314
osd.3 is down since epoch 261, last address 10.19.1.102:6809/3694
[root@ceph-node1 ceph]#
```

- You can try and restart the OSD daemon:

    # systemctl start ceph-osd@<id>

- If the OSD daemon cannot start, then review the following common issues:
    - Validate that the OSD and journal partitions are mounted:

    # ceph-disk list

```
[root@ceph-node2 ~]# ceph-disk list
/dev/dm-0 swap, swap
/dev/dm-1 other, xfs, mounted on /
/dev/sda :
 /dev/sda2 other, LVM2_member
 /dev/sda1 other, xfs, mounted on /boot
/dev/sdb :
 /dev/sdb2 ceph journal, for /dev/sdb1
 /dev/sdb1 ceph data, active, cluster ceph, osd.1, journal /dev/sdb2
/dev/sdc :
 /dev/sdc2 ceph journal, for /dev/sdc1
 /dev/sdc1 ceph data, active, cluster ceph, osd.3, journal /dev/sdc2
/dev/sdd :
 /dev/sdd2 ceph journal, for /dev/sdd1
 /dev/sdd1 ceph data, active, cluster ceph, osd.6, journal /dev/sdd2
/dev/sr0 other, unknown
[root@ceph-node2 ~]#
```

- If you
  have
  and t|

idate that you
default 32768
·rocess.

d_max =

Validate that the change was made:

```
# sysctl -a | grep kernel.pid_max
```

- If you receive ERROR: missing keyring, cannot
  use cephx for authentication, then the OSD is
  missing its keyring and you will need to register the
  OSD's keyring:

```
# ceph auth add osd.{osd-num} osd 'allow *'
  mon 'allow rwx' -i /var/lib/ceph/osd/ceph-
  {osd-num}/keyring
```

- If you receive ERROR: unable to open OSD
  superblock on /var/lib/ceph/osd/ceph-<id>,
  then the OSD daemon cannot read the underlying
  filesystem. Review /var/log/messages or dmesg for
  any errors against the device backing the OSD node and
  replace the faulty media.
- If you receive the FAILED
  assert(!m_filestore_fail_eio || r !=
  -5) error at /var/log/ceph/ceph-
  osd.<id>.log, then review /var/log/messages or
  dmesg for any errors against the device backing the OSD
  node and replace the faulty media.

- If the OSD daemon is running but is *still* marked as down then review the following issues:
    - Check the OSD log file `/var/log/ceph/ceph-osd.<id>` for a `wrongly marked me down` message and verify that any recovery or scrubbing activity was occurring at the time the OSD was marked down. The cluster log file located on the monitor node `/var/log/ceph/ceph.log` can be reviewed for these events. These operations can take an extended amount of time in certain scenarios and can cause the OSD to not respond to heartbeat requests and be marked down by its peers.

      You can increase the grace period OSDs will wait for heartbeat packets, but this is **not recommended**. The default is 20 seconds, and this can be set in the `[osds]` section of the conf file:

      ```
      osd_heartbeat_grace = 20
      ```

    - If no scrubbing or recovery occurred at the time of the OSD wrongly being marked down then, validate in the `ceph health detail` command whether any *blocked* or *slow* requests are seen against any OSDs:

      ```
      # ceph health detail
      ```

    - See whether you can find a commonality between the OSDs that have the *blocked* or *slow* requests logging. If a common OSD node is seen, then you likely have a network issue on that OSD node; if a common rack is seen, then you likely have a network issue on that rack. You can sort the down OSDs by executing the following:

      ```
      # ceph osd tree | grep down
      ```

- How to troubleshoot slow requests or blocked requests on an OSD:
  - A slow request is a request that has been in the OSD `op_queue` for 30 seconds or more and has not been serviced. This is configurable by setting the `osd_op_complaint_time`, default 30 seconds. It is not recommended that you change this, as that can lead to false reporting issues.
  - Main causes of these issues are network issues, hardware issues, and system load.
  - To begin troubleshooting these issues, you will first want to validate whether the OSDs with the *slow* requests are sharing any common hardware or networking; if they are, then the hardware/network is the likely suspect.
  - You can drill down further into the slow requests by dumping the historic ops on the OSD while the slow requests are logging:

  ```
  # ceph daemon osd.<id> dump_historic_ops
  ```

  - This can tell you the type of slow request and can help pinpoint where to look further. The types of common slow requests are as follows:
    - `waiting for rw locks`: OSD is waiting to acquire a lock on PG for OP
    - `waiting for sub ops`: OSD is waiting for a replica OSD to commit the OP to the journal
    - `no flag points reached`: OP hasn't reached any major OP milestone
    - `waiting for degraded object`: OSD hasn't replicated an object a certain number of times yet

- Using Linux tools such as `iostat` can help determine a poorly performing OSD that can be leading to slow requests. Reviewing for high await times can help pinpoint a poorly performing disk. More information on the `iostat` utility can be found at `http://man7.org/linux/man-pages/man1/iostat.1.html`:

```
# iostat -x 1
```

- Using Linux tools such as *netstat* can help determine a poorly performing OSD node that may be leading to slow *requests*. Refer to the earlier recipes on *Troubleshooting network issues*:

```
# netstat -s
```

Troubleshooting placement groups

As with the Ceph daemons issues, placement group issues will usually first be seen in the `ceph health detail` or `status` commands. They are usually accompanied by OSDs that are in a down state or a clock skew issue on the monitors. Prior to moving forward with troubleshooting, placement groups validate that all of your Ceph monitors are *up* and in quorum and that all Ceph OSDs are in the up/in state. The upcoming recipes will show you how to troubleshoot some of the more common Ceph placement group issues you may come across in your Ceph cluster.

How to do it...

Before you begin troubleshooting PG states, validate that the Ceph monitors are all up and in quorum and that any available OSDs are also in the up/in state:

1. How to handle *stale* placement groups:
    - A PG is labeled stale by the Ceph monitor when it does not receive a status update of the PG from the primary OSD or if a peer OSD reports the primary OSD as down.
    - The stale PG state is commonly seen after recently bringing the Ceph cluster up and when the PGs have not completed peering.

- If the PG is stuck in a stale state, then validate with `ceph health detail` about which OSDs are currently down in the PG's acting set and attempt to bring that OSD online. If you're unable to bring it online, refer to the previous section on *Troubleshooting OSDs*:

```
# ceph health detail
# systemctl start ceph-osd<id>
```

2. How to handle *unclean* placement groups:
    - A PG is labeled *unclean* if it has not been `active+clean` for 300 seconds, as defined by the `mon_pg_stuck_threshold`.
    - A PG labeled *unclean* has not properly replicated its objects for the required replication size on the pool.
    - An *unclean* PG is usually due to an OSD being down. Review the `ceph health detail` and `ceph osd tree` for any down OSDs and resolve as necessary:

```
# ceph osd tree | grep down
# ceph health detail
```

3. How to handle *inconsistent* placement groups:
    - A PG is marked *inconsistent* when there is a mismatch between objects on its replicas. Examples include differences in object size and objects missing in the replica after recovery completion.
    - These errors are typically flagged by *scrubbing* on the Ceph cluster.
    - In order to determine why the PG is flagged as inconsistent, we can do the following:
        - Issue a `deep-scrub` on the inconsistent placement group:

```
# ceph pg deep-scrub <pg.id>
```

        - Review the `ceph -w` command for a message related to `deep-scrub` on that PG.

```
# ceph -w |grep <pg.id>
```

fits one of the

```
d>: soid
attr _, missing
```

```
d>: soid
 != known digest
!= known size
```

```
d>: soid
= known size
```

- `<pg.id> deep-scrub stat mismatch, got <mismatch>`
- `<pg.id> shard <osd>: soid <object> candidate had a read error, digest 0 != known digest <digest>`

- If the error reported fits one of the these scenarios, then the PG can be safely repaired and have a `deep-scrub` rerun to validate the repair:

```
# ceph pg repair <pg.id>
# ceph deep-scrub <pg.id>
```

- If the output indicates one of the following, then *do not* repair the PG and open a case with Red Hat support for assistance or reach out to the Ceph community:
  - `<pg.id> shard <osd>: soid <object> digest <digest> != known digest <digest>`
  - `<pg.id> shard <osd>: soid <object> omap_digest <digest> != known omap_digest <digest>`

4. How to handle down placement groups:
   - When a PG is in a *down* state, it will not actively be serving client I/O.
   - A down PG is typically due to a peering failure and a down or several down OSDs.

- To determine the cause for a down PG, we need to query the PG:

  ```
  # ceph pg <pg.id> query
  ```

- When reviewing the PG query, there is a section in the command called `recovery_state`. This section highlights the PG's current recovery and will flag any issues that are blocking the current recovery:

```
"recovery_state": [
    {
        "name": "Started\/Primary\/Active",
        "enter_time": "2017-09-25 23:05:04.494547",
        "might_have_unfound": [
            {
                "osd": "2",
                "status": "already probed"
            },
            {
                "osd": "6",
                "status": "already probed"
            },
            {
                "osd": "7",
                "status": "not queried"
            }
        ],
        "recovery_progress": {
            "backfill_targets": [],
            "waiting_on_backfill": [],
            "last_backfill_started": "MIN",
            "backfill_info": {
                "begin": "MIN",
                "end": "MIN",
                "objects": []
            },
            "peer_backfill_info": [],
            "backfills_in_flight": [],
            "recovering": [],
            "pg_backend": {
                "pull_from_peer": [],
                "pushing": []
            }
        },
        "scrub": {
            "scrubber.epoch_start": "0",
            "scrubber.active": 0,
            "scrubber.state": "INACTIVE",
            "scrubber.start": "MIN",
            "scrubber.end": "MIN",
            "scrubber.subset_last_update": "0'0",
            "scrubber.deep": false,
            "scrubber.seed": 0,
            "scrubber.waiting_on": 0,
            "scrubber.waiting_on_whom": []
        }
    },
    {
        "name": "Started",
```

- If the recovery is blocked: peering is blocked by down osd then bring the down OSD back up to recover the PG. Otherwise if the OSD process cannot be started review the *Troubleshooting OSDs* section for further methods into OSD investigation.

5. How to handle *inactive* placement groups:
    - When a PG is *inactive* it will not be serving client I/O.
    - A PG is set to inactive state when it has not been active for 300 seconds, as defined by the `mon_pg_stuck_threshold`.
    - PG's that are inactive are usually due to OSDs that are in a *down* state. Use the `ceph health detail` and `ceph osd tree` commands to determine the *down* OSDs:

    ```
    # ceph health detail
    # ceph osd tree | grep down
    ```

6. How to handle placement groups that have *unfound objects*.
    - Unfound objects exist when Ceph is aware that newer copies of the object exists but is unable to find them. As Ceph cannot find the newer copies, it cannot complete recovery so marks the objects unfound.
    - A cluster that has placement groups with unfound objects usually has experienced an OSD node failure or OSD flapping scenarios where OSDs in the PGs acting were continually dropping offline and coming back online before completing recovery on the objects.
    - The `ceph health detail` command will flag PGs with unfound objects and will help us determine which OSDs need investigation:

    ```
    # ceph health detail
    ```

    - We can query the PG to determine further details on the OSDs that are required to be probed for the missing objects by viewing `recovery_state` as done previously with *down* placement groups:

    ```
    # ceph pg <pg.id> query
    ```

    - Resolve any of the OSDs that are in a *down* state in order to recover the unfound objects.
    - If you're unable to recover these objects, open a support ticket with Red Hat support or reach out to the Ceph community for assistance.

There's more...

Now that you have a general idea about troubleshooting the different components within Ceph, you are well on your way to be able to handle a failure in your Ceph cluster without panicking. But what happens if your Ceph cluster finds itself in an unrepairable state, and no matter what you do, you are unable to recover the cluster? The Ceph community is a large and extremely knowledgeable community that is always willing to help out a fellow Cepher. For more information on the Ceph community, refer to `http://ceph.com/community/` and join the Ceph community irc channels and mailing lists: `http://ceph.com/irc/`

14
Upgrading Your Ceph Cluster from Hammer to Jewel

In this chapter, we will cover the following recipe:

- Upgrading your Ceph cluster from Hammer to Jewel

Introduction

Now that you have reviewed the *Ceph Cookbook – Second Edition* and gone through the recipes in this book to familiarize yourself with Ceph Jewel and the changes that came in the Ceph Jewel release, it's time to upgrade your current running production cluster from Ceph Hammer to the latest stable Jewel! In this chapter, we will be demonstrating the online rolling update process to take you from the Hammer release (0.94.10) to Jewel. We will be upgrading each node in the cluster sequentially, only proceeding to the next node after the previous node is done. It is recommended that you update the Ceph cluster nodes in the following order:

1. Monitor nodes.
2. OSD nodes.
3. MDS nodes.

Upgrading your Ceph cluster from Hammer to Jewel

In this recipe, you will be upgrading your Ceph cluster from Hammer to Jewel.

How to do it...

We will be upgrading a CentOS 7 server running Ceph Hammer 0.94.10 to the latest stable Jewel release, 10.2.9.

Upgrading the Ceph monitor nodes

Upgrading a Ceph monitor is a simple process and should be done one monitor at a time. At a high level, you will need to enable the Jewel repositories, update the permission on the monitor directories, and reboot the monitor to complete the upgrade. Let's have a further look in detail at how to upgrade the Ceph monitor:

1. Update to Ceph `yum` repositories by editing the `ceph.repo` file in `/etc/yum.repos.d` from Hammer to Jewel in all of your Ceph nodes and clients:

```
[ceph]
name=Ceph packages for $basearch
baseurl=https://download.ceph.com/rpm-jewel/el7/$basearch
enabled=1
priority=1
gpgcheck=1
type=rpm-md
gpgkey=https://download.ceph.com/keys/release.asc

[ceph-noarch]
name=Ceph noarch packages
baseurl=https://download.ceph.com/rpm-jewel/el7/noarch
enabled=1
priority=1
gpgcheck=1
type=rpm-md
gpgkey=https://download.ceph.com/keys/release.asc

[ceph-source]
name=Ceph source packages
baseurl=https://download.ceph.com/rpm-jewel/el7/SRPMS
enabled=0
priority=1
gpgcheck=1
gpgkey=https://download.ceph.com/keys/release.asc
```

2. As `root`, stop the monitor process on the first monitor you will be upgrading:

   ```
   # sudo /etc/init.d/ceph stop mon
   ```

3. As `root`, once the process is stopped successfully, update the packages:

   ```
   # sudo yum update -y
   ```

4. As `root`, update the owner and group permissions of the monitor directories to the Ceph user. With the Jewel release, Ceph processes are no longer managed by the `root` user, but instead by the Ceph user:

```
# chown -R ceph:ceph /var/lib/ceph/mon
# chown -R ceph:ceph /var/log/ceph
# chown -R ceph:ceph /var/run/ceph
# chown ceph:ceph /etc/ceph/ceph.client.admin.keyring
# chown ceph:ceph /etc/ceph/ceph.conf
# chown ceph:ceph /etc/ceph/rbdmap
```

```
[root@ceph-node1 yum.repos.d]# chown -R ceph:ceph /var/lib/ceph/mon
[root@ceph-node1 yum.repos.d]# chown -R ceph:ceph /var/log/ceph
[root@ceph-node1 yum.repos.d]# chown -R ceph:ceph /var/run/ceph
[root@ceph-node1 yum.repos.d]# chown -R ceph:ceph /etc/ceph/ceph.client.
admin.keyring
[root@ceph-node1 yum.repos.d]# chown -R ceph:ceph /etc/ceph/ceph.conf
[root@ceph-node1 yum.repos.d]# chown -R ceph:ceph /etc/ceph/rbdmap
[root@ceph-node1 yum.repos.d]#
```

5. If using SELinux in enforcing or permissive mode, then you will need to relabel the SELinux context on the next reboot. If SELinux is disabled, this is not required:

```
# touch /.autorelabel
```

6. We then need to replay device events from the kernel as `root`:

```
# udevadm trigger
```

7. As `root`, we will need to enable the MON process:

```
# systemctl enable ceph-mon.target
# systemctl enable ceph-mon@<hostname>
```

8. Finally, reboot the monitor node to complete the upgrade:

```
# shutdown -r now
```

```
[root@ceph-node1 yum.repos.d]# udevadm trigger
[root@ceph-node1 yum.repos.d]# systemctl enable ceph-mon.target
[root@ceph-node1 yum.repos.d]# systemctl enable ceph-mon@ceph-node1
Created symlink from /etc/systemd/system/ceph-mon.target.wants/ceph-mon@
ceph-node1.service to /usr/lib/systemd/system/ceph-mon@.service.
[root@ceph-node1 yum.repos.d]# shutdown -r now
```

9. Once the monitor node comes back online, validate the Ceph cluster status and
    review the newly installed Ceph version; then you can move on to the next
    monitor node, following the same upgrade steps:

    ```
    # ceph status
    # ceph -v
    ```

```
[root@ceph-node1 yum.repos.d]# ceph -s
    cluster 878d051b-62af-4aed-b9f6-5d06326011a8
    health HEALTH_WARN
            crush map has legacy tunables (require bobtail, min is firef
ly)
    monmap e1: 3 mons at {ceph-node1=10.19.1.101:6789/0,ceph-node2=10.1
9.1.102:6789/0,ceph-node3=10.19.1.103:6789/0}
            election epoch 16, quorum 0,1,2 ceph-node1,ceph-node2,ceph-n
ode3
    osdmap e47: 9 osds: 9 up, 9 in
     pgmap v82: 128 pgs, 1 pools, 0 bytes data, 0 objects
            307 MB used, 161 GB / 161 GB avail
                128 active+clean
[root@ceph-node1 yum.repos.d]# ceph -v
ceph version 10.2.9 (2ee413f77150c0f375ff6f10edd6c8f9c7d060d0)
[root@ceph-node1 yum.repos.d]#
```

10. You will notice a new HEALTH_WARN reporting crush map has legacy
    tunables (require bobtail, min is firefly). We will resolve this
    message after upgrading the OSD nodes.

11. Once all monitor nodes have completed the upgrade, let's verify they are all running Jewel 10.2.9:

    ```
    # ceph tell mon.* version
    ```

    ```
    [root@ceph-node1 yum.repos.d]# ceph tell mon.* version
    mon.ceph-node1: ceph version 10.2.9 (2ee413f77150c0f375ff6f10edd6c8f9c7d
    060d0)
    mon.ceph-node2: ceph version 10.2.9 (2ee413f77150c0f375ff6f10edd6c8f9c7d
    060d0)
    mon.ceph-node3: ceph version 10.2.9 (2ee413f77150c0f375ff6f10edd6c8f9c7d
    060d0)
    [root@ceph-node1 yum.repos.d]#
    ```

Upgrading the Ceph OSD nodes

Upgrading the OSD nodes is a similar process to upgrading the monitor nodes and should be done one OSD at a time. At a high level, the upgrade process includes enabling the Jewel repositories, updating the ownership of the OSD directories, and restarting the OSD. Let's review the following steps for a detailed upgrade procedure for the Ceph OSDs:

1. While upgrading the OSD nodes, some placement groups will enter a degraded state because one of the OSDs backing the PGs might be down or restarting. We will set two flags on the cluster prior to upgrading the OSD nodes, which will prevent the cluster from marking an OSD as out and triggering recovery. We will be upgrading a single OSD node at a time and moving to the next node once all PGs are active+clean:

    ```
    # ceph osd set noout
    # ceph osd set norebalance
    ```

2. Verify that the Ceph yum repositories have been updated by viewing the ceph.repo file in /etc/yum.repos.d. We updated this from Hammer to Jewel in *step 1*.

3. Stop any running OSD processes on the first OSD node you are updating:

    ```
    # sudo /etc/init.d/ceph stop osd.<id>
    ```

4. Once all the OSD processes on the node are stopped, as root update the packages:

    ```
    # yum update -y
    ```

5. As `root`, update the owner and group permissions of the OSD directories to the Ceph user:

```
# chown -R ceph:ceph /var/lib/ceph/osd
# chown -R ceph:ceph /var/log/ceph
# chown -R ceph:ceph /var/run/ceph
# chown -R ceph:ceph /etc/ceph
```

```
[root@ceph-node1 yum.repos.d]# chown -R ceph:ceph /var/lib/ceph/osd
[root@ceph-node1 yum.repos.d]# chown -R ceph:ceph /var/log/ceph
[root@ceph-node1 yum.repos.d]# chown -R ceph:ceph /var/run/ceph
[root@ceph-node1 yum.repos.d]# chown -R ceph:ceph /etc/ceph
[root@ceph-node1 yum.repos.d]#
```

6. If using SELinux in enforcing or permissive mode, then you will need to relabel the SELinux context on the next reboot. If SELinux is disabled, this is not required:

```
# touch /.autorelabel
```

7. We then need to replay device events from the kernel as `root`:

```
# udevadm trigger
```

8. As `root`, we will need to enable the Ceph OSD process for each OSD:

```
# systemctl enable ceph-osd.target
# systemctl enable ceph-osd@<id>
```

9. Finally, reboot the OSD node to complete the upgrade:

```
# shutdown -r now
```

```
[root@ceph-node1 yum.repos.d]# udevadm trigger
[root@ceph-node1 yum.repos.d]# systemctl enable ceph-osd.target
[root@ceph-node1 yum.repos.d]# systemctl enable ceph-osd@0
Created symlink from /etc/systemd/system/ceph-osd.target.wants/ceph-osd@
0.service to /usr/lib/systemd/system/ceph-osd@.service.
[root@ceph-node1 yum.repos.d]# systemctl enable ceph-osd@1
Created symlink from /etc/systemd/system/ceph-osd.target.wants/ceph-osd@
1.service to /usr/lib/systemd/system/ceph-osd@.service.
[root@ceph-node1 yum.repos.d]# systemctl enable ceph-osd@2
Created symlink from /etc/systemd/system/ceph-osd.target.wants/ceph-osd@
2.service to /usr/lib/systemd/system/ceph-osd@.service.
[root@ceph-node1 yum.repos.d]# shutdown -r now
```

10. Once the OSD node comes back online, validate the Ceph cluster status and review the newly installed Ceph version; then you can move on to the next OSD node, following the same upgrade steps:

```
# ceph -s
# ceph tell osd.* version
```

```
[root@ceph-node1 vagrant]# ceph tell osd.* version
osd.0: {
    "version": "ceph version 10.2.9 (2ee413f77150c0f375ff6f10edd6c8f9c7d
060d0)"
}
osd.1: {
    "version": "ceph version 10.2.9 (2ee413f77150c0f375ff6f10edd6c8f9c7d
060d0)"
}
osd.2: {
    "version": "ceph version 10.2.9 (2ee413f77150c0f375ff6f10edd6c8f9c7d
060d0)"
}
osd.3: {
    "version": "ceph version 10.2.9 (2ee413f77150c0f375ff6f10edd6c8f9c7d
060d0)"
}
osd.4: {
    "version": "ceph version 10.2.9 (2ee413f77150c0f375ff6f10edd6c8f9c7d
060d0)"
}
osd.5: {
    "version": "ceph version 10.2.9 (2ee413f77150c0f375ff6f10edd6c8f9c7d
060d0)"
}
osd.6: {
    "version": "ceph version 10.2.9 (2ee413f77150c0f375ff6f10edd6c8f9c7d
060d0)"
}
osd.7: {
    "version": "ceph version 10.2.9 (2ee413f77150c0f375ff6f10edd6c8f9c7d
060d0)"
}
osd.8: {
    "version": "ceph version 10.2.9 (2ee413f77150c0f375ff6f10edd6c8f9c7d
060d0)"
}
[root@ceph-node1 vagrant]#
```

11. Once you have validated that all PGs are in an active+clean state and *all* OSDs are up/in, we can remove the noout and norebalance flags from the cluster:

    ```
    # ceph osd unset noout
    # ceph osd unset norebalance
    ```

12. We will want to set the require_jewel_osds flag and the sortbitwise flag to verify that only OSDs running Jewel or higher can be added to the Ceph cluster, and enable a new method of handling bits. When the sortbitwise flag is set, the PGs will need to repeer but this should occur quickly with minimal impact:

    ```
    # ceph osd set require_jewel_osds
    # ceph osd set sortbitwise
    ```

```
[root@ceph-node1 vagrant]# ceph osd unset noout
unset noout
[root@ceph-node1 vagrant]# ceph osd unset norebalance
unset norebalance
[root@ceph-node1 vagrant]# ceph osd set require_jewel_osds
set require_jewel_osds
```

13. Finally, we can set out CRUSH tunables to optimal profile on the cluster. Setting this optimal profile may incur some data movement in the cluster. Also, verify that any clients have previously been upgraded to Jewel prior to enabling optimal tunables, and if using kernel clients that your client supports Jewel tunables (http://docs.ceph.com/docs/master/rados/operations/crush-map/#tunables):

    ```
    # ceph osd crush tunables optimal
    ```

14. Verify that your cluster is in `HEALTH_OK` and all PGs are in an `active+clean` state:

```
[root@ceph-node1 vagrant]# ceph -s
    cluster 878d051b-62af-4aed-b9f6-5d06326011a8
     health HEALTH_OK
     monmap e1: 3 mons at {ceph-node1=10.19.1.101:6789/0,ceph-node2=10.1
9.1.102:6789/0,ceph-node3=10.19.1.103:6789/0}
            election epoch 44, quorum 0,1,2 ceph-node1,ceph-node2,ceph-n
ode3
     osdmap e83: 9 osds: 9 up, 9 in
            flags sortbitwise,require_jewel_osds
      pgmap v219: 128 pgs, 1 pools, 0 bytes data, 0 objects
            318 MB used, 161 GB / 161 GB avail
                 128 active+clean
[root@ceph-node1 vagrant]# 
```

Congratulations, you have upgraded your Ceph cluster from Hammer to Jewel!

Upgrading the Ceph Metadata Server

When upgrading a Ceph MDS, you will want to upgrade a single MDS at a time.

See also

The following upstream Ceph documentation can be helpful when looking to upgrade your production Ceph cluster:

- http://docs.ceph.com/docs/master/install/get-packages/
- http://docs.ceph.com/docs/master/install/upgrading-ceph/#upgrading-ceph
- http://docs.ceph.com/docs/master/start/quick-start-preflight/
- http://docs.ceph.com/docs/master/release-notes/
- http://docs.ceph.com/docs/master/release-notes/#id851

Index

Printed in Great Britain
by Amazon